The Women Founders

Sociology and Social Theory 1830–1930

A Text/Reader

Patricia Madoo Lengermann
George Washington University

Gillian Niebrugge
American University

WAVELAND
PRESS, INC.
Long Grove, Illinois

After a hundred years
Nobody knows the place. . . .
—*Emily Dickinson*

TO THE MEMORY OF OUR PARENTS

Dorothy Edith Gocking Madoo and Roslan Mahaiste Madoo
(1912–1989)   *(1912–1960)*

Dixie Lee Sours Niebrugge and Jackson Samuel Niebrugge
(1918–1992)   *(1914–1981)*

For information about this book, contact:
Waveland Press, Inc.
4180 IL Route 83, Suite 101
Long Grove, IL 60047-9580
(847) 634-0081
info@waveland.com
www.waveland.com

Printed in the United States of America

17 16 15 14 13

ACKNOWLEDGMENTS

Agatha Christie once remarked in an interview that "where two people are writing the same book, each believes he gets all the worries and only half the royalties." We, however, have worried this book together every step of the way. Nor is the book a product only of our joint work; we are indebted to a great many people. As will become obvious, we are intellectually indebted to Mary Jo Deegan, who more than any single person has kept alive the knowledge of women's contributions to sociology and without whose scholarship this book would not have been possible; to Dorothy E. Smith, whose theories inform these pages and whose work sets a standard of excellence; and to George Ritzer, whose vision of sociology as a multi-paradigm science makes a pathway for works such as this one. Elizabeth Kirchen provided the admirable translations of Marianne Weber that enhance this volume, her own passionate intellectual energy, and wry support (leaving messages on our answering machine at odd hours of the day and night—"Imagine the worse mess you've ever been in; now square that."). We have been both improved and encouraged by the intelligence and generosity with which our reviewers responded to this manuscript. They gave hours of time and offered up their best thoughts on both content and phrasing, and we are enormously indebted to Abby Ferber, Kate Hausbeck, Susan Hoecker-Drysdale, Terry Kandal, E. Doyle McCarthy, Eleanor Miller, Mary Rogers, and two anonymous reviewers of Chapters 5 and 7. Our editors were Jill Gordon, whose immediate support of the idea of such a book gave us this opportunity, and Kathy Blake, who oversaw its development and our progress with tact, grace, vision, and gentle humor.

The production was supervised by Susan Trentacosti with efficiency and steadying doses of calm. Our research was greatly aided by Louise Rossmann, Reference Librarian at Wells College, who helped us get many original texts through interlibrary loan; Mary Pryor, Archivist at Rockford College, who took the time to locate a key document in our understanding of Jane Addams; the staff of the Dana Porter Library and of its Rare Book Collection at the University of Waterloo in Ontario; and Suzy Taraba, Public Services Librarian at the University of Chicago. We are indebted to students and colleagues at The George Washington University, Northern Virginia Community College, and Wells College, where we developed the understandings that frame the discoveries presented here. Dan Niebrugge and Barbara Lantz provided good counsel in moments that felt like crises. Finally we would like to thank Bentley's (the Bar to Be At) and York Street Kitchen of Stratford, Ontario, where much of this manuscript was outlined and the community of Stratford, which maintains the beautiful parks system where we walked and talked this book into being.

CONTENTS

CHAPTER 1

Present at the Creation— Women in the History of Sociology and Social Theory

A sociology is a systematically developed consciousness of society and social relations.
—Dorothy E. Smith

This is a book about social theory and about the history of sociology. It makes three claims: that women have always been significantly involved in creating sociology; that women have always made distinctive and important contributions to social theory; and that women's contributions to sociology and social theory have been written out of the record of the discipline's history. Our first claim is indebted to a contemporary effort by feminists to reconstruct women's contribution to the history of the social sciences (Broschart, 1991a,b; Collins, 1990; Costin, 1983; Deegan, 1988, 1991; Fish, 1981, 1985; Fitzpatrick, 1990; Hill, 1989; Hoecker-Drysdale, 1994; Keith, 1991; Lemert, 1995; Lengermann and Niebrugge-Brantley, 1996; McDonald, 1994; Reinharz, 1992, 1993; Rosenberg, 1982; Terry, 1983). Our second claim is the particular focus of this book: the explication of the social theories of the women founders of sociology. Our third claim is the topic of this chapter which explores how the writing out of the women founders occurred as part of a politics of gender and a politics of knowledge within the discipline.

Our analysis focuses on the lives and social theories of fifteen women who were present at and active in the creation of sociology: Harriet Martineau (1802–1876), Jane Addams (1860–1935), Charlotte Perkins Gilman (1860–1935), Anna Julia Cooper (1858–1964), Ida B. Wells-Barnett (1862–1931), Marianne Weber (1870–1954), Beatrice Potter Webb (1858–1943), and the group we label "the Chicago Women's School of Sociology"—Edith Abbott (1876–1957), Grace Abbott (1878–1939), Sophonisba Breckinridge (1866–1948), Florence Kelley (1859–1932), Frances Kellor (1873–1952), Julia Lathrop (1858–1932), Annie Marion MacLean (ca. 1870–1934), and Marion Talbot (1858–1947). These women, all significant participants in the development of sociology, have emerged in our study as only the beginning of a history that includes many other women.[1]

1

One of the ways a discipline or a profession socializes new members is by telling its history as an account of its authoritative texts, discoveries, thinkers, and ideas—the discipline's "canon." The history sociologists tell themselves matters because it reaffirms for the teller and the audience a sense of identity: who sociologists are, what sociologists do, which aspects of social life sociologists look at (Halbwachs, 1992). Different nations produce somewhat different histories of Western sociology (Donald Levine, 1995). In developing the thesis of this chapter and this book, we focus primarily on the way American sociology has constructed its history of the discipline, a focus reflecting our own location within the American tradition. But we argue that all national traditions have written women out and that this writing out distorts and diminishes sociology's understanding of itself and what it does. In recovering women's presence in the creation of sociology and social theory, we rediscover the role sociology once played in the shaping of various Western societies, the directions it has gone, the paths it might have chosen.

The history of sociology is typically told as the history of its theorists and their theories. This is a choice. It could be told as a history of major empirical works (see, for example, Bulmer, Bales, and Sklar, 1991; Kent, 1981; Madge, 1963; Platt, 1996; Reinharz, 1992) or the development of specialized fields such as criminology or collective behavior. But there are sound reasons for choosing to study sociology as a history of its theories, as long as we remember we are making a choice. A "theory"—the word comes from the Greek verb "to see"—can be understood as a lens that directs the eye towards a given reality so that one focuses on some of its features while filtering out others. If we had no theory to guide our attention, all things would present themselves to us as of equal importance, "a booming, buzzing reality" in William James's phrase. A social theory systematically directs one's attention to certain features of human social relations; social theories can be distinguished from each other by the features they emphasize.

The history of sociology's theories is conventionally told as a history of white male agency—an account of the theoretical contributions of a "founding" generation of men, Auguste Comte, Herbert Spencer, and Karl Marx, writing in the middle of the nineteenth century, expanded by a second, "classic" generation of men, Emile Durkheim, Max Weber, Georg Simmel, George Herbert Mead, and Robert E. Park, who wrote between 1890 and 1930. This history is presented as an account of the natural way things occurred, a chronicle beyond the powers of human tellers to change. In contrast, we portray this history as a social construction arising out of the discipline's power arrangements, and like all histories, reflecting an ongoing conflict between exclusionary and inclusionary values and practices (Becker, 1971; Lemert, 1995; D. Smith, 1987). In this chapter we first establish the fact that women were a significant presence in the creation of sociology. Then we explore how they came to be written out of sociology's history. We conclude with an exploration of the reasons for their contemporary reintroduction into the sociological canon.

A SIGNIFICANT PRESENCE: WOMEN AS SOCIOLOGISTS, 1830–1930

The claim that a group has been "written out" of history is different from the claim that a group has been "invisible." "Invisibility" suggests not being seen, that is, never having one's presence acknowledged as significant—a concept applied by many African Americans to their experience of marginalization (e.g., Collins, 1990; Cooper, 1892; DuBois, 1903; Ellison, 1952; Lorde, 1984; Rollins, 1985). "Being written out" suggests having once been seen as a presence in a community and then having been erased from its record. For several reasons, the case of the fifteen women sociologists treated in this volume is an instance of erasure rather than invisibility. First, almost all these women were well-known public figures in their lifetime, larger than the fledgling discipline of sociology they helped create; like the work of Marx, Max Weber, or Durkheim, their work has relevance for all the social sciences. Second, they created social theory and did sociology in the same times and places as the male founders (see Figures 1-1 and 1-2). Third, they were widely recognized by their contemporaries, including male sociologists, as significant social analysts. Fourth, they all acted as members of a sociological community, meeting at least one of the following criteria: employment as a sociologist, membership in a national sociological association, publication framed by an explicit concern with sociological principles, self-identification as a sociologist and recognition by contemporaries as a sociologist (Käsler, 1981; Deegan, 1991). We introduce some of the evidence for these claims in the brief descriptions of the women that follow; we develop this evidence more fully in subsequent chapters.

Martineau—whose *Illustrations of Political Economy* (1832–1834) outsold even Charles Dickens (Hoecker-Drysdale 1992)—was Britain's preeminent woman of letters until her death, writing social analysis, journalism, history, novels, children's stories, and travel books. Long identified in the history of sociology for her 1853 translation and abridgement of Comte, she was herself writing sociology as early as 1834, drafting what would become the first major statement of method, *How to Observe Morals and Manners* (1838b) and testing her methodology in her classic study *Society in America* (1836). Addams was the founder of Hull-House, the famous Chicago social settlement; a major spokesperson for Progressive reform on behalf of immigrants, trade unions, women, children, working-class people, and African Americans; and consistently named in public opinion polls as one of the most admired Americans (Davis, 1973; Daniel Levine, 1971). At Hull-House, she administered a major research institution, drawing on her experiences there to formulate a social theory in eight major books and some 200 articles. She self-identified as a sociologist; taught sociology; was a member of the American Sociological Society (ASS)—until 1959 the name of the American Sociological Association (ASA); published in the *American Journal of Sociology* (*AJS*); and had significant relationships with Mead, Park, W. I. Thomas, Albion Small, and Ernest Burgess (Deegan, 1988). Gilman was widely regarded as the leading feminist intellectual of her day. Her *Women and Economics* (1898) went through nine printings by 1920, was translated into seven languages, and was the bible of many women's college student bodies (Ceplair, 1991). Besides the classic feminist novella *The Yellow Wallpaper* (1892) and some 2,000 pieces of journalism, poetry, and prose, she wrote six significant works of formal social theory, including *Women and Economics, Human Work* (1904), and *The Man-Made World* (1911). She also published in the *AJS*, was a member of the ASS, and maintained intellectual relationships with Lester Ward and E. A. Ross.

Wells-Barnett spearheaded national and international anti-lynching campaigns, writing major analyses of lynching—*Southern Horrors* (1892) and *A Red Record* (1895)—and

FIGURE 1-1 Lifelines of Women and Men Founders of Sociology

| 1790 | 1800 | 1810 | 1820 | 1830 | 1840 | 1850 | 1860 | 1870 | 1880 | 1890 | 1900 | 1910 | 1920 | 1930 | 1940 | 1950 | 1960 |

Auguste Comte 1798–1857
Harriet Martineau 1802–1876
Karl Marx 1818–1883
Herbert Spencer 1820–1903
Anna Julia Cooper 1858–1964
Emile Durkheim 1858–1917
Julia Lathrop 1858–1932
Georg Simmel 1858–1918
Marion Talbot 1858–1947
Beatrice Potter Webb 1858–1943
Florence Kelley 1859–1932
Jane Addams 1860–1935
Charlotte Perkins Gilman 1860–1935
Ida B. Wells-Barnett 1862–1931
George Herbert Mead 1863–1931
W. I. Thomas 1863–1947
Robert E. Park 1864–1944
Max Weber 1864–1920
Sophonisba Breckinridge 1866–1948
Annie Marion MacLean ca. 1870–1934
Marianne Weber 1870–1954
Frances Kellor 1873–1952
Edith Abbott 1876–1957
Grace Abbott 1878–1939

4

carrying the battle to Britain, where she often spoke to crowds in the thousands. She was an active organizer for African American civil rights, helping to found the National Association for the Advancement of Colored People (NAACP). Cooper's major book *A Voice from the South* (1892) received superlative reviews from black and white publications alike, establishing her as a prominent intellectual and spokesperson for African American women; she was one of two women to address the world's first Pan-African Conference in London in 1900. Cooper and Wells-Barnett created a genuine American non-Marxian conflict theory in which they spoke of the sociological framing of their argument; but American racism made tentative any relationship between them and white professional sociology, although both knew and worked with black sociologist W. E. B. DuBois. Marianne Weber lived at the center of German sociological circles and debated the ideas of both Simmel and her husband Max in her own writings. She was a leading figure in the German feminist movement, the first woman to be elected to a German parliament, and the author of nine books of social analysis and sociology including her monumental work on the legal position of women, *Ehefrau und Mutter in der Rechtsentwicklung (Marriage, Motherhood, and the Law)* (1907), and her collected essays, *Frauenfragen und Frauengedanken (Reflections on Women and Women's Issues)* (1919). She secured Max's position within sociology after his death by editing and publishing ten volumes of his work and writing her important interpretive biography of him.

Webb was tutored by Spencer, self-identified as a sociologist, taught sociology, worked as a social investigator on the major empirical study of her age (Charles Booth's *Life and Labour of the People of London*), and did her own independent investigations, leading to the socialist reform classic *The Co-operative Movement in Great Britain* (1891). With her husband Sidney, she researched and co-authored eleven voluminous works of empirical sociology that formed the blueprint for the British welfare state. All the members of the Chicago Women's School of Sociology (hereafter referred to as the Chicago Women's School or the Chicago Women) wrote prolifically as social analysts, all publishing in the *AJS*. Many were prominent public figures: Kelley headed the National Consumers' League (1899–1932); Lathrop (1912–20), and then Grace Abbott (1920–34), served as chief of the Children's Bureau, the highest-ranking woman in the federal government at that time; Edith Abbott and Breckinridge founded the University of Chicago's School of Social Service Administration (1922); Talbot was dean of women at the University of Chicago (1893–1925); Kellor was a founder and executive officer of the American Arbitration League (1926–53). Kelley knew Friedrich Engels, maintained a correspondence with him until his death, and did the first English translation of *The Condition of the Working Class in England in 1844*; MacLean studied with Small, Mead, and Charles Henderson; Kellor also studied with Henderson; Edith Abbott, Grace Abbott, and Breckinridge are all referenced in Park and Burgess's *Introduction to the Science of Sociology*; Talbot served as an associate editor of the *AJS* from its founding by Small to her retirement in 1925.

These women knew each other or each other's work. Gilman, Webb, Weber, and Wells-Barnett all visited Hull-House, which was, of course, the working base for Addams and most of the Chicago Women. Many of them read Gilman's *Women and Economics*—Webb, Weber, Addams, Kelley, Lathrop, and Talbot. Addams published with Wells-Barnett on

FIGURE 1-2 Coordinates: Key Works of Women Founders, Key Works of Male Founders, and Key Events in History

This chart gives (1) key works generally considered part of the established canon of writings by male sociologists, (2) works representative of the writings done by women founders, some of which might find their way into an expanded canon, and (3) historical markers that indicate either events useful for placing people in past time or concerns of particular import to the women theorists.

Dates	Male canon	Women founders' representative statements	Historical markers
Prologue			American Revolution, 1776–83 French Revolution, 1789–99 Wollstonecraft, *The Vindication of the Rights of Women*, 1790 Napoleonic Wars, 1799–1815
1830s	Comte, Volume I of *The Positive Philosophy*, 1830 Comte uses term "sociology" in lecture, 1839	Martineau, "Essays on the Art of Thinking," 1832 Flora Tristan, *Peregrinations of a Pariah*, 1833–1834 Martineau, *Society in America*, 1836 Martineau, *How to Observe Morals and Manners*, 1838 Martineau writes 1837 letter about editing new journal of "sociology"	Slavery abolished in British Empire Abolitionist activity in United States Victoria crowned, 1837
1840s	Comte, entire six volumes of *The Positive Philosophy*, 1842 Marx, *The German Ideology*, 1846 Marx and Engels, *The Communist Manifesto*, 1848	Tristan, *The London Journal of Flora Tristan, or The Aristocracy and Working Class of England*, 1840 Martineau, *Eastern Life: Past and Present*, 1848 Martineau, *Household Education*, 1849	Liberal middle-class revolutions in Europe against monarchy, aristocracy, 1848 Seneca Falls Women's Rights Convention, 1848
1850s	Spencer, *Social Statics*, 1850 Marx, *The Eighteenth Brumaire*, 1852	Martineau translates Comte's *Positive Philosophy*, 1853 Martineau, "Female Industry" in *Edinburgh Review*, 1859 Florence Nightingale writes reports to governors of her nursing homes, 1853–54	Crimean War, 1856 Darwin, *The Origin of the Species*, 1859
1860s	Spencer, *First Principles*, 1862 Spencer, *Reasons for Dissenting from M. Comte*, 1864 Marx, *Capital*, 1867	Nightingale, *Notes on Hospitals*, 1863 Martineau, "Modern Domestic Industry," *Edinburgh Review*, 1862 Martineau works as journalist to keep Britain from joining US Civil War on side of Confederacy	Civil War in United States, 1861–65 Emancipation of serfs in Russia Emancipation Proclamation, United States, 1863 John Stuart and Harriet Taylor Mill, *On the Subjection of Women*, 1869

1870s	Spencer, *Principles of Sociology*, 1876–96	Nightingale, *Introductory Notes on Lying-In Institutions*, 1871 Posthumous publication of Martineau's *Autobiography*, 1876	Unification of Germany under Bismarck, 1871 End of Reconstruction, beginning of segregation, Jim Crow laws, lynch law in United States
1880s	Engels, *The Origins of the Family*, 1884 Tönnies, *Gemeinschaft und Gesellschaft*, 1887	Kelley, "On Some Changes in the Legal Status of the Child since Blackstone," *The International Review*, 1882 Cooper delivers "Womanhood a Vital Element in the Regeneration and Progress of a Race" to convention of black clergy of Protestant Episcopal Church, at Washington, DC, 1886 (becomes first essay in *A Voice from the South*) Kelley, "The Need for Theoretical Preparation for Philanthropic Work" in *On the Need and Opportunity for College-Trained Women in Philanthropic Work*, 1887 Kelley, translation of Engels's *The Condition of the Working Class in England in 1844*, 1887 Webb, "The Dock Life of East London," in *Nineteenth Century*, 1887 Webb, "East London Labour" *Nineteenth Century*, 1888 Webb, "Pages from a Working-Girl's Diary," *Nineteenth Century*, 1888	Civil Rights cases in United States make it possible for private individuals (and corporations) to discriminate on basis of race, 1883 Haymarket Massacre one sign of United States labor unrest, 1886 American Federation of Labor formed, 1886 Hull-House, Chicago settlement, founded by Addams and Ellen Gates Starr, 1889 Women's suffrage campaign continues Progressive Era of reform in United States begins in late 1880s
1890s	Durkheim, *The Division of Labor in Society*, 1893 Durkheim, *The Rules of Sociological Method*, 1895 Durkheim, *Suicide*, 1897	Webb, *The Co-operative Movement in Great Britain*, 1891 Cooper, *A Voice from the South*, 1892 Wells-Barnett, *Southern Horrors*, 1892 Addams, "The Objective Value of a Social Settlement" and "The Subjective Necessity for Social Settlements" in *Philanthropy and Social Progress*, 1893 Wells-Barnett, *A Red Record*, 1895	Women's suffrage campaign continues Bismarck replaced as German chancellor, 1890 University of Chicago founded, 1891 Columbian Exposition in Chicago to mark 500th anniversary of Columbus's voyage; African Americans protest their exclusion; 1892 University of Chicago Department of Sociology founded, 1893 Pullman Strike, 1894 *American Journal of Sociology* founded, 1895

(continued)

FIGURE 1-2 (continued)

Dates	Male canon	Women founders' representative statements	Historical markers
		Hull-House Maps and Papers, by Residents of Hull-House, a Presentation of Nationalities and Wages in a Congested District of Chicago, Together with Comments and Essays on Problems Growing out of Social Conditions, 1895 (includes essays by Addams, Kelley, and Lathrop; project organized by Kelley) Gilman, *Women and Economics,* 1898 MacLean, "Two Weeks in a Department Store," *AJS,* 1899 (early participant-observation study)	*Plessy v Ferguson* upholds segregationist doctrine "separate but equal," 1896 Spanish-American War, 1898
1900s	Cooley, *Human Nature and the Social Order,* 1902 Max Weber, "Methodology of the Social Sciences," 1903–17 (originally series of essays in journals) Simmel, "The Metropolis and Mental Life," 1903 Max Weber, *The Protestant Ethic and the Spirit of Capitalism,* 1904 Sumner, *Folkways,* 1906 Simmel, *The Philosophy of Money,* 1907 Simmel, *Conflict and the Web of Group Affiliations,* 1908 Simmel, *Soziologie* 1908 Cooley, *Social Organization,* 1909	Kelley, "Principles of the Consumers' League," *AJS,* 1899 Gilman, *On Children,* 1900 Marianne Weber, *Fichte's Sozialismus und Sein Verhältnis zur Marx'schen Doktrin,* 1900 Addams, *Democracy and Social Ethics,* 1902 Gilman, *Human Work,* 1904 Kellor, *Out of Work,* 1904 Kelley, *Some Ethical Gains through Legislation,* 1905 Addams, *Newer Ideals of Peace,* 1907 Weber, *Marriage, Motherhood, and the Law,* 1907	McKinley reelected; assassinated; Theodore Roosevelt becomes president, pledging *square deal* to control corporate mergers Pan-African Conference, London, 1900; Cooper and W. DuBois among US delegates International Lady Garment Workers Union established, 1900 Muckraking begins about 1902 Ida B. Tarbell begins publishing *History of the Standard Oil Trust,* 1903 Queen Victoria dies 1903; Edward VII succeeds Upton Sinclair's *The Jungle* leads to Pure Food and Drug and Meat Inspection Acts, 1906 Women's suffrage campaign continues

1910s	Durkheim, *The Elementary Forms of Religious Life*, 1912 Pareto, *General Treatise*, 1915 Max Weber, *The Religion of China* and *The Religion of India*, 1916 Mead lectures at University of Chicago Thomas and Znaniecki, *The Polish Peasant*, 1918	Addams, *Twenty Years at Hull-House*, 1910 Edith Abbott, *Women in Industry*, 1910 Talbot, *The Education of Women*, 1910 Gilman, *The Man-Made World, or Our Androcentric Culture*, 1911 Addams, *The Long Road of Women's Memory*, 1916 Weber, *Reflections on Women and Women's Issues*, 1919 (collection of essays written over nearly 20 years)	NAACP founded, 1910 Federal Children's Bureau established; Lathrop of Hull-House becomes first head, 1912 Progressive Party convention; Addams seconds nomination of Teddy Roosevelt, 1912 Women's suffrage campaign continues World War I begins in Europe, 1914 Communist Revolution in Russia, 1917 United States enters World War I, 1917 German military leaders leave it to newly formed German republic to formally surrender, ending World War I, 1918 German women get vote under new German Republic, 1918 Treaty of Versailles ends war, punishes Germany, promises League of Nations, 1919
1920s	Max Weber publishes first part of *Economy and Society*, 1920 Park and Burgess, *Introduction to the Science of Sociology*, 1921 Posthumous publication of Max Weber's *Economy and Society*, 1921	Gilman, *His Religion and Hers*, 1923 Weber edits and publishes Max Weber's essays to complete *Economy and Society*, 1921 Breckinridge, "The Home Responsibilities of Women Workers and the 'Equal Wage,'" *Journal of Political Economy*, 1923 Cooper, *Slavery and the French Revolutionists*, 1925 Weber, *Max Weber: A Life*, 1926 Webb, *My Apprenticeship*, 1926	19th Amendment grants women right to vote in United States, 1920 Era of Jazz Age chronicled by F. Scott Fitzgerald in United States Mussolini comes to power in Italy, 1922 First labor government in Great Britain, 1924 Worldwide Great Depression begins, 1929

lynching on at least two occasions, one of which was in a remarkable issue of *Survey* in February of 1913 in which Addams, Wells-Barnett, Breckinridge, and DuBois all analyze the problem of race.[2] Addams, Wells-Barnett, Kelley, and Breckinridge participated in the founding of the NAACP. Hull-House residents, including Addams, Lathrop, and Kelley, used Webb's *The Co-operative Movement in Great Britain* in preparation for their own venture into cooperative housing for working women. The persons most outside this network are Martineau, a full generation earlier than the rest of the women, and Cooper, whose life course rarely took her to Chicago. Yet Edith Abbott knew and responded to Martineau's work on women's employment in America, and Gilman refers to Martineau's struggle to overcome gender barriers to her career as a social analyst. And Cooper spoke in Chicago in 1893 at the white feminist Women's Congress, was active, as was Wells-Barnett, in the National Federation of Colored Women's Clubs and the African American settlement house movement, and wrote a sympathetic response to Gilman's suicide.

These women knew that they were part of a larger movement to create a science of society and had their own sense of what that science should be: a project of social critique in which research and theory had as a morally necessary focus the description, analysis, and correction of social inequality. The women vary in terms of the particular inequality focused on—gender, class, race, ethnicity, age, or combinations thereof; the relative balance between research and theory, and the choice of research strategy and theoretical method. Working out this commitment to critical social theory, these women engaged with sociology and the sociological community at the moment in which the discipline was itself emerging. Their varying relationships to that community thus reflect both the instability of sociology's emerging identity and the effects of gender, class, and race on access to what would become a formal academic enterprise, the province of educated white men. But at the moment these women were writing, sociology was as much their intellectual project as the men's; it is only in the retelling that they have disappeared.

GENDER AND KNOWLEDGE: THE POLITICS OF ERASURE

Despite their work in sociology and social theory and their visibility to their contemporaries, the women founders disappeared as a significant presence from sociology's record, surviving only in marginalized positions. Martineau is remembered as Comte's translator; Weber, as handmaiden to genius; Webb, as Sidney's partner; Addams, as secular saint; Gilman, as the eccentric genius of *The Yellow Wallpaper;* and the Chicago Women, as social workers and reformers. Cooper is quoted by DuBois but acknowledged only as "a woman of the race" (Washington, 1988).[3] This erasure can be understood in terms of a series of power processes involving the conferral or denial of *authority,* understood as "a form of power that is a distinctive capacity to get things done in words" (D. Smith, 1987:29). Nearly all the women founders were aware of the importance of authority, linked it, as Smith does, to an ability to do things in words, and recognized its attainment as a particular problem for women.[4] In this section we focus on authority as a factor in two intricately interrelated politics that determined the women's fate—a politics of gender and a politics of knowledge.

In order to understand women's precarious relation to authority in this context, it is instructive to look at Addams's career. We choose Addams because of her stature as a presence in American society, because her relation to the male sociologists is so well documented (Deegan, 1988), because her published works were acknowledged by her contemporaries as sociology, and because she self-identified as a sociologist. Figure 1-3 presents an abbreviated portrait of Addams's reputation in sociology, offering an exemplar of the power processes that erased women from the history of sociology.

A Politics of Gender

The erasure of the women founders is most basically explained in terms of women's tenuous hold on authority in a man-made culture; that tenuousness can be understood through an analysis of how one person is "present" to, or known in consciousness by, another person. We develop this analysis through a feminist reworking of the phenomenological theory of Alfred Schutz, (Lengermann and Niebrugge-Brantley, 1995; Schutz, 1967, 1973; Schutz and Luckmann, 1973).

For Schutz, the capacity to know another person is learned in the situation of face-to-face relating, the essential relation of human life, in which one consciousness recognizes the other as a human "like himself." Schutz calls this the "thou-orientation," or "consociate," relation.[5] When individuals move out of the face-to-face, or consociate, relation, they enter what Schutz generally categorizes as the "contemporary" relation. No longer physically present to each other, individuals are present to each other in consciousness—know each other—through mental constructs, or "typifications." A typification may be based on previous firsthand experience, information from mutual acquaintances, documents produced by or telling about the other, or actions the other is known to have undertaken. When a person dies, he becomes a "predecessor" in Schutz's schema and even more subject to a rigid and lasting typification. Over time, as those who knew an individual also die, the predecessor is increasingly remembered through artifacts—things the person made or wrote, or things others made or wrote about the person. In an academically based profession like sociology, the key artifacts for typifying predecessors are their writings, which may become part of the canon.

Factoring gender into this model alters it in significant ways. As much feminist scholarship shows, women become present to male consciousness in face-to-face relations not as I-thou—I and a being like myself—but as I-*other* (e.g., Anzaldua, 1990; Benjamin, 1988; Chodorow, 1978; Collins, 1990; DeBeauvoir, 1947/1963; Keller, 1985; Lengermann and Niebrugge-Brantley, 1995; Minnich, 1990; Olsen, 1972; Smith, 1987). The women founders, though strong individual presences, were viewed by their male associates through the veil of male privilege as "the less-than-being," "the being who need not be taken seriously"—as *she who lacks authority*. The women founders were aware of how they were regarded in their face-to-face relations with men. Martineau in the introduction to *Society in America*, reports, "It has been frequently mentioned to me that my being a woman was [a] disadvantage" in doing social research (1836/1837:I:xii). Cooper writes of an encounter with a male authority figure in which her decision to "go to college . . . was received with about the same incredulity and dismay as if a brass button on [his coat] had propounded a new method for squaring the circle or trisecting the arc"

FIGURE 1-3 **A Brief Overview of Addams's Career in Sociology**

Note: Texts marked with an * are those identified by Levine in *Visions of the Sociological Tradition* (1995) as key statements interpreting the history of sociology and shaping the canon.

Moment I: Addams's presence in mainstream sociological circles, 1894–1920

1894 Small and Vincent mention Hull-House in *An Introduction to the Study of Society*
1895 Addams contributes to *Hull-House Maps and Papers,* a pioneering work of critical empirical sociology: her contribution is entitled "The Settlement as a Factor in the Labor Movement" and puts the settlement on the side of organized labor—a radical step in 1895; Charles Zeublin of the University of Chicago also contributes to this volume. Not reviewed in *AJS* which does not begin publication until March 1895.
1896 Addams publishes "A Belated Industry" in Volume 1 of the *AJS*
1899 Addams publishes "Trade Unions and Public Duty" in Volume 4 of *AJS;* co-teaches summer course at University of Chicago with Kelley
1902 Addams publishes *Democracy and Social Ethics,* reviewed by Henderson in Volume 8 of *AJS* that same year
1905 Addams publishes "Problems of Municipal Administration" in Volume 10 of *AJS*
1907 Addams publishes *Newer Ideals of Peace,* reviewed by Mead in Volume 13 of *AJS* that same year
1908 Addams publishes "Comment on an Article by John R. Commons, 'Class Conflict in America'" in Volume 13 of *AJS*
1909 Addams publishes *The Spirit of Youth and the City Streets*
1910 *The Spirit of Youth and the City Streets* is reviewed by Harriet Thomas and William James in Volume 15 of *AJS;* Addams publishes *Twenty Years at Hull-House*
1912 Addams publishes "Recreation as a Public Function in Urban Communities," in Volume 17 of *AJS*
1914 Addams publishes *A New Conscience and an Ancient Evil,* reviewed in Volume 18 of *AJS* by Kelley; publishes "A Modern Devil Baby" in Volume 19 of *AJS*
1916 Addams publishes *The Long Road of Women's Memory*
1919 Addams presents "Americanization" at the annual meeting of the ASS (published in 1920 in *Papers and Proceedings of the American Sociological Society*)
NB: The scarcity between 1914 and 1919 of Addams's publication in sociology journals is explainable by her general marginalization in US society because of her continuing opposition to World War I and to US entry into that war.

Moment II: Addams's marginalization in male accounts of the discipline

---

1921 Park and Burgess's *Introduction to the Science of Sociology** mentions two texts by Addams, *Twenty Years at Hull-House* and *The Spirit of Youth and the City Streets;* and lists *Hull-House Maps and Papers* in the bibliography.
1922 Emory S. Bogardus mentions Addams twice in *A History of Social Thought,* in Chapter 24 "The Trend of Applied Sociology"
1928 Pitrim Sorokin's *Contemporary Sociological Theory** mentions Addams once

---

Moment III: Addams's erasure from textual accounts

1937 Talcott Parsons's *The Structure of Social Action** makes no mention of Addams
1951 Robin Williams's *American Society: A Sociological Interpretation* does not mention Addams
1955 Bogardus does not include Addams in the third edition of *The Development of Social Thought;* similarly, Nicholas S. Timasheff does not include Addams in *Sociological Theory: Its Nature and Growth,* which will be a major theory text for the 1950s and early 1960s
1960 Don Martindale's *The Origins and Types of Sociological Theory* does not mention Addams
1963 Lewis Coser's *Masters of Sociological Theory;* does not mention Addams
1966 Robert Nisbet's *The Sociological Tradition** does not mention Addams
1970 Alvin Gouldner's *The Coming Crisis in Western Sociology** does not mention Addams
NB: Introductory sociology texts in the 1960s and 1970s also typically do not include Addams.
1981 Jonathan Turner and Leonard Beeghley's *The Emergence of Sociological Theory* does not mention Addams
1983 George Ritzer's first edition of *Sociological Theory* does not mention Addams

---

Moment IV: Addams's tentative reemergence

[**1965** Historian Christopher Lasch publishes an edited collection entitled *The Social Thought of Jane Addams*]
1988 Mary Jo Deegan publishes *Jane Addams and the Men of the Chicago School, 1892–1918*
1991 Deegan publishes *Women in Sociology: A Bio-Bibliographical Sourcebook,* placing Addams in company of other women in sociology
1996 Ritzer includes Addams in the second edition of *Classical Sociology*

(1892:77–78). Even Webb, who typically chose to deny gender discrimination, devotes pages in both her 1889 diary entry and her 1926 autobiography to the conversation in which Professor Alfred Marshall of Cambridge tried to discourage her from writing *The Co-operative Movement in Great Britain* (1891); Marshall told her, *"'A book by you on the Co-operative Movement I may get my wife to read to me in the evening to while away the time, but I shan't pay any attention to it'"* (italics hers) (Webb, 1926:352).

When the woman is a contemporary, a living but not directly present other, her claim to authority becomes even more fragile, for she cannot override by sheer force of character the typification "woman" by which she is stereotyped and diminished in male consciousness. Marianne Weber recounts how in 1893 before her wedding to Max, she was sent by his family to housekeeping school and wrote to him for books to read. He responded with concern that she should carve out a domestic place of her own: "[M]y mind tells me . . . you will have a more secure position . . . if [your] focal point is not in the purely intellectual-philosophical realm . . . but [in] a domain of practical activity . . . . For . . . in the intellectual sphere . . . I have naturally greater resources" (Weber, 1926/1975:186–187).[6] In 1899, Kelley actively lobbied Governor Theodore Roosevelt for the position of New York State Inspector of Factories (a job similar to one she had held in Illinois). She wrote Roosevelt, sent him copies of her publications, got Lillian Wald (the founder of the Henry Street Settlement in New York City) to press her case, and had Addams come from Chicago to meet with the governor. But Roosevelt decided that "'the time was not ripe'" to appoint a woman and instead appointed a man who, though admitting he knew nothing about the job requirements, had also been actively lobbying for the position. Roosevelt advised him to talk to Kelley: "'She knows more about enforcing the factory law than any man I know of, and I want you to keep in touch with her'" (Sklar, 1995:293–294). Despite her close link to the male sociologists at the University of Chicago, Addams's work, as shown in Figure 1-3, was marginalized by them almost from the beginning. In their *Introduction to the Science of Sociology,* the required text for sociology students between 1921 and 1940, Park and Burgess put together some 800 pages of readings with approximately 200 pages of their own text. They refer to two books by Addams but present no readings from her. In contrast, there are 43 references to Simmel, including ten readings. This contrast between Addams and Simmel is taken for granted today because the history of the discipline has taught that this is how they should rank; but here in the *Introduction,* Park and Burgess were establishing that ranking.

Once a woman dies and becomes a predecessor, she is truly subsumed within the assumptions of patriarchy: "The universe of ideas, images, and themes—the symbolic modes that are the general currency of thought—have been either produced by men or controlled by them. In so far as women's work and experience have been entered into it, it has been on terms decided by men" (D. Smith, 1987:19). In academic sociology, a key element in the maintenance of the predecessor is the canon, and women have been excluded from sociology's canon (Sprague, 1997). A simple test may be done here by the reader: refer back to the list of women at the beginning of this chapter and ask yourself how many times you have ever read their writing or discussed their ideas as the central topic of a sociology class. Inclusion in the canon—or on a microscale, in the syllabus—is more than an activity of selection; it asks the reader to orient toward a work seriously, that is, to see in the work the quality of authority. The importance of this request that the reader orient seriously toward a work is shown in a classic study that discovered that students' spontaneous responses to literary works often produced rankings much at odds with the established canon; the author of that study, I. A. Richards concluded: "Without the control of this . . . mysterious, traditional authority, poets of the most established reputations would very quickly and surprisingly change their places in general approval" (1929/1962:297).

Patriarchal marginalization of the woman as predecessor is illustrated in the professional fates of Addams and Martineau. The social theory texts cited in Figure 1-3, all written by men, all marginalize Addams. This process is also evident in a lengthy poem Burgess wrote in response to Addams's death, a poem that effectively trivializes Addams's intellectual achievement by sentimentalizing her for her maternal "spirit": "'Jane Addams, mother of the poor and helpless, / And of all humanity; . . . / . . . Great neighbor / Of the poor, rarely gifted in sympathy, . . . / The look of brooding in your eyes, compassion / For man's inhumanity to man; . . . / Your spirit stays to bless our thought and work. . .'" (the full 93 lines of this poem are given in Deegan, 1988:150–151).[7] Similarly, Martineau's obituaries blur, distort, and finally erase her contribution. John Morley, writing for the generation that would follow Martineau, allowed that she had "'a sure eye for social realities,'" but chose to dwell on her character, claiming that she possessed "'fine qualities, which would mostly be described as manly'"—"'industry and energy . . . a splendid sincerity, a magnificent love of truth'" (cited in Pichanick, 1980:242). Morley's gendering of his assessment foreshadows Martineau's fate. If "industry and energy . . . a splendid sincerity, a magnificent love of truth" are "manly," what is left for the woman scholar?[8]

A Politics of Knowledge

The marginalization of the women founders produced by the politics of gender was accelerated within the sociological community by the outcome of a debate over the purpose of sociology and the social role of the sociologist—an outcome determined by professional power relations that can be understood as a politics of knowledge. This debate moved among positions on a continuum variously described as "objectivity versus advocacy" (Furner, 1975), "scientistic" timelessness versus historical specificity (Ross, 1991), or "the objective service intellectual" versus "the purposivist" reformer (M. Smith, 1994). In the period between 1890 and 1947, sociology's academic elites arrived at the consensus that the appropriate role for the sociologist was that of the intellectual committed to scientific rigor, value-neutrality, and formal abstraction. This consensus de-legitimated the work of the women founders, and many men, who practiced the alternative position of a critical, activist sociology of advocacy. (Aspects of the history of this politics in American sociology can be found in Bannister, 1987; Diner, 1980; Furner, 1975; Halliday and Janowitz, 1992; Kuklick, 1973; Lemert, 1995; Lengermann, 1979; Donald Levine, 1995; Rosenberg, 1982; Ross, 1991; Silva and Slaughter, 1989; M. Smith, 1994; Turner and Turner, 1990, and Wilner, 1985.)

We can trace the emergence of this consensus through four representative statements by male founders of academic sociology. In 1895, in the lead article in the first issue of the *AJS*, editor Albion Small took a middle ground in this debate, calling for scientific knowledge while endorsing a practical purpose for the new journal and for sociology: "no subject which pertains to men's pursuits is beneath the notice of sociology"; contributors were to be "men and women who are gathering the materials of social philosophy from the most diverse sources"; contents would range from "methodology" to "social amelioration" to "social conditions"; and the purpose was to increase people's understanding so that they can form "more effective combinations for the promotion of the general welfare" (Small, 1895:14). But by 1916, in the twentieth anniversary issue, Small spoke for a decades-long move in academic sociology away from social reform towards pure research and academic recognition. The sociological community was "growing more and more dissatisfied with the ways in which . . . men were proceeding . . . in the interest of social betterment" like the "cheerful social dowagers of both sexes who thought they were solving social problems over teacups." Sociology's academic reputation was now seen to depend on scientific rigor: "Whether [sociologists] retain the academic recognition they have won will depend on whether they turn out to be at least as scientific as the most responsible of their colleagues" (Small, 1916:768; 861–63). In 1921, in their definitive text *Introduction to the Science of Sociology,* Park and Burgess described sociology as a project of pure and generalized scientific investigation: "a fundamental science . . . not mere congeries of social-welfare programs and practices. . . . [S]ociology is the abstract science of human experience and human nature" (1921:42–43). By 1947, on the fiftieth anniversary of the *AJS*, then-editor Louis Wirth consolidated the shift toward technical expertise, abstraction, and value-neutrality. He described sociology as having begun with "the crumbs that dropped off the table of . . . better-established academic disciplines, . . . such topics as poverty, delinquency and crime, insanity, marriage and divorce, slums, and other pathologies, together with such subjects as the community, voluntary groups, classes and races" (Wirth, 1947:276). He dismissed many early sociologists as "social workers, social reformers, social prophets, and social critics who, for want of any other academic refuge, had identified themselves with the adolescent science of sociology" (Wirth, 1947:273). Wirth's essay is important because it is essentially unreflective; he assumes that anyone reading the *AJS* in 1947 would share this view.

But every one of the women founders defined as a major concern the topics Wirth dismissed: poverty, class, and race, that is, social inequality; gender issues like marriage and divorce; and the ways that communities and voluntary groups function. And many male sociologists had shared these concerns.[9]

The primary explanation for the growing emphasis on scientistic expertise was sociology's move into the university as its "legitimate" work site, a move that was part of its quest for professional authority, social status, and job and salary security. Many potential work sites were open to sociology in the 1890s—social service agencies, research and policy-making groups, settlement houses, politics, religion, labor organizations, and various Progressive pressure groups. These possibilities are often overlooked in histories of social science and sociology, partly because the work of the women founders in this period is not considered and partly because the historians themselves write from, and thus privilege, an academic location. Nevertheless, higher education was unquestionably a growth industry, enrolling 2 percent of all college-age persons in 1890 and 15 percent by 1940 (Ross, 1991:161). The effect of this expansion was multiplied by the doubling of the US population in that period. In this work site, American sociology established itself "as an autonomous academic discipline [with] smashing success" (Oberschall, 1972:187), moving from four instructors offering courses in 1880 to 225 instructors and 59 departments by 1900 (Morgan, 1983:43), to "almost every major university and college [having] an independent department of sociology" by 1947 (Wirth, 1947:279).

Securing and expanding this work site meant that the sociological community became permeated by academic expectations and power arrangements. The university, whether private or public, depended on the economic support of powerful corporate and governmental groups aligned with capitalism. Under these circumstances, university administrations, senior faculty, and research foundations typically worked to distance departments and schools from the politics of trouble-making. Even in the midst of Progressive reform, economics professor Richard T. Ely reported President Harper of the University of Chicago saying, "'The labor movement may be all right but we get our money from the corporations and I am with the capitalists every time'" (cited in Sklar, 1995:295). Many universities purged or pressured their more radical faculty, including social scientists Henry Carter Adams, Edward W. Bemis, John R. Commons, Richard T. Ely, E. A. Ross, W. I. Thomas, and Thorstein Veblen (Deegan, 1988; Fitzpatrick, 1990; Ross, 1991; Sklar, 1995; M. Smith, 1994). For instance, after being dismissed from Cornell University for openly supporting labor in the Haymarket Massacre (1886), Adams advised fellow social scientists to "avoid controversial topics and become technical experts for legislators or regulatory commissions" (M. Smith, 1994:23); and economist Edward Bemis, after dismissals by the University of Chicago and Kansas State Agricultural College, got an appointment by a reform mayor in Cleveland and developed a model city water system (Campbell, 1988). Within academic culture these pressures were reworked to form a set of criteria for academic legitimacy to which academic sociologists had to conform: a subject matter distinct from that of other disciplines, a value-neutral expertise, a rhetoric consistent with academic decorum, a routinized way of credentialing new members, an established body of literature—a canon—through which new members were socialized, and a respect for academic rank and professional publication (Furner, 1975; Donald Levine, 1995; Minnich, 1990; D. Smith, 1987, 1990; Stinchcombe, 1982).

The academic work site made it all but impossible for women to interact with men as professional equals in face-to-face relations. Between 1890 and 1940 across all disciplines, women constituted on average about one-quarter of the faculty (Bernard, 1964; Carter, 1981; Morgan, 1978; Misra, Kennelly, and Karides, 1997). This rate overstates women's standing in academic sociology because it includes the faculty in women's colleges; includes the faculty in "women's disciplines" such as home economics, education, and library science; and fails to distinguish between regular appointments and the part-time, non-tenured, low-rank, low-pay slots that women typically fill.[10] In the profession as a whole in this period, no woman held senior rank in any of the leading sociology departments, no woman served as president of the American Sociological Society, and articles by women accepted for publication in the leading journals, the *American Journal of Sociology* and the *American Sociological Review*, constituted less than ten percent of all papers published (Hughes, 1975).[11]

The trend toward scientism in the academically situated social sciences has occasionally been slowed or redirected by reformist moments in the larger society. One such moment helped make possible the sociological production of the women founders—the Progressive liberationist mobilization between 1890 and 1915 by labor, immigrant groups, African Americans, an educated segment of the middle class, and the women's movement of first-wave feminism (see Figure 1-2). Another such moment occurred in the 1960s and 1970s under the impacts of the African American civil rights movement, the anti–Vietnam War movement, and the movement of second-wave feminism. But for the most part the trend toward scientism in academic sociology was encouraged by a general conservatism in American society and politics. The seeming anomaly in this linkage of societal conservatism to professional scientism is, of course, the 1930s, a period of economic crisis, labor militancy, capitalist opposition, and the commitment of national government to reform—a commitment characterized by Franklin Roosevelt in the 1932 presidential campaign: "The country needs and, unless I mistake its temper, the country demands bold, persistent experimentation." This cry might have seemed a call for a sociology of advocacy; and indeed many New Deal programs had earlier been advocated by the women founders (see Chapters 3 and 7). But by and large, academic sociology offered what it was asked to supply—technical expertise in the evaluation and implementation of New Deal policies. This response is evidenced by the absence of critical writing in the major sociology journals (Wilner 1985), the expansion of statistical sociology under William Ogburn at the University of Chicago (Bannister, 1987), the work done by H. L. Henderson at Harvard to shape sociology and other social sciences into practices of technical expertise (Buxton and Turner, 1992), the movement in the ASS led by L. L. Bernard to assert a wholly scientific sociology (Bannister, 1987), and the growing population of sociologists working for the federal government in Washington in the 1930s (Lengermann, 1979).

By the mid-1930s, sociology's narrative of itself had undergone a major reshaping, which marginalized many male thinkers and completed the erasure of the women founders. This reworking of sociology's intellectual record legitimated the combination of structural functionalist theory and survey research being developed by Talcott Parsons at Harvard and Robert Merton and Paul Lazarsfeld at Columbia, a combination offering a formal, value-neutral, universalized theory and methodology for the study of society. Parsons's landmark work *The Structure of Social Action* (1937) argued for a natural convergence toward a definition of sociology as the study of consensus and order in the social system—a convergence he traces in the works of four historically unrelated thinkers, Durkheim in France, Max Weber in Germany, Vilfredo Pareto in Italy, and Alfred Marshall in Britain. In 1921, Park and Burgess had given only three minor references each to Weber and Marshall (both of whom essentially fared no better than Addams), no mention to Pareto, and only moderate attention to Durkheim; their major figures—measured by references, readings, and permeating presence—had been Simmel, Park himself, W. I. Thomas, Small, Spencer, Charles Horton Cooley, and Charles Darwin.

Two points emerge from this broad-brush portrait of the politics of knowledge within sociology. First, the operative canon in modern sociology is a social construction, not a natural development. Second, its configuration legitimates a patterning of sociology that is conceivable only because of the earlier marginalization of the women founders. One could not look to Martineau, Addams, Gilman, Cooper, Wells-Barnett, Marianne Weber, Webb or the Chicago Women for one's founders and exemplars and remain secure in a definition of sociology that emphasizes social consensus over social inequality, detached analysis over activist engagement, and abstraction over critique.

BRINGING THE WOMEN BACK IN

The chapters that follow explore the lives, work, and significance of the women founders of sociology. Each chapter can be read as a self-contained unit in the order of the reader's choosing. Our ordering is guided by three objectives: to begin with Martineau (Chapter 2) as a member of the founding generation of sociologists; to conclude with the Chicago Women and Webb (Chapters 7 and 8) as representative of an empirical tradition; and to introduce the other thinkers in the order in which they might be most familiar in reputation and most accessible in works available for further study—Addams (Chapter 3), Gilman (Chapter 4), Cooper and Wells-Barnett (Chapter 5), and Weber (Chapter 6).

We begin each chapter with a biographical sketch, because all knowledge is situated and sociologists develop their theories from given cultural locations (McCarthy, 1996). While the lives of the male founders are part of the history and legend of the profession, almost non-reflectively framing the study of their theories, the women's lives are not so known. These biographies are necessary to allow the reader to locate the women founders in history and society. The women themselves were aware of their situatedness, often leaving significant autobiographical statements, as in the case of Martineau, Addams, Gilman, Cooper, Wells-Barnett, Weber, Webb, Kelley, Breckinridge, Talbot, and MacLean.

We then analyze the theory, summarizing its underlying assumptions, explicating its major themes, and introducing key vocabulary:

- Martineau's project is to develop a method for studying the relationship of a society's "morals" to its "manners" by finding the social indicators, "the THINGS," that measure degrees of liberty and domination, best shown, she believes, in the treatment of disempowered groups—women, the poor, racial minorities, children, and the handicapped.
- Addams focuses on how people align ethical conduct and material interests, on how the sociologist can study this alignment through empathetic participation in the lives of the disempowered and through analysis of societal trends, and on how American society in her own time can become a "socialized democracy."
- Gilman creates a formal critical theory relating the determining features of social life (consciousness, work, and gender) and showing how gender inequality ("the sexuo-economic relation") corrupts the human potential to think and work cooperatively, producing "an androcentric culture" instead of a human one. She develops a detailed program for achieving gender equality.
- Cooper and Wells-Barnett formulate a sociology from the standpoint of the disempowered, using the combination of race and gender as a double lens through which to uncover societal practices of "domination" and to discover the principles for a society based in social "justice."

- Weber describes the social world from the standpoint of women, using their experience of "authority and autonomy," "work," and "culture" to critique both the world in place and universalized male understandings of that world.
- The Chicago Women use social research to support their theory that there is "a public interest" in the designing of ameliorative social policies for specific categories of the disempowered—immigrants, the working class, children, women, and African Americans.
- Webb seeks to solve the problem of "poverty amidst riches" through the use of "social investigation to inform public policy."

We conclude the analysis in each chapter with a discussion of the relation of the theorist or theorists to the established canon and to the contemporary feminist paradigm. Each chapter then offers selected writings by the theorist or theorists discussed.

As the preceding summary of themes shows, the women founders created a range of theories. But those theories all share a moral commitment to the idea that sociology should and could work for the alleviation of socially produced human pain. The ethical duty of the sociologist is to seek sound scientific knowledge, to refuse to make that knowledge an end in itself, to speak for the disempowered, and to advocate social reform. This sense of moral purpose should not be misread as a carryover into social science of nineteenth-century "womanly virtues" described in American social history as "the cult of true womanhood" (e.g., Welter, 1966/1973). For in key respects the sociology of the women founders is guided by rules similar to those of contemporary feminist scholarship: that theory and research should be empirically grounded and empowering of the disempowered, that the correct relationship between researcher and subject is one of mutuality of recognition, that the social theorist should reflexively monitor herself as a socially located actor, and that social analysis should build from situated accounts to a general and critical theory of society (Benjamin, 1988; Collins, 1990; Fonow and Cook, 1995; Mies, 1983; Reinharz, 1983, 1992; Haraway, 1988).

In choosing to claim these women as part of our tradition as sociologists, we reaffirm that sociology is a discipline that has a history of speaking directly to and pressing for action on the most immediate problems confronting any society in which it is practiced. The significance of the re-introduction of these ideas is twofold. First, it shows us that the ideas of contemporary feminist sociology have a long and genuinely illustrious tradition in the discipline. Second, it confronts us with a problem at the very heart of the discipline: the tension between exclusive and inclusive principles and practices. These issues are the subject of the epilogue of this book.

This present volume is not a triumph of truth per se, though we believe it represents a truth about the history of sociology and social theory and contributes importantly to our understanding of our heritage as sociologists and social theorists. The same processes that operated to exclude the women, the interworkings of a politics of gender with a politics of knowledge, are operating now to make possible their re-emergence. The women founders are being rediscovered by sociologists because of a much larger, social movement towards greater inclusivity—most notably the global feminist movement of the second and, now, third wave along with mobilization by people of color and by gays and lesbians. This societal power realignment now affects the inner dynamics of the sociological profession. Within sociology, it is collective feminist action that makes possible the recovery of the women founders: the emergence of Sociologists for Women in Society in 1971, the creation of the ASA section on sex and gender in 1972, the establishment of *Gender & Society* in 1986, and the organization of the ASA Section on Race, Class, and Gender in 1996. A move towards a more inclusive history, thus, takes more than good-will. It must rest on a continuing mobilization by those excluded, a mobilization that creates the possibility of a dialogue among empowered equals (Collins, 1996). In speaking of women's gains within contemporary society, feminist sociologists "warn of the danger of overlooking . . . that 'such accomplishments [are] the result of feminist action. It is easy to forget'" (Ferree and Hess, 1985, in Roby, 1992:20). The story that unfolds in the chapters that follow demonstrates how tenuous such gains are, how implacable are the forces for exclusion, and above all, that *it is easy to forget.*

ENDNOTES

1. Among the other women are Helen Campbell, Janie Porter Barrett, Mary McLeod Bethune, Katharine Bement Davis, Ellen Irene Diggs, Frances R. Donovan, Ethel Sturgess Dummer, Isabel Eaton, Lucille Eaves, Emma Goldman, Amy Hewes, Leta Stetter Hollingworth, Susan Kingsbury, Alexandra Kollontai, Alice Masaryk, Florence Nightingale, Elsie Clews Parsons, Gertrud Simmel, Anna Garlin Spencer, Jessie Taft, Mary Church Terrell, Mary van Kleeck, and Lillian Wald.

2. The *Survey* was a magazine founded in the merger of several social work journals; it was edited by Paul U. Kellogg, and Addams served on its editorial board. This magazine served as a major vehicle for social reformers who saw themselves as engaged in sociology. It also offered a more popular version, *Survey Graphic,* because its editorial board took communication with a general public as a primary duty.

3. DuBois and Cooper were acquaintances and he knew exactly who she was and what she had written. Further, as Mary Helen Washington (1988) points out, Cooper encouraged DuBois in several projects, including one of his best-known works, *Black Reconstruction;* but there is no corresponding record of DuBois encouraging Cooper.

4. Addams, as early as 1881, recognizes that women need to acquire "*auctoritas* . . . the right of the speaker to make himself heard" (1881:37). Cooper argues that women's voices have been silenced and that progressive change will occur only when *"women have had a chance to grasp, master, and wield [the world's] dogmas"* (1892:58) (see Chapter 5). In *The Man-Made World* (1911), Gilman analyzes the consequences of men's having seized the authority to define words and meanings. Wells-Barnett in her analyses of lynching, explicitly states that she will use reports from white newspapers so that "[o]ut of their own mouths shall the murderers be condemned" (1895:15).

5. The most intimate and important form of the "thou-orientation" relation is the we relation, in which two people in a face-to-face relation are mutually aware of each other, know that each is aware of the other, and think of self and other as "we."

6. In her laudatory biography of Max, Marianne Weber's characteristic presentation of herself is one of admiring self-effacement. But on occasion, as after this letter, she asserts herself, here writing cryptically that she "did what her own conscience prompted" although she

could not have anticipated that "her marriage would some day depend . . . on her independent intellectual existence" (Weber 1926/1975:186–188).

7. Lest it be thought that most "in memoriam" poems follow this pattern, the reader might look, for instance, at W. H. Auden's tribute on the death of William Butler Yeats. Nor would one expect a male social theorist to be eulogized with the sentimentality Burgess accords Addams.

8. Apparently, what is left is to be a translator of the men. Park and Burgess, in *Introduction to the Science of Sociology,* begin by citing from Martineau's translation of Comte (she is credited in a footnote). They say of Comte: "Comte did not, to be sure, create sociology. He did give it a name, a program, and a place among the sciences" (Park and Burgess 1921:1). While that claim may surely be made, Park and Burgess could as easily have looked to Martineau and written: "Martineau did not, to be sure, create sociology. She was using the name as early as 1837, and she did give it a program, and a place among the sciences and a purpose in society." (See Hill, 1989, Hoecker-Drysdale, 1992, and Chapter 2 in this text.)

9. Indeed, even in the 1920s, Park and Burgess and the students they trained did not practice their stated goals of abstraction but continued a social science that bears striking resemblance to much of the work done by the women founders of the Chicago School, with a focus on descriptions of urban life, ethnicity, poverty, and deviance in case-specific field studies, framed by a regional mapping of social functions.

10. Thus, these figures could include MacLean, ghettoized for much of her career in the University of Chicago's Extension School, and Edith Abbott, who at points was employed only as an instructor of social statistics in the University of Chicago sociology department—as well as Addams and Kelley, who co-taught one summer course in sociology at the university.

11. The data for 1925–45 are taken from Hughes 1975; the data for 1895–1924 are our own counts. The only anomalous volume is Volume 14 of the *AJS* for 1908–9, in which women published eleven out of 52 articles, or about twenty percent of the total.

Harriet Martineau (1802–1876)— The Beginnings of a Science of Society

BIOGRAPHICAL BACKGROUND

Harriet Martineau was born in Norwich, England, on June 12, 1802, and died on June 27, 1876, in Ambleside, at The Knoll, the home she had designed and built for herself in England's Lake District from her earnings as Britain's foremost woman of letters. She had kept the pledge she had made to herself on her 27th birthday, when she faced a choice between earning her living by the needle or by the pen, with sewing being the more certain source of income: "I believe myself possessed of no uncommon talents, and of not an atom of genius; but as various circumstances have led me to think more accurately and read more extensively than some women, I believe that I may so write on subjects of universal concern as to inform some minds and stir up others" (Martineau, 1877:III:33). She wrote successfully across a range of disciplines—sociology, literature, children's literature, history, and political commentary.

Her foundational statements on the nature of society and the rules of sociological method were made in the 1830s, primarily in two closely related works, *Society in America* (1836) and *How to Observe Morals and Manners* (1838b). Our focus in this biographical sketch is on the intellectual and personal paths that led her to the project of founding a science of society; we then give a brief overview of the remainder of her career, emphasizing her continued work in sociology. The sources for our biographical sketch are Martineau's remarkably vivid *Autobiography* (1877); Susan Hoecker-Drysdale's scholarly, thoughtful, and readable study *Harriet Martineau: First Woman Sociologist* (1992); Michael R. Hill's excellent introduction to his much-needed reissue of *How to Observe Morals and Manners* (1838/1989); and studies of Martineau from other disciplines by Pichanick (1980), Robert K. Webb (1960), and Yates (1985).

Founding a Science of Society

Three biographical factors are crucial to Martineau's development as a sociologist: (1) an early life shaped by the Unitarian convictions and manufacturing interests of her middle-class family and by personal unhappiness caused in part by a progressive loss of hearing; (2) a series of crises in the late 1820s that interrupted—or rescued her from—a conventional life and let her design a life of her own; (3) her conviction that she should use her talent for writing to serve society as a public educator.

Early Life   Martineau grew up in an environment which prized standing for one's opinions regardless of public consequence, being able to state those opinions clearly in a rational argument, and seeking through steady reflection to align one's own behavior with the transcendent principles governing the universe. Thus, from childhood on, she was interested in the search for those principles—natural, social, and ethical—that pattern the world.

She was the sixth of eight children born to Thomas and Elizabeth (Rankin) Martineau in Norwich, a prosperous industrial town with an intellectual culture centered in the English Dissenting tradition. Dissenters belonged to a range of Protestant sects—Baptist, Methodist, Quaker, Presbyterian, and Unitarian—that refused to accept Anglicanism, the state religion of Britain, and were thus barred from various civil rights such as voting and attending university. The Martineaus were Unitarians, a particularly intellectual sect that deemphasized the significance of a personal God, focusing instead on the human duty to search for and live by the principles through which God ordered the world. Unitarians emphasized education and sought more education for their daughters than was common in British society. Martineau was primarily educated at home, with a couple of experiences of schooling in more formal settings; but like all women of her time, and to her lifelong regret, she was barred from university.

Her father Thomas was a manufacturer of textiles, who earned for his family a comfortable, cultivated middle-class lifestyle. Harriet Martineau's sense of the manufacturing or capitalist class was always to be affected by the particular conditions of her father's work as a small-scale capitalist. Thomas Martineau worked hard as the personal supervisor of his workers, a manufacturer whose prosperity was linked to his workers' well-being, and a businessman burdened by taxation and government regulation. But this mode of manufacturing, based in the coordination of skilled and semiskilled craftspersons, was superseded in his lifetime by the vast mechanized, steam-driven complexes of Yorkshire and the British Midlands. This "industrial revolution" transformed owner–worker relations in ways Harriet Martineau did not always fully grasp—even though this industrial revolution, by the 1820s, had swept away her family's business and the prosperity of most of Norwich (Webb, 1960). These experiences made "political economy," as the emerging science of economics was then known, a prime topic of discussion in her home, a topic that would be her initial entry into social science writing.

The Martineaus were thus placed in two ways outside the British establishment: they were small manufacturers in a country in which political power still belonged to the landed gentry and they were Dissenters from an established church which exercised political power and meant to keep it. This social placement made them, like most Unitarians, political progressives rather than revolutionaries: they had much to gain from reform but

Harriet Martineau, age 31

even more to lose from revolution. From this tempered stance, Unitarians responded to the intellectual arguments of the American and French Revolutions, sought political reform in Britain, and worked for the rights of other oppressed groups, particularly for the abolition of slavery in the British Empire.

Martineau, by her own account, was frequently ill as a child and at once both timid and willful. This may have produced some withdrawal of affection by her mother, as Harriet interpreted—or Mrs. Martineau may only have been caught up in the management of a large household. Martineau's life was further complicated by a serious and permanent loss of most of her hearing when she was twelve, a disability her family seems not to have immediately recognized—she did not get her prized ear trumpet until 1820. The deepest comfort of her growing up was in reading, study, and writing. Martineau developed a lifelong habit of disciplined self-education and writing, realizing in these projects the values of Unitarianism, the admiration of her family for scholarship, and a respite from the daily stress of being hearing impaired. Her earliest publication was an anonymous essay in 1822, "Female Writers on Practical Divinity," in the Unitarian journal the *Monthly Repository,* which won her family's praise even before they knew its authorship.

Crisis and Change   The course of Martineau's life was dramatically affected by two events in the 1820s—the decline of the family fortune and the breaking of her engagement. Beginning with a nationwide economic crisis in 1824, the Martineau textile business fell into a steady decline, which accelerated with the death of her father in 1826; the business collapsed entirely in 1829. (The economic crisis was caused by financial speculation, and all her life Martineau opposed this aspect of capitalist investment.) During this same period, Martineau, with much reservation, became engaged to a Unitarian minister with weak nerves. In Hoecker-Drysdale's judgment, she seems to have become engaged more out of convention than affection. When he collapsed into insanity, Martineau's response was relief; she refused to visit him, asked for her letters back, and a month after his death reported herself in "high spirits" (Hoecker-Drysdale, 1992:24). The collapse of the family business had left the Martineau women to support themselves. Two sisters went out to work as governesses. It was agreed within the family that Martineau, because of her deafness, would stay in the family home with her mother and attempt to earn a living by sewing and writing. Martineau began writing fictional tales on economic issues and requested payment for the ethical and philosophic pieces she was contributing to the *Monthly Repository.* Offered £15 a year by that journal's editor, she began to write prolifically. In 1830, a banner year, she turned out 52 pieces for the *Repository,* plus a novel, a book-length religious history, and essays for three contests sponsored by the Unitarian Association.

In 1831, on a visit to Dublin financed by the Unitarian prize money, Martineau got the idea that was to launch her firmly in the English literary and political world of her day: the conviction that the reading public was ready for a series of short tales that would illustrate the principles of political economy. After a long struggle, she finally managed to interest a publisher, but on very harsh terms: she had to get 500 subscriptions in advance; the publisher would take half the profits, could cancel after five volumes, and a thousand copies of the first two volumes had to be sold in two weeks. The first volumes of *Illustrations of Political Economy* were published in 1832, and the series became a runaway best-seller. Writing the *Illustrations,* Martineau turned out 25 volumes in 24 months; each volume of about 33,000 words was made pocketbook size for easy portability and told a story that taught principles of political economy, which were summarized at the end. By 1834, the series was selling at the phenomenal rate of "10,000 per month. This can be compared with the sales of other well-known authors of the period: J. S. Mills' *Principles* sold 3,000 copies in four years; Dickens's novels, which had been serialized first, had a sale of 2,000 or 3,000 copies and were considered very successful; . . . She seems to have outsold nearly everyone" (Hoecker-Drysdale, 1992:33–34).

Interpreting her own life to this point, Martineau saw that the great changes of the 1820s—the loss of money and the end of the engagement—had liberated her:

> I, who had been obliged to write before breakfast or in some private way, had henceforth liberty to do my own work in my own way; for we had lost our gentility. . . . [B]y being thrown, while it was yet time, on our own resources, we have worked hard and usefully, won friends, reputation and independence, seen the world abundantly, abroad and at home, and, in short, have truly lived instead of vegetated. (1877: I:142)

Writing as a Calling   *Illustrations of Political Economy* established Martineau in the public mind in the role she was to maintain for the rest of her long life: public educator on the critical theories and issues of her day. Writing for a general public let her be financially self-supporting, influence public policy, answer the call of duty to others by educating them, and, perhaps, achieve a sociality her deafness threatened. This complex of motivations led to an astounding productivity throughout a long life. Martineau's ability to write with exceptional rapidity was the result of the method of composition in which she had trained herself with rigid self-discipline: "I have always made sure of what I mean to say, and then written it down without care or anxiety,—glancing at it again only to see if words were omitted or repeated, and not altering a single phrase in a whole work" (1877:I:121–123). In all her writing, Martineau kept as her primary goal accessibility to a general public, a predominant concern in the *Illustrations:* "the works which profess to teach [political economy] have been written for the learned, and can only interest the learned. . . . We cannot see why the truth and its application should not be made more clear and interesting at the same time by pictures of what those principles are actually doing in communities" (1832–1834:I:viii–xi). The *Illustrations* are, as Martineau was the first to admit, derivative; but they gave her sufficient financial security, confidence, and reputation to allow more independence of thought.

The new turn in her thinking was toward the creation of a science of society and began in 1834 when she sailed to America for a change after the exhausting production of the *Illustrations*. She spent two years in America and wrote three books out of her experience: *Society in America, How to Observe Morals and Manners,* and *Retrospect of Western Travel* (1838d). Martineau loved the two-year American adventure—from the trip over, on which she tied herself to the mast during a hurricane in order to have the full experience of it, to her travels all over America, and her conversations with people from all classes there. She opens *Society in America* with a brief account of where she went, describing an itinerary that would daunt even the modern traveler. Landing in New York City, she eventually went as far south as New Orleans, as far west as the new city of Chicago, and as far north as Mackinac Island (Michigan). She visited twenty states (of the then twenty-four), traveling by foot, horse, carriage, and boat. She made repeated visits, especially to New England and New York. In Washington, she visited Congress, had dinner with President Jackson, and met "almost every senator and representative" (1836/1837: I:x–xiv). The American visit gave a new liberality to Martineau's thinking that shows itself in *Society in America,* perhaps her single most radical piece of social analysis. In it she espouses with force and clarity racial equality, the emancipation of the slaves, the abolitionist cause, the rights of women, and the need for equalization of property. She liked the Americans, and they, for the most part, seem to have liked her (see Webb, 1960, chap. 1). She made significant and lasting friendships, most importantly with William Lloyd Garrison, the abolitionist leader, and Maria Westin Chapman, another abolitionist whom Martineau later named her literary executor.

The experience with the abolitionist cause gave Martineau the opportunity to practice what she had long preached—courage of conviction. Martineau had written against slavery as early as 1830 but had not identified with the American abolitionists, whose confrontational strategies she questioned. She was initially welcomed as a guest in the homes of slave owners in the South, although she was uncomfortable and testifies to bearing witness against slavery there. But in her second visit to Boston she attended an abolitionist meeting, where she was passed a note asking her if she would speak to the gathering. In the *Autobiography,* she recalls: "The moment of reading this note was one of the most painful of my life. I felt that I could never be happy again if I refused what was asked of me: but, to comply was probably to shut against me every door in the United States but those of the Abolitionists" (1877:II:30). Choosing conscience over the possibilities for social science research, Martineau spoke and thereafter found her life threatened, her plans for a return trip to the South cut off, and her ability to visit easily with many people in the North abridged.

Returning to England in 1836, Martineau saw *Society in America* through publication, revised and published *How to Observe Morals and Manners,* and wrote a number of major review articles in which she applied her social science perspective. Reviewing the Annals of the Female Anti-Slavery Society in an article entitled "The Martyr Age of the United States" (1838c), she highlighted both her anti-slavery views and her unwavering conviction of the importance and heroism of women. "Domestic Service" (1838a) gave a detailed sociological analysis of the complex practice of paid household labor as an exemplar of class tensions. She ended the decade with the well-received novel *Deerbrook* (1839), which broke convention by offering middle-class heroes in a novel of manners and which Charlotte Brontë and George Eliot both credited with inspiring their later efforts.

Subsequent Career

The 1840s anticipated the pattern of much of the rest of Martineau's life: prolific writing both in sociology and in other genres, battles with illness, a willingness to seek new adventures, and involvement in intellectual and political controversy. Between 1839 and 1844 she was ill, apparently with gynecological problems. Even while ill, Martineau continued writing—*The Hour and the Man* (1841a), a fictional account of Toussaint L'Ouverture, the black liberator of Haiti, and *The Playfellow* (1841b), an enormously popular series of children's adventure stories. Finally cured—she felt, through mesmerism—Martineau wrote two studies of illness, *Life in the Sick-Room* (1844), an account from the standpoint of the patient, and *Letters on Mesmerism* (1845). The latter caused controversy because hypnotism was new and unconventional. But her recovery was complete, and by 1845 she had purchased land at Ambleside and designed and built The Knoll. She tried to run this home as a model farm and household venture, raising her own food and ensuring the fair treatment of her domestic staff. She continued her sociological analyses in *Eastern Life: Past and Present* (1848)—an account of her 1846 trip through the Middle East, which treats religion as a social construction rather than divine revelation—and *Household Education* (1849), a treatise on childhood socialization which calls for parents to be a refuge offering essentially unconditional love.

The 1850s followed the pattern of the 1840s. In *Letters on the Laws of Man's Nature and Development* (1851), co-authored with a younger friend and philosopher, Henry George Atkinson, Martineau argued that the mind can be studied scientifically as a material reality that forms ideas out of experience. She rejected the idealist thesis that the mind has immanent categories issuing directly from God. The book was received primarily as her declaration of atheism—a charge she described as true "in the vulgar sense,—that of rejecting the popular theology,—but not in the philosophical sense, of denying a First Cause" (1877:II:351). In 1852 she wrote *Letters from Ireland,* a book of travel and social analysis. In 1853, Martineau made the contribution to sociology for which she has been most remembered up to now, the translation of Auguste Comte's six-volume *Positive Philosophy.* The work was much more than a translation; it was a systematic condensation that clarified many of the original's main ideas:

> As for my method of working at my version, about which I have often been questioned,—it was simple enough.—I studied as I went along . . . the subjects of my author, reviewing all I had ever known about them, and learning much more. [Then], I simply set up the volume on a little desk before me, glanced over a page or a paragraph, and set down its meaning in the briefest and simplest way I could. Thus, my work was not mere translation: it involved quite a different kind of intellectual exercise . . . the work of condensation. (1877:II:391)

Martineau's two-volume edition made Comte accessible to English readers, and Comte liked it so much he had it retranslated into French. Martineau seems to have found Comte's vision of societal growth a parallel to her own intellectual journey from "theology" to "metaphysics" to "positive philosophy." In 1855, Martineau was again ill;

fearing she was dying, she wrote her three-volume autobiography, surely one of the most delightful and insightful works of this genre in English. Her other significant sociological work in this decade was a major review article, "Female Industry" (1859), which surveyed women's work in Great Britain and argued for the importance of that labor to the national wealth.

From the 1850s on, Martineau concentrated on a career as a journalist and public commentator, writing "leaders," that is, editorial opinion pieces, for English journals such as Charles Dickens's *Household Words* and the liberal newspaper the *Daily News,* to which she contributed some 1,600 pieces—editorials, opinion pieces, letters, and obituaries. Pichanick summarizes the range of issues on which she wrote: "economic, social and political conditions; war in Crimea . . . imperial policy in Ireland, India, and the colonies . . . education at all levels of society . . . public health, political, legal and prison reform . . . the rights of women . . . abolition and civil war in the United States, questions concerning the working class" (1980:204–205). Martineau's influence in these years was enormous; during the American Civil War one British politician claimed that "'[i]t was Harriet Martineau alone who was keeping English public opinion about America on the [Union] side through the press'" (William Edward Forster cited in Pichanick, 1980:213).

In her last year, Martineau (1877) gradually reduced her range of activity, finally confining herself to her bedroom at The Knoll; she died peacefully, leaving an obituary she had written for herself: "She saw the human race . . . advancing under the law of progress; . . . she enjoyed her share of the experience, and had no . . . reluctance or anxiety about leaving the enjoyment of such as she had" (1877:III:462).

GENERAL SOCIAL THEORY

Assumptions

Martineau had chosen from childhood a life built around study, reading, and writing. Though typically seen as a writer of the Victorian period, she was thirty-five years old when Victoria came to the throne in 1837. Her formative experiences thus reflect the intellectual conditions in England of the first third of the nineteenth century—some diffuse and popular, such as the British response to political revolutions abroad and the general belief in progress; others technical and scholarly, including debates within Unitarian religion, Lockean psychology, utilitarian economics, and positivist philosophy.

Born in the middle of England's desperate involvement in the Napoleonic Wars, Martineau absorbed the rhetoric of the American and French Revolutions as well as the English intellectuals' ambivalence towards revolution. From the literature of these two revolutions (including her reading of Mary Wollstonecraft's *A Vindication of the Rights of Women*), she took the basic idea of human equality, especially as it related to women's equality and to opposition to slavery. In her commitments to women's equality and racial equality, themes that are hallmarks of her sociology, she is a radical thinker.

Like most of her contemporaries, she believed in progress, that is, that the governing principle of human history is a movement towards betterment. Progress was sometimes seen as a frequently interrupted but discernible direction in human events; sometimes it was portrayed as a trend marked by a series of distinguishable stages. As the nineteenth century advanced, the idea of progress became intertwined with notions of biological evolution as the first principle of the universe. Martineau's use of progress is closest to the first form of this theory—that progress is a discernible potential. Her sociology is distinguished by her effort to arrive at a comprehensive definition of what would constitute betterment in human social affairs.

From her Unitarianism, Martineau derived an understanding of people as active moral and ethical beings, for Unitarianism theology focused on personal responsibility rather than reliance on the worship of an omnipotent God. A central question in her sociology is how this moral and active nature is realized or distorted in the processes of human social life. A corollary of Unitarianism in Martineau's day was the doctrine of necessarianism, which argued that God had in an original moment created a universe and set in motion natural laws that governed that universe—laws to which God, too, was subject. Martineau took several ideas from necessarianism: that the world operates according to fixed and discoverable principles which govern human life as well as the natural world; that the human qualities of reason and conscience make each individual responsible for her or his actions; that the individual must be aware that any choice is both the product of past actions and the producer of future states in which choice must again be made; and that the spiritual life is built on the study of this orderly functioning of the universe.

From her reading of philosophers like Joseph Priestley and David Hartley on the necessarianism theme, and of their intellectual predecessors such as John Locke, Martineau derived a psychology. All ideas come from experience; no ideas are innate (thus, there is no original sin, no impulse to evil born within each person). But the mind is not a passive receptor. Its active quality comes from what Hartley calls the principle of association of ideas—ideas themselves stimulate other ideas and thus it is possible for the mind to formulate laws and principles. Martineau's faith in education, which always informs her work as a sociologist, is based in this theory that the mind develops in response to its environment, that sound intellectual and moral development is produced by an environment that consciously trains minds.

Although Martineau later renounced political economy—"the pretended science is no science at all, strictly speaking" (1877:II:245)—she did take principles with her from her study of political economy, most significantly the widely held principle of utilitarian economics that the purpose of societal action is to secure the greatest good for the greatest number. At the time that Martineau wrote *Illustrations of Political Economy,* the idea had sparked two schools. One argued that people needed to be encouraged by rewards or punishments to align their actions with the good of the whole. The other, represented most famously by Adam Smith, argued that there was a principle of "identity of interests" in society—if people pursue their individual interests, the "invisible hand of the market" will produce the greatest good for the greatest number; governments need only take a laissez-faire approach to the economy and let free competition work. Martineau, all her life, vacillated between these two approaches. Her commitment to the values of individual freedom and moral agency led her on numerous occasions to oppose "reform" intended to regulate the market in the interest of the workers, seeing this reform as an interference with the principle of identity of interests. Yet she was also deeply committed to the principle of equality, and she never doubted that some equalization of material resources is necessary to that principle. Education was her strategy for resolving this conundrum: people do not need to be forced to align their interest with the good of the whole, but can be educated to choose freely such alignment.

In 1830, Martineau found another explication of social principles in the positivist philosophy of Henri Saint-Simon (1760–1825), Comte's teacher. Saint-Simon's primary thesis was that society and science had progressed to a point where society might use science to discover and improve its social and moral arrangements. Martineau's reading of Saint-Simon may have encouraged her to turn her quest for scientific principles to the design of a science of society.

Major Themes   Martineau sought to create a science of society that would be systematic, grounded in empirical observation, and accessible to a general readership, enabling people to make personal and political decisions guided by a scientific understanding of the principles governing social life. Like other founders of sociology, she worked relatively alone, experimenting with ways to name what she was doing. "Sociology" was one general term in her vocabulary; Hoecker-Drysdale reports that in 1837 Martineau wrote her brother James that she had been offered the editorship of a new journal intended "to treat of philosophical principles, abstract and applied, of sociology" (1992:70–71). But she more frequently describes her work as the science of society or the science of morals, and she speaks of the sociologist as the student of society, the student of morals, the observer, or the traveler. She uses the term "the traveler" in her most theoretical work, *How to Observe Morals and Manners* (1838b), because here she is trying to imagine the conditions under which her audience might really be called to think and observe sociologically. In our description of her ideas, we will use the terms "sociologist," "student of society," and "observer."

To create a science of society, Martineau had to develop both rules of scientific inquiry and an understanding of society itself. This she did primarily in two closely related works in the 1830s: *How to Observe Morals and Manners,* a guide to sociological fieldwork written during her voyage to America (revised and published after her American experiences), and *Society in America,* a sociological analysis based in two years of fieldwork. She continued to do sociological analyses for the rest of her life. In the remainder of this section, we describe Martineau's sociology in terms of her development of a subject matter, an epistemology, a methodology, and a critique of domination.

1. For Martineau, the subject matter of sociology is a society's distinguishing configuration of morals and manners. "Morals and manners" is the general term Martineau uses to describe the subject matter of sociology. By "morals" she means a society's collective ideas of prescribed and proscribed behavior; by "manners," the patterns of action and association in a society. Martineau argues that "manners are inseparable from morals, or, at least, cease to have meaning when separated" (1838b:220), that is, that patterns of interaction are intertwined with, and infused with meaning from, the collective ideas of a people. The phrase "morals and manners" is not a sentimental Victorianism. Martineau, like Comte and later Durkheim, is searching for a label for the phenomenon of a society's shared understandings. She uses, as they do, many different terms—for example, "virtues," "principles," "institutions," "common mind." Within the modern functionalist paradigm, this phenomenon is described as "norms," "values," "institutions," and "culture." But, unlike the functionalists, Martineau does not treat morals as the controlling overlayer that determines action or manners. Rather, she sees manners—patterns of action and association—revolving around collective ideas in complex ways: motivated by them, contradicting them, reworking them. And she sees that morals exist in varying modes of generality and formalism, in everything from legal constitutions to epitaphs to popular songs.

For Martineau the work of the sociologist is to describe, explain, and evaluate the relationship between manners and morals in a given society at a given moment in time. To do this the sociologist must (1) "trace . . . the circumstances" under which that relationship arises (1838b:27), (2) generalize about what qualities of morals and manners are " 'fixed and essential' " in a society (1838b:10), and (3) note and explain "anomalies" or contradictions between action and meaning (1836/1837:I:132). Among the circumstances Martineau herself studies are a society's geography, material resources, population density, history, relation to other societies, and ethnic homogeneity or heterogeneity. To discover what is fixed and essential about a people's morals and manners, the sociologist has to view individuals in a particular way. Martineau argues that while "[t]here are two aspects under which every individual . . . may be regarded"—one way certainly is as a self-directing person—the interest of the sociologist is in studying the individual in a second way, "as a being infinitely connected with all other beings, with none but derived powers, with a . . . directed will; a transparent medium through which the workings of principles are to be . . . revealed" (1836/1837:II:93). From this latter perspective, the individual is the medium, or link, between a society's morals or principles, on the one hand, and its manners or interactional practices on the other.

In her fieldwork in America, rather than in her formulation of *How to Observe,* Martineau discovers the need for the sociologist to deal with anomalies, that is, with contradictions between a society's declared morals and its habituated manners. The anomalies of US society become her chief theme in *Society in America.* Anomaly is a particularly striking feature of American society because that society has so self-consciously and formally stated its moral principles in the Declaration of Independence and the Constitution. Martineau focuses especially on the principles of the Declaration of Independence which promise "that all men are created equal" and describe governments as "deriving their just powers from the consent of the governed." The manners she holds most in contradiction with, or anomalous to, these principles are slavery, the subjection of women, the inequality resulting from the pursuit of wealth in property, and the flagrant cynicism about the elected representatives of government. Focus on these anomalies leads her to formulate as a basic principle of social change that a tension between morals and manners cannot continue unresolved in a society.

America offers Martineau an ideal field in which to explore her essential insight that morals and manners are always being socially constructed and modified, though people living in a society are not always aware of this ongoing construction of social reality. She finds America sociologically fascinating because what she calls "the process of world-making" is so visible, or transparent, there, as compared to England, where custom hides so much:

> In England, everything comes complete and finished under notice. . . . Each man may be aware of some one process of formation, which it is his business to conduct; but all else is present to him in its entirety. . . . [In America], old experience is all reversed. . . . It is an absorbing thing to watch the process of world-making;—both the formation of the natural and conventional world. I witnessed both in America. (1836/1837:I:155–156)

2. For Martineau the epistemological validity of sociological knowledge depends on three interconnected practices—impartiality, critique, and sympathy. For Martineau the key epistemological issue in sociology is how the observer can produce fair and accurate generalizations about the society observed. The appropriate orientation for the observer is one of "impartiality," which for Martineau encompasses not only a proscription against ethnocentrism but a prescription for independent standards of judgment and the practice of sympathetic understanding. Martineau's discussion of impartiality is an original and nuanced understanding of the idea of objectivity in sociology. In the first instance, impartiality means "the exclusion of prejudice, both philosophical and national." The sociologist must not carry ethnocentric or personal prejudices to the study of another society, or infuse the actions observed with meanings brought from her or his own biography or society. The sociologist must not "be perplexed or disgusted by seeing the great ends of human association pursued by means which he could never have devised and to the practice of which he could not reconcile himself" (1838b:13).* The student of society must be ever conscious that "actions and habits do not always carry their moral impress visibly to all eyes" (1838b:17) and must seek to discover the meaning actions have for the actors.

It is essential to understand that for Martineau impartiality is not value-neutrality. The sociologist is a moral being who must critically but fairly assess the moral status of the society observed. This calls for impartial standards of evaluation. One standard to use is the set of principles a society declares for itself. In *Society in America,* Martineau proposes "to compare the existing state of society in America with the principles on which it is professedly founded; thus testing Institutions, Morals, and Manners by an indisputable, instead of an arbitrary standard" (1836/1837:I:iv).* Thus, she takes as her standard the opening paragraphs of the Declaration of Independence, which she interprets to mean that in America all people bear the moral obligation to participate in government except "the unrepresented; and they in theory are none" (1836/1837: I:5). Martineau concludes that American society is in an anomalous situation, partially constrained by the principles of equality it has formally declared, but "from a want of faith in the infallible operation of the principles of truth and the rule of justice . . . [the United States] is acting out in its civilization an idea but little more exalted than those operating among nations far less favoured . . . in . . . political freedom"

---

*An asterisk following a citation in the text means that the passage quoted is given in fuller context in the readings at the end of the chapter.

(1836/1837:II:154). A second standard for impartial judgment, explicitly invoked in most of Martineau's own analyses and formally commended to the sociologist, is "the only general one," the standard of "the relative amount of human happiness" (1838b:13).* Martineau offers this as a trans-societal, or universal, principle by which the morals and manners explicit or implicit in societies may and must be judged. In her own sociological analyses, she applies this utilitarian principle of the greatest happiness for the greatest number to some very specific concerns about how this is to be achieved, calling on the corollary principles of justice and fairness, especially in the treatment of the less powerful. With the principle thus expanded, she explores it by dealing with cases of its violation in acts of domination (see Theme 4, following).

But the sociologist can neither see impartially nor judge correctly without the skill of *sympathy*—a skill that distinguishes the student of society from the student of geology or general statistics. The student of society who lacks sympathy, writes Martineau, is "like one who, without hearing the music, sees a roomful of people begin to dance." Martineau criticizes alike the observer in America "who has never felt any strong political interest, and cannot sympathize with American sentiment about the majesty of social equality" and those American observers of English society who "have no antiquarian sympathies." The former "can never understand the political religion of the United States; the sayings of the citizens by their own fire-sides, the perorations of the orators in town-halls, installations of public servants, and the process of election"; the latter cannot understand that contemporary British society would not invent the pomp of "the royal state-coach, with eight horses covered with trappings" but maintain them out of a respect for tradition.* The sociologist who lacks the sympathy or empathy to grasp the meaning of such public events will never be able to analyze the far more significant and complex phenomena of the community and the home— "even if the roofs of all the houses of a city were made transparent to him, and he could watch all that is done in every parlor, kitchen, and nursery in a circuit of five miles" (1838b:44–45).* The emphasis on sympathy will for the contemporary reader link Martineau to the interpretive, or Weberian, tradition in sociology. Just as significant and perhaps more intriguing is Martineau's focus on domestic life as a central subject for sociological analysis, a theme that recurs throughout her career. This focus shows that from the very beginning, there has been a feminist sociology—a sociology from the standpoint of women.

3. Martineau's methodology is to seek representative objectifications of the manners and morals of the society being studied. Martineau gives as her first rule of sociological method: "the grand secret of wise inquiry into Morals and Manners is to begin with the study of THINGS, using the DISCOURSE OF PERSONS as a commentary upon them" (1838b: 63).* She frames this rule with a detailed discussion of why to choose things over discourse, how to choose things, what kinds of things to choose, and how to make and organize observations of the things chosen.

The methodological problem facing the sociologist is finding accurate and fair representations that will show what is fixed and essential in the manners and morals of a people. Martineau sees a number of problems in arriving at representativeness through interviews with and statements by people. The sociologist can talk with or listen to only a limited number of people and has no way to confirm that that sample constitutes an accurate cross-section of the general population. Diversity of circumstance renders the opinions of some people more accessible, visible, and prominent in a society. If the sociologist receives consistent opinions from those interviewed, he or she may falsely conclude that there is more consensus than actually exists; on the other hand, wide diversity of opinion may lead the sociologist to make generalizations based on personal predisposition.

Martineau, thus, recommends the study of those "Things" that embody or objectify the "common mind," "the voice of the people," "the condition of the masses": "The eloquence of Institutions and Records, . . . be they what they may, whether architectural remains, epitaphs, civic registers, national music, or any of the thousand manifestations of the common mind which may be found among every people, afford more information on Morals in a day than converse with individuals in a year" (1838b:64).* With remarkable inventiveness, she looks for a way to catch the manners of a people in things, focusing on the kinds of collective activity people engage in. She suggests both the indicator of manners to be looked for and the questions to be asked about it:

> General indications must be looked for. . . . In cities, do social meetings abound? and what are their purposes and character? Are they most religious, political or festive? . . . Are women there? In what proportions, and under what law of liberty? What are the public amusements? . . . In country towns, how is the imitation of the metropolis carried on? . . . In the villages, what are the popular amusements? Do the people meet to drink or to read, to discuss, or play games, or dance? (1838b: 64–65)*

Even conversations with people, or "discourse," can be treated as a thing. In her chapter, "Discourse," she does not deal with the meaning of what people say about things, but rather makes discourse a thing itself by suggesting a typology of possible discourse styles: "In one country less regard is paid to truth in particulars, to circumstantial accuracy than in another. One nation has more sincerity; another more kindliness. One proses; another is a light and sportive. . . . One flatters the stranger; one is careless of him. . . . Such characteristics of the general discourse may be noted as a corroboration of suppositions drawn from other facts" (1838b:222–223).

In deciding what things to observe, the sociologist should begin with universal features of collective life: age and gender differences; the requirements for subsistence, such as food, clothing, and shelter; the conditions of mortality—birth, reproduction, illness, death; the necessity to devise rules or procedures for collective living; the need for domesticity and affection. To make safe generalizations about a whole society, Martineau advises the sociologist to select things that are particular manifestations of these universal features of human social life. The table of contents of *How to Observe* shows how she operationalizes this directive (see Figure 2-1).

For instance, Martineau looks at the universal experience of death in the sections on suicide, epitaphs, and health (in which she considers mortality rates). She considers burial arrangements and epitaphs to be hugely significant things because they indicate the morals and manners of a people around an unavoidable fact of social life—people die and something must be done with the body. In her interpretation, the pyramids of Egypt show that class privilege is not leveled by death; the use of the village cemetery in England as a playground and area of easy gossip, on the other hand, suggests a sense of community that transcends the distinction between life and death; the epitaphs in the cemeteries of Paris show a

FIGURE 2-1

Table of Contents from *How to Observe Morals and Manners,* giving Martineau's sense of key social indicators, key social structures, and key social values.

CHAP. I. Religion
  Churches
  Clergy
  Superstitions
  Suicide

CHAP. II. General Moral Notions
  Epitaphs
  Love of Kindred and Birth-Place
  Talk of Aged and Children
  Character of Prevalent Pride
  Character of Popular Idols
  Epochs of Society
  Treatment of the Guilty
  Testimony of Criminals
  Popular Songs
  Literature and Philosophy

CHAP. III. Domestic State
  Soil and Aspect of the Country
  Markets
  Agricultural Class

  Manufacturing Class
  Commercial Class
  Health
  Marriage and Women, Children

CHAP. IV. Idea of Liberty
  Police
  Legislation
  Classes in Society
  Servants
  Imitation of the Metropolis
  Newspapers
  Schools
  Objects and Form of Persecution

CHAP. V. Progress
  Charity
  Arts and Invention
  Multiplicity of Objects

CHAP. VI. Discourse

view of death characterized by a sense of hopeless loss and desolation, while those in New England proclaim the strength and hope of family ties continuing in an afterlife. Such indicators may suggest what behaviors a group considers good, how it interprets the loss of a member, and hence how it defines its own continuity.

It would be a mistake to treat the social indicators in Figure 2-1 simply as a sort of researcher's checklist. These chapter headings and subheadings provide us with a sketch of what Martineau considers to be the fundamental organization of society as well as what she sees as measures of the degree to which a given society is realizing human happiness. Theoretically, she defines a society's realization of human happiness in terms of ideals of fairness and justice—and the absence of practices of domination. She treats of general attitudes towards authority and the potential for domination in her fourth chapter, "Idea of Liberty." Her sense of progress (the topic of her fifth chapter) focuses on the movement toward an expanded spirit of community, best measured by the types of charity practiced in a society. She advises early on and repeatedly that the sociologist look to the status of women in any society as the standard for judging its state of domestic morals.

Martineau devotes considerable space to the mechanics of data-gathering—devising a journal format that meets one's needs, regular journal keeping, interviewing without intimidating, writing up the results of interviews as soon as possible, and frequent reevaluation of research protocols. She also suggests by example the use of typologies as a tool in the comparative study of societies. For instance, in looking for social indicators of domination, Martineau focuses on a society's practice of charity, using a typology of charitable efforts which ranks the lowest type of charity as that which is concerned only with "relieving immediate pressure of distress in individual cases" and the highest as that which directs efforts at "prevention rather than alleviation." Progress is measured by the degree to which "[t]he helpless are . . . aided expressly on the ground of their helplessness,—not from the emotions of compassion excited by the spectacle of suffering in particular cases, but in a nobler and more abstract way" (1838b:208, 214). In reporting one's results, Martineau urges giving the reader vivid verbal sketches of one's observations. This strategy she explicitly adheres to in *Society in America*. And in the linked creation and publication of *Society in America* and *How to Observe*, we have in sociology the first juxtaposition of a statement of methodology and a research application of that methodology. If nothing else establishes Martineau as the first modern sociologist, this fact does.

4. For Martineau sociology is a critical science with an ethical imperative to oppose domination. For Martineau, the supreme right of all individuals, the key to each person's pursuit of happiness within the general good, is the right to act as a moral being. "If there be any human power and business and privilege which is absolutely universal, it is the discovery and adoption of the principle and laws of duty. As every individual, whether man or woman, has a reason and a conscience, this is a work which each is thereby authorized to do for him or herself" (1836/1837:II:229–230). The opposite of autonomy, or self-direction, is domination, the enforced "submission of one's will to another" (1838a:411).* Domination in its most immediate and visible form may be found in interactions between individuals in which one person uses another person as an instrument, denying the other's independent subjectivity. Domination also exists in societal practices that limit people's ability to function as free moral agents.

In *How to Observe*, Martineau presents three formal criteria for estimating the degree of domination within a society: (1) the condition of less powerful or disempowered actors—women, prisoners, those in need of charity; (2) the society's idea of liberty, which will show its attitudes towards authority and autonomy, and (3) the society's progress in providing all people with the means whereby to be self-directing moral agents. These criteria inform her investigation of American society, in which she finds four major practices of domination—slavery, the treatment of women, the reification of public opinion, and the fetishizing of wealth. These excite her analysis because they are clear anomalies within the framework of America's declared first principles of equality before the law, the consent of the governed, and the institution of government as a way to secure the rights to life, liberty, and the pursuit of happiness.

In "The Morals of Slavery" (one of several chapters in which she explores the morals of various institutions—economy, commerce, manufacture, and politics), Martineau examines the attempt to justify slavery as an example of the complex relation between manners and morals. She asks, "What social virtues are possible in a society of which injustice is the primary characteristic? in a society which is divided into two classes, the servile and the imperious?" (1836/1837:II:106).* She says slaveholders claim mercy as the chief, but that this is a meaningless virtue, deriving as it does from a fundamental injustice: "human beings are totally subjected to the will of other human beings, who are under no other external control than the law which forbids killing and maiming,—a law which is difficult to enforce in individual cases" (1836/1837:II:112–113).* Martineau argues that the institution of slavery subverts the moral potential of everyone within it: the slave; the white slave owners—men, women, and children; other whites who are in contact with it—so-called free whites in the South and the merchants of the North who trade in slave-produced goods. She focuses on the corrupting influence of slavery on sexuality and marriage, between and within black and white populations. With a degree of directness which we will not see again in the writing of sociologists until we begin to study the work of Anna Julia Cooper and Ida Wells-Barnett writing a half century later, she discusses the widespread sexual exploitation of black women by white men and the fact of sexual attraction between the races. She traces the pain this exploitation causes black men, the impotence and complicity of white women, and the destruction of the character of the white man who is not true to his white wife and either abuses or fails to acknowledge his relationship with the black woman. For Martineau, the entire domestic structure, which she sees as the primary unit in society, is poisoned by the institution of slavery. She recognizes the connection among race, color, and slavery in her chapter, "The Citizenship of People of Color," that is, "free" people of color who are denied their legal rights as citizens of the United States.

For Martineau the domination of women closely parallels the domination of slaves, and she forcefully draws this comparison. Like the slave, the woman is seen and describes herself as being indulged, but "indulgence is given her as a substitute for justice. Her case differs from that of the slave, . . . just so far as this; that the indulgence is large and universal, instead of petty and capricious. In both cases, justice is denied on no better plea than the right of the strongest" (1836/1837:II:227). Laws denying women political and economic rights erode the woman's capacity for moral agency. Martineau traces the consequences of this denial of legal and moral autonomy, this contradiction of the principle of consent of the governed, for other aspects of society—the state of marriage, the possibilities for women's work, the health of both women and children, the socialization and education of girls, and sexuality.

In Martineau's analysis, Americans' subservience to public opinion undermines their moral independence and their capacity to practice republican government. Martineau sees Americans living in a state of perpetual self-censorship because of their fears of public opinion. She asks the reader to consider "[w]hat harm the 'force of public opinion' . . . can inflict upon a good man or woman, which can be compared with the evil of living in perpetual caution" (1836/1837:II:159). In the case of slavery, Americans edit their opinions by arguing that speaking against slavery may harm the Union. "But is it possible that such do not see that if slavery be wrong, and if it be indeed bound up with the Union, the Union must fall?" (1836/1837:I:134). The great danger is that people come to associate supposed public opinion with majority rule; and "[i]n a country where the will of the majority decides all political affairs, there is a temptation to belong to the majority" (1836/1837:II:154). This temptation means that men often seek office by "declar[ing] a coincidence of opinion with the supposed majority" (1836/1837:I:85). Martineau says that nothing caused her more sorrow during her research in America than the contempt Americans had for office seekers precisely because those office seekers bowed to public opinion—the same public opinion that their constituents also obeyed.

Martineau also analyzes the anomaly for the American republic of the frenetic pursuit of wealth. This configuration of manners and morals leads, in two ways, to domination. First, it produces a stratificational arrangement analogous to race and gender, for "[w]ealth is power, and large amounts of power ought not to rest in the hands of individuals" in a republic (1836:/1837:I:175).* Second, the pursuit of wealth reduces people's capacity for moral agency because it promotes anxiety and limits reflection. Martineau sees Americans as dissatisfied because they lack the leisure in which to think about appropriate directions for their lives: "Leisure, some degree of it, is necessary to the health of every man's spirit. Not only intellectual production, but peace of mind cannot flourish without it." Martineau stresses that America is wealthy enough to offer sufficient leisure to everyone if there were "community of property" (1836/1837:II:180).* She believes Americans will achieve "an equalization of property" when they recognize the costs of the fetishizing of wealth—crime, anxiety, and ill health.

Looking at practices of domination as a critical sociologist, Martineau produces a critique of America that may be tested against that society today: she sees the society's promise blighted and distorted by racism, sexism, an irrational pursuit of money, and the fear-worship of public opinion by officials and voters alike.

MARTINEAU'S RELEVANCE FOR THE HISTORY AND PRESENT PRACTICE OF SOCIOLOGY

Martineau and the Canon of Sociology

Martineau's place in sociology's history is as a member of its first generation of founders. Up to now this generation has been interpreted by sociologists in terms of the works of three major male thinkers, Auguste Comte, Herbert Spencer, and Karl Marx, who are seen as having established the main macrostructural traditions—functionalism and Marxian conflict theory.[1] Each of these men produced broad definitional statements which presented a view of the overarching dynamics of history, society, and evolution and located the social analyst's work in the twin tasks of expanding scientific understanding of these dynamics and of proceeding deductively to the interpretation of any given society. Of these three, only Marx grounds his theory in any direct observations of social life.

If we include Martineau's work as part of this initial definitional activity (and in publication it is almost the earliest block of sociological writings, overlapping only with Comte), we discover that from the very beginning there were other paradigmic traditions present in sociology. Martineau's work shows us that there has always been (1) a concern with the meanings that actions have for actors, (2) a sense that the place to begin to do sociology is in the field, (3) a definition of the subject matter of sociology as the diversity of human life, (4) a commitment to the idea that gender matters, and (5) an understanding that a critique of society in terms of its *multiple* oppressive practices is the moral responsibility of the sociologist. In different configurations these five points show us that Martineau represents in the founding generation both the interpretive paradigm, typically presented as having been introduced by the second generation of founders, and the feminist paradigm, only intermittently presented as a sociological paradigm with a tradition. Thus, Martineau's place in the canon is essential for a full understanding of the complexity of sociology's history. We expand on this idea by comparing Martineau's sociology with that of Comte, Spencer, and Marx and then, in the next section, by explicating the elements of a feminist paradigm visible in her work.

Abstracts versus Grounded Theory   Comte, Spencer, and Marx all have as a primary project the creation of an abstract, general social theory, and they present this theory in a style seemingly unconstrained by issues of accessibility to a general public.[2] Martineau is distinguished from the men in that she seeks to create an empirically grounded, narratively vivid sociology that shows the concrete realities of people's lives in a style accessible to a general public. She wishes to educate the public in what will later be called the "sociological imagination" (Mills, 1957/1977), both by showing them the product of this imagination—fair and accurate pictures of social life—and by teaching them how to observe manners and morals for themselves. Her goal is to enable people to bring an understanding informed by social science to their duties as independent moral agents within the social and political arenas.

Evolution: Major versus Minor Theme   The male founders all advance as a major thesis the principle of the unilinear development of societies. In the theories of all three, the course of human history is a movement from simple, primitive, and vulnerable forms of collective life towards complex social systems which increasingly approach the possibility of what they hold to be the greatest realizable human good. For Comte, this good is social stability in a hierarchically organized society, self-consciously guided by social scientific principles; for Spencer, social equilibrium among the institutions of an industrial and democratic society; for Marx, a technical-industrial order in which the apparatus of production is collectively owned and products are distributed according to a principle of equity.

Martineau also believes in a principle of progress towards the good society, which she measures in terms of the amount and distribution of happiness, which, for her, is equivalent to the degree to which all people function as full moral agents. Such a society requires a fair distribution of material goods, leisure for reflective choice, cultivation of intellectual and fine arts, full public education, equality between men and women, self-government, a spirit of moderation, and a respect for all types of honest work. But Martineau is distinguished from the men in that she does not make a principle of unilinear development in society a central theme, nor does she locate any society in its entirety on some general continuum towards this good. Instead, she studies a society's various configurations of manners and morals—for example, religion, politics, marriage, gender, economy, race, and class—and develops a series of subtypologies of progress. In religion, she distinguishes two excessive modes, the licentious and the ascetic, and the appropriate mode, which she calls "the moderate" (1838b:68); in class stratification, she distinguishes among societies that have only two classes, "proprietors and labourers," societies marked by complex gradations, and "the most advanced," those societies in which the labor and capitalist functions are mingled and "classes least distinguishable" (1838b: 190–191). When all these typologies are brought into play, no society, in Martineau's view, fully realizes the good and almost every society has some progressive features.

Structure versus Meaning The male founders conceive of social systems as systems of interrelated structures: Comte explores the relation of intellectual institutions like religion, education, and science to practical institutions like the economy and politics; Spencer, using an image of the society as organism, traces the functional relations among institutions like religion, polity, and economy; Marx, reversing Comte, argues the effect of economy on all other institutions, including the intellectual, but interpolates class relations as the mechanism of association among institutions. Martineau is distinctive in this generation for moving beyond an analysis of social structure to an investigation of the relations between large-scale, or macro, social arrangements and the micro-dynamics of daily living. She emphasizes critical empirical observation of people's actions and meanings as those are typified in morals and principles, manifested in interaction, and present in intra-psychic states, such as mood and motive. Except in situations of extreme suffering and poverty, she, unlike Marx, does not see material circumstance determining morals, but rather influencing them. Her interest remains in what the people intend, why they choose the intentions they do, how they fail or succeed in those intentions, and what anomalies exist between declared formal principles and lived everyday morals and manners. To understand all this, Martineau focuses on the everyday world as subject matter; this focus distinguishes her not only from Comte, Spencer, and Marx, but also from the sociologist whom at first glance she may seem most to resemble—Emile Durkheim.

Martineau and Durkheim It is possible for us to describe Martineau as anticipating Durkheim when we compare Martineau's first methodological rule, "the grand secret of wise inquiry into Morals and Manners is to begin with the study of THINGS, using the DISCOURSE OF PERSONS as a commentary upon them" (Martineau, 1838b:63), and Durkheim's dictum in *The Rules of Sociological Method* that "[t]he first and most fundamental rule is: *Consider social facts as things*" (Durkheim,1896/1938:14]. But such a view trivializes and marginalizes Martineau's achievement. She makes her statement some sixty years before Durkheim and makes it decisive and central to her methodology. Moreover, her development of the concept of "things" is different from Durkheim's in important ways, ways that tell us much about her—and his—idea of society and social life.

Most important is the difference in the choice of things to be observed. Durkheim typically chooses what contemporary feminist Dorothy E. Smith (1987) would call "the texts of the relations of ruling"—law, religious doctrines, and government records; Martineau just as typically chooses things from what Smith calls "the actualities of lived experience"—what people eat when they gather in a pub, whether people gather to drink or read or dance, what goods are offered in a market, and whether the home is the center of social life or amusements are always planned to take place away from home. Where Durkheim focuses on statistical records of suicide, Martineau wishes to look at epitaphs in graveyards. Where Durkheim wishes to look at laws as indicators of the social consensus, Martineau is skeptical about the empirical significance of law, which she sees as an expression of social consensus only in a fully democratic republic—an ideal as yet unrealized even in the United States. Martineau chooses rather to seek indicators of society's attitudes toward freedom and control, which she calls their idea of liberty. She believes this idea can be measured in people's attitudes towards the police, in the presence and quality of newspapers, and in the ways persecution for opinion is carried out (1838b:204).

Durkheim wishes to look at what constrains people to do what they would not otherwise do; Martineau wishes to understand what meanings are present in what people do and to judge those meanings in terms of human progress. Durkheim's operationalization of the concept of "things" offers a formulation for the functionalist paradigm in sociology; Martineau's, for the interpretive and feminist paradigms. This latter difference is made clear by Durkheim's lack of interest in domination and the centrality of domination in Martineau's thought.

Harriet Martineau and the Tradition of Feminist Sociology

From its inception as an intellectual endeavor in the middle third of the nineteenth century, sociology has had a feminist paradigm. Four key themes of this paradigm are woven through Martineau's sociology: (1) a gendered standpoint, (2) a focus on women's lives and work, (3) an exploration of domination and inequality in terms of issues of vantage point and differences among women, and (4) a commitment to not merely analyzing the world but changing it.

A Gendered Standpoint   Martineau writes and does sociology both self-consciously and unself-consciously as a woman. Her standpoint as a woman is reflected in her presentation of self to readers, her response to women's situation, her choice of things to study, and her style of doing sociology and sociological theory. She opens *Society in America* by explicitly addressing the issue of her gender: "It has been frequently mentioned to me that my being a woman was [a] disadvantage" in doing social research (1836/1837:I:xiii).* Martineau's answer reflects both her gendered standpoint and her woman-centeredness as she argues that women have the advantage in social research because they can more easily gain access to domestic life, which she defines as the strategic site for the study of morals and manners. Repeatedly, she reverses the male practice of emphasizing the so-called public sphere and marginalizing the private. She suggests that it is fairly easy to study the public sphere and that what is important—and difficult—is to study the private sphere. She remarks on men's failure to realize the importance of the domestic: "Men know very little about it, and would fain appear to know less than they do. . . . Men never think of the subject if they can help it . . . They consider it an evil which it is their wives' business to manage and to bear" (1838a:408).*

Later in *Society in America,* she responds as a woman to her own description of the condition of women in her chapter "Political Non-Existence of Women," which Pichanick has called "a too much neglected early manifesto in the women's rights campaign" (1980:93). Tracing the history of women's lack of and loss of civil rights in the United States, Martineau asks "[h]ow the political condition of women [can] be reconciled" with the universalistic and inclusive claims of the Declaration of Independence (1836/1837:II: 148).* In scathing prose, she answers that it cannot and disputes the arguments Americans give to explain this anomaly. To the frequently repeated assertion that women themselves agree with or acquiesce in their position, she says that, in the first place, "such acquiescence proves nothing but the degradation of the injured party." But in the second place, "this acquiescence is only partial; . . . I, for one, do not acquiesce. . . . I know that there are women in America who agree with me in this. The plea of acquiescence is invalidated by us" (1836/1837:II:151–152).*

A gendered standpoint shapes Martineau's style of doing sociological theory, as it does the men's. We said earlier that a primary difference between Martineau and her male contemporaries of the first generation of sociologists is that they aim for abstract general theory, while she seeks an empirically grounded, descriptively rich theory. The male theorists are all distanced by their gender from contact with the direct daily maintenance of social life; Comte lived the life of a recluse, Spencer inherited a private fortune and was able to keep a domestic staff, and Marx worked on his manuscripts while his wife and daughters managed domestic life without money. Martineau, in contrast, is never far away from the daily experience of herself and other women who practically and materially create and maintain the life of the household.

Focus on Women's Lives and Work   Central to Martineau's social theory is the basic feminist question, "Where are the women?" The question she poses for all sociological investigators is, "Are women present, and under what law of liberty?" (1838b:65).* Answering this question leads her to investigate women's lives and work and to explore domination and inequality in terms of the issues of vantage point and of differences among women. She portrays women as agentic, active members of, rather than passive furnishings in, the social world; their agency takes many forms—moral self-direction, independent will, and practical action. Her first publication is on women as writers on theological issues (1822); she pictures women as workers in her *Illustrations of Political Economy;* she does at least three lengthy sociological investigations of women's paid labor—"Domestic Service" (1838a), "Female Industry" (1859), and "Modern Domestic Service" (1862); when she focuses on abolitionist efforts in the United States, she does so through the lens of the annual reports of the Female Anti-Slavery Society of 1835, 1836, and 1837 (1838c). At the end of her life, she is involved in a battle against attempts by the British government to protect soldiers' sexual activity by punishing prostitutes—and any other women—suspected of carrying contagious diseases; here, she again addresses, as she has at other points in her career, the question of the conditions that lead women to sex work as a means of livelihood.

In her studies of women's work, she uses statistical data to prove the significance of women's work for the economy and the society, gives a history of women's employment, presents an overview of its variety, talks about the hardships of various occupations, argues for the need for further training, and praises achievements by women. In these analyses, Martineau emphasizes the limitations placed on women's agency by patriarchal practices and the negative effects of this for the total society. She focuses on the interconnections among restrictive education, limited employment opportunities, the forced choice of marriage, and male jealousy of women workers. She argues, further, that marriage and family life are impaired by this mistreatment of women. Marriage is "debased by being considered the one worldly object in life,—that on which maintenance, consequence, and power depend" (1836/1837:I:178). She reasons that the inevitable result of marriage for money must be "that the sanctity of marriage is impaired and that vice succeeds. Anyone must see at a glance that if men and women marry those whom they do not love, they must love those whom they do not marry" (1836/1837:II:243).

Differences among Women   Martineau's critique of domination and inequality is a central tenet of her sociology (see Theme 4, earlier in this chapter). Her analyses of domestic service bring together gender, class, and ethnicity and are perhaps her most concentrated efforts at feminist sociology. She sees domination at the heart of the conundrum of domestic service: "The peculiarity in the life of domestic service is subjection to the will of another. . . . A servant enters a family for the very purpose of fulfilling the will of the employer. . . . How troublesome and fundamentally vicious an arrangement this is, becomes apparent when we consider the difficulty of settling where this obedience to another's will is to stop" (Martineau, 1838a:411).*

Domestic service, she argues, "is important, both in itself and because it is symptomatic of some things out of itself" (1838a:408–409).* One of the things outside itself is class tension, particularly as those tensions materialize in the relation between employer and employee. The problems inherent in domestic service are also symptomatic of the fact that class relations often have an embedded and historic subtext in ethnic differences. Martineau's study of domination in domestic service leads her to differences between women based in class and ethnicity and to the problem of collisions in vantage points. Women's overall subordination often heightens their irresponsible use of power, rather than lessening it. The outcome of tensions between women of different classes, made the worse by women's overall subordination, is encapsulated for Martineau in a fact she cites in her major review articles on women's work: "Next to governesses the largest class of female patients in lunatic asylums is Maids of All Work" (1838a:423; 1859:307; 1862:426).* She explores interactions between employer and employee in terms of a collision in vantage points caused by lack of vocabulary and procedures for training in domestic skill and by a lack of imagination about the differences between the various actors:

> [W]ho that does not live by manual labor understands the feelings of those who do? . . . What was the Maid-servant once, and what has her rearing been? She was early used to hard work and self-denial. . . . She has been used to do other people's bidding, but she has not been used to other people's ways. She goes to service, full of fear and undefined expectations. For some time her mistress has patience with her; but mistresses are not aware of the time it takes to overcome the small habits of a life. (1838a: 424–426)*

The maid servant in turn is unaware that she has any rights in the relationship and is often disdainful of or irritated by her employers' chosen activities: reading and writing, for example, seem to her leisured frivolity.

Social Change   Martineau is essentially a liberal feminist who believes in progress. She interprets progress to be the movement toward the greatest good for the greatest number, and that good to be the right of each individual to act as an independent, self-directing moral being. Her career and her theory of change are concerned with how progress occurs. She believes: (1) that progress requires a transformation of desire; (2) that a transformation of desire cannot be coerced—indeed, to coerce change is to engage in domination and to engage in domination is to move against progress; (3) that transformation of desire occurs through reflection; (4) that reflection can occur gradually and naturally as people repeatedly live and think through an experience; and (5) that reflection can also be produced abruptly and radically by a call to conscience.

Martineau finds examples of both types of change in her studies of America. She believes that Americans will eventually renounce their consuming pursuit of wealth and that equalization of property will occur. But she insists it will not happen by revolution; it will happen, rather, "[w]hen the people become tired of their universal servitude to worldly anxiety,—when they have fully meditated and discussed the fact" that this pursuit of wealth is a source of pain rather than joy (1836/1837:II:185). The abolitionist movement illustrates the other way in which change occurs. Change here is the result not of a gradual process of reflection but of a clear call to conscience produced by an anomaly between the formal principles one has professed and the daily morals and manners one is practicing. Some persons seeing the anomaly, whether it be slavery or wealth, "rise up to overthrow it"; they rise up not because they necessarily see more than other people but because they have "minds gigantic, not in understanding, but in faith" (1836/1837:I:132; 197).

It is the role of the public educator—and Martineau defined the sociologist as a public educator—to help in this transformation of desire, by urging people to reflection on their own lives and by making a call to conscience on behalf of the threatened and disempowered.

ENDNOTES

1. The immediate comparison that can be made of Martineau's work is to Alexis de Tocqueville's *Democracy in America* (1835/1840). But neither Tocqueville nor Martineau is typically included by sociologists in their reconstruction of their history. Tocqueville is, however, by far, the better-remembered commentator on America, a testimony to the gender politics that we discuss in Chapter 1.
2. *The Communist Manifesto* (1848) by Marx and Friedrich Engels is the exception to this style.

READING 2-1

Excerpts from *How to Observe Morals and Manners*

This is Martineau's programmatic statement of sociological method, a statement framed by a significant theoretical consideration of the nature of society, the subject matter of sociology, and the significance of sociological study. Throughout, she refers to the sociological researcher as the "observer" or the "traveller"; the latter term is partly a strategy to include the average reader in the idea and possibility of sociological investigation, and partly the consequence of the fact that Martineau wrote this as a guide to her own two years of fieldwork in the United States between 1834 and 1836. The research report on that fieldwork, Society in America, *is presented, in excerpted form following these selections from* How to Observe.

EXCERPT FROM PART I, "REQUISITES FOR OBSERVATION"

This selection is excerpted from pages 1–45. It defines the sociologist's task as the comparative study of the morals and manners of societies; emphasizes the scientific nature of this field of investigation; sets a standard by which the researcher can critically assess a society in terms of the degrees of happiness realized for its members; and warns against narrow ethnocentrism on the part of the researcher, who must, above all, take the quality of sympathy or empathy to fieldwork.

The observer of Men and Manners stands as much in need of intellectual preparation as any other student. This is not, indeed, generally supposed, and a multitude of travellers act as if it were not true. . . . [N]o misgiving prompts [this traveller] to say, "I can give you little general information about the people I have been seeing; I have not studied the principles of morals; I am no judge of national manners."

Source: Harriet Martineau, *How to Observe Morals and Manners* (London: Charles Knight and Company, 1838).

There would be nothing to be ashamed of in such an avowal. No wise man blushes at being ignorant of any science which it has not suited his purpose to study. . . . [T]he natural philosopher . . . or the classical scholar [should not] be ashamed to own himself unacquainted with the science which, of all the sciences which have yet opened unto men, is, perhaps, the least cultivated, the least definite, the least ascertained in itself, and the most difficult in application. . . .

. . . Which of us would undertake to classify the morals and manners of any hamlet in England, after spending the summer in it? . . . Who pretends to explain all the proceedings of his next-door neighbour? . . .

. . . If it be thus with us at home, amidst all the general resemblances, the prevalent influences which furnish an interpretation to a larger number of facts, what hope of a trustworthy judgment remains for the foreign tourist, however good may be his method of travelling, and however long his absence from home? He looks at all the people along his line of road, and converses with a few individuals from among them. If he diverges, from time to time, from the high road,—if he winds about among villages, and crosses mountains, to dip into the hamlets of the valleys,—he still pursues only a line, and does not command the expanse; he is furnished at best with no more than a sample of people; and whether they indeed be a sample, must remain a conjecture which he has no means of verifying. He converses, more or less, with, perhaps, one man in ten thousand of those he sees . . . .

What is to be done? Let us first settle what is not to be done.

The traveller must deny himself all indulgences of peremptory decision, not only in public on his return, but in his journal, and in his most superficial thoughts. . . .

Natural philosophers do not dream of generalizing with any such speed as that used by the observers of men; yet they might do it with more safety, at the risk of an incalculably smaller mischief. . . . [B]ut if a traveller gives any quality which he may have observed in a few individuals as a characteristic of a nation, the evil is not speedily or easily remediable. Abject thinkers, passive readers, adopt his words; parents repeat them to their children; and townspeople spread the judgment into the villages and hamlets—the strongholds of prejudice; future travellers see according to the prepossessions given them, and add their testimony to the error, till it becomes the work of a century to reverse a hasty generalization. . . .

Above all things, the traveller must not despair of good results from his observations. Because he cannot establish true conclusions by imperfect means, he is not to desist from doing anything at all. Because he cannot safely generalize in one way, it does not follow that there is no other way. . . .

It ought to be an animating thought to a traveller that, even if it be not in his power to settle any one point respecting the morals and manners of an empire, he can infallibly aid in supplying means of approximation to truth, and of bringing out "what is fixed and essential in a people." This should be sufficient to stimulate his exertions and satisfy his ambition. . . .

There are two parties to the work of observation on Morals and Manners—the observer and the observed. This is an important fact which the traveller seldom dwells upon as he ought; yet a moment's consideration shows that the mind of the observer—the instrument by which the work is done, is as essential as the material to be wrought . . . I shall point out what requisites the traveller ought to make sure that he is possessed of before he undertakes to offer observations on the Morals and Manners of a people.

He must have made up his mind as to what it is he wants to know. . . . [This] method is the only one which promises any useful results. . . .

What does the traveller want to know? He is aware that wherever he goes, he will find men, women, and children; strong men and weak men; just men and selfish men. He knows that he will everywhere find a necessity for food, clothing, and shelter; and everywhere some mode of general agreement how to live together. He knows that he will everywhere find birth, marriage, and death; and therefore domestic affections. What results from all these elements of social life does he mean to look for? . . .

The . . . considerations just mentioned must be subordinated to the grand one,—the only general one,—of the relative amount of human happiness. Every element of social life derives its importance from this consideration. The external conveniences of men, their internal emotions and affections, their social arrangements, graduate in importance precisely in proportion as they affect the general happiness of the section of the race among whom they exist. Here then is the wise traveller's aim,—to be kept in view to the exclusion of prejudice, both philosophical and national. He must not allow himself to be perplexed or disgusted by seeing the great ends of human association pursued by means which he could never have devised and to the practice of which he could not reconcile himself. . . .

His more philosophical belief, derived from all fair evidence and just reflexion, is, that every man's feelings of right and wrong, instead of being born with him, grow up in him from the influences to which he is subjected. We see that in other cases,—with regard to science, to art, and the appearances of nature,—feelings grow out of knowledge and experience; and there is every evidence that it is so with regard to morals. The feelings begin very early; and this is the reason why they are supposed to be born with men; but they are few and imperfect in childhood, and, in the case of those who are strongly exercised in morals, they go on enlarging and strengthening and refining through life. See the effect upon the traveller's observations of his holding this belief about conscience! Knowing that some influences act upon the minds of all people in all countries, he looks everywhere for certain feelings of right and wrong which are as sure to be in all men's minds as if they were born with them. For instance, to torment another without any reason, real or imaginary, is considered wrong all over the world. In the same manner, to make others happy is universally considered right. At the same time, the traveller is prepared to find an infinite variety of differences in smaller matters. . . .

The traveller having satisfied himself that there are some universal feelings about right and wrong, and that in consequence some parts of human conduct are guided by general rules, must next give his attention to modes of conduct, which seem to him good or bad, prevalent in a nation, or district, or society of smaller limits. His first general principle is, that the law of nature is the only one by which mankind at large can be judged. His second must be, that every prevalent virtue or vice is the result of the particular circumstances amidst which the society exists.

The circumstances in which a prevalent virtue or vice originates, may or may not be traceable by a traveller. If traceable, he should spare no pains to make himself acquainted with the whole case. If obscure, he must beware of imputing disgraces to individuals, as if those individuals were living under the influences which have made himself what he is. He will not blame a deficiency of moral independence in a citizen of Philadelphia so severely as in a citizen of London, seeing, as he must do, that the want of moral independence is a prevalent fault in the United States, and that there must be some reason for it. . . .

The observer must have sympathy; and his sympathy must be untrammelled and unreserved. If a traveller be a geological inquirer, he may have a heart as hard as the rocks he shivers, and yet succeed in his immediate objects: if he be a student of the fine arts, he may be as silent as a picture, and yet gain his ends; if he be a statistical investigator, he may be as abstract as a column of figures, and yet learn what he wants to know: but an observer of morals and manners will be liable to deception at every turn, if he does not find his way to hearts and minds. . . .

. . . A stranger who has never felt any strong political interest, and cannot sympathize with American sentiment about the majesty of social equality, and the beauty of mutual government, can never understand the political religion of the United States; and the sayings of the citizens by their own fire-side, the perorations of orators in town-halls, the installations of public servants, and the process of election, will all be empty sound and grimace to him. He will be tempted to laugh,—to call the world about him mad,—like one who, without hearing the music, sees a room-full of people begin to dance. The case is the same with certain Americans who have no antiquarian sympathies, and who think our sovereigns mad for riding to St. Stephen's in the royal state-coach, with eight horses covered with trappings, and a tribe of grotesque footmen. . . . If an unsympathizing stranger is so perplexed by a mere matter of external arrangement,—a royal procession, or a popular election,—what can he be expected to make of that which is far more important, more intricate, more mysterious,—neighbourly and domestic life? If he knows and feels nothing of the religion of these, he could learn but little about them, even if the roofs of all the houses of a city were made transparent to him, and he could watch all that is done in every parlour, kitchen, and nursery in a circuit of five miles.

EXCERPT FROM PART II, "WHAT TO OBSERVE"

This selection is excerpted from pages 61–66. It is the most famous passage in the book, and it discusses the problem of sampling respondents, and the necessity of studying "things" that objectify a society's morals and manners. Each of these concepts is clarified by Martineau's selection of research indicators.

A good many features compose the physiognomy of a nation; and scarcely any traveller is qualified to study them all. The same man is rarely enlightened enough to make investigation at once into the religion of a people, into its general moral notions, its domestic and economical state, its political condition, and the facts of its progress;—all of which are necessary to a full understanding of its morals and manners. Few have even attempted such an inquiry of this extent. . . . [T]he traveller hears and notes what this and that and the other person says. If three or four agree in their statements on any point, he remains unaware of a doubt, and the matter is settled. If they differ, he is perplexed, does not know whom to believe, and decides, probably, in accordance with the prepossessions of his own. The case is almost equally bad, either way. He will hear of only one side of every question if he sees only one class of persons,—like the English in America, for instance, who go commonly with letters of introduction from merchants at home to merchants in the maritime cities. . . . Such partial intercourse is fatal to the observations of the traveller; but it is less perplexing and painful at the time than the better process of going from one set of people to another, and hearing what they have to say. No traveller in the United States can learn much of the country without conversing equally with farmers and merchants, with artizans and statesmen, with villagers and planters; but, while discharging this duty, he will be so bewildered with the contrariety of statements and convictions, that he will often shut his note-book in a state of scepticism as to whether there be any truth at all shining steadily behind all this tempest of opinions. . . . The plain truth is—it is beginning at the wrong end.

The grand secret of wise inquiry into Morals and Manners is to begin with the study of THINGS, using the DISCOURSE OF PERSONS as a commentary upon them.

Though the facts sought by travellers relate to Persons, they may most readily be learned from Things. The eloquence of Institutions and Records, in which the action of the nation is embodied and perpetuated, is more comprehensive and more faithful than that of any variety of individual voices. The voice of a whole people goes up in the silent workings of an institution; the condition of the masses is reflected from the surface of a record.

The institutions of a nation,—political, religious, or social,—put evidence into the observer's hands as to its capabilities and wants which the study of individuals could not yield in the course of a lifetime. The Records of any society, be they what they may, whether architectural remains, epitaphs, civic registers, national music, or any of the thousand manifestations of the common mind which may be found among every people, afford more information on Morals in a day than converse with individuals in a year. Thus also must Manners be judged of. . . . General indications must be looked for, instead of generalizations being framed from the manners of individuals. In cities, do social meetings abound? and what are their purposes and character? Are they most religious, political or festive? If religious, have they more the character of Passion Week at Rome, or of a camp-meeting in Ohio? If political, do the people meet on wide plains to worship the Sun of the Celestial Empire, as in China; or in town-halls, to remonstrate with their representatives, as in England; or in secret places, to spring mines under the thrones of their rulers, as in Spain? If festive, are they most like an Italian carnival, where everybody laughs; or an Egyptian holiday, when all eyes are solemnly fixed on the whirling Dervishes? Are women there? In what proportions, and under what law of liberty? What are the public amusements? . . . In country towns, how is the imitation of the metropolis carried on? Do the provincials emulate most in show, in science, or in the fine arts?—In the villages, what are the popular amusements? Do the people meet to drink or to read, to discuss, or play games, or dance? What are the public houses like? Do the people eat fruit and tell stories? or drink ale and talk politics? or call for tea and saunter about? or coffee and play dominoes? or lemonade and laugh at Punch? . . . A traveller who bears all this in mind can hardly go wrong. Every thing that he looks upon will instruct him, from an aqueduct to a punch-bowl, from a penitentiary to an aviary, from the apparatus of a university to the furniture of an alehouse or a nursery. . . .

It appears to me that the Morals and Manners of a nation may be included in the following departments of inquiry—the Religion of the people; their prevalent Moral Notions; their Domestic State; their Idea of Liberty; and their Progress, actual or in prospect.

EXCERPT FROM PART II, CHAPTER II, "GENERAL MORAL NOTIONS"

This selection is excerpted from pages 101–37. It contains Martineau's description of the things a sociologist can study that reveal the attitudes and aspirations of ordinary people in a society. This excerpt gives a sense of the richness of her sociological imagination and presents us with research possibilities still useful today.

. . . In speaking of the popular notion of a Moral Sense, it was mentioned that so far from there being a general agreement on the practice of morals, some things which are considered eminently right in one age or country are considered eminently wrong in another; while the people of each age or country, having grown up under common influences, think and feel sufficiently alike to live together in general agreement as to right and wrong. It is the business of the traveller to ascertain what this general agreement is in the society he visits. . . .

He will find no better place of study than the Cemetery,—no more instructive teaching than Monumental Inscriptions. The brief language of the dead will teach him more than the longest discourses of the living.

He will learn what are the prevalent views of death; and when he knows what is the common view of death, he knows also what is the aspect of life to no small number;—that is, he will have penetrated into the interior of the morals . . . [T]he pyramids of Egypt tell at least that death was not regarded as the great leveller,—that kings and peasants were not to sleep side by side in death, any more than in life. . . . In contrast with these are the church-yards of English cities, whose dead thus lie in full view of the living; the school-boy tumbles his hoop among them, and the news of the day is discussed above their place of rest. . . .

Much may be learned from the monumental inscriptions of all nations. . . . One common rule, drawn from a universal sentiment, has presided at the framing of all epitaphs for some thousands of years. "De mortuis nil nisi bonum" [of the dead, speak only good] is the universal agreement of mourners.* It follows that epitaphs must everywhere indicate what is there considered good.

The observer must give his attention to this. Among a people "whose merchants are princes," the praise of the departed will be in a different strain from that which will be found among a war-like nation, or a community of agriculturists. . . .

Even the nature of public services commemorated, where public service is considered the highest praise, may indicate much. It is a fact of no small significance whether a man is honoured after death for having made a road, or for having founded a monastery, or endowed a school. . . .

The traveller must talk with Old People, and see what is the character of the garrulity of age. He must talk with Children, and mark the character of the aspirations of childhood. He will thus learn what is good in the eyes of those who have passed through the society he studies, and in the hopes of those who have yet to enter upon it. Is it the aged mother's pride that her sons are all unstained in honour, and her daughters safe in happy homes? or does she boast that one is a priest, and another a peeress? . . .

---

*An exception to this may meet the eye of a traveller once in a lifetime. There is a village church-yard in England where the following inscription is to be seen. After the name and date occurs the following:

  He was a Bad Son,
  A Bad Husband,
  A Bad Father.
  "The wicked shall be turned into Hell."

Side by side with this lies the inquiry into the great Epochs of the society visited. . . . Nations, too, date from what interests them most. It is important to learn what this is. The major date of American citizens is the Revolution; their minor dates are elections, and new admissions into the Union. The people at Amsterdam date from the completion of the Stadt Huis; the Spaniards from the achievement of Columbus; the Germans from the deeds of Luther; the Haytians from the abduction of Toussaint L'Ouverture . . .

The treatment of the Guilty is all-important as an index to the moral notions of a society . . . What the traveller has to observe then is, first, whether there has been any amelioration of the treatment of criminals in countries where the people have a voice upon it: and, in countries despotically ruled, whether the public sentiment is moved about the condition of state criminals, and whether men treat one another vindictively in their appeals to the laws of citizenship; . . .

. . . Up to a comparatively high point of civilization, the law makes free with life, long after the private expenditure of it has been checked or has ceased. Duels, brawls, assassinations, have nearly been discontinued, and even war in some measure discountenanced, before the law duly recognises the sacredness of human life. But the time comes. . . . Capital punishments are restricted,—are further restricted,—are abolished. Such is the process. It is now all but completed in the United States: it is advancing rapidly in England. . . .

The Songs of every nation must always be the most familiar and truly popular part of its poetry. They are uniformly the first fruits of the fancy and feeling of rude societies; and, even in the most civilized times, are *the only* poetry of the great body of the people. Their influence, therefore, upon the character of a country has been universally felt and acknowledged. . . .

It appears that popular songs are both the cause and effect of general morals: that they are first formed, and then react. In both points of view they serve as an index of popular morals. The ballads of a people present us, not only with vivid pictures of the common objects which are before their eyes,—given with more familiarity than would suit any other style of composition,—but they present also the most prevalent feelings on subjects of the highest popular interest. If it were not so, they would not have been popular songs. The traveller cannot be wrong in concluding that he sees a faithful reflection of the mind of a people in their ballads.

EXCERPT FROM PART II, CHAPTER IV, "IDEA OF LIBERTY"

This selection is excerpted from pages 183–205. Martineau here pursues a key theme, the need to ascertain the relative balance between the amount of domination and the amount of moral autonomy, or liberty, in a society.

The same rule—of observing Things in preference to relying upon the Discourse of persons—holds good in the task of ascertaining the Idea of Liberty entertained and realized by any society. The Things to be observed for this purpose are those which follow. . . .

[T]he Police of a country [are] a sure sign of the idea of liberty existing within it. Where the soldiery are the guards of the social order, it makes all the difference whether they are royal troops,—a destructive machinery organized against the people,—or a National Guard, springing up when needed from among the people, for the people's sake. . . .

Such are some of the relations of the people to authority. . . . In some regions, all men go armed: in others, it is penal to wear arms: in others, people may do as they please. In some countries, there are costumes of classes enforced by law: in others, by opinion: while fashion is the only dictator in a third. In some societies citizens must obtain leave from the authorities to move from place to place: in others, strangers alone are plagued with passports: in others, there is perfect freedom of locomotion.

It is taken for granted that the traveller is informed, before he sets out, respecting the form of Government and general course of Legislation of the nation he studies. He will watch both, attending upon the administration as well as the formation of laws,—visiting, where it is allowed, the courts of justice as well as the halls of parliament. But he must remember that neither the composition of the government, nor the body of the laws, nor the administration of them, is an evidence of what idea of liberty at present is among the people, except in a democratic republic, where the acts of government are the result of the last expression of the national will. . . .

Whether the society is divided into Two Classes, or whether there is a Gradation, is another important consideration. Where there are only two, proprietors and labourers, the Idea of Liberty is deficient or absent. The proprietary class can have no other desires on the subject than to repress the encroachments of the sovereign above them, or of the servile class below them: and in the servile class the conception of liberty is yet unformed. . . .

There are two pledges of the advancement of the idea of liberty in a community:—the one is the mingling of the functions of proprietor and labourer throughout the whole of a society ruled by a representative government; the other is the graduation of ranks by some other principle than hereditary succession. . . .

In close connexion with this, he must observe the condition of Servants. . . . In an Irish country-house, the guest sometimes finds himself desired to keep his wardrobe locked up.—In England, he perceives a restraint in the address of each class to the class above it.—In France, a washerwoman speaks with as much ease to a duchess as a duchess to a washerwoman.—In Holland, the domestics have chambers as scrupulously neat as their masters'.—In Ireland, they sleep in underground closets.—In New York, they can command their own accommodation.—In Cuba, they sleep, like dogs, in the passages of the family dwellings. . . .

A point of some importance is whether the provincial inhabitants depend upon the management and imitate the modes of life of the metropolis, or have the principles and manners of their own. Where there is least freedom and the least desire of it, everything centres in the metropolis. Where there is the most freedom, each "city, town, and vill," thinks and acts for itself. . . .

Newspapers are a strong evidence of the political ideas of a people;—not individual newspapers; for no two, perhaps, fully agree in principles and sentiment, and it is to be feared that none are positively honest. Not by individual newspapers must the traveller form his judgment, but by the freedom of discussion which he may find to be permitted, or the restraints upon discussion imposed. The idea of liberty must be low and feeble among a people who permit the government to maintain a severe censorship; and it must be powerful and effectual in a society which can make all its complaints through a newspaper,—be the reports of the newspapers upon the state of social affairs as dismal as they may.

READING 2-2

Excerpts from *Society in America*

Martineau's most famous research statement is based on two years of fieldwork in the United States. The analytic structure of the study is anticipated in her companion methodological work, How to Observe Morals and Manners, *excerpted in the previous reading.*

EXCERPT FROM "INTRODUCTION"

This selection is excerpted from Volume I, pages i–xv. Here, Martineau outlines her strategy for studying the

Source: Harriet Martineau, *Society in America,* 2 vols. (New York: Saunders and Otley, 1837).

relation between morals and manners in the United States, and describes how she did her fieldwork.

In seeking for methods by which I might communicate what I have observed in my travels, without offering any pretension to teach the English, or judge the Americans, two expedients occurred to me; both of which I have adopted. One is, to compare the existing state of America with the principles on which it is professedly founded; thus testing Institutions, Morals, and Manners by an indisputable, instead of an arbitrary standard, and securing to myself the same point of view with my readers of both nations.

In working according to this method, my principal dangers are two. I am in danger of not fully apprehending the principles on which society in the United States is founded; and of erring in the application of the facts which came under my notice. In the last respect, . . . I can only explain that I have spared no pains to discover the truth, in both divisions of my task; and invite correction, in all errors of fact. . . .

The other method by which I propose to lessen my own responsibility, is to enable my readers to judge for themselves, better than I can for them, what my testimony is worth. For this purpose, I offer a brief account of my travels, . . . and a report of the principal means I enjoyed of obtaining a knowledge of the country. . . .

I landed at New York on the 19th of September, 1834; paid a short visit . . . to . . . New Jersey, . . . and passed through New York again on my way to . . . the Hudson, and Stockbridge, Massachusetts. . . . I travelled through the State of New York, . . . to the Falls of Niagara. . . . I embarked on Lake Erie, landing in the back of Pennsylvania, and travelling down . . . to Pittsburgh . . . over the Alleghanies to Northumberland, [to] . . . Philadelphia . . . Baltimore . . . and Washington. . . . I enjoyed peculiar opportunities of witnessing the proceedings of the Supreme Court and both houses of Congress. I was acquainted with almost every eminent senator and representative,

both on the administration and opposition sides; and was on friendly and intimate terms with some of the judges of the Supreme Court. I enjoyed the hospitality of the President, and of several of the heads of departments. . . . I arrived at Montpelier, the seat of Mr. and Mrs. Madison, . . . I proceeded to Charlottesville, and passed two days amidst the hospitalities of the Professors of Mr. Jefferson's University, . . . [I went on] to Richmond, where the Virginia legislature was in session; . . . then North and South Carolina to Charleston . . . and Columbia, South Carolina. . . . I traversed the southern States, . . . Georgia, . . . Alabama . . . New Orleans . . . Tennessee . . . Kentucky . . . I descended the Ohio to Cincinnati, [then to] Virginia, . . . arriving at New York again on the 14th of July, 1835. The autumn was spent [in] . . . Massachusetts . . . Rhode Island . . . New Hampshire and Vermont. . . . My last journey was . . . far into the west, . . . proceeding by Lake Erie to Detroit, and across the territory of Michigan . . . to Chicago . . . and by the Lakes Michigan, Huron, and St. Clair to Detroit, visiting Mackinaw by the way. . . . I sailed from New York for England on the 1st of August, 1836, having been absent just two years.

In the course of this tour, I visited almost every kind of institution. The prisons . . . the insane and other hospitals . . . the literary and scientific institutions; the factories of the north; the plantations of the south; the farms of the west. I lived in houses which might be called palaces, in log-houses, and in a farm-house. I travelled . . . in wagons . . . stages . . . on horseback . . . steamboats. I saw weddings and christenings; . . . watering places and . . . country festivals . . . land sales, and . . . the slave market.

. . . I have respected and beloved friends of each political party; and of nearly every religious denomination; among slave-holders, colonizationists, and abolitionists; among farmers, lawyers, merchants, professors, and clergy. I travelled among several tribes of Indians; and spent months in the southern States, with negroes ever at my heels.

Such were my means of information. . . .

It has been frequently mentioned to me that my being a woman was one disadvantage; and my being previously heard of, another. In this I do not agree.

I am sure, I have seen much more of domestic life than could possibly have been exhibited to any gentleman travelling through the country. The nursery, the boudoir, the kitchen, are all excellent schools in which to learn the morals and manners of a people: and, as for public and professional affairs,—those may always gain full information upon such matters, who really feel an interest in them,—be they men or women. . . .

As for the other objection, I can only state my belief, that my friends and I found personal acquaintance so much pleasanter than any previous knowledge by hearsay, that we always forgot that we had heard of each other before. . . .

I laboured under only one peculiar disadvantage, that I am aware of; but that one is incalculable. I mean my deafness. This does not endanger the accuracy of my information, I believe, as far as it goes; because I carry a trumpet of remarkable fidelity; . . . by which I gain more in *téte-á-tétes* than is given to people who hear general conversation. . . . But I am aware that there is no estimating the loss, in a foreign country, from not hearing the casual conversation of all kinds of people, in the streets, stages, hotels. . . . This was my peculiar disadvantage. . . . I mention it, that the value of my testimony may be lowered according to the supposed worth of this circumstance.

EXCERPT FROM PART I, CHAPTER III, SECTION IV "ALLEGIANCE TO LAW"

This selection is excerpted from Volume I, pages 120–34. Martineau has made the theoretical discovery of the issue of anomaly—a relation of contradiction between morals (or principles) and manners (or interactional patterns). Here, she explores anomaly and its implications.

The law, in a republic, is the embodiment of the will of the people. As long as the republic is in a natural and healthy state, containing no anomaly, . . . the function of the law works easily, and is understood and reverenced. . . .

If there be any anomaly among the institutions of a republic, the function of the law is certain to be disturbed, sooner or later: and that disturbance is usually the symptom by the exhibition of which the anomaly is first detected, and then cured. . . . It will be so with slavery; and with every institution inconsistent with the fundamental principles of democracy. The process is easily traceable. The worldly interests of the minority,—of perhaps a single class,—are bound up with the anomaly:—of the minority, because, if the majority had been interested in any anti-republican institution, the republic would not have existed. The minority may go on for a length of time in apparent harmony with the expressed will of the many,—the law. But the time comes when their anomaly clashes with the law. . . . [I]t takes time to awaken the will of the majority; and till it awakes, the interest of the faction is active and overbears the law . . . There is no fear that the majority will ultimately succumb to the minority,—the harmonious law to the discordant anomaly. . . .

One compound fallacy is allowed daily to pass unexposed and unstigmatized. "You make no allowance," said a friend who was strangely bewildered by it,—"you make no allowance for the great number of excellent people who view the anomaly and the law as you do, but who keep quiet, because they sincerely believe that by speaking and acting they should endanger the Union." This explains the conduct of a crowd of excellent people . . . who revile or satirize the abolitionists, and, for the rest, hold their tongues. But is it possible that such do not see that if slavery be wrong, and if it be indeed bound up with the Union, the Union must fall? . . . I regard it as a false and mischievous assumption that slavery is bound up with the Union: but if I believed the dictum, I should not be for "putting off the evil day." Every day which passes over the unredressed wrongs of any class which a republic holds in her bosom; . . . every day which adds a sanction to brute force, and impairs the sacredness of law; every day which prolongs impunity to the oppressor and discouragement to the oppressed, is a more evil day than that which should usher in the word of renovation.

But the dictum is not true. . . .

Let citizens but take heed individually to respect the law, and see that others do,—that no neighbour transgresses it, that no statesman despises it unrebuked, that no child grows up ignorant or careless of it; and the Union is secure as the ground they tread upon. If this be not done, everything is in peril, for the season; not only the Union, but property, home, life and integrity.

EXCERPT FROM PART II, CHAPTER V, SECTION I "MORALS OF SLAVERY"

This selection is excerpted from Volume II, pages 106–36. As is already evident in the preceding excerpt, slavery is for Martineau the most serious of anomalies in US society. She explores the tension between that institution and the society's principles with vivid detail in this chapter. She deals, in a straightforward analysis, with the then taboo issues of sexuality and race.

This title is not written down in a spirit of mockery; though there appears to be a mockery somewhere, when we contrast slavery with the principles and the rule which are the test of all American institutions—the principles that all men are born free and equal; that rulers derive their just powers from the consent of the governed; and the rule of reciprocal justice. This discrepancy between principles and practices needs no more words. But the institution of slavery exists; and what we have to see is what the morals are of the society which is subject to it.

What social virtues are possible in a society of which injustice is the primary characteristic? in a

society which is divided into two classes, the servile and the imperious? . . .

. . . [M]ercy, indulgence, patience was often pleaded to me in defence of the system. . . . The fallacy of this is so gross as not to need exposure anywhere but on the spot. I was . . . weary of explaining that indulgence can never atone for injury: that the extremest pampering, for a life-time, is no equivalent for rights withheld, no reparation for irreparable injustice. . . .

. . . The inherent injustice of the system . . . nourishes a whole harvest of false morals towards the rest of society.

The personal oppression of the negroes is the grossest vice which strikes a stranger in the country. It can never be otherwise when human beings are wholly subjected to the will of other human beings, who are under no external control than the law which forbids killing and maiming;—a law which it is difficult to enforce in individual cases. . . .

A young negress had escaped . . . and was alarmed by constables, under the direction of her master, entering the house [where she had been hiding]. . . . She flew up the stairs to her chamber in the third story, and drove a heavy article of furniture against the door. The constables pushed in, notwithstanding, and the girl leaped from the window into the paved street. Her master looked at her as she lay, declared she would never be good for anything again, and went back to the South. The poor creature, her body bruised, and her limbs fractured, was taken up, and kindly nursed; and she is now maintained in Boston, in her maimed condition, by the charity of some ladies there. . . .

. . . Let any one look at the positive licentiousness of the south, and declare if, in such a state of society, there can be any security for domestic purity and peace. The Quadroon connexions in New Orleans are all but universal, as I was assured. . . .

The Quadroon girls of New Orleans are brought up by their mothers to be what they have been: the mistresses of white gentlemen. . . . The girls are highly educated, externally, and are, probably, as beautiful and accomplished a set of women as can be found. Every young man early selects one, and establishes her in one of those pretty and peculiar houses . . . in the Remparts. . . . The connexion now and then lasts for life: usually for several years. In the latter case, when the time comes for the gentleman to take a white wife, the dreadful news reaches his Quadroon partner. . . . The Quadroon ladies are rarely or never known to form a second connexion. Many commit suicide: more die broken-hearted. Some men continue the connexion after marriage. . . .

What security for domestic purity and peace there can be where every man has had two connexions, one of which must be concealed; and two families, whose existence must not be known to each other. . . .

There is no occasion to explain the management of the female slaves on estates where the object is to rear as many as possible, like stock, for the southern market: not to point out the boundless licentiousness caused by the practice. . . .

It is well known that the most savage violences that are now heard of in the world take place in the southern and western States of America. Burning alive, cutting the heart out, and sticking it on the point of a knife, and other such diabolical deeds, the result of the deepest hatred of which the human heart is capable. . . . They arise out of the licentiousness of manners. The negro is exasperated by being deprived of his wife. . . . If the negro attempts to retaliate, . . . the faggots are set alight about him. . . .

Let us, however, see what is the very best state of things. Let us take the words and deeds of some of the most religious, refined and amiable members of society. It was this aspect of affairs which grieved me more, if possible, than the stormier one which I have presented. The coarsening and hardening of mind and manners among the best; the blunting of the moral sense among the most conscientious. . . .

A southern lady, of fair reputation for refinement . . . , told the following story . . . with obvious unconsciousness that she was saying anything remarkable. . . . She had possessed a pretty mulatto girl, of whom she declared herself fond. A young man came to stay at her house, and fell in love with the girl. "She came to me," said the lady, "for protection; which I gave her." The young man went away, but after some weeks, returned saying he was so much in love with the girl that he could not live without her. "I pitied the young man," concluded the lady; "so I sold the girl to him for 1,500 dollars." . . .

The degradation of women is so obvious a consequence of the evils disclosed above, that the painful subject need not be enlarged on. By the degradation of women, I do not mean to imply any doubt of the purity of their manners. . . . Their degradation arises, not from their own conduct, but from that of all other parties about them. Where the generality of men carry secrets which their wives must be the last to know; where the busiest and more engrossing concerns of life must wear one aspect to the one sex, and another to the other, there is an end to all wholesome confidence and sympathy, and woman sinks to be the ornament of her husband's house, the domestic manager of his establishment, instead of being his all-sufficient friend. . . .

Of course, the children suffer, perhaps the most fatally of all, under the slave system. What can be expected of from little boys who are brought up to consider physical courage the highest attribute of manhood; pride of section and of caste its loftiest grace; . . . What is to be expected of little girls who boast of having got a negro flogged for being impertinent to them. . . .

[T]he gentry of the south do not know what freedom is . . . many seem unconscious of the state of coercion in which they themselves are living; . . . coercion, not only from their fear, from their being dependent for their hourly comforts upon the extinguished or estranged will of those whom they have injured; but coercion also from their own laws. The laws against the press are as peremptory as in the most despotic countries of Europe. . . .

What is to be thought of the freedom of gentlemen subject to the following law? "Any person or persons who shall attempt to teach any free person of colour, or slave, to spell, read or write, shall . . . be fined . . . five hundred dollars."

What is to be thought of the freedom of gentlemen who cannot emancipate their own slaves, except by consent of the legislature.

EXCERPT FROM PART I, CHAPTER III, SECTION VII "POLITICAL NON-EXISTENCE OF WOMEN"

This selection is excerpted from Volume I, pages 148–54. In this powerful feminist statement, Martineau explores the second major anomaly in the United States—the disenfranchisement of women. The status of women is a concern discussed in other sections of this work, for example, in relation to their economic and their domestic circumstances.

One of the fundamental principles announced in the Declaration of Independence is, that governments derive their just powers from the consent of the governed. How can the political condition of women be reconciled with this?

Governments in the United States have power to tax women who hold property; to divorce them from their husbands; to fine, imprison, and execute them for certain offences. Whence do these governments derive their powers? They are not "just" as they are not derived from the consent of the women thus governed.

Governments in the United States have power to enslave certain women; and also to punish other women for inhuman treatment of such slaves. Neither of these powers are "just"; not being derived from the consent of the governed.

Governments decree to women in some States half their husbands' property; in others one-third. In some, a woman, on her marriage, is made to yield all her property to her husband; in others, to retain a portion, or the whole, in her own hands. Whence do governments derive the unjust power of thus disposing of property without the consent of the governed?

The democratic principle condemns all this a wrong; and requires the equal political representation of all rational beings. Children, idiots, and criminals, during the season of sequestration, are the only fair exceptions.

The case is so plain that I might close it here; but it is interesting to inquire how so obvious a decision has been evaded as to leave to women no political rights whatever. . . . No plausible answer has, as far as I can discover, been offered; for the good reason, that no plausible answer can be devised. The most principled writers on government have on this subject sunk into . . . despotism. . . .

Jefferson says . . . "Women to prevent depravation of morals, and ambiguity of issue, could not mix promiscuously in the public meetings of men. . . ." As if there could be no means of conducting public affairs but by promiscuous meetings! As if there would be more danger in promiscuous meetings for political business than in such meetings for worship, for oratory, for music, for dramatic entertainments,—for any of the thousand transactions of civilized life! The plea is not worth another word. . . .

Mill says, . . . "In this light, women may be regarded, the interest of almost all of whom is involved, either in that of their fathers or in that of their husbands." . . .

The word "almost," in Mr. Mill's second sentence, rescues women from the exclusion he proposes. As long as there are women who have neither husbands nor fathers, his proposition remains an absurdity.

The interests of women who have fathers and husbands can never be identical with theirs, while there is a necessity for laws to protect women against their husbands and fathers. This statement is not worth another word.

Some who desire that there should be an equality of property between men and women, oppose representation, on the ground that political duties would be incompatible with the other duties women have to discharge. The reply to this is, that women are the best judges here. . . . But their guardians follow the ancient fashion of deciding what is best for their wards. . . . The Georgian planter perceives the hardship that freedom would be to his slaves. And the best friends of half the human race peremptorily decide for them as to their rights, their duties, their feelings, their powers. In all these cases, the persons thus cared for feel that the abstract decision rests with themselves; that, though they may be compelled to submit, they need not acquiesce.

It is pleaded that half of the human race does acquiesce in America in the decision of the other half, as to their rights and duties. And some instances, not only of submission, but of acquiescence, there are. Forty years ago, the women of New Jersey went to the poll, and voted at state elections [because the election law said "inhabitants" without qualification of sex]. A motion was made to correct the inadvertence; and it was done, as a matter of course; without any appeal, as far as I could learn, from the persons about to be injured. Such acquiescence proves nothing but the degradation of the injured party. . . . Acquiescence like this is an argument which cuts the wrong way for those who use it.

But this acquiescence is only partial; and, to give any semblance of strength to the plea, the acquiescence must be complete. I, for one, do not acquiesce. . . . I know that there are women in England who agree with me in this—I know that there are women in America who agree with me in this. The plea of acquiescence is invalidated by us.

It is pleaded that, by enjoying the protection of some laws, women give their assent to all. This needs but a brief answer. Any protection thus conferred is, under woman's circumstances, a boon bestowed at the pleasure of those in whose power she is. A boon of any sort is no compensation for the privation of something else. . . .

I cannot enter upon the commonest order of pleas of all;—those which relate to the virtual influence of woman; her swaying the judgment and will of man through the heart; and so forth. One might as well try to dissect the morning mist. . . .

The truth is, that while there is much said about "the sphere of woman," two widely different notions are entertained of what is meant by that phrase. The narrow, and, to the ruling party, the more convenient notion is that sphere appointed by men, and bounded by their idea of propriety;—a notion from which any and every woman may fairly dissent. The broad and true conception is of the sphere appointed by God, and bounded by the powers which he has bestowed. . . .

That woman has the power to represent her own interests, no one can deny till she has been tried. . . . The principle being once established, the methods will follow, easily, naturally, and under a remarkable transmutation of the ludicrous into the sublime. . . .

The principle of the equal rights of both halves of the human race is all we have to do with here. It is the true democratic principle which can never be seriously controverted, and only for a short time evaded. Governments can derive their just powers only from the consent of the governed.

EXCERPT FROM PART III, CHAPTER I, "IDEA OF HONOUR" AND PART I, CHAPTER III, SECTION I "OFFICE"

This selection is excerpted from Volume II, pages 155–68 and Volume I, pages 84–108. It explores the consequences for people and for political life of the third great American anomaly—the fear of public opinion in a democracy that formally promotes free expression of opinions.

It is true that it is better to live for honour than for wealth: but how much better, depends upon the idea of honour. . . . Where the honour is to be derived from present human opinion, there must be fear, ever present, and perpetually exciting to or withholding from action. In such a case, as painful a bondage is incurred as in the pursuit of wealth.

This regard to opinion shows itself under various forms in different parts of the country, and under dissimilar social arrangements. . . .

The Americans of the northern States are, from education and habit, so accustomed to the caution of which I speak, as to be unaware of its extent and singularity. . . . They may travel over the world, and find no society but their own which will submit to the restraint of perpetual caution, and reference to the opinions of others. They may travel over the whole world, and find no country but their own where the very children . . . talk of the effect of actions upon people's minds. . . .

"Mrs. B," said a child of eleven to a friend of mine, "what church do you go to?"—"To Mr. ——'s." "O, Mrs. B. are you a Unitarian?"—"No." "Then why do you go to that church?"—"Because I can worship best there." "O, but Mrs. B., think of the example,—the example, Mrs. B.!" . . .

When the stranger has recovered a little from the first disagreeable impression of all this caution, he naturally asks what there can be to render it worth while. To this question, I never could discover a satisfactory answer. What harm "the force of public opinion," or "publicity," can do to any individual; what injury "bad hands" can inflict upon a good man or woman, which can be compared with the evil of living in perpetual caution, I cannot image. . . . This bondage, this torment is worse than the worst that the "force of public opinion" can inflict, even if such force should close the prospect of political advancement, of professional eminence, and of the best of social privileges. . . . It will be well for Americans, particularly those of the east and south, when their idea of honour becomes as exalted as that which inspired their revolutionary ancestors. Whenever they possess themselves of the idea of their democracy, as it was possessed by the statesmen of 1801, they will moderate their homage of human opinion, and enhance their worship of humanity. Not till then will they

live up to their institutions, and enjoy that internal freedom and peace to which the external are but a part of the means. . . .

[from "Office":] . . . The temptation to propitiate opinion becomes powerful when a citizen desires to enter the legislature, or to be the chief magistrate of the State. The peril increases when he becomes a candidate for Congress; and there seems to be no expectation whatever that a candidate for the presidentship, or his partizans, should retain any simplicity of speech, or regard to equity in the distribution of places and promises. All this is dreadfully wrong. . . .

The primary mistake is in supposing that men cannot bear to hear the truth. It has become the established method of seeking office, not only to declare a coincidence of opinion with the supposed majority, on the great topics on which the candidate will have to speak and act while in office, but to deny, or conceal, or assert anything else which it is supposed will please the same majority. The consequence is, that the best men are not in office. . . .

. . . The first principles in the United States [are] "rulers derive their just powers from the consent of the governed;" and that . . . the best men are chosen to serve. Both these pre-suppose mutual faith. Let the governed once require honesty as a condition of their consent; let them once choose the best men, according to their most conscientious conviction, and there will be an end of this insulting and disgusting political scepticism. . . . [A]nd the spirit of the constitution, now drooping in some of its most important departments, will revive.

I write more in hope than in immediate expectation. I saw much ground for hope, but very much also for grief. Scarcely anything that I observed in the United States caused me so much sorrow as the contemptuous estimate of the people entertained by those who were bowing the knee to be permitted to serve them.

. . . All the evidence on the subject that I could collect, went to prove that the people can bear, and do prefer to hear, the truth. It is a crime to withhold it from them; and a double crime to substitute flattery.

EXCERPT FROM PART II, CHAPTER III, SECTION II "PROPERTY"

This selection is excerpted from Volume II, pages 175–86. Here, Martineau identifies the fourth great US anomaly—inequality of wealth in a republic of equals. She makes the radical suggestion that wealth should be equalized in order to give all people greater leisure for moral autonomy and happiness; but she feels that a community must choose this course for itself, rather than having it imposed by a radical faction.

I found it an admitted truth, through the United States, that enormous private wealth is inconsistent with the spirit of republicanism. Wealth is power; and large amounts of power ought not to rest in the hands of individuals. . . .

There is, as there ought to be, as great a horror in America as everywhere else of the despotism that would equalise property arbitrarily. . . . Such aggression upon property can never take place, or be seriously apprehended in a republic where all, except drunkards and slaves, are proprietors, and where the Declaration of Independence claims for every one, with life and liberty, the pursuit of happiness. There will be no attacks on property in the United States.

But it appears to me inevitable that there will be a general agreement, sooner or later, on a better principle of property than that under which all are restless; under which the wisdom and peace of the community falls far below what their other circumstances would lead themselves and their well wishers to anticipate. . . .

. . . Leisure, some degree of it, is necessary to the health of every man's spirit. Not only intellectual production, but peace of mind cannot flourish without it. It may be had under the present system, but it is not. With community of property, it would

be secured to every one. The requisite amount of work would bear a very small proportion to that of disposable time. . . .

The professional men of America are dissatisfied. . . . Very severe toil is necessary to maintain a respectable appearance, . . .

The merchants are dissatisfied. . . . In comparison with merchants generally, they are happy: but in comparison with what men are made to be, they are shackled, careworn, and weary, as the slave. . . .

Are the mechanic and farming classes satisfied? No. . . . They, too, are aware that life must be meant to be passed far otherwise than in providing the outward means of living. . . . No thinking man or woman, who reflects on the amount of time, thought, and energy, which would be set free by the pressure of competition and money-getting being removed,—time, thought, and energy now spent in wearing out the body, and in partially stimulating and partially wasting the mind, can be satisfied under the present system. . . .

. . . When the people become tired of their universal servitude to worldly anxiety,—when they have fully meditated and discussed the fact that ninety-nine hundredths of social offences arise directly out of property; that the largest proportion of human faults bear a relation to selfish possession; that the most formidable classes of diseases are caused by over or under toil, and by anxiety of mind; they will be ready for the inquiry whether this tremendous incubus be indeed irremovable; and whether any difficulties attending its removal can be comparable to the evils it inflicts. . . .

It is objected that the majority of society in America would have a horror of any great change like that contemplated. . . . Well: as long as this is the case, they have no change to dread; for all such alteration must proceed from their own will. . . . When we look at a caterpillar, we like to anticipate the bright day when it will be a butterfly. If we could talk about it with the caterpillar, it would probably be terrified at the idea, and plead the exceeding danger of being high up in the air. . . .

The principal fear, expressed or concealed, of those who dislike the mere mention of the outgrowth of individual property is lest they should be deprived of their occupations, objects, and interests. But no such deprivation can take place till they have arrived at preferring other interests than money, and at pursuing their favourite occupation with other views than of obtaining wealth. "O, what shall I ever do without my currant leaves?" might the caterpillar exclaim. "How shall I ever get rid of the day, if I must not crawl along the twigs any more?" By the time it has done with crawling, it finds a pair of wings unfolding, which makes crawling appear despicable in comparison. . . . Men may safely dismiss all care about the future gratification of their tastes under new circumstances, as long as it happens to be the change of tastes which brings about the change of circumstances. . . .

. . . Whenever a healthy hunger enables the popular mind to assimilate a great principle, there are always strong and skillful hands enough to do the requisite work.

READING 2-3

Excerpt from "Domestic Service"

This selection is excerpted for pages 407–32. One of Martineau's many explorations of women's wage work, this systematic sociological analysis illustrates her woman-centered viewpoint, her concerns with interactional and vantage point tensions between women relating across lines of class and ethnic differences in a situation characterized by domination, and her ability to join quantitative and qualitative analyses.

Any one relation of employers and employed serves as an exponent of the rest . . . But if there

Source: Harriet Martineau, "Domestic Service," *London and Westminster Review* 7 and 29 (1838), pp. 405–32.

is one which more certainly than any other includes all the feelings which have descended through a hundred generations of rich and poor, it is that of Domestic Service. . . . It is important, both in itself and because it is symptomatic of some things out of itself.

. . . [T]he subject of Domestic Service is considered a low, trifling, and almost ludicrous one. Men know very little about it, and would fain appear to know less than they do. The very words call up in their minds images of mops and brooms, or of squabbles about giving away cold meat, summonses of pilfering cooks to police offices, and such disagreeable things. Men never think of the subject if they can help it: they put away all knowledge of it as a nuisance. They consider it an evil which it is their wives' business to manage and to bear. A gentleman swore at a police office lately, that he had never seen his housemaid; and he was actually unable to identify her. . . .

The numbers concerned show that the relation is important in itself. The number of domestic servants in the United Kingdom is considerably above a million. The census of 1831 presents us for the first time with the estimate. Seventy-five in a thousand of the female population, and eighteen in a thousand of the male population are domestic servants. It is strange that this large class has been the subject of so little philosophical observation and reflection. . . .

. . . [T]hese considerations would be sufficient to justify a grave review of the subject of domestic service in Great Britain; but it is chiefly as an exponent of the general relation between employers and employed that we adopt it. One recommendation of this choice is that this is perhaps the mildest exemplification that can be brought of the opposition of interests and tempers between the two classes concerned. . . .

The peculiarity in the life of domestic service is subjection to the will of another. There may be more or less of this, avowedly or virtually, in other modes of life; but of no other is it the distinguishing peculiarity. . . . A servant enters a family for the very purpose of fulfilling the will of the employer; and obedience to orders is the first requisite demanded. . . .

How troublesome and fundamentally vicious an arrangement this is, becomes apparent when we consider the difficulty of settling where this obedience to another's will is to stop, and that the system is a *tertium quid* from the mixture of two other systems quite opposite in their principles—slavery and contract. . . .

. . . Very few individuals are to be trusted with irresponsible power over other human beings; and those few are not to be looked for among such as are themselves suffering under arbitrary power, as every woman is. . . .

. . . Whence arises the eminent badness of [this relation] in England? One most important fact appears to be, that the fierce evils of the Norman Conquest are smouldering in this relation. The old Saxon enmity burns in the bosoms of the working classes of England; and in none so naturally as those who have to render service to superior rank. . . . The sufferers under it are unconscious of the cause. Thousands upon thousands struggle and inflict, who never heard the name of Saxon or Norman. . . . The feelings have been transmitted, without the traditions of those times, among the common people of England. . . .

. . . The want is [also] of sympathy—of mutual knowledge. There is perhaps no parallel instance of two classes of people living in such close conjunction amidst so entire a mutual ignorance, as in that of masters and servants. They see one another many times a day; but, the blind sides of their minds being mutually presented, they might as well be living on different halves of the globe for anything they know of each other. A country girl once in a grand flight of imagination, supposing herself Lady Anne, was asked what she would do if she was really Lady Anne:—"Swing on a gate all day, and eat bread and butter." Such is the notion of aristocratic privilege. A clergy-

man who is an author, spends the greater part of his days with book or pen in hand. His wife's housemaid, after various symptoms of indignation, broke forth one day with exclamations against the waste of time of people who are always amusing themselves with reading and writing, while others are toiling away in their service. Such is the notion of professional labour. On the other hand, who that does not live by manual labour understands the feelings of those who do? . . .

What was the Maid-servant once, and what has her rearing been? She was early used to hard work and self-denial; over-powered with sleep in her chair, and suddenly rousing herself in the fear of letting the baby fall. She has been used to do other people's bidding, but she has not been used to other people's ways. Her mother's are all she has seen. The family room has been swept out by her on Saturday afternoon. The little matter of crockery has been washed up when wanted. The potatoes have been set on the table at any angle. She has never spoken with strangers except by accident, and then she has got out her speech as she best might. She goes to service, full of fear and expectation. For some time her mistress has patience with her; but mistresses are not aware of the time it takes to overcome the small habits of a life. If, after some weeks, the dishes are not set straight on the table, if there is a spot on the tablecloth, or the fresh mustard is forgotten—if she twists the corner of her apron in answering strangers—if she does a thing last which she was told to do first, alas for her. . . . If she breaks a piece of china, she is perhaps terrified with the common threat that the value of the article shall be deducted from her wages. She does not know that her mistress has no right to do this, and she has not an advocate at hand to inform her of the nature of her contract. Her wages have long been laid out in her own mind; and now she does not know how much of her first earnings she must forego. . . . She trembles at the sound of her mistress's bell, waits upon her looks, is relieved to see her go abroad, and sorry to see her return. . . .

It is commonly said that Education is the remedy for this as for other social evils. This is true; but the education must begin with the master. What is commonly called an education is a great good; but if it has failed to teach employers the truth which lies at the bottom of social reform, it will probably fail to impart it to the employed.

This great truth is, that *mutual service is honourable, and not disgraceful.* . . .

. . . The self-education of the employing class—the study of the philosophy of Work, and the cultivation of sympathy with human feelings, will help to rectify the position of the one party; and the influence of their improvement upon those beneath them will tend to dissolve the prejudices and temper the feelings of the other.

Jane Addams (1860–1935)— Ethics and Society

BIOGRAPHICAL BACKGROUND

Jane Addams was born on September 6, 1860, in Cedarville, Illinois, and died on May 21, 1935, in Chicago. In her lifetime she became the most prominent woman in America. Her extraordinary success, as both a social reformer and a social theorist, owed much to the quality of mind insightfully described by Charlotte Perkins Gilman: "Her mind had more 'floor space' in it than any other I have known. She could set a subject down, unprejudiced, and walk all around it, allowing fairly for every one's point of view" (Gilman, 1935:184). The sources of information about her life are enormous: some 30,000 pieces of correspondence; news reports; memoirs by people who knew her; her public statements; and her writings, especially the autobiographical volumes *Twenty Years at Hull-House* (1910b) and *The Second Twenty Years at Hull-House* (1930). There is as yet no feminist biography of Addams, though she is discussed insightfully by several feminist scholars (e.g., Gordon, 1994; Marilley, 1995; Muncy, 1991; Scott, 1964). The two major biographies of her are the laudatory, richly detailed *Jane Addams* by her nephew James Weber Linn (1935) and the intelligent but uneven study of her as an American legend, *American Heroine* by Allen F. Davis (1973). The major treatment of her place in sociology is Mary Jo Deegan's landmark study *Jane Addams and the Men of the Chicago School, 1892–1918* (1988). *The Jane Addams Papers* (Bryan, Slote, Angury, 1996) offer a wealth of facts not readily available elsewhere. In the biographical sketch that follows, we explore five factors that shaped Addams as a sociologist and social theorist: (1) a quest for the right to speak and be heard, (2) Hull-House, the Chicago settlement she founded, (3) relationships with other women, (4) the social reform and social science movements of the Progressive Era (1880–1914), and (5) her own character and temperament.

The Quest for Authority

In her senior essay at Rockford Female Seminary in 1881, Addams interpreted the story of Cassandra, the prophetess who foresaw the doom of Troy, as a problem for all women: "to be in the right and always to be disbelieved and rejected." She argues that women must find a way to attain "what the ancients called *auethoritas* [*sic*], right of the speaker to make themselves heard" (Addams, 1881:37). Our thesis is that Addams's life project was to find a way that she as a woman in a patriarchal world could act and speak with *auctoritas*—with dignity, influence, consequence.

By her account, she grew up with a model of male *auctoritas* in her father, John Huy Addams, a successful businessman and lawyer who provided a comfortably middle-class living for his family, was active in local civic affairs, and served in the Illinois state legislature for many years, serving for part of that time with Abraham Lincoln. Only two when her mother, Sarah Weber Addams, died, Jane was nurtured by her four surviving older siblings and came to idolize her father. When she was eight, her father married a widow with two sons, Anna Hostetter Haldeman, for whom Jane seems to have felt a genuine affection and through whom she was introduced to a lifestyle—of elegant furniture, music, discussions of literature, and formal entertaining—that may have helped her to be at ease among the wealthy she later won as patrons for Hull-House.

Addams was sent to the village school, where she was diligent but unprecocious. At seventeen, despite her wish to go East to Smith College, she followed her father's desires and enrolled, like her sisters before her, at Rockford Female Seminary. Despite her seeming dislike of the school's religious emphasis, Addams emerged as a leader and an intellectual, showing that quality of mind that Nancy Miller attributes to women's intellectual experience—"'not coldly cerebral but impassioned'" (cited in Heilbrun 1988:16). She began to take her writing seriously, saving her college essays and contributing to the literary magazine. On more than one occasion, she wrote on the question of women's role in the world. She graduated as class valedictorian in 1881.

The seven years after her graduation were marked by false starts, uncertainty, ill health, and travel. She set and abandoned plans for schooling; dealt emotionally and practically with family crises—her father's death in 1881, managing his estate and her inheritance, her stepmother's desire for companionship, a brother's nervous breakdown, and a sister's family problems; underwent painful spinal surgery and a long convalescence, and traveled twice to Europe, with her stepmother and friends in 1883–85, and with two college friends in 1887–88. On these trips, she seems to have been a typical young American woman tourist, similar to the heroines Henry James was creating in his fiction—except that no male romantic interest emerged for her. Perhaps if she had settled into the role of maiden aunt, a possibility she saw for herself, this period would be interpreted as typical; but given the life she eventually made, the years 1881–87 emerge as lacking in focus.

Addams seems to have reached the decision to found a settlement in 1888. Though her letters of that time make little reference to her decision, her 1910 autobiographical account *Twenty Years at Hull-House* presents a significant sociological interpretation of this decision—an experience of what feminists today label "bifurcated consciousness" (D. Smith 1979, 1987). In her account of her 1883 tour of the poverty-ridden East End of London, she recalls seeing from the top of an omnibus poor people bidding frantically for spoiled cheap

Jane Addams, age 36

food. She writes, "I have never since been able to see a number of hands held upward, even . . . when they belong to a class of chubby children who wave them in eager response to a teacher's query, without a certain revival of this memory, a clutching at the heart reminiscent of the despair and resentment which seized me then" (1910b:68). But Addams, in remembering the incident, is shocked not just by what she had seen but by her own reaction to it. She had experienced her mind retreating to literature: "at the very moment of looking down the East London street from the top of the omnibus, I had been sharply and painfully reminded of 'The Vision of Sudden Death' which had confronted De Quincey one summer's night as he was being driven through rural England on a high mail coach" (1910b:69–70). In the story, De Quincey tells of a moment of horror in which he is too paralyzed to act because he is remembering a passage from the *Iliad*. Addams analyzes this division in her consciousness as the outgrowth of her social position as a young, educated, privileged-class woman. Her learning had paralyzed her in a confrontation with real experience, taking her away from action rather than towards it. She feels that she, like others of the first generation of college women, "had taken [her] learning too quickly, . . . had lost that simple and almost automatic response to the human appeal, that old healthful reaction resulting in activity" (1910b:71).

Yet, for the next two years, Addams did nothing. Then, on her second European trip, when the experience of bifurcation repeated itself in another retreat from life into literature, Addams saw that she had been substituting "a dreamer's scheme" that she would someday do some kind of reforming work, for the reality of action. "I . . . made up my mind that next day, whatever happened, I would begin to carry out the plan, if only by talking about it" (1910b:87). She began the next day to talk to her traveling companion, college friend Ellen Gates Starr, who joined her in her plan. In June 1888, five years after her visit to the East London slums, she returned to England to study Toynbee Hall, the prototype of the "settlement," a social experiment in which young university men of Addams's class were trying to bridge the widening gap between social classes by going to live among the poor.

The Hull-House Experience

By January 1889, Addams and Starr were in Chicago searching for a location and financial and relational support for their settlement. They chose Chicago's nineteenth ward, a desperately poor neighborhood of immigrants, tenements, and sweatshops, where they rented the second floor of a subdivided former mansion on Halsted Street, which they named "Hull-House" after Chicago millionaire Charles Hull, the original owner.

Addams always insisted that she and Starr had no clear plan beyond that of going to live among the poor "as a neighbor"—a role that informs much of Addams's sociology. They began by inviting their neighbors in for social evenings aimed at bringing "culture"; they quickly realized that the immigrants had rich cultures of their own that they needed help preserving in America, and the evenings shifted to celebrating those. As they came to know the neighborhood, Addams and Starr evolved from seeing themselves as culture bearers to focusing on the practical issues of poverty.

They were joined almost from the beginning by other young women, and some men, who came as "residents" to Hull-House. Residents paid room and board and used whatever skills they had to respond as neighbors, leading Hull-House into a wide variety of efforts: providing meeting space for groups—trades unions, anarchists, socialists, and women's associations; supplying services for children—a kindergarten, nursery, playgrounds, clinic, summer camp; space and support for study groups, social clubs, and educational programs; cooperative apartments for working women and, later, housing for working men; a clearinghouse for social services to help deserted women, injured workers, evicted tenants, the unemployed, and people dealing with institutions like the county hospital and the state asylum. Hull-House expanded from a single floor to a city-block complex of buildings including an art gallery, coffeeshop, gymnasium, library, theater, museum of labor, dining rooms, music rooms, and housing facilities.

Energetic and political, the residents pushed Addams into more systematic efforts at reform.[1] She aided Florence Kelley in coordinating an extensive study of the Hull-House neighborhood that would become one of the groundbreaking research works of American and of feminist sociology: *Hull-House Maps and Papers: A Presentation of Nationalities and Wages in a Congested District of Chicago, Together with Comments and Essays on Problems Growing out of the Social Conditions* (hereafter, *Hull-House Maps and Papers*) (see Chapter 7). The authorship is given as "By Residents of Hull-House a Social Settlement." This cumbersome title records the growth of Addams and Hull-House between 1889 and 1895. Hull-House existed now as a collaborative effort. The project of the settlement had moved from some vague sense of outreach to the poor to creating structures for social amelioration. The residents now wrote and spoke not only as neighbors but as social scientists. Addams's own contribution to the study, "The Settlement as a Factor in the Labor Movement," shows a growth in critical understanding of class and structural relations and a commitment to social action when that seemed called for—even when it was unpopular, as the labor movement often was.

As a reformer and social activist, Addams participated in meetings of labor congresses, social settlements, women's rights groups, and peace groups. She was an arbitrator in the 1894 Pullman Strike, for the Ladies' Garment Workers' Union (1903), and in the Hart, Schaffner, and Marx strike (1910). She lobbied successfully to establish the Illinois Factory Inspector Office (1893), the Cook County Juvenile Court (1898), the Illinois Child Labor Act (1902), and the federal Children's Bureau (1909–12). She served as a member of the National Child Labor Committee (1904) and the Chicago Board of Education (1905–9), as the first woman president of the National Conference of Charities and Corrections (1909), as vice president of the National American Woman Suffrage Association (1911–14), as a delegate to the Progressive Party convention (1912), as president of the International Committee of Women for Permanent Peace (1915), as a delegate taking the women's peace plan to the belligerent capitals of Europe (1915)—and as garbage inspector (1895) and postmistress of the nineteenth ward (1897). She fought several political campaigns against the ward's corrupt alderman (1895–1900), even though women were not allowed to vote, and spoke and wrote for women's suffrage (1906–20). She helped organize the National Association for the Advancement of Colored People, the Women's Peace Party, the National Consumers' League, and the National Women's Trade Union League.

Through all this, Addams worked successfully to retain leadership of Hull-House, and to keep Hull-House independent of encroaching institutions like the University of Chicago. She maintained this independence by being a highly effective fundraiser, matching the interests of wealthy patrons, the needs of the community, and the residents' abilities; she formalized some of this patronage in a "fellowship system" providing stipends for the residents who did the work of Hull-House (Hamilton, 1943; Knight, 1991; Muncy, 1991). Much of this patronage came from wealthy women.

The Confidence of Women

Through her relations with other women, Addams drew confidence in her ability to speak and act with *auctoritas*. From her Hull-House base, Addams formed connections with many other women involved in social reform and in social science. One group, whom we call the "Chicago Women's School of Sociology" (see Chapter 7), created a sociology and a sociological theory at the same time that men at the University of Chicago were building what was to become known as the Chicago School in American sociology. The former network included women who studied or taught at the University of Chicago, and Hull-House residents who did research from that base. Besides Addams, this network included Edith and Grace Abbott, Sophonisba Breckinridge, Florence Kelley, Frances Kellor, Julia Lathrop, Annie Marion MacLean, Virginia Robinson, Anna Garlin Spencer, Jessie Taft, and Marion Talbot. These women were part of a larger network of women, the first full generation of women to be active in the government of the United States at city, state, and federal levels. Gordon (1994) has done a brief collective biography of 76 leaders of this network, including Addams, who can be linked by correspondence with at least two-thirds of these women. This leadership's "constituency numbered many thousands. For example, in the Northeast alone in 1911–1913, there were eight hundred settlement workers and seventeen hundred paid and volunteer women 'social workers' in 49 social welfare institutions" (Gordon, 1994:72). Addams reached out to still other networks through lectures in women's colleges, settlement houses, and small towns. This elaborate network of women challenged their traditional segregation in the private sphere and exclusion from the public sphere (Fitzpatrick, 1990; Gordon, 1994; Rosenberg, 1982; Scott, 1964). To do this, the women had to be relationally inventive. Hull-House was the result of such inventiveness, as were other settlement houses organized by women, an array of women's clubs and associations, academic programs carved as niches in male-dominated universities, and the powerful informal networks of women activists, scholars, and clubwomen formed out of these bases.

Hull-House offered an extraordinary world of female friendship, mental stimulation, professional advice and collegiality, and practical and material support. Alice Hamilton, a physician and medical pioneer who lived at Hull-House for 22 years, writes: "The life there satisfied every longing—for companionship, for the excitement of new experiences, for constant intellectual stimulation, and for the sense of being caught up in a big movement" (1943:69). The Hull-House women often formed intense and lifelong relations of many types.[2] Addams usually controlled her public presentation of self and was addressed as Miss Addams by Hull-House residents except for an inner circle, like Kelley and Lathrop, who called her J. A. Yet she developed deep friendships and had two major love relations. The first, with Ellen Gates Starr, was critical to the founding of Hull-House because, in her passionate devotion to Addams, Starr may have had more confidence in Addams than Addams had in herself. But in the 1890s, Addams transferred much of her affection to Mary Rozet Smith, a volunteer at Hull-House, and later a trustee. Smith, the daughter of a wealthy Chicago family, provided Addams with close to unconditional love. She filled the role of Addams's constant supporter and helpmate, financing Hull-House projects, buying clothes for Addams, worrying over her health, paying for their vacations, bringing Addams into the elegant home she shared with her parents, and above all, giving Addams a constant sense of being loved by one person in particular.[3]

When Addams wrote sociology, she did not have the men of the academy as her primary audience, but the thousands of women she knew through social reform work, lecture tours, personal correspondence, and as the intended readership for her articles in popular magazines. She understood the work that she and other women activists were doing to be sociology—a sociology created primarily by women out of their life experiences.

The Social Reform and Social Science Movements

The years 1880–1920 in America mark a period of massive social change and social dislocation. One response to these changes was the development of a vast composite of reform movements in America generally known as Progressivism. The city of Chicago was the epicenter both of these changes and of the Progressive reform impulse. Chicago was America's fastest growing urban center, its population of largely immigrant or first generation Americans growing from 150,000 in 1860 to more than two million by 1920. It was home to the first urban skyscraper, the agricultural commodities exchange, the world's biggest stockyards, enormous fortunes produced by manufacturing and commerce—and a level of urban poverty and squalor that shocked foreign and middle-class American visitors alike. In Chicago, exploited workers listened to both anarchist and socialist organizers, and violent labor disputes, like the Pullman Strike of 1894, were a frequent occurrence. William Jennings Bryan gave his famous "Cross of Gold" speech there, and Jane Addams was hailed as the first woman to second the nomination of a presidential candidate (Theodore Roosevelt), at the Progressive Party convention of 1912.[4] Addams's career and her social thought must be understood against this urban and national backdrop; her public persona, her *auctoritas,* and her social theory were shaped by and helped to shape the Progressive reform agenda (see "Assumptions" later in this chapter).

Almost from the beginnings of Hull-House, Addams worked not only as a social reformer but also as a sociologist, part of that sector of Progressive thinking and activity that L. L. and Jessie Bernard (1943) have called "the social science movement." The social science movement expressed the continuing Progressive belief that science must control the changes that science had wrought. Sociologists who were part of this movement defined the responsibility of the sociologist as the reform and improvement of society. Addams was a life-long active participant in professional sociology. She was a member of the American Sociological Society from its founding in 1895 and a frequent contributor to the *American Journal of Sociology,* including an article in its first volume. Beginning with her contribution to *Hull-House Maps and Papers* in 1895, she wrote numerous sociological studies and nine books of social theory and analysis: *Democracy and Social Ethics* (1902), *Newer Ideals of Peace* (1907), *The Spirit of Youth and the City Streets* (1909), *Twenty Years at Hull-House* (1910), *A New Conscience and an Ancient Evil* (1912), *Women at The Hague* (1915) *The Long Road of Woman's Memory* (1916), *Peace and Bread in Time of War* (1922), and *The Second Twenty Years at Hull-House* (1930). She defined herself as doing sociology, referring to life in a settlement as "sociology," and noting with pride that the founding of Hull-House preceded by three years the founding of the first department of sociology in the United States (1930:405). Addams found in the reform social science and sociology movements a relatively fluid area of scholarship in which her social theory could be introduced and recognized—work as a sociologist was another path to *auctoritas.*

Character and Temperament

In the period between 1889 and 1915, Addams achieved, perhaps beyond her dreams, the *auctoritas,* the influence and credibility, that women lacked. Biographer Davis correctly summarizes her success—"Probably no other woman in any period in American history has been venerated and worshiped the way Jane Addams was in the period before World War I" (1973:200)—citing as one indicator, her prominence in public opinion polls. Much of this success and that of Hull-House turned on Addams's character and temperament. She had a much remarked on gift for appreciating the points of view of other people, empathizing with the position of the other, while holding to her own views. The richest vein in her sociological analysis may be her exploration and description of the experience of multiple vantage points in social interaction. This sensitivity to others' views made her prefer compromise over either defeat or victory. Some Addams associates felt disappointed at the least and betrayed at the worst by her preference for compromise over confrontation.

Yet ultimately Addams did sacrifice the *auctoritas* she had so diligently earned for a principle—that of world peace. With the outbreak of World War I, she became increasingly active in the peace movements she had long endorsed, helping to organize the Woman's Peace Party, presiding at the First International Congress of Women at The Hague, serving as president of the International Committee of Women for Permanent Peace, and, in her most daring move, traveling with other delegates to take the women's plan for peace to the leaders of the warring nations. In the United States, which was moving towards entry into the war, Addams was first ridiculed for this special diplomacy and then condemned as a traitor who slighted the bravery of Allied fighting men. Even with United States entry, Addams, unlike many peace party members, refused to change her antiwar stance. The end of the war brought no respite. For her efforts to get food to the defeated and starving Germans, she was pilloried as "pro-German." For her continuing championship of freedom of expression for socialists and anarchists, she was decried as a "Red Sympathizer." Addams was visibly depressed by the ongoing attacks. Yet she held to principle, returning to Europe to become president of a new organization, the Women's International League for Peace and Freedom. In the last fifteen years of her life, she tried to reestablish her credibility; part of that effort gained her the Nobel Peace Prize in 1931, four years before her death.

Hull-House itself slowly withered away, and Addams's considerable achievements both as a social reformer and a social theorist were written out of the record; she became a name to be learned in school, not a mind to be reckoned with. In 1937, two years after Addams's death, Talcott Parsons published *The Structure of Social Action,* which identified sociology with the formal theoretical efforts of European men of Addams's generation. Fifty years later, in 1988, Mary Jo Deegan began the task of restoring the work of Jane Addams to the canon of thinkers who had helped create and establish American sociology.

GENERAL SOCIAL THEORY

Assumptions

Addams participated in several interconnected discourse communities, that is, groups of people having varying degrees of formal affiliation but sharing common concerns and vocabulary: the women's movement, Progressivism, reform social darwinism, philosophic pragmatism, social gospel Christianity, and the social settlement movement. A review of the key concerns within each discourse community can help us gauge where Addams is original and where she is concurring in or debating with widespread understandings of her day. Addams's participation in all these communities was shaped by the ethical posture of her middle-class, Midwestern, Protestant background. While her later religious faith is unclear, she always understood herself as one of those to whom much had been given and therefore of whom much was expected, as a moral agent to be guided by her conscience, and having an absolute duty to act for good in the world.

She brought this orientation to her position as a member of the first generation of college-educated women, a cohort made possible by post–Civil War prosperity. These women faced the anomic situation of needing to define their role in a society that prepared them by education to do almost anything and then denied them any field for action except domesticity. In response to this situation, the women's movement focused on strategies that would gain women access in the public sphere, most especially on strategies for winning the vote. Discussions often concerned the appropriate philosophic arguments for claiming a *right* to vote. Addams's response was to invoke "the social ethic" as the duty now incumbent upon all people, but especially upon women like herself. Her writings about suffrage took issue with the liberal feminist argument that women have the same inalienable natural rights as men and thus can claim political and social equality. She rejected the individualistic emphasis in the natural rights argument which she felt made no allowances for the human capacity for collective rather than individualistic morality. She argued for women's suffrage not as an individual right, but as a civic duty now essential to social progress.

Addams's class and religious background made her at home in the Progressive community. There, theoretical discussions explored the appropriate responsibilities of the state. Rejecting the prevailing laissez-faire position of minimalist involvement with issues of social and economic justice, Progressives claimed that constitutional principles and social science logic demanded an activist enlightened state. Addams's writings reflect these views. She, too, felt that reformist action must counterbalance capitalist expansionism in order to ameliorate the human pain produced by that expansion, and that government was the only social structure with power and resources adequate to this task. But she was concerned that the state envisioned in some reform arguments may act without the necessary knowledge of the everyday life of its citizens.

The laissez-faire philosophy of government claimed social science legitimacy by invoking the social darwinist theories of Herbert Spencer, which held that social evolution and societal progress would only be impeded by government regulation. The Progressives advanced an alternative social science thesis, "reform social darwinism," which held that humans had evolved to a point where their intelligence could and must assume control of evolution. According to this thesis, evolutionary law demanded that people find ways to work in combination with each other to secure a social environment in which all people could develop fully. Government should be an expression of this combined intelligence. Addams's views on her duty as a practical sociologist fit comfortably within this social science ethos, and her theory reflects reform social darwinism with its mix of history and evolutionary imagery. Her theory also reflects her relationships with the male sociologists at the University of Chicago, most especially George Herbert Mead, W. I. Thomas, Charles Henderson, Charles Zeublin, and Albion Small (these relationships are explored in detail in Deegan 1988).

The Progressive and reform social darwinist arguments with laissez-faire ideology were not simply academic debates. They were fought in some of the most important court cases in American history: *Wabash, St. Louis & Pacific R.R. Co. v. Illinois* (1886), *Chicago, Milwaukee & St. Paul R.R. Co. v. Minnesota* (1890), *U.S. v. E. C. Knight Co.* (1895), *In Re Debs* (1895), *U.S. v. Trans-Missouri Freight Association* (1897), *Smyth v. Ames* (1898), *Swift & Co. v. U.S.* (1905), and *Lochner v. New York* (1905). In this last case, in a dissenting opinion, Justice Oliver Wendell Holmes, Jr. criticized the majority decision as being based "upon an economic theory" and warned that "the 14th Amendment does not enact Mr. Herbert Spencer's *Social Statics*." Addams's arguments about the role of the state developed in this context of intense legal debate over government's right to regulate economic and social conditions.

Addams's own commitments to Progressivism and social activism were further legitimated by another discourse community, that of philosophic pragmatism. Addams had significant personal ties with many of the major formulators of this philosophy, including John Dewey, William James, and George Herbert Mead (see Deegan 1988). Pragmatism addressed the issue of the connection between truth and action, knowledge and life experience. James (1907) claimed that the truth of any proposition lay in its practical consequences, its usefulness, its workability. In this sense, no idea could be true that did not work. Dewey saw human intelligence as a finely tuned set of habits for solving problems of any type—moral, scientific, practical, or theoretical—and defined truth as a problem-oriented hypothesis "tested and confirmed" in experience (1922:98–99, 101). Pragmatism gave Addams a philosophic framework for her conviction that the truth of any sociological theory lay in its ability to present solutions to real life issues and for her earlier resolution that the answer to her life crisis lay in action not in study.

Progressive beliefs were also confirmed by the religious discourse within the Protestant Christian churches known as the "social gospel." The doctrine of the social gospel urged ministers to act as bridge between classes, to use "the great teaching powers of the pulpit sanely and wisely to open the minds of the people to the moral importance of the social questions," and to call their congregations to a ministry of works among the poor and op- pressed (Rauschenbusch, 1907:369). Addams worked frequently with ministers, but she was careful not to self-define as a social gospeler: "For Addams, social gospel is a part of a larger movement which is not necessarily religious. Social gospel is the Christian expres- sion of humanitarianism, which is first" (Murphy-Geiss, 1995:22).

The social settlement movement brought together the Progressive reform agenda, so- cial science reformers, and social gospel ministers. Begun in the 1880s in England, the settlement movement spread rapidly to and in America: in 1891 there were 6 settlements in the United States; in 1897, 74; by 1900, 100; by 1905, 200; and by 1910, 400 (Davis, 1967:12). Discussions within the movement focused on the purpose of the settlement, what it should be for residents, how it should orient to its neighbors, its appropriate role in political activism. Addams saw the social settlements as "a subjective necessity" for the educated young people who went there as residents, reuniting them with the life from which their education and privilege had divorced them (1893). She came increasingly to appreciate and speak for the vantage points of her neighbors. She developed an intellec- tual justification of the settlements as morally propelled to political action by their con- nections with their poor neighbors, and she used Hull-House as a platform from which to argue for reform.

Major Themes

Addams wrote social theory as part of her larger project of achieving ameliorative social change in her own society and time. Her chief proposition is that the times require a *so- cial ethic* as the prevailing principle of conduct in society: people must learn to identify their individual interests with the common good, and the common good must be defined so as to recognize that an injury to one is an injury to all. Her social theory is devoted to a careful explication of the need for this ethic and the conditions necessary to achieve it.

Addams was a theorist who distrusted theory, recognizing its capacity to distance the thinker from the immediate realities of what had to be done. She consciously crafted her social theory so as to avoid this danger—grounding and testing her theoreti- cal claims in her experiences and observations of Hull-House and of Progressive ac- tivism, writing with a commitment to accessibility, taking as her prototype of the soci- ologist not the academic but the settlement resident, someone learning from the actualities of lived experience. Because of this commitment to learning from experi- ence, Addams develops an organic rather than a linear theory, proceeding by means of narrative or illustration rather than argument, and presenting through the narrative the major themes of her sociology. The discussion that follows is true to Addams's themes, though we impose some analytic linearity, describing her theory in terms of its episte-mology, its method, its view of the individual, and its concept of society.

1. For Addams the work of the sociologist is to analyze the situation-at-hand in order to bring about ameliorative social change in the world in which the situation occurs. Addams's understanding of sociology begins in the idea that it is a work to be done. She acts on the pragmatist principle that life can be learned only through experience, and social life, only through interactive participation in society. The sine qua non of her theorizing is that "social perspective and sanity of judgment come only from contact with social experience" (1902/1907:7).* It is easy to misread this claim as simply the re-searcher's truism that one must have empirical data for one's generalizations. But Addams means something much more specific and demanding: she means an active and sustained participation in the actualities of people's lives—a participation tested finally by a desire to help alleviate and to make "common lot" with people's problems and needs. For Ad-dams this participation was life and work "as a neighbor" at Hull-House. In her first theo-retical statement on the idea of the settlement, "The Subjective Necessity for Social Settle-ments," Addams described the orientation necessary for the residents: "They must be content to live quietly side by side with their neighbors, until they grow into a sense of re-lationship and mutual interests. . . . They are bound to see the needs of their neighbor-hood as a whole, to furnish data for legislation, and to use their influence to secure it" (1893/1910b:126–127). Her two main epistemological principles—(1) that knowledge of social life can be gained only through direct social experience, and (2) that the knower is responsible toward the subject and situation as they become known—apply equally to the social analyst, the would-be reformer, the Hull-House resident, the individual citizen.

Addams insists that the situation-at-hand for social analysis is the lived experience of in-dividual actors. The sociologist can discover that experience by combining "sympathetic understanding" with "the information of the statistician" (Addams 1910a, p. 70). Although she herself nearly always used case studies, she was also a consistent supporter of quantita-tive studies and a contributor to one of the early works in American sociology combining quantitative and qualitative research, *Hull-House Maps and Papers* (1895). The re-searcher's aim is to construct a knowledge of the social world as the sum of the experiences of human subjects with a variety of interests and viewpoints. To do this, Addams combines elements similar to Weberian *verstehen* with symbolic interactionist participant observation to form a method we might label "sympathetic observation." She first describes this tech-nique in the inaugural volume of the *AJS* in her study of paid domestic labor: "An attempt is made to present this industry from the point of view of those women who are working in households for wages. . . . The opinions in it have been largely gained through experi-ences in a Woman's Labor Bureau, and through conversations held there with women re-turning from . . . 'situations' in Chicago households of all grades" (1896:536).

Addams situates the knower as an ethical being within the situation-to-be-known. For her, the sociologist is ethically bound to move from knowledge gained in social research

---

*An asterisk following a citation in the text means that the passage quoted is given in fuller context in the read-ings at the end of the chapter.

to the project of social amelioration, which may culminate in political action. A stance of value-neutrality would invalidate the knowledge gained; knowledge must suggest a course of action, and the social analyst is not morally free to ignore that course of action or consider it as something apart from the research project. Social research must lead to social amelioration, and political action must be informed by social research that is linked to lived experience. In her contribution to *Hull-House Maps and Papers,* Addams establishes the logical connection between experience and amelioration:

> A settlement accepts . . . that the sharing of the life of the poor is essential to the understanding and bettering of that life. . . . The social injury of the meanest man not only becomes its concern, but by virtue of its very locality it has put itself into a position to see, as no one but a neighbor can see, the stress and need of those who bear the brunt of the social injury. . . .
>
> If the settlement is convinced that . . . lack of organization tends to the helplessness of the isolated worker, and is a menace to the entire community, then it is bound to pledge itself to industrial organization . . . And at this point the settlement enters into what is more technically known as the labor movement. (1895:183–184, 187)*

The researcher also has a moral responsibility not to lose the subject's viewpoint in the sociological accounting. Addams actively sought strategies for monitoring her accounts. She made it a point never to speak to "a Chicago audience on the subject of the Settlement and its vicinity without having a neighbor to go with me, that I might curb any hasty generalization by the consciousness that I had an auditor who knew conditions more intimately than I could hope to do"(1910b:96). As a further act of her self-monitoring, she never allowed herself to forget the economic realities of her relation to her neighbors:

> Of course there was always present the harrowing consciousness of the difference in economic condition between ourselves and our neighbors. Even if we had gone to live in the most wretched tenement, there would always have been an essential difference between them and ourselves, for we should have had a sense of security in regard to illness and old age and the lack of these two securities are the specters which most persistently haunt the poor. (1910b:133–134)

Her insistence on an interactional relationship between the researcher and the subject of research, her belief in the ethical qualities of that relationship, and her respect for her subjects' meanings frame her method for doing theory.

2. Addams's method of doing theory is to report and analyze the situation-at-hand as a narrative of multiple vantage points. Addams's typical method of theory-building is to develop tentative generalizations through narratives. We use "narrative" here in a fairly traditional sense, one that would have been understood by Addams, to mean a story involving characters and events, told in chronological sequence and making some attributions of cause.[5] Addams tells stories out of her experiences as a neighbor—a strategy that allows her to stay true to the situation-at-hand and the lived experiences of the various actors. This technique brings her to the most consistent theme in her social theory: the collision in viewpoints between differently situated actors. Her accounts of such collisions are often reflexive, including the viewpoint of the resident/social analyst, who is understood, as are all of the participants, as an individual with class, ethnicity, gender, and interest. We offer as one example a narrative in which Addams compares the efforts and standards of the Hull-House residents with those of the Hull-House neighbors in regard to funerals:

> [A] delicate little child was deserted in the Hull-House nursery. An investigation showed that it had been born ten days previously in the Cook County hospital, but no trace could be found of the unfortunate mother. The little child lived for several weeks, and then, in spite of every care, died. It was decided [by the residents] to have it buried by the county authorities, and the wagon was to arrive at eleven o'clock; about nine o'clock in the morning the rumor of this awful deed reached the neighbors. A half dozen of them came, in a very excited state of mind, to protest. They took up a collection out of their poverty with which to defray a funeral. The residents of Hull-House were then comparatively new in the neighborhood and did not realize that they were really shocking a genuine moral sentiment of the community. In their crudeness, they instanced the care and tenderness which had been expended upon the little creature while it was alive; that it had had every attention from a skilled physician and a trained nurse, and even intimated that the excited members of the group had not taken part in this, and it now lay with the nursery to decide that it should be buried as it had been born, at the county's expense. It is doubtful if Hull-House has ever done anything which injured it so deeply in the minds of some of its neighbors. It was only forgiven by the most indulgent on the ground that the residents were spinsters, and could not know a mother's heart. No one born and reared in the community could possibly have made a mistake like that. No one who had studied the ethical standards with any care could have bungled so completely. (1902/1907:240–242)

Social theory is not typically told as or created through narrative. In choosing to develop a sociology through narrative, Addams commits herself to a vision of social life as grounded in the historic experiences of individual people in interaction with each other in real places at real times. In her narratives, people are portrayed as ordering their lives not only in time and space but in terms of values, or what Addams calls ethics. They make value judgments about their own actions, their past, their future, and other people; they assign meaning to events. Addams's narratives turn on the conflict between different vantage points or the conflict in consciousness, the bifurcated consciousness, in the mind of a single protagonist, nearly always a woman. Often the protagonist is a "social type"—a character who is in fact a composite of many people located at a similar "intersection of biography and history" (Mills, 1959/1977:6).

In one of Addams's most extensive theoretical uses of narrative, the chapter "Charitable Effort" in *Democracy and Social Ethics,* she tells the story of a relation that was both prominent in her own day and significant to her sociology: the relation between the charity visitor and the client. The charity visitor represents a social type, an educated young woman, potentially like Addams herself, seeking to use her education in service. The client, and the client's family and neighbors, are representative of the growing number of city poor who, Addams stresses, have "come to grief only on the industrial [economic] side" and "may possess other charms and virtues."* Addams develops the plot of the narrative through the conflict between vantage points as represented by the charity visitor and the client, and through the internal conflict experienced by each in trying to understand the other. The charity visitor wrestles with the conflict between her orders from the agency to instruct and uplift her client family and her dawning realization that her class privilege makes such instruction tantamount to hypocrisy. The clients struggle to utter the platitudes seemingly expected of them in return for charity, while suspending belief in what the "neighborhood mind" knows to be the realities—for instance, that the saloon, condemned in those clichés, is a place where a man can get a loan to pay the rent when the charity visitor is miles away. Capturing this complex of experiences in the encounter in "Charitable Effort," Addams moves the reader through time—the charity visitor arrives at the client family's home, lectures, departs, and returns—and yet suggests an endless round of encounters between typical charity visitors and typical client families (1902/1907:13–19).

3. Addams understands the individual social being as an embodied, agentic subjectivity, motivated by interests and ethics. Addams makes the individual the basic unit of her theory, building much of her critique of the world in place out of her ideas about the individual. She sees the individual not only in terms of consciousness, will, and sociability, but also as a person-in-a-body. The theme of the embodied person allows Addams to stay empirically grounded in the actualities of her subjects' lives, to keep her reader so grounded, to test theory by practical solutions, and to assess the world in place by its impact on the body. Her analyses are marked by a rich, and often poignant, imagery of the body which evokes the intersection of class, gender, ethnicity, and age in the individual biography:

> [S]ome frightened women had bidden me to come quickly to the house of an old German woman, whom two men from the county agent's office were attempting to remove to the County Infirmary. The poor old creature had thrown herself bodily upon a small and battered chest of drawers and clung there, clutching it so firmly that it would have been impossible to remove her without also taking the piece of furniture. She did not weep nor moan nor indeed make any human sound, but between her broken gasps for breath she squealed shrilly like a frightened animal caught in a trap. The little group of women and children gathered at her door stood aghast at the realization of the black dread which always clouds the lives of the very poor when work is slack, but which constantly grows more imminent and threatening as old age approaches. The neighborhood women and I hastened to make all sorts of promises of support of the old woman and the county officials, only too glad to be rid of their unhappy duty, left her to our ministrations. (1910b:155–156)

These embodied people are characterized by a complex inner life, marked first of all by an agentic subjectivity—a capacity to think and to will. Addams emphasizes that the actor has purposes of his or her own. "We are not," she writes, "content to include all men in our hopes, *but have become conscious that all men are hoping* and are part of the same movement of which we are a part" (italics ours) (1902/1907:179). This capacity of the individual to hold to her or his own purposes even in the most repressive or degrading circumstances is an object of wonder to her—and a fact of social life that must be taken into account by other social actors, both as a normative duty and a practical reality.

Addams's theory of human development revolves around the way the will is nourished, shaped, and thwarted. Childrearing should nourish the child's capacity for self-actualizing will; parents need to understand and respect the "attempts of a child to assert his individuality, which so often takes the form of opposition to the wishes of the family and the rule of the household" (1902/1907:92). The capacity to will is always shaped by the experiences life presents to the mind. One obligation of ethical personhood is to try to broaden one's range of experiences ("narrowness of interest" is one of Addams's most damning descriptions). But for children, and many disempowered people, experiences are limited by circumstances of class, and these circumstances shape the focus of agency: "[T]he child who is prematurely put to work is constantly oppressed by this never ending question of the means of subsistence, and even little children are sometimes almost crushed with the care of life through their affectionate sympathy" (1902/1907:43).* Much of Addams's ameliorative project involves attempting to reduce the stress on individual will by improving the structural conditions that thwart and distort the will of powerless people. At the same time she is highly critical of reformers and philanthropists whose projects refuse to recognize the legitimacy of the will of the people they seek to help; she sees such a reformer as the "type of humanitarian who loves the people without really knowing them . . . and expects the people whom he does not know to foreswear altogether the right of going their own way, and to be convinced of the beauty and value of his way" (Addams, 1905:425–426).*

The social being is propelled to action not only by interests dictated by practical judgment, but by a need for ethics which is rooted in human propensities for sociability and kindness. The desire for sociability may manifest itself in so everyday an interaction as that Addams labels "'aesthetic sociability' which impels any one of us to drag the entire household to the window when a procession comes into the street or a rainbow appears in the sky" (1916:6).* Often this need for sociability is made apparent by the effects of its absence. In her *AJS* study of domestic workers, Addams suggests that domestic workers, although lacking the vocabulary to describe what is missing, frequently abandon positions because of "isolation": "Many a girl who complains of loneliness, and who relinquishes her situation with that as her sole excuse, feebly tries to formulate her sense of restraint and social mal-adjustment. She sometimes says that she 'feels so unnatural all the time'" (1896:548).

Addams sees the desire for sociability as a basic motive in the construction of ethical conduct, illustrating this motive in the working of the corrupt political machine. She argues: "After all, what the corrupt alderman demands from his followers and largely depends upon is a sense of loyalty. . . . All this is perfectly legitimate, and all in the line of the development of a strong civic loyalty, if it were merely socialized and enlarged" (1902/1907:267–268). The voter who is involved with the political machine has come to understand that city government does directly affect individual lives and has abandoned the notion that each person is independently making a life.

The idea of human beings desiring sociability was being explored in sociology by Addams's contemporaries; but Addams is distinctive in focusing on human beings not only as sociable but as actively seeking to be kind. One of the points in her theoretical framing is that all people, no matter how materially hard-pressed, desire "an outlet for more kindliness," seek "to do a favor for a friend," hope that "kindheartedness . . . shall be given some form of governmental expression" (1907:13). To summarize this persistent desire for kindliness, she uses the French phrase, *"l'imperieuse bonté* by which they designate those impulses towards compassionate conduct which will not be denied" (1907:21). In the current state of municipal government, Addams says, the citizen can find the expression of kindness only in the ward politician who delivers the Christmas turkey, pays for and attends the funeral, or helps arrange bail but expects a vote in return. But she believes it is possible to educate the citizen to see kindness in and feel gratitude toward the collectivity, "the city which supplies . . . a Kindergarten, . . . the Board of Health which properly placarded a case of scarlet-fever next door, . . . the city authorities who provided . . . a playground" (1902/1907:266–267). Addams frequently turns to analyses of trades unions' actions as an example of the force of an appeal to human kindness and decency (e.g., 1902/1907, 1905, 1907).

In human relationships, agency and the impulses to sociability and kindness are inextricably interwoven as people seek a standard of ethics, or correctness—to give their actions intelligibility as being not only practical but moral, or good. "Ethics" is the term Addams uses to name individual and collective standards for right conduct in social interaction, and she has as her major thesis that the times require a collective, or social, ethic (see Theme 4, following). For a social ethic to prevail, people must learn to practice kindness through the collectivity rather than only as individuals. One way to establish a social rather than individual ethic is to appeal to this potential for kindness—a potential that is reciprocal, it is both gratitude for kindness received and the desire to do kindness to others.

4. Addams's social theory outlines society's essential characteristics, describes their particular configuration in American society, and analyzes how that configuration must change if America is to be transformed into a socialized democracy. Addams sees society as people in interaction in multiple relational sites, in real time and space—in cities, ghettos, homes, factories, schools, union meetings, political party headquarters, social gatherings, courts, shops. These sites are linked together in a variety of ways—by the movement of individuals from one site to another, by functional interdependence, by recurring patterns of organization in sites of the same kind (e.g., the middle-class household), by coalitions specifically framed to pursue shared interests, and by hierarchical coordination. In these relational sites, people pursue practical interests—livelihood, wealth, power, material goods, sociability, and intimacy.

In these relational sites people also seek to realize ethical interests as a variable in any relation. While an ethical code originates with the human impulses to sociability and kindness, it becomes established in the individual and in society only through habituated practice in social interaction: "for by our daily experience we have discovered that we cannot mechanically hold up a moral standard, then jump at it in rare moments of exhilaration when we have the strength for it, . . . [rather] the strength to attain it must be secured from interest in life itself" (1902/1907:5–6).* Ethics are historically conditioned and "each generation has its . . . contemporaneous and current standard by which alone it can adequately judge of its own moral achievements" (1902/1907:2).*

This understanding of society informs Addams's description of the United States in her own time. For Addams the *historical* fact of her day is that connections among people are becoming increasingly intense and complex as America transforms from agricultural to industrial, from rural to urban, from homogeneity to heterogeneity. This transformation calls for new practices of sociability and ethics. The central *social* fact is that people must achieve a social ethic aligned with the current state of material production. She interprets the need for ethical realignment in response to industrial change not as economic determinism but as the response of human intelligence in one area of life to changes wrought by human intelligence in another. The chief *contradiction* is that the new forms of social organization are still pervaded by the old ethics: the individual ethic which calls for one to be moral through personal achievement; the family ethic (or "family claim") which calls for loyalty to one's own immediate kin and a few other intimates; and the militaristic ethic which rewards participation in group-approved collective violence. But the times call for a social ethic which requires that each individual identify with the larger, heterogeneous, even anonymous community of which he or she is a part. This identification must be learned through experience and enacted in all forms of association.

Addams is critical of the persistence of these earlier ethics because they lead people to misunderstand their present situation—"to pride one's self on the results of personal effort when the time demands social adjustment, is utterly to fail to apprehend the situation" (1902/1907:2–3)*—and because they all, in varying ways, legitimate domination. Addams locates the cause of industrial conflict in the attempt to maintain an individual ethic of control in the face of a socialization of production, taking as an example the Pullman Strike of 1894: "[A] large manufacturing concern has ceased to be a private matter; not only a number of workmen and stockholders are concerned in its management but the interests of the public are so involved that the officers of the company are in a real sense administering a public trust" (1902/1907:143). This individual ethic provided millionaire businessman George Pullman with a rationale for domination in which he built and regulated a company town for his workers, allowing them no say in its governance because "[h]e honestly believed that he knew better than they what was for their good" (1902/1907:144). In the modern household, Addams says, the family ethic leads women, in particular, away from a recognition that one's true group is the neighborhood, the community, or the society—as well as the family. The woman must "extend her sense of responsibility to many things outside of her own home if she would continue to preserve the home" (1910c:21). Further, the family ethic encourages the housewife to practice domination of her servants' lives, denying them freedom to be with their families in order to secure the quality of life in her own family. Addams traces many problems of current municipal government to the survival of militaristic ethics. She sees the founders of both the nation and its cities as having an idea of government as that which operates by "penalties, coercion, compulsion." This sense of "force of arms" carried over into municipal governments creates "a municipal administration in America which concerns itself only grudgingly with the social needs of the people, and is largely reduced to the administration of restrictive measures" (1907:52).

It is important to reiterate that Addams sees her analysis of contemporary American society as historically specific; she is *not* saying that as a general rule change starts with the material and moves to the ethical. Indeed, in her call for social change, she suggests a possible reversal: changes in ethical standards may change the organization of production.

The first change Addams calls for is in consciousness and habits of interaction. People must learn to identify their individual interests with the common good, to see themselves not in an individual struggle for the good things of life but as participants in a group effort to that end. The only way to acquire this consciousness is through interactive practice; the social ethic must be learned just as the family ethic is, through the living of it: "We have met the obligations of our family life, not because we had made resolutions to that end, but spontaneously, because of a common fund of memories and affections, from which the obligation naturally develops, and we see no other way in which to prepare ourselves for the larger social duties" (1902/1907:5–6).* This interactive practice must be based in a principle of equity and a process of collective and democratic decision-making. The principle of equity is that "no group of people are of so much less importance than another, that a valuable side of life pertaining to them should be sacrificed for the other" (1902/1907:124). To work successfully, collective decision-making requires the form of "imagination" that makes possible "the realization of the experiences of other people" (1902/1907:9). Addams argues that it will be a slow and difficult process to learn to relate as equals across lines of difference and to arrive at decisions collectively. She acknowledges that "[w]e have all been at times entertained by the futile efforts of half a dozen highly individualized people gathered together as a committee. Their aimless attempts to find a common method of action have recalled the wavering motion of a baby's arm before he has learned to coordinate his muscles." But she insists that the process is as important as the outcome, that the "associated effort . . . which appears ineffective . . . may represent a finer social quality than the more effective individual action" (1902/1907:137–138).

The second change called for is the invention of new forms and sites of association. The settlement house was such invention, and Hull-House itself fostered other new forms of association: trades unions (especially for women), educational clubs, women's associations, consumer leagues, study groups, investigative task forces, and ventures into cooperatives, such as the founding of an apartment house for young women working in factories. Addams's account of a women's cooperative apartment house project sponsored by Hull-House shows her program for social change being played out: the decision to cooperate is based in a desire to stand as one; the idea arises from the women themselves out of their lived experience of vulnerability during a strike which threatened their rent money; the decision is implemented after careful investigation; the decision is facilitated by the presence of the settlement as a place to meet; and the settlement is there because of a faith that the age now demands a social ethic (1910b:135–137).

A third change is that people must use their new associational forms to urge the state to act responsibly towards all its citizens because only the state can counterbalance the growing concentrations of wealth and power in the relations of capitalist industry. Addams analyzes the state's inadequacies as arising out of a desire not to act at all, a predilection for misdefining its activities in militaristic and formalistic rather than ethical terms, and a tendency, when it does act, to do so through the ward politician rather than established ethical procedures. In a neighborhood like Chicago's 19th ward, "the policy of the public authorities of never taking an initiative . . . is obviously fatal [because] there is so little initiative among the citizens" (1910b:98). But this lack of initiative comes from the fact that the state has allowed "industrial conditions" to force "the workers below the standard of decency." Since "the very existence of the State depends upon the character of its citizens, . . . it becomes possible to deduce the right of State regulation" in and of this situation (1910b:229). For the state to be reformed, citizens have to take a continuing interest in its administration, mobilize to make it the channel of their own ethical impulses, and promote reform legislation aimed at "municipal housekeeping."[6] Municipal housekeeping means caring for the community in a collective and cooperative way so that government becomes an agent for health, for security in old age, for regulation of working conditions and wages, "in short, all that organization and activity that . . . would prevent a lowering of the standard of life" (1902/1907:166).

ADDAMS'S RELEVANCE FOR THE HISTORY AND PRESENT PRACTICE OF SOCIOLOGY

Addams and the Canon of Sociology

While Martineau belongs to the founding generation of sociologists, that is, those sociologists writing between 1830 and 1870, Addams and the rest of the women discussed in this text belong to the next generation of social theorists, those who created sociology in the period between 1890 and 1930. The contribution of this classic generation is usually understood in terms of (1) a continuation of functionalism in the work of Emile Durkheim, Vilfredo Pareto, and possibly, Robert E. Park, (2) the emergence of the interpretive paradigm with the work of Max Weber, Mead, and Georg Simmel, and (3) the establishment of sociology as an academic discipline. Adding Addams to this classic generation gives new insights into the construction of the distinction between theory and application, the choice of an appropriate voice for writing sociological theory, the critical possibilities of the interpretive paradigm, and the ongoing problematic of the social actor as constrained or agentic.

Theory versus Application   At the moment in the history of sociology during which Addams was doing her most creative work, the distinction, which we now take for granted, between theory and practice, between academic work and applied sociology, was not yet in place. This distinction was formed in Addams's lifetime, as a result of the move by parts of the sociological community to secure professional status by establishing themselves as academics within the university (see Chapter 1). In this movement the profession divorced itself and sociology from activism and application. In keeping with the norms of the university, a division of labor was worked out within sociology so that those who think were, and are, able to claim for themselves more status within the profession than those who do. Addams refused this forced choice, holding to her first tenet in sociology that sociological theory must be used for social amelioration and that theory can be created only through active social involvement.

In this professional struggle, there was a subtext of gender, race, and class exclusiveness. Only white privileged-class men could hope to claim a tenured university position in the early twentieth century. Marginalizing practice in sociology meant marginalizing women, and many men, who worked with dedication to define sociology, doing what is now called "applied sociology" in settlements, other voluntary associations, and government agencies. Further, as Deegan (1988) shows, this distinction meant that the canonized figures of this period—Durkheim, Max Weber, Simmel, and Mead—are remembered in terms of their pure theory rather than in terms of their sociological practice or social activism. These selective memories significantly rework the careers of Durkheim, Mead, and W. I. Thomas, to name but three. Restoring Addams to the canon strengthens the argument about the necessary relation between theory and practice. That argument is now present in Marxian sociology, in the growing field of feminist sociology, and in black feminist thought.

A Distinctive Theoretical Voice   The men now canonized as representing the classic period sought to create sociological theory in a tone that signaled that it was apart from daily life, involving an act of consciousness different from that in everyday life (Schutz and Luckmann, 1973). This approach to theory was one route to professional status. When the men write, they only rarely use "I," and the "I" is understood to refer not to the living, breathing writer but to a universalized actor portrayed for a moment as relating from his consciousness to the world. For the men, theory begins with the construction of general, decontextualized, ahistorical concepts that transcend lived experience—Weber's famous typologies of power, action, and stratification; Durkheim's equally famous typologies of the structural causes of suicide; and Mead's concept of the self.

Addams writes sociological theory in a different voice—personal, involved, grounded, and humorous. She keeps herself present in her theoretical accounts as "Jane Addams of Hull-House," an embodied consciousness with gender, class, ethnicity, age, and location, who responds with emotions—horror, dismay, humor, irony, delight, anger—to the situations she analyzes. She rejects the idea of Hull-House as a social laboratory in which she will observe as a scientist; she writes instead as a neighbor. From this position as a neighbor, she begins her theory with a retelling of the situation-at-hand, and the theoretical principle emerges out of the situation as retold. Her retelling is done in the form of narrative rather than that of ideal typification (see Theme 2, preceding). In this form the sociological account has a built-in limit on its degree of generalizability because the actors and situations are presented not as universals but as deeply contextualized, historical types such as the charity worker, the client, and the neighbor.

An Expanded Interpretive Paradigm   Addams is part of the interpretive tradition: like Max Weber, she is interested in the meanings people assign to their actions; like Mead, she sees the self as produced through relationships; like Simmel and Mead, she describes the dynamics of relationship. But Addams's strategy for exploring actors' meanings is to engage in ongoing sympathetic participant observation of their daily lives. And her interest extends to how meanings interact in very concrete situations; to the problem, later taken up by the ethnomethodologists, of the incomprehension among actors of each others' meanings and the work done in such situations to sustain relationships; and to how larger social arrangements are present and enacted in daily life. Her work is an early example of the institutional ethnography advocated in contemporary sociology by Dorothy E. Smith and her students. Additionally, Addams gives a distinctive mark to interpretive sociology by insisting that people are moral agents propelled to action not only by needs for sociability and meaning but by their desire to understand themselves, their relationships, and the world in terms of principles of right and wrong.

Constraint versus Agency   As part of their move towards establishing the academic legitimacy of sociology, the male theorists of the classic period all claimed that the special competence of their discipline lay in the analysis of society understood as a complex pattern of relational and meaning structures. This claim led them all to a theoretical problematic, that of the relation between society, so defined, and the individual, understood as a thinking, willful being. Despite their very different theories, the men of the classic generation all arrive at a similar conclusion about the nature of this relation—that society determines, to a greater or lesser degree, individual ideas, will, and action. In Durkheim and Mead, this is presented as a universal truth; in Weber and Simmel, it is a characteristic of modern society, with its burgeoning systems of objective culture (Simmel) or bureaucratized social process (Weber). For Durkheim, the socially determined individual is a sociological good, for it is only when individuals conform to the collective consciousness that social order is possible. For Simmel and Weber, the overdetermined individual is a source of grave concern, a malaise of modernity. For Mead, this direction in his theoretical work is untenable. To avoid its full implications, he resorts to the sketchily developed concepts of the "I," or willful self, and the "me," or conforming self, as an ever-present tension in the self; though the enactment of the "I" is at any moment in the social process a remarkable or aberrant event, rather than a typical one.

Addams is to be distinguished from these other theorists, perhaps most dramatically, in her refusal to portray the individual as socially determined. Indeed, she starts with the opposite premise, that the individual is agentic, that is, willful, desirous, irrepressible, even in the most overwhelming social circumstances. This is what she observed as a neighbor in the world around her, and it delights and fascinates her. This vision sets her off from the male theorists whose conclusions were arrived at by a distancing from the everyday and a move toward the purely theoretical orientation. Moreover, Addams's individual is willful not only egoistically but socially and ethically—wishing to relate to others, to have an opportunity to be kind, and to be able to assess his or her actions as being good or bad. Addams sees the conditions of modernity as offering an enormously expanded opportunity for such ethical agency through the enactment of the social ethic in a socialized democracy. The steps for realizing this social ethnic make up her theoretical agenda.

Addams and the Tradition of Feminist Sociology

Addams's configuration of the feminist paradigm is marked by (1) a gendered standpoint, (2) a focus on women's lives, (3) the exploration of multiple vantage points, (4) the invention of a research methodology respectful of these multiple vantage points, and (5) a commitment to change.

A Gendered Standpoint Addams always locates herself as a woman in her theory, alerting the reader that she is actively present in the account and that she brings a woman's consciousness to her analyses. She sees and responds actively and feelingly to gender in the world:

> I cannot recall without indignation a recent experience. I was detained late one evening in an office building . . . . As I came out at eleven o' clock, I met in the corridor . . . a woman whom I knew, on her knees scrubbing the marble tiling. As she straightened up to greet me, she seemed so wet from her feet up to her chin, that I hastily inquired the cause. Her reply was that she left home at five o'clock every night and had no opportunity for six hours to nurse her baby. Her mother's milk mingled with the very water with which she scrubbed the floors. (1910b:174–175)

Through self-reflection, Addams comes to recognize herself as a social type: a woman of a particular class, ethnicity, time, and place, an intersection of biography and history. She especially identifies herself as one of the first generation of college-educated women, facing the problem of women's autonomy, most especially their right to decide for themselves the ethical direction for their lives—a problem she theorizes as a conflict between the family claim and the social ethic. Her knowledge of herself as a social type shapes her awareness of differences among women. The woman scrubbing on her knees is a real person whom Addams knows, but she is also the embodiment of the working-class mother. Awareness of difference, in turn, makes Addams realize the limits of her own class background in dealing with the problems facing her Hull-House neighbors. And this awareness leads her to one of her major themes, the recognition, exploration (and enjoyment) of the phenomenon of multiple vantage points.

Focus on Women's Lives   Women are central to Addams's social analysis: women's work—as domestics, factory workers, housewives, charity visitors, and sweatshop laborers; women's lives over the life cycle—as young wage workers, educated idealists, victims of prostitution, as mature wives and mothers burdened with the ethical and practical work of household and community, as old women facing with terror the threats of isolation, illness, and destitution; women's situation in the family—as household managers, mothers, and daughters—constricted ethically and practically by the morality of the family claim; and women as citizens whom she calls to political action, through unions, club federations, settlements, consumer leagues, and political party participation.

Addams is a cultural feminist, that is, she believes that women bring a different ethical and practical orientation to life situations and that public life in the United States in her lifetime particularly needs this orientation. She traces many of the problems of the cities to the contrast between the prevailing masculine militaristic orientation to city government and her sense of government as civic housekeeping:

> If American cities have failed . . . , may we not say that city housekeeping has failed partly because women, the traditional housekeepers, have not been consulted as to its multiform activities? . . .
>
> It is difficult to see what military prowess has to do with the multiform duties, which, in a modern city, include the care of parks and libraries, superintendence of markets, sewers, and bridges, the inspection of provisions and boilers, and the proper disposal of garbage. (1907:184–185)

In *The Long Road of Women's Memory,* Addams explores how women's minds work, especially the minds of old women. Addams sees women using memory in two different but complementary ways: for "interpreting and appeasing life for the individual" and as "a selective agency in social reorganization"—memory is a way that women realign themselves with the larger impersonal forces that have shaped their lives and in that realignment they may prepare the way for social change (1916:xi–xiii).

Multiple Vantage Points   For Addams, the existence of multiple vantage points is proof of the quality that most interests her in human beings: the capacity of individuals to hold to their own ideas, their own desire, their own will, despite pressure from other people and especially from people more powerful than themselves. People's attempt to communicate from differing vantage points is proof of the desire for sociability and of the fact that society must finally be a cooperative venture. The denial by some people of other people's vantage point is an essential element in domination. Addams's typical mode of analyzing multiple vantage points is through a narrative that illustrates a particular social issue. For example:

> The head of a kindergarten training-class addressed a club of working women, and spoke of the despotism which is often established over little children. She said that so-called determination to break a child's will many times arose from a lust of dominion, and she urged the ideal relationship founded upon love and confidence. But many of the women were puzzled. One of them remarked to the writer [Addams] as she came out of the club room, "If you did not keep control over them from the time they were little, you would never get their wages when they are grown up." Another one said, "Ah, of course she (meaning the speaker) doesn't have to depend upon her children's wages. She can afford to be lax with them, because even if they don't give money to her, she can get along without it." (1902/1907:46)

Framing the contrasting views of the kindergarten teacher and the working-class mothers, Addams shows how multiple vantage points are created by structural location. She draws the reader into participation in the analysis by arguing against the domination of the child but then showing the rationale for the working-class mothers' thinking. Addams's overall argument is that oppressive social structures reproduce themselves in the actions of the oppressed, actions which in the circumstances of their oppression are reasonable and necessary for survival. Only a change in structure can make possible a retreat from domination. What Addams never lets go of—and never allows her reader to let go of—is the complexity of the problem, the absence of simple solutions.

A Feminist Research Method   Addams invented a research methodology that is respectful of multiple vantage points in both its method of inquiry and its mode of presentation—a methodology guided by what contemporary feminist researchers would describe as "mutuality of recognition" (see Benjamin, 1988; Mies, 1983; Reinharz, 1983). This is the ideal she repeatedly expresses when she talks about her relationship to her subjects as "that of a neighbor." Several corollaries flow from the general epistemological proposition of mutuality of recognition. The researcher is obliged to recognize and reflexively monitor her/himself as a socially located actor engaged in a project. This project is not a separate, "objective" research undertaking, but an activity socially located in the researcher's interest and meanings. In her famous early statement "The Subjective Necessity for Social Settlements," Addams explicitly acknowledges that she is engaged in her work because of her own need to express values and purpose. Addams actively worked to monitor her activities, using her Hull-House neighbors as auditors and openly acknowledging the implications of the differences in financial status between herself and her neighbors. Addams, like other feminist sociologists, faced at least two acts of translation in constructing a knowledge of the social world: (1) the task of enabling subjects' lived, personal, historically specific experiences to be expressed in accounts which can be shared without losing the individuality of the original accounts and (2) the task of translating those accounts into the symbol system of sociology. As we have discussed, she solved these problems of translation in part through her use of narrative. The problem of translating these accounts into the symbol system of sociology confronted Addams in a way quite different from the way it presents itself to the modern researcher, as there was in a sense no sociological symbol system when she wrote—everything was being formed and Addams was part of this formation. Addams both formulated a theory and found a style of presentation that allowed her to keep the personal and particular while moving to analysis of structural and political issues.

Commitment to Change   Addams assumes change; for her the fundamental question is not whether change will occur but how to direct that change to produce a socialized democracy, that is, a society infused with values now central to the contemporary feminist agenda—*inclusivity, empowerment,* and *respect for vantage-point.*

Addams sees change as immanent in the contradictions of U.S. society in her time: between the social organization of work and the individual control of production; between the social dependency of all people on each other and the old ethics of individuality, militarism, and family; between the social production of wealth and the inequity of its distribution; between the stated claims of education to foster civic cooperation and the educational practice of rewarding individual competitiveness. For change to be accomplished, people must translate the discomfort they feel about these contradictions into habituated practices of daily interaction to develop associations that are cooperative, democratic, and diverse in membership, welcoming people across racial, ethnic, class, and gender lines. It is in the process of trying to produce reform that people acquire the new ethical habits they are working to realize in the world. Addams argues that the vanguard in this effort for change must be the working class and women. The labor movement in its "inner concept" if not always in its "outward action" aims to be democratic, cooperative, and inclusive, to organize around a key expression of the social ethic that "'[t]he injury to one . . . become the concern of all'" (1895:183). Women are potentially key actors in the movement for progressive change for two reasons. Their traditional ethical location within the family claim, while restricting their view of the group for whom they are responsible, nevertheless prepares them for the ongoing daily practice of being responsible for others. And the consequence of this responsibility for others is that women know practically what is needed to care for people. Above all, Addams rests her hope for change in her distinctive sense of the nature of the social actor in the modern world:

> In the midst of the modern city which, at moments, seems to stand only for the triumph of the strongest, the successful exploitation of the weak, . . . there comes daily . . . . an accretion of . . . people, who carry in their hearts the desire for mere goodness. They regularly deplete their scanty livelihoods in response to . . . pity, and independent of the religions they have professed, of the wrongs they have suffered, and of the fixed morality they have been taught, have an unquenchable desire that charity and simple justice shall regulate men's relations. (1907:12–13)

ENDNOTES

1. From here on, we speak of Addams rather than Addams and Starr. Ellen Gates Starr, who awaits a full biography, for a considerable period was a social activist, joining picket lines and even being arrested. Eventually, she left Hull-House and converted to Roman Catholicism. But she and Addams always remained in touch.

2. Alice Hamilton introduced her sister Margaret to fellow resident Clara Landsberg to whom Margaret became romantically attached, and the three eventually retired together. Children's Bureau head Julia Lathrop met and mentored Grace Abbott, whom she had named as her successor at the Children's Bureau. Residents Sophonisba Breckinridge and Edith Abbott, partners in the building of the University of Chicago's School of Social Service Administration, formed an affectionate triad with Marion Talbot, the creator of the University of Chicago School of Household Administration (see Deegan, 1996; Fitzpatrick, 1990; Richards, 1993).

3. We have tried to describe this relation as it would have been seen by Addams and Smith; they did speak of themselves as "married to each other," but probably within the context of "Boston marriages." They were not politically lesbian and we do not know what their sexual relations were (which would in part depend on the standard one used to categorize "sexual"). (See Cook, 1977; Davis, 1973; Faderman, 1991; Rosenberg-Smith, 1975.)

4. There seems to be some debate about whether Mary Lease may have seconded a nomination at the Populist Convention of 1892. But newspapers in Addams's day reported her seconding speech for Theodore Roosevelt as a "first."

5. This definition combines several ideas from E. M. Forster's discussion in *Aspects of the Novel* (1927/1955).

6. Addams's actual words seem to have been "city housekeeping" or "civic housekeeping." But the idea, which she repeated many times, became popularly remembered as "municipal housekeeping." Perhaps this memory comes from the title of the speech in which she first outlined the orientation, "The Modern City and the Municipal Franchise for Women" (her 1906 speech to the National American Woman Suffrage Association).

Excerpt from "The Settlement as a Factor in the Labor Movement"

This selection is excerpted from pages 183–203. This is Addams's theoretical contribution to the famous volume of critical research and theory by Hull-House residents—a landmark yet forgotten classic in sociology. It is important to understand that Addams views the settlement as the site for doing sociology, as she chooses to define that field. This statement is thus about the role of sociology in class relations in capitalist society. Addams's analysis of these relations is radical, and informed by both observation and theoretical reading. The sociological settlement has a distinct and activist role to play in class relations and the labor movement—a role framed by Addams's sociological theory of ethics in society.

One man or group of men sometimes reveal to their contemporaries a higher conscience by simply incorporating into the deed what has been before but a philosophic position. By this deed the common code of ethics is stretched to a higher point.

Such an act of moral significance, for instance, was John Burns's loyalty to the dockers' strike of East London. "The injury to one" did at last actually "become the concern of all;" and . . . the man who does not share that concern drops below the standard ethics of his day. . . .

When the social conscience, if one may use the expression, has been thus strikingly formulated, it is not so hard for others to follow, . . . weakly and stumblingly, perhaps, . . . yet they have a code of ethics upon which the first man was vague. . . . A settlement accepts the ethics of its contemporaries that the sharing of the life of the poor is essential to the understanding and bettering of that life; but by its very existence it adopts this

Source: Jane Addams, "The Settlement as a Factor in the Labor Movement," in *Hull-House Maps and Papers . . .* (Boston: Crowell, 1895), pp. 183–204.

modern code somewhat formally. The social injury of the meanest man not only becomes its concern, but by virtue of its very locality it has put itself into a position to see, as no one but a neighbor can see, the stress and need of those who bear the brunt of the social injury. A settlement has not only taken a pledge towards those thus injured, but it is placed where the motive power for the fulfillment of such a pledge is constantly renewed. Propinquity is an unceasing factor in its existence.

A review of the sewing-trades, as seen from a settlement, will be sufficient to illustrate this position.

Hull-House is situated in the midst of the sweaters' district of Chicago. The residents came to the district with the general belief that organization for working people was a necessity. They would doubtless have said that the discovery of the power to combine was the distinguishing discovery of our time; that . . . it is already operating to such an extent in commercial affairs, that the manufacturer who does not combine with others of his branch is in constant danger of failure; . . . and that working people likewise cannot be successful unless they too, learn skillfully to avail themselves of this power.

This was to the residents, as to many people, an accepted proposition, but not . . . the driving force of a conviction. The residents have lived for five years in a neighborhood largely given over to the sewing-trades, which is an industry totally disorganized. . . . [T]hey have gradually discovered that lack of organization in a trade tends to the industrial helplessness of the workers in that trade. If in all departments of social, political, and commercial life, isolation is a blunder, . . . in industrial affairs isolation is a social crime; for it there tends to extermination.

This process of extermination entails starvation and suffering, and the desperate moral disintegration which inevitably follows in their train, until the need of organization in industry gradually assumes a moral aspect. The conviction arrived at entails a social obligation.

No trades are so overcrowded as the sewing-trades; for the needle has ever been the refuge of the unskilled woman. . . . This subdivision and low wage have gone so far, that the woman who does home finishing alone cannot possibly gain by it a living wage. The residents of Hull-House have carefully investigated many cases, and are ready to assert that the Italian widow who finishes the cheapest goods, although she sews from six in the morning until eleven at night, can only get enough to keep her children clothed and fed; while for her rent and fuel she must depend upon charity or the hospitality of her countrymen. . . .

The Hebrew tailor, the man with a family to support, who, but for this competition of unskilled women and girls, might earn a wage upon which a family could subsist, is obligated, in order to support them at all, to put his little children at work as soon as they can sew on buttons.

. . . The mother who sews on a gross of buttons for seven cents, in order to buy a blue ribbon with which to tie up her little daughter's hair . . . commits unwittingly a crime against her fellow-workers, although our hearts . . . ache with pity over her misery.

The maternal instinct and family affection is woman's most holy attribute; but if she enters industrial life, that is not enough. She must supplement her family conscience by a social and industrial conscience. She must widen her family affection to embrace the children of the community. She is working havoc in the sewing-trades, because with the meager equipment sufficient for family life she has entered industrial life. . . .

If the settlement, then, is convinced that in industrial affairs lack of organization tends to the helplessness of the isolated worker, and is a menace to the entire community, then, it is bound to pledge itself to industrial organization, and to look about it for the lines upon which to work. And at this point the settlement enters into what is more technically known as the labor movement.

The labor movement may be called a concerted effort among the workers in all trades to obtain a more equitable distribution of the product, and to secure a more orderly existence for the laborers. How may the settlement be of value to this effort?

. . . [T]he most obvious line of action will be organization through the trades-unions, a movement already well established.

The trades-unions say to each workingman, "Associate yourself with . . . fellow-workers. . . . It is the only possible way to prevent cuts in the rate of wages, and to regulate the hours of work. Capital is organized, and has influence with which to secure legislation in its behalf. We are scattered and feeble because we do not work together."

Trades-unionism, in spite of the many pits into which it has fallen, has the ring of altruism about it. It is clearly the duty of the settlement to keep it to its best ideal . . . This keeping to the ideal is not so easy as the more practical work of increasing unions, although that is difficult enough. . . .

It was perhaps natural, from the situation, that the unions organized at Hull-House should have been those in the sewing-trades. The shirtmakers were organized in the spring of 1891. . . .

The cloakmakers were organized at Hull-House in the spring of 1892. Wages had been steadily falling, and there was a great depression among the workers of the trade. . . . The men had urged organization for several years, but were unable to secure it among the women. One apparently insurmountable obstacle had been the possibility of securing any room, save one over a saloon, that was large enough and cheap enough for a general meeting. To a saloon hall the women had steadfastly refused to go. . . . The first meeting at Hull-House was composed of men and girls, and two or three of the residents. The meeting was a revelation to all present. The men, perhaps forty in number, were Russian-Jewish tailors, many of whom could command not even broken English. They were ill-dressed and grimy, suspicious that Hull-House was a spy in the service of the capitalists. They were skilled workers, easily superior to the girls when sewing on a cloak, but shamefaced and constrained in meeting with them. The American-Irish girls were well-dressed, and comparatively at ease. They felt chaperoned by the presence of the residents, and talked volubly among themselves. These two sets of people were held together only by the pressure upon their trade. They were separated by strong racial differences, by language, by nationality, by religion, by mode of life, by every possible social distinction. The interpreter stood between the two sides of the room, somewhat helpless. He was clear upon the economic necessity for combination; he realized the mutual interdependence; but he was baffled by the social aspect of the situation. The residents felt that between these men and girls was a deeper gulf than the much-talked of "chasm" between the favored and unfavored classes. The working-girls before them, who were being forced to cross such a gulf, had a positive advantage over the cultivated girl who consciously, and sometimes heroically, crosses the "chasm" to join hands with her working sisters.

There was much less difference of any sort between the residents and working-girls than between the men and the girls of the same trade. It was a spectacle only to be found in an American city, under the latest conditions of trade-life. Working-people among themselves are being forced into a social democracy from the pressure of the economic situation. It presents an educating and broadening aspect of no small value. . . .

But the labor movement is by no means so simple as trades-unionism. A settlement finds in the movement devoted men . . . who insist that industrial organization must be part of the general re-organization of society. The individualists, for instance, insist that we will never secure equal distribution until we have equality of opportunity. . . , that the sole function of the State is to secure the freedom of each, guarded by the like freedom of all, and that each man free to work for his own existence and advantage will by this formula work out our industrial development. . . . Opposite to him, springing up in discussion every

time he speaks, is the socialist in all varieties. The scientific socialist reads his Karl Marx, and sees a gradual and inevitable absorption of all the means of production and of all capital by one entity, called the community. . . . He sees in the present tendency towards the concentration of capital, and in the growth of trusts and monopolies, an inevitable transition to the socialistic state. . . . In the former cases we had the ex-propriation of the mass of the people by a few usurpers; in the latter we have the ex-propriation of a few usurpers by the mass of the people. . . .

Between these two divergent points of view we find many shades of opinion . . . ; but perhaps a presentation of these two . . . will illustrate how difficult a settlement finds it to be liberal in tone, and to decide what immediate measures are in the line of advantage to the labor movement and which ones are against it.

. . . The crucial question of the time is, "In what attitude stand ye toward the present industrial system? Are you content that greed and seizing upon disadvantage and the pushing of the weaker to the wall shall rule your business life, while in your family and social life you live so differently?" . . . If these questions press upon all of us, then a settlement must surely face the industrial problem as a test of its sincerity, as a test of the unification of its interests with the absorbing interests of its neighbors. Must it, then, accept the creeds of one or the other schools of social thought[?] . . . Can it find the moral question involved? Is there a line of ethics which its action ought to follow? . . .

A glance at the labor movement shows that the preponderating force has been given to what may be called negative action. . . .

A movement cannot be carried on by negating other acts; it must have a positive force, a driving and self-sustaining motive-power. A moral revolution cannot be accomplished by men who are held together merely because they are all smarting under a sense of injury and injustice, although it may be begun there.

Men thus animated may organize for resistance, they may struggle bravely together, and may destroy that which is injurious, but they cannot build up, associate and unite. They have no common, collective faith. The labor movement in America bears this trace of its youth and immaturity. . . .

It is doubtless true that men who work excessively certain weeks in the year, and bear enforced idleness harassed by a fear of starvation . . . are too far from that regulated life . . . in which the quiet inculcation of moral principle is possible. . . . The labor movement is bound, therefore, to work for shorter hours and increased wages and regularity of work, that education and moral reform may come to the individual laborer; that association may be put upon larger principles, and assume the higher fraternal aspect. . . .

The settlement may be of value if it can take a larger and steadier view than is always possible to the workingman, smarting under a sense of wrong; or to the capitalist, seeking only to "quiet down," without regard to the historic significance of the case, and insisting upon the inalienable right of "invested capital," to a return of at least four per cent, ignoring human passion. It is possible to recall them both to a sense of the larger development.

A century ago there was an irresistible impulse, an upward movement, among the mass of people to have their share in political life,—hitherto the life of the privileged. . . . There is a similar demand at the close of this century on the part of working-people; but this time it is for a share in the results of industry. . . .

. . . It is singular that in America, where government is founded upon the principle of representation, the capitalist should have been so slow to accord this right to the workingmen; that he should refuse so steadily to treat with a "walking delegate," and so long maintain that no "outsider" could represent the men in his shop.

We must learn to trust our democracy, giant-like and threatening as it may appear in its uncouth strength and untried application. . . .

As the tendency to warfare shows the primitive state of the labor movement, so also this division on class lines reveals its present undeveloped condition. The organization of society into huge battalions with syndicates and corporations on the side of capital, and trades-unions and federations on the side of labor, is to divide the world into two hostile camps, and to turn us back into class warfare and class limitations. . . .

. . . As the labor movement grows older its leaders may catch the larger ethical view which genuine experience always gives; they may have a chance to act free from the pressure of threat or ambition. They should have nothing to gain or lose, save as they rise or fall with their fellows. In raising the mass, men could have a motive-power . . . much greater than the motive for individual success. . . .

Is it too much to hope that as better organized and older trades-unions are fast recognizing a solidarity of labor, and acting upon the literal notion of brotherhood, that they will later perceive the larger solidarity which includes labor and capital, and act upon the notion of universal kinship? . . .

A settlement may well be dismayed when it sees workingmen apathetic to higher motives, and thinking only of stratagems by which to outwit the capitalists; or when workingmen justify themselves in the use of base measures, saying they have learned the lessons from the other side. Such an attitude at once turns the movement from a development into a struggle, and the sole judge left between the adversaries must in the end be force. Class interests become the governing and motive power, and the settlement can logically be of no value to either side. Its sympathies are naturally much entangled in such as struggle, but to be of value it must keep its judgment clear as to the final ethical outcome—and this requires both perceptions and training.

Fortunately, every action may be analyzed into its permanent and transient aspects. The transient aspect of the strike is the anger and opposition against the employer, and too often the chagrin of failure. The permanent is the binding together of the strikers in the ties of association and brotherhood, and the attainment of a more democratic relation to the employer; and it is because of a growing sense of brotherhood and of democracy in the labor movement that we see in it a growing ethical power.

Hence the duty of the settlement in keeping the movement from becoming in any sense a class warfare is clear. . . . A class working for a class, and against another class, implies that within itself there should be trades working for trades, individuals working for individuals. The universal character of the movement is gone from the start, and cannot be caught until an all-embracing ideal is accepted. . . .

The settlement is pledged to insist upon the unity of life, to gather to itself the sense of righteousness to be found in its neighborhood, and as far as possible in its city; to work towards the betterment not of one kind of people or class or people, but for the common good. The settlement believes that just as men deprived of comradeship by circumstances or law go back to the brutality from which they came, so any class or set of men deprived of the companionship of the whole, become correspondingly decivilized and crippled. No part of society can afford to get along without others.

The settlement, then, urges first, the organization of working people in order that as much leisure and orderly life as possible may be secured to them in which to carry out higher aims of living; in the second place, it should make a constant effort to bring to bear upon the labor movement a consciousness of its historic development; and lastly, it accentuates the ultimate ethical aims of the movement.

READING 3-2

Excerpts from *Democracy and Social Ethics*

This is Addams's programmatic statement of the significance of ethics in social life, the need for American society to adopt a social ethic of collective participation and responsibility, and the importance of social analysis and theory in supporting and expanding these claims.

EXCERPT FROM CHAPTER I, "INTRODUCTION"

This selection is excerpted from pages 1–12. Its general thesis is that ethics are essential in social life; that the times call for a new and social ethic, understood as a systematic expansion of the democratic principle; and that this ethical transformation requires a broader understanding of the lives and perspectives of society's various groups. Social research and social theory will assist in the creation of a social morality.

It is well to remind ourselves, from time to time, that "Ethics" is but another word for "righteousness," that for which many men and women of every generation have hungered and thirsted, and without which life becomes meaningless.

Certain forms of personal righteousness have become to a majority of the community almost automatic. It is as easy for most of us to keep from stealing our dinners as it is to digest them, and there is quite as much voluntary morality involved in one process as in the other. . . . In the same way we have been carefully reared to a sense of family obligation, to be kindly and considerate to the members of our own households, and to feel responsible for their well-being. As the rules of conduct have become established in

Source: Jane Addams, *Democracy and Social Ethics* (New York: Macmillan, 1902/1907).

regard to our self-development and our families, so they have been in regard to limited circles of friends. . . .

But we all know that each generation has its own test, the contemporaneous and current standard by which alone it can adequately judge of its own moral achievements, and that it may not legitimately use a previous and less vigorous test. The advanced test must indeed include that which has already been attained; but if it includes no more we fail to go forward. . . .

To attain individual morality in an age demanding social morality, to pride one's self on the results of personal effort when the time demands social adjustment, is utterly to fail to apprehend the situation. . . .

All about us are men and women who have become unhappy in regard to their attitude toward the social order itself. . . . These men and women have caught a moral challenge raised by the exigencies of contemporaneous life; . . . all are increasingly anxious concerning their actual relations to the basic organization of society.

The test which they would apply to their conduct is a social test. They fail to be content with the fulfillment of their family and personal obligations, and find themselves striving to respond to a new demand involving a social obligation; they have become conscious of another requirement, and the contribution they would make is toward a code of social ethics. The conception of life which they hold has not yet expressed itself in social changes or legal enactment, but rather in a mental attitude of maladjustment, and in a sense of divergence between their consciences and their conduct. They desire both a clearer definition of the code of morality adapted to present day demands and a part in its fulfillment, both a creed and a practice of social morality. In the perplexity of this intricate situation at least one thing is becoming clear: if the latter day moral idea is in reality that of a social morality, it is inevitable that those who desire it must be brought in contact with the moral experiences of the many in order to procure an adequate social motive.

. . . We may indeed imagine many . . . saying: "Cast our experience in a larger mould if our lives are to be animated by the larger social aims. We have met the obligations of our family life, not because we had made resolutions to that end, but spontaneously, because of a common fund of memories and affections, from which the obligation naturally develops, and we see no other way in which to prepare ourselves for the larger social duties." Such a demand is reasonable, for by our daily experience we have discovered that we cannot mechanically hold up a moral standard, then jump at it in rare moments of exhilaration when we have the strength for it, but that even as the ideal itself must be a rational development of life, so the strength to attain it must be secured from interest in life itself. . . . We are thus brought to a conception of Democracy not merely as a sentiment which desires the well-being of all men, nor yet as a creed which believes in the essential dignity and equality of all men, but as that which affords a rule of living as well as a test of faith.

. . . To follow the path of social morality . . . implies that diversified human experience and resultant sympathy which are the foundation and guarantee of Democracy . . . [for w]e realize . . . that social perspective and sanity of judgment come only from contact with social experience; that such contact is the surest corrective of opinions concerning the social order, and concerning efforts, however humble, for its improvement. Indeed, it is a consciousness of the illuminating and dynamic value of this wider and more thorough human experience which explains in no small degree that new curiosity regarding human life which has more of a moral basis than an intellectual one. . . .

. . . We have learned as common knowledge that much of the insensibility and hardness of the world is due to the lack of imagination which prevents a realization of the experiences of other people. . . . We know . . . that if we grow contemptuous of our fellows, and consciously limit our intercourse to certain kinds of people whom we have previously decided to respect, we not only tremendously circumscribe our range of life, but limit the scope of our ethics.

. . . Thus the identification with the common lot which is the essential idea of Democracy becomes the source and expression of social ethics. . . .

The six following chapters are . . . [n]o attempt . . . to reach a conclusion, nor to offer advice beyond the assumption that the cure for the ills of Democracy is more Democracy, but the quite unlooked for result of the studies would seem to indicate that while the strain and perplexity of the situation is felt most keenly by the educated and self-conscious members of the community, the tentative and actual attempts at adjustment are largely coming through those who are simpler and less analytical.

EXCERPTS FROM CHAPTER II, "CHARITABLE EFFORT"

This selection is excerpted from pages 13–32. Addams, like Martineau, saw a society's treatment of its poor as the clearest measure of its ethical progress. Here she uses the organization of charity to show the ethical confusion present in American society in her time. In an extended use of narrative, she also develops her theme of collisions between situated vantage points.

Probably there is no relation in life which our democracy is changing more rapidly than the charitable relation—that relation which obtains between benefactor and beneficiary; at the same time there is no point of contact in our modern experience which reveals so clearly the lack of equality which democracy implies. . . .

. . . Formerly when it was believed that poverty was synonymous with vice and laziness, and that the prosperous man was the righteous man charity was administered harshly with a good conscience; for the charitable agent really blamed the individual for his poverty. . . . We have learned since that time . . . to judge men by their social

virtues as well as by their business capacity . . . and we naturally resent being obliged to judge poor people so solely upon the industrial side. . . . It is largely in this modern tendency to judge all men by one democratic standard, while the old charitable attitude commonly allowed the use of two standards, that much of the difficulty adheres. We know that unceasing bodily toil becomes wearing and brutalizing, and our position is totally untenable if we judge large numbers of our fellows solely upon their success in maintaining it.

The daintily clad charitable visitor who steps into the little house made untidy by the vigorous efforts of her hostess, the washerwoman, is no longer sure of her superiority to the latter; she recognizes that her hostess after all represents social value and industrial use, as over against her own parasitic cleanliness and a social standing attained only through status.

The only families who apply for aid to the charitable agencies are those who have come to grief on the industrial side. . . . The charity visitor, let us assume, is a young college woman, well-bred and open-minded. . . . The members of her assigned family may have other charms and virtues—they may possibly be kind and considerate of each other, generous to their friends, but it is her business to stick to the industrial side. As she daily holds up these standards, it often occurs to the mind of the sensitive visitor, whose conscience has been made tender by much talk of brotherhood and equality, that she has no right to say these things; that her untrained hands are no more fitted to cope with actual conditions than those of her brokendown family. . . .

Added to this is a consciousness, in the mind of the visitor, of a genuine misunderstanding of her motives by the recipients of her charity, and by their neighbors. Let us take a neighborhood of poor people, and test their ethical standards by those of the charity visitor, who comes with the best desire in the world to help them out of their distress. A most striking incongruity, at once apparent, is the difference between the emotional kindness with which relief is given by one poor neighbor to another poor neighbor, and the guarded care with which relief is given by a charity visitor to a charity recipient. The neighborhood mind is at once confronted not only by difference of method, but by an absolute clashing of two ethical standards. . . .

When they see the delay and caution with which relief is given, it does not appear to them a conscientious scruple, but as the cold and calculating action of a selfish man. It is not the aid that they are accustomed to receive from their neighbors, and they do not understand why the impulse which drives people to "be good to the poor" should be so severely supervised. . . .

When the agent or visitor appears among the poor, and they discover that under certain conditions food and rent and medical aid are dispensed from some unknown source, every man, woman, and child is quick to learn what the conditions may be, and to follow them. Though in their eyes a glass of beer is quite right and proper when taken as any self-respecting man should take it; though they know that cleanliness is an expensive virtue which can be required of few; though they realize that saving is well-nigh impossible when but a few cents can be laid by at a time; though their feeling for the church may be something quite elusive of definition and quite apart from daily living: to the visitor they gravely laud temperance and cleanliness and thrift and religious observance. . . .

If a poor woman knows that her neighbor next door has no shoes, she is quite willing to lend her own, that her neighbor may go decently to mass, or to work; for she knows the smallest item about the scanty wardrobe, and cheerfully helps out. When the charity visitor comes in, all the neighbors are baffled as to what her circumstances may be. They know she does not need a new pair of shoes, and rather suspect that she has a dozen pairs at home; which, indeed, she sometimes has. . . . [H]er most generous gift is considered niggardly, compared with what she might do. She ought to get new shoes for the family all round, "she sees well enough that they need them." It is not more than the neighbor herself would do, has practically done, when she lent her own shoes. . . .

The visitor says, sometimes, that in holding her poor family so hard to a standard of thrift she is really breaking down a rule of higher living which they formerly observed. . . . She says sometimes, "Why must I talk always of getting work and saving money, the things I know nothing about? If it were anything else I had to urge, I could do it; anything like Latin prose, which I had worried through myself, it would not be so hard." But she finds it difficult to connect the experiences of her youth with the experiences of the visited family.

This selection is excerpted from pages 43–44. In another narrative based in sympathetic participation, Addams shows how economic pressure can distort will and moral development; her project, to be achieved through both her activism and her theory, is to bring about social change in America that will remove these pressures from the lives of people in general, and children in particular.

The child who is prematurely put to work is constantly oppressed by this never ending question of the means of subsistence, and even little children are sometimes almost crushed with the cares of life through their affectionate sympathy. The writer knows a little Italian lad of six to whom the problems of food, clothing, and shelter have become so immediate and pressing that, although an imaginative child, he is unable to see life from any other standpoint. The goblin or bugaboo, feared by the more fortunate child, in his mind, has come to be the need of coal which caused his father hysterical and demonstrative grief when it carried off his mother's inherited linen, the mosaic of St. Joseph, and, worst of all, his own rubber boots. He once came to a party at Hull-House, and was interested in nothing save a gas stove which he saw in the kitchen. He became excited over the discovery that fire could be produced without fuel. "I will tell my father of this stove. You buy no coal, you need only a match. Anybody will give you a match." He was taken to visit at a country-house and at once inquired how much rent was paid for it. On being told carelessly by his hostess that they paid no rent for that house, he came back quite wild with interest that the problem was solved. "Me and my father will go to the country. You get a big house, all warm, without rent." Nothing else in the country interested him but the subject of rent, and he talked of that with an exclusiveness worthy of a single taxer.

Excerpt from "Problems of Municipal Administration"

This selection is excerpted from pages 425–39. This paper illustrates Addams's theory of the democratic state and her critique of American government in her own time, not in terms of a popular outcry about corruption, but in terms of (1) the persistence of a militaristic ethic in government and (2) the absence of a truly democratic process which rests in a faith in the humanity and virtue of the average citizen.

We are accustomed to say that the machinery of government incorporated in the charters of the early American cities, as in the federal and state constitutions, was worked out by men who were strongly under the influence of the historians and doctrinaires of the eighteenth century. . . .

We are only now, however, beginning to suspect that the present admitted failure in municipal administration, the so-called "shame of American cities," may be largely due to the inadequacy of those eighteenth-century ideals, with the breakdown

---

Source: Jane Addams, "Problems of Municipal Administration," *American Journal of Sociology* 10 (1905), pp. 425–44.

of the machinery which they provided, and further, to the weakness inherent in the historic and doctrinaire method when it attempts to deal with growing and human institutions.

These men were the legitimate successors of the seventeenth-century Puritans in their devotion to pure principle, . . . and represented that first type of humanitarian who loves the people without really knowing them, which is by no means an impossible achievement . . . expect[ing] the people whom he does not know to forswear altogether the right of going their own way, and to be convinced of the beauty and value of his way.

. . . It was inevitable, therefore, that they should have remained quite untouched by that worldly wisdom which counsels us to know life as it is, and by that very modern belief that, if the world is ever right at all, it must go right in its own way.

. . . Were self-government to be inaugurated by the advanced men of the present moment, as the founders were doubtless the advanced men of their time, they would make the most careful research into those early organizations of village communities, folkmotes and *mirs,* those primary cells of both social and political organization, where people knew no difference between the two, but quite simply met to consider in common discussion all that concerned their common life. They would investigate the craft guilds and *artels,* which combined government with daily occupation, as did the self-governing university and free town. . . .

But our eighteenth-century idealists, unconscious of the compulsions of origins and of the fact that self-government had an origin of its own, timidly took the English law as their prototype. . . . They depended upon penalties, coercion, compulsion, and remnants of military codes to hold the community together; and it may be possible to trace much of the maladministration of our cities to these survivals, to the fact that our early democracy was a moral romanticism, rather than a well-grounded belief in social capacity and in the efficiency of the popular will.

All might have gone well upon this doctrinaire plan, . . . if there had not been a phenomenally rapid growth in cities upon an entirely changed basis. Multitudes of men were suddenly brought together in response to the nineteenth-century concentration of industry and commerce—a purely impersonal tie. . . . Added to this unprecedented growth from industrial causes, we have in American cities multitudes of immigrants, coming in successive migration, often breaking social ties which are as old as the human family, and renouncing customs which may be traced to the habits of primitive man. Both the country-bred and immigrant city dwellers would be ready to adapt themselves to a new and vigorous civic life founded upon a synthesis of their social needs, but framers of our carefully prepared city charters did not provide for this expanding demand at the points of congestion. They did not foresee that after the universal franchise has once been granted, social needs and ideals are bound to enter in as legitimate objects of political action. . . . We have, therefore, a municipal administration in America which is largely reduced to the administration of restrictive measures.

. . . [T]he mechanical method of civic control . . . inevitably produces . . . the so-called . . . professional politician, . . . who easily adapts himself to an illegal avoidance of the external fixed conditions by assuming that those conditions have been settled by doctrinaires who did not in the least understand the people, while he, the politician, makes his appeal beyond those to the real desires of the people themselves. He is thus not only the "people's friend," but their interpreter. It is interesting to note how often simple people refer to "them," meaning the good and great who govern, but do not understand, and to "him," meaning the alderman who represents them in these incomprehensible halls of state, as an ambassador to a foreign country to whose borders they could not possibly penetrate and whose language they do not speak. . . .

As this type of politician is successful from his alliance with crime, there also inevitably arises from time to time a so-called reformer, who . . . dramatically uncovers the situation. . . . In portraying the evil he is fighting, he does not recognize, or at least does not make clear, all the human kindness upon which it has grown. In his speeches he inevitably offends a popular audience, who know that the political evil exists in all degrees and forms of human weakness, but who also know that these evils are by no means always hideous. They resent his overdrawn pictures of vice and of the life of the vicious; their sense of fair play, and their deep-rooted desire for charity and justice, are outraged.

If I may illustrate from a personal experience: Some years ago a famous New York reformer came to Chicago. . . . He proceeded to describe the criminals of lower New York in terms and phrases which struck at least one of his auditors as sheer blasphemy against our common human nature. I thought of the criminals whom I knew, of the gambler for whom each Saturday I regularly collected his weekly wage of $24, keeping $18 for his wife and children, and giving him $6 on Monday morning. His despairing statement, "The thing is growing on me, and I can never give it up," was the cry of a man who, through much tribulation, had at least kept the loyal intention. . . . I recalled the first murderer whom I had ever known—a young man who was singing his baby to sleep, and stopped to lay it in its cradle before he rushed down-stairs into his father's saloon, to scatter the gang of boys who were teasing the old man by giving him their orders in English which he could not understand, and refusing to pay for the drinks which they had consumed. . . .

For one short moment I saw the situation from the point of view of humbler people who sin often through weakness and passion, but seldom through hardness of heart; and I felt that such sweeping condemnations and conclusions as the speaker was pouring forth could never be accounted for righteousness in a democratic community. . . .

In point of fact, government ignores industrial questions as the traditional ostrich hides his head in the sand. . . . It is merely a question as to whether industry in relation to government is to be discussed as a matter of popular interest and concern at the moment when that relation might be modified and controlled. . . .

Again we see the doctrinaire of the eighteenth century preferring to hold to his theory of government and ignoring the facts, as over against the open-minded scientist of the present day who would scorn to ignore facts because they might disturb his theory.

Excerpts from *The Long Road of Woman's Memory*

In this book, Addams presents, in vivid detail, data from her Hull-House observations and interviews, in order to explore women's consciousness, particularly the functions of memory for old, poor, ethnic women.

EXCERPT FROM "INTRODUCTION"

This selection is excerpted from pages ix–xv. Here, Addams sets up her study of women's memories—her question about its functions for the women and for society; her data-gathering measures, that is, observation and conversation "as a neighbor," and her conclusions that memory (1) transmutes a painful past into acceptance and reconciliation for the individual woman and (2) shows how people in consciousness adjust to social change.

For many years at Hull-House I have at intervals detected in certain old people, when they spoke of

Source: Jane Addams, *The Long Road of Woman's Memory* (New York: Macmillan, 1916).

their past experiences, a tendency to an idealization. . . .

. . . Sir Gilbert Murray in his life of Euripides . . . writes that the aged poet . . . declared that he could transmute into song traditional tales of sorrow and wrong-doing because, being long past, they had already become part mystery and part music: "Memory, that Memory who is the Mother of the Muses, having done her work upon them."

Here was an explanation which I might have anticipated; it was the Muses again at their old tricks . . . equally at home with the aged whose prosaic lives sadly need such interference. . . .

The subject, however, was not so easily disposed of, for certain elderly women among these selfsame neighbors disconcertingly took quite another line from that indicated by Euripides. To my amazement, their reminiscences revealed an additional function of memory, so aggressive and withal so modern that it was quite impossible, living as I was in a Settlement with sociological tendencies, to ignore it.

It was gradually forced upon my attention that these reminiscences of the aged, even while softening the harsh realities of the past, exercise a vital power of selection which often necessitates an onset against the very traditions and conventions commonly believed to find their stronghold in the minds of elderly people. . . .

In the light of this later knowledge, I was impelled to write . . . this book, bas[ed] upon conversations held with various women of my acquaintance whose experience in family relationships or in the labor market had so forced their conduct to a variation from the accepted type that there emerged an indication of selective groping toward another standard. . . .

. . . I found that the two functions of Memory—first, its important role in interpreting and appeasing life for the individual, and second its activity as a selective agency in social reorganization—were not mutually exclusive, and at moments seemed to support each other.

EXCERPT FROM CHAPTER I, "TRANSMUTING THE PAST," AND CHAPTER II, "REACTING ON LIFE"

This selection is excerpted from pages 1–21 and from page 25. In this stunning ethnographic account, Addams explores the role of memory and folklore in the individual's adjustment to and acceptance of a painful past and present.

Quite as it would be hard for any one of us to select the summer in which he ceased to live that life when all the real happenings are in the future, so it must be difficult for old people to tell at what period they began to regard the present chiefly as a prolongation of the past. There is no doubt, however, that such instinctive shiftings and reversals have taken place for many old people who, under the control of Memory, are actually living much more in the past than in the ephemeral present. . . .

This permanent and elemental function of Memory was graphically demonstrated at Hull-House during a period of several weeks when we were reported to be harboring within its walls a so-called "Devil Baby."

The knowledge of his existence burst upon the residents of Hull-House one day when three Italian women, with an excited rush through the door, demanded that he be shown to them. No amount of denial convinced them that he was not there, for they knew exactly what he was like with his cloven hoofs, his pointed ears and diminutive tail; the Devil Baby had, moreover, been able to speak as soon as he was born and was most shockingly profane.

The three women were but the forerunners of a veritable multitude; for six weeks from every part of the city and suburbs the streams of visitors to this mythical baby poured in all day long and so far into the night that the regular activities of the settlement were almost swamped.

The Italian version, with a hundred variations, dealt with a pious Italian girl married to an atheist. Her husband in a rage had torn a holy picture from the bedroom wall saying that he would quite as soon have a devil in the house as such a thing, whereupon the devil incarnated himself in her coming child. As soon as the Devil Baby was born, he ran about the table shaking his finger in deep reproach at his father, who finally caught him and, in fear and trembling, brought him to Hull-House. . . .

The Jewish version . . . was to the effect that the father of six daughters had said before the birth of a seventh child that he would rather have a devil in the family than another girl, where upon the Devil Baby promptly appeared.

Save for a red automobile which occasionally figured in the story and a stray cigar which, in some versions, the new-born child has snatched from his father's lips, the tale might have been fashioned a thousand years ago.

. . . [T]he visitors to the Devil Baby included persons of every degree of prosperity and education. . . .

For six weeks as I went about the house, I would hear a voice at the telephone repeating for the hundredth time that day, "No, there is no such baby"; . . . "We didn't send it anywhere, because we never had it"; "I don't mean to say that your sister-in-law lied, but there must be some mistake"; "There is no use getting up an excursion from Milwaukee, for there isn't any Devil Baby at Hull-House". . . . As I came near the front door, I would catch snatches of arguments that were often acrimonious: . . . "We have taken three lines of cars to come and we have as much right to see it as anybody else"; "This is a pretty big place, of course you could hide it easy enough". . . .

We had doubtless struck a case of what the psychologists call the "contagion of emotion" added to that "aesthetic sociability" which impels any one of us to drag the entire household to the window when a procession comes into the street or a rainbow appears in the sky. The Devil Baby of course was worth many processions and rainbows. . . . It was a very serious and genuine matter with the old women, this story so ancient and yet so contemporaneous, and they flocked to Hull-House from every direction; those I had known for many years, others I had never known and some whom I had supposed to be long dead. But they were all alive and eager; something in the story or in its mysterious sequences had aroused one of those active forces in human nature which does not take orders, but insists only upon giving them. We had abruptly come in contact with a living and self-assertive human quality!

During the weeks of excitement it was the old women who really seemed to have come into their own, and perhaps the most significant result of the incident was the reaction of the story upon them. . . . They are accustomed to sit at home and to hear the younger members of the family speak of affairs quite outside their own experiences. . . . The story of the Devil Baby evidently put into their hands the sort of material with which they were accustomed to deal . . . as if they had made good at last and had come into a region of sanctions and punishments which they understood. . . .

. . . Many of them who came to see the Devil Baby had been forced to face tragic experiences, the powers of brutality and horror had had full scope in their lives and for years they had had acquaintance with disaster and death. Such old women do not shirk life's misery by feeble idealism, for they are long past the stage of make-believe. They relate without flinching the most hideous experiences: "My face has had this queer twist for now nearly sixty years; I was ten when it got that way, the night after I saw my father do my mother to death with his knife.". . .

None of them had a word of blame for undutiful children or heedless grandchildren, because apparently the petty and transitory had fallen away from their austere old age, the fires were burnt out, resentments, hatreds, and even cherished sorrows had become actually unintelligible. . . .

One old woman actually came from the poorhouse. . . . It was no slight achievement for the penniless and crippled old inmate to make her escape. She had asked "a young bar-keep in a saloon across the road" to lend her ten cents, offering as security the fact she was an old acquaintance at Hull-House who could not be refused so slight a loan. . . . [I]t was clear that she would consider herself well repaid by a sight of the Devil Baby and that not only the inmates of her own ward, but those in every other ward in the house would be made to "sit up" when she got back. . . .

As she cheerfully rambled on, we weakly postponed telling her there was no Devil Baby, . . . [and] I found myself for the first time vaguely wishing that I could administer comfort by the simple device of not asserting too dogmatically that the Devil Baby had never been at Hull-House.

Our guest recalled with great pride that her grandmother has possessed second sight; then her mother had heard the Banshee three times, and that she, herself, had heard it once . . . and I suspected that she cherished a secret hope that when she laid her eyes upon [the Devil Baby] . . . he would afford proof that her family-long faith in such matters was justified. . . .

. . . [Another] old woman, sturdy in her convictions, although long since bedridden, . . . had doggedly refused to believe that there was no Devil Baby at Hull-House, unless "herself" told her so. . . . As I walked along the street and even as I went up the ramshackle outside stairway . . . I was assailed by a veritable temptation to give her a full description of the Devil Baby, which by this time I knew so accurately. . . .

I found my mind hastily marshaling arguments for not disturbing her belief in the story which had so evidently brought her a vivid interest long denied her. . . . She could live only a few months at the very best, I argued to myself; why not give her this vivid interest. . . .

. . . I was still arguing the case with myself when I stood on the threshold of her room and caught the indomitable gleam of her eye, fairly daring me to deny the existence of the Devil Baby, her slack dropsical body so responding to her overpowering excitement that for the moment she looked alert in her defiance and positively menacing.

But, as in the case of many another weak soul, the decision was taken out of my hands, my very hesitation was enough, for nothing is more certain than that the bearer of a magic tale never stands dawdling on the door-step. Slowly the gleam died out of the expectant old eyes, the erect shoulders sagged and pulled forward, and I saw only too plainly that the poor old woman had accepted one more disappointment in a life already overflowing with them. She was violently thrown back into all the limitations of her personal experience and surroundings, and that larger life she had anticipated so eagerly was as suddenly shut away from her as if a door had been slammed in her face.

. . . [A]s a result of this experience, I gradually lost the impression that the old people were longing for a second chance at life, . . . and I became more reconciled to the fact that many of them had little opportunity for meditation . . . .

The vivid interest of so many old women in the story of the Devil Baby may have been an unconscious, although powerful, testimony that tragic experiences gradually become dressed in such trappings in order that their spent agony may prove of some use. . . .

[from page 25:] During the weeks when the Devil Baby seemed to occupy every room in Hullhouse, I was conscious that all human vicissitudes are, in the end, melted down into reminiscence, and that a metaphorical statement of the basic experiences implicit in human nature itself, however crude in form the story may be, has a singular power of influencing daily living.

EXCERPT FROM CHAPTER IV, "INTEGRATING INDUSTRY"

This selection is excerpted from pages 85–92. Addams continues her exploration, through conversation, of the consciousness of old, poor, ethnic women. Here she shows memory working as an aid to social change, from a consciousness based in the family ethic to one that begins to grasp the social ethic.

In some of the reminiscences related by working women I was surprised, not so much by the fact that memory could integrate the individual experience into a sense of relation with the more impersonal aspects of life, as that the larger meaning had been obtained when the fructifying memory had had nothing to feed upon but the harshest and most monotonous of industrial experiences.

I held a conversation with one such woman when she came to confess that her long struggle was over and that she and her sister had at last turned their faces to the poorhouse. She clearly revealed not only that she had caught a glimpse of the great social forces of her day, but that she had had the ability to modify her daily living by what she had perceived.

Perhaps, under the shadow of a tragic surrender, . . . she talked more fully of her hard life than I had ever heard her before in the many years I had known her. She related in illuminating detail an incident of her long effort of earning, by ill-paid and unskilled labor, the money with which to support her decrepit mother and her imbecile sister. For more than fifty years she had never for a moment considered the possibility of sending either of them to a public institution, although it had become almost impossible to maintain such a household after the mother, who lived to be ninety-four years old, had become utterly distraught. . . .

She told of her monotonous years in a box factory, where she had always worked with the settled enmity of the other employees. They regarded her as a pace setter, and she, obliged to work fast and furiously in order to keep three people, and full of concern for her old mother's many unfulfilled needs, had never understood what the girls meant when they talked about standing by each other.

She did not change in her attitude even when she found the prices of piece work went down lower and lower, so that at last she was obliged to work overtime late into the night in order to earn the small amount she had previously earned by day. She was seventy years old when the legality of the Illinois Ten Hour Law was contested, and her employer wanted her to testify in court that she was opposed to the law because she could not have supported her old mother all those years unless she had been allowed to work nights. She found herself at last dimly conscious of what it was that her long time enemies, the union girls, had been trying to do, and a subconscious loyalty to her own made it impossible for her to bear testimony against them. She did not analyze her motives but told me that, fearing she might yield to her employer's request, in sheer panic she had abruptly left his factory and moved her helpless household to another part of the city on the very day she was expected to appear in court. In her haste she left four days unpaid wages behind her, . . . She had unknowingly moved into a neighborhood of cheap restaurants, and from that time on she worked in any of them which would employ her until now at last she was too feeble to be of much use to anybody.

Although she had never joined the Union which finally became so flourishing in the box factory she had left, she was conscious that in a moment of great temptation she had refrained from seeking her own advantage at the expense of others. As she bunglingly tried to express her motives, she said, "The Irish—you know I was ten years old when we came over—often feel like that: it isn't exactly that you are sorry after you have done a thing, not so much that you don't do it because you know you will be sorry afterwards, nor that anything in particular will happen to you if you do it, but that you haven't the heart for it, that it goes against your nature."

When I expressed my admiration for her prompt action she replied: "I have never told this before except to one person, to a woman who was organizing for the garment workers and who came to my house one night about nine o'clock, . . . The organizer was looking for some of the women living in our block who had been taking work from the shops ever since the strike was on. She was clean tired out, and when I offered her a cup of tea she said quick as a flash, 'You are not a scab, are you?' I just held up my poor old hands before her face, swollen red from scrubbing and full of chilblains, and I told her that I couldn't sew a stitch if my life depended on it.

"When I offered her the second cup of tea . . . I said to her, 'My hands aren't the only reasons I'm not scabbing. I see too much of the miserable wages these women around here get for their sweatshop work, and I've done enough harm already with my pace setting'. . . . She smiled at me and nodded her head over my old cracked cup, 'You are a Union woman all right,' she said. 'You have the true spirit whether you carry a card or not.'" . . .

The old woman repeated the words as one who solemnly recalls the great phrase which raised him into a knightly order, revealing a secret pride in her unavowed fellowship with Trades Unions, for she had vaguely known at the time of the Ten Hour trial that powerful federations of them had paid for the lawyers and gathered the witnesses. . . .

It was in keeping with the drab colored experiences of her seventy hard years that her contribution to the long struggle should have been one of inglorious flight, nevertheless she had gallantly recognized the Trades Union organizer as a comrade in a common cause. She cherished the memory of one golden moment when she had faintly heard the trumpets summon her and had made her utmost response.

When the simple story of a lifetime of sacrifice to family obligations and of one supreme effort to respond to a social claim came to an end, I reflected that for more than half a century the narrator had freely given all her time, all her earnings, all her affections, and yet during the long period had developed no habit of self-pity. At a crucial moment she had been able to estimate life, not in terms of her self-immolation but in relation to a hard pressed multitude of fellow workers.

CHAPTER 4

Charlotte Perkins Gilman (1860–1935)— Gender and Social Structure

BIOGRAPHICAL BACKGROUND

Charlotte Anna Perkins Stetson Gilman was born in Hartford, Connecticut, on July 3, 1860. Ill with cancer, she died in Pasadena, California, painlessly by her own hand on August 17, 1935. Shortly before her death, she wrote in her autobiography, *The Living of Charlotte Perkins Gilman:* "The one predominant duty is to find one's work and do it, and I have striven mightily at that" (1935:335). No précis of her life could be more exact. She published over 2,000 works (Scharnhorst 1985) in a wide range of genres—fiction, serious poetry and light verse, satire, essay, journalism, and social analysis and sociology. Best known today for her novella *The Yellow Wallpaper* (1892), in her own day she was recognized as a leading feminist thinker for her sociological study *Women and Economics* (1898). Gilman's critical and feminist social theory permeates her writing in all genres; but our presentation of her sociology draws on *Women and Economics* and her other five formal statements of social theory—*Concerning Children* (1900), *The Home* (1903), *Human Work* (1904), *The Man-Made World, or Our Androcentric Culture* (1911), and *His Religion and Hers* (1923).

Gilman has received two major feminist biographies: Mary A. Hill's multi-volume, still-in-progress work—*Charlotte Perkins Gilman: The Making of a Radical Feminist, 1860–1896* (1980); *Endure* (1985), an edition of the diaries of Gilman's first husband Charles Walter Stetson, and *A Journey from Within* (1995), an edition of Gilman's letters between 1897 and 1900 to the man who became her second husband, Houghton Gilman; and Ann J. Lane's one-volume interpretive study of the whole life, *To Herland and Beyond* (1990). Larry Ceplair gives an intelligent and feminist overview of Gilman's life in the introductory essays in *Charlotte Perkins Gilman: A Non-Fiction Reader* (1991). There are also Gilman's autobiography (1935) and her diaries (ed. by Knight, 1994).

Our purpose here is to suggest the particular genius—and it was more than talent—that Gilman brought to her sociological work. Gilman herself described the nature of that genius: "I have nothing to offer the world but what I *think*. . ."; "I like a few salient and relevant facts—and then far seeing generalization" (cited in Ceplair, 1991:29, 31). She possessed what Henry James attributes to all great artists: "The power to guess the unseen from the seen, to trace the implications of things, to judge the whole piece by the pattern" (1888/1985:437). Most of the pattern came from her own life experience. That life experience was crucially shaped by gender, a fact that she had the prescience to see, not as a personal dilemma, but as *the* social structure determining and distorting the shape of society and individual lives. We divide her life into two phases, "Formation and Crisis" and "Recovery and Invention."

Formation and Crisis

In retrospect, Gilman's move toward sociology seems to begin in the interweaving of four biographical factors: (1) Gilman's recognition of herself as a woman moved by desire, that is, wanting to set and execute projects; (2) the emergence of this desire in a family situation that was irregular and precarious; (3) the location of that desire and family within a culture that disapproved of desire in a woman; and (4) the crisis in desire Gilman experienced in her own attempt at family, marriage, and motherhood between 1884 and 1888.

Female Desire   Feminist sociologist and psychoanalyst Jessica Benjamin (1988) argues that Freud's question "What do women want?" should really be phrased "Do women want?"—that women are taught not to seek individual agency, but to find their fulfillment in helping others to set and execute projects. If this insight holds true for women at the end of the twentieth century in America, it is an even more accurate description of the condition of women in the last half of the nineteenth century.

In her autobiography, Gilman defines her real birth of self as a moment at age fifteen when she discovered in an argument with her mother her own capacity to will, to hold on to her own desire. She reports herself learning "that neither [my mother], nor any one, could *make* me do anything. One could suffer, one could die if it came to that, but one could not be coerced. I was born" (1935:34). The will she discovered in that moment would manifest itself repeatedly throughout her life, most painfully in sets of relations—with women for whom she felt a love she for the most part could not act on, and in the demands of marriage and motherhood which pushed her into nervous collapse. There are painful passages from Gilman's letters recording her love for other women: to Martha Luther in 1881, "'It is no longer friendship between us, it is love'" (cited in Hill, 1980, 83–84); to Grace Channing in December 1890, " 'It is awful to be a man inside and not able to marry the woman you love! When Martha married it cracked my heart a good deal—your loss will finish it. . . . I think of you with a great howlin' selfish heartache. I want you—I love you—*I* need you *myself!*' " (cited in Lane, 1990: 150); to Houghton Gilman in 1899 about her love for Adeline Knapp in California in the 1890s, "Adeline Knapp has (I suppose she has) letters of mine most fully owning the really passionate love I had for her. . . . I told you that I loved her that way. You ought to know that there

Charlotte Perkins Gilman, age about 30

is a possibility of such letters being dragged out someday. . . . Fancy the San Francisco papers with a Profound Sensation in Literary Circles! . . . Mrs. Stetson's Love Affair with a Woman" (Gilman, 1995:246). Gilman's route to sociology arises from the essential tension between her wish to pursue her own agency and her wish to be approved by a conventional world that felt women should not want agency.

The Family   Gilman's family life as a child was a series of lessons in the gendered configurations of desire and in status inconsistency. Through her father, Frederick Beecher Perkins, she was connected to one of the most influential families in nineteenth century America. Among her great-uncles and great-aunts were Henry Ward Beecher (1813–1873), a lionized preacher; Catharine Beecher (1800–1878), a champion of women's education who helped create "the cult of domesticity"; and Harriet Beecher Stowe (1811–1896), the author of *Uncle Tom's Cabin* whom Abraham Lincoln called "the little lady who made the big war." But Gilman's father was, as Lane says, "a failed Beecher" (1990:26), who got kicked out of Yale before graduating, dabbled in librarianship, and attempted fiction and satire, in which he described himself as one who "lacked an 'instinctive desire' for the good will of others and sought instead to live out his own life for himself'" (Lane, 1990:32). Certainly this description fits his behavior toward his wife and children, whom he deserted when Gilman was about two, thereafter providing only irregular support and refusing to visit his former wife as she lay dying. Gilman summarizes the life of her mother, Mary Fitch Westcott, as "one of the most painfully thwarted I have ever known. . . . The most passionately domestic of home-worshiping housewives, she was forced to move nineteen times in eighteen years. . . . Absolutely loyal, as loving as a spaniel no ill treatment can alienate, she made no complaint" (1935: 8–9). Gilman's father gave her a model of male desire, the determination to live free; she admired his intellect, she cherished the Beecher connection, she resented his desertion. Gilman's mother gave her a model of the feminine ideal as the era expressed it: loyal, loving, self-denying, seeking not her own will but the well-being of others.

The general difficulties of the family were both complicated and to some degree alleviated by status inconsistency. Through the Beecher family connection, Gilman was often invited to "good" homes; through her father she had some idea of what it meant to be educated, and she was given a brief, interrupted stint at the Rhode Island School of Design; yet she grew up as a poor relation, living off the kindness of relatives, writing her father for support money, moving frequently, irregularly schooled, while possessed of the hope and challenge of being "a Beecher." The reader of her autobiography and the various biographical works is struck by how little practical preparation she had for achieving anything—save the first thing she really did to end her adolescence, getting married.

Culture   Gilman grew to maturity during a period of widespread debate over the nature and place of woman, a debate sparked by new opportunities for women in the post–Civil War expansion and by women's own mobilization for wider public participation. One strand in this debate had its origins in the pre–Civil War "cult of true womanhood" described by Barbara Welter: "The attributes of True Womanhood, by which a woman judged herself and was judged by her husband, her neighbors and society could be divided into four cardinal virtues—piety, purity, submissiveness and domesticity" (1966/1973:96). This radical denial of women's agency was modified by another strand of the debate, "the cult of domesticity," represented most forcefully by Gilman's great-aunt Catharine Beecher (see Sklar, 1973). Catharine Beecher, single and self-supporting all her life, attempted to help women find meaning in domestic life by arguing that it was demanding, required scientific management and was a source of empowerment: "Are you not only a housekeeper, but a *mother?* . . . training young minds . . . who will transmit what they receive from you to their children . . . until a *whole nation* will have received its character and destiny from your hands!" (Beecher, 1846/1977:124). A third strand was women's quest for greater political participation and more education. Political mobilization involved not only the struggle for suffrage but the formation of powerful organizations like the Women's Christian Temperance Union and the women's club movement. Further, by 1880, there were 40,000 women enrolled in institutions of higher learning, making them a third of the total student body (Lane, 1990:68). The fourth strand was a backlash against the gains by women. In the last three decades of the nineteenth century, male writers from all backgrounds weighed in to support the "biology-is-destiny" argument.

Gilman was surrounded by questions of gender in the painful extremes of her immediate family, the contradictory role models of her aunts, and the culture itself. She reflects in her life and in her sociology both a loyalty to certain ideals enunciated in the cult of true womanhood and an opposition to ideologies like those she attacked in *Women and Economics* that reduced woman to " 'very much less than man; . . . not even half the race at present, but rather a part of it [set off] for the continuance of the species' " (1898:172). All this debate was framed by an expanding literature of feminism to which Gilman would make a major contribution.

1881–1888: Conventionality and Crisis   In 1881, Gilman was 21, still living at home, still receiving from and giving emotional and financial support to her mother. She recalls herself as at once undecided and yet confident: "by no means definite" but with "a tremendous sense of power, . . . of ability to do whatever I decided to undertake" (1935: 71). She began writing for publication, sending articles and poems to various magazines including *Woman's Journal,* the official publication of the American Woman Suffrage Association. In the autumn of 1881, Gilman's first love, Martha Luther, became engaged.[1] Grieving for Martha, Gilman, in January 1882, met Charles Walter Stetson, a handsome artist, who immediately began courting her. A reluctant Gilman did not agree to marry

Stetson until March 1883, and they did not marry until May 1884. Their daughter Katharine Beecher Stetson was born on March 23, 1885.

It is hard to disentangle from the record where Gilman's breakdown in this period began—in the courtship, the marriage, her illness in the pregnancy, after the birth. She associated marriage with loss of agency, but tried to rally by giving herself a stern definition of love: "Now Love is more than *wanting. Love* is the infinite desire to benefit, a longing to *give* not merely a hungry wish to take" (Gilman, 1994:841–842). Stetson brought to the courtship and the marriage a conventional series of expectations: "I doubt not that when marriage comes she will look to me for advice, and make me the ruler of the house" (Stetson, 1985:139–140). But the absolute fact that emerges from the diaries, letters, and records is that Gilman was miserable when at home trying to be a wife and mother and happy and productive the moment she escaped: "I lay on that lounge and wept all day. . . . I went to bed crying, woke in the night crying, sat on the edge of the bed in the morning and cried" (Gilman, 1935:91). As one way of curing herself, she visited a longtime friend, Grace Channing, in Pasadena, California, where her spirits lifted as she wrote, painted, and completed a play with Channing. But upon her return home to Providence, she again fell into periods of despondency: out of the house, stimulated and hopeful; but with each return to domesticity, unable to hold together.

Early in 1887, Stetson and her mother got Gilman to see Dr. S. Weir Mitchell, a leading "nerve" specialist. Mitchell prescribed complete rest and avoidance of any mental activity: "'Live as domestic a life as possible. Have your child with you all the time. . . . And never touch pen, brush or pencil as long as you live.'" Gilman reports that following that advice she "came perilously close to losing my mind" (1935:96). But Gilman did not lose her mind and would later turn the experience with Mitchell into *The Yellow Wallpaper's* account of a woman going mad through enforced idleness. Despite depression, Gilman forced an agreement out of Stetson for a trial separation and kept writing, publishing that same year "The Right to Earn Money" in *Woman's Journal.* With Channing's support, Gilman took Katharine and returned to California. Although never again wholly free of depression, she began the process of recovery that led to one of the most productive careers in the history of sociology. At the heart of her sociology would be an analysis of gender as the main cause of social pain and dysfunction.

Recovery and Invention

1888–1898: A Decade of Productivity   Between 1888, when she returned to Pasadena, and 1898, when she published *Women and Economics,* Gilman created the public persona she was to be for most of the rest of her life. To do this she had to earn her living, disentangle her private life, find a public for her work, and make space to think, to do the thing she truly could do.

She began to earn her living anyway she could, sewing, painting, teaching, writing. For a while she worked as a writer and lecturer in Southern California; then she moved to the San Francisco–Oakland Bay area and ran a boardinghouse. There she had several passionate affairs (including the one with Adeline Knapp); nursed her mother who was dying of cancer; handled newspaper attacks made on her during her divorce (by mutual agreement) from Stetson; aided in Stetson's forming an alliance with Grace Channing which led to their marriage in 1894; and sent her daughter Katharine to live with Channing and Stetson, occasioning more newspaper attacks. All of this was not done without a price, and some of that price was paid by people other than Gilman. While our summary account may seem the stuff of melodrama, it serves to suggest how explosive and demanding those years were. Through all this, Gilman launched herself as a public presence. When truly thrown back on her own resources, she could rise to the occasion; what seemed to defeat her was the sense of being hemmed in by expectations—especially expectations of gender.

In 1888, that first year of independence, she wrote some thirty articles, twenty poems, and ten children's verses, selling them for small sums (ranging from two to ten dollars) to progressive newspapers. One of the poems, "Similar Cases," which satirized the belief that human nature could not change, became a rallying cry for Nationalism, one branch of Progressive mobilization. Los Angeles, only a few miles from Pasadena, was a center of Nationalism, and the popularity of "Similar Cases" led to Gilman's being asked to address the local Nationalist Club there. It was her first public lecture, and it was a huge success. She joined the California lecture circuit and was drawn into a variety of women's networks as well as labor reform organizations. Gilman brought to the Nationalist Club lecture circuit, according to one early California supporter, "'a voice clear, compelling, yet conversational, easily reaching to the farthest end of the hall, entirely devoid of effort; . . . [T]he women in the audience had never heard such plain statements of clear facts, and they had never heard anything of the kind from any woman'" (Ceplair, 1991:35). She also brought a willingness to deal with women's issues, to combine themes of women's equality with Nationalist goals of economic justice and social good (Hill, 1980:183). The circle of groups she lectured for expanded, to include the Socialist Society, the Social Purity Society, the Women's Christian Temperance Union, the Friday Morning Club. All these groups were part of the burgeoning women's club movement, itself a major component of Progressivism (see "Assumptions" later in this chapter). Her publications from this decade show a concern with themes that would be central to her sociology—women's economic independence, the working of human consciousness, the capacity of human beings to change human nature, the need for economic justice.

Leaving California in 1895, she embarked on a five-year period of almost constant travel and lecturing, which she called her years "at large," expanding her networks as she moved. She met Susan B. Anthony, Elizabeth Cady Stanton, and sociologist Lester Ward, who admired her "Similar Cases" and whose theory of reform social darwinism attracted Gilman as an intellectual field. She spent time at Hull-House at the invitation of Jane Addams, whom she had met in San Francisco; while she was depressed by the surrounding poverty, she nevertheless toyed with the idea of starting a settlement. At a socialist convention in England, she met some of the major British Fabians—Sidney and Beatrice Webb and George Bernard Shaw—and upon her return she began writing for the *American Fabian*. During these years, she increasingly systematized her ideas.

In 1897 she renewed her acquaintance with a cousin, George Houghton Gilman, seven years younger and a Wall Street lawyer (though not a wealthy one). Gilman began writing to him while she was on lecture tours; her letters got longer and longer, becoming "like morning prayers to me" (Gilman, 1995:109). As she engaged in this self-examination by letter (which Houghton may have taken as courtship—and it did turn into that), she complained of depression and yet was capable of incredible productivity. On July 1, 1897, two days before her 37th birthday, she wrote: "Got hold of a new branch of my theory . . . Now I can write the book" (Gilman, 1995:53). On August 31, 1897, in Laconia, New Hampshire, a place and day Gilman recalls in her autobiography, she began writing *Women and Economics*. Following the pattern of a lifetime, she moved five times between then and October 8, 1897, when she finished the first draft, 35,600 words—enough to get a publication offer. *Women and Economics,* Gilman's programmatic statement of feminist sociological analysis, was published in 1898.

1898–1916: Confidence and Productivity   *Women and Economics* enjoyed a response not always accorded works of genius—an enormously favorable immediate reception. It was reviewed widely and positively. *The Nation* called it "the most significant utterance on the subject [of women] since Mill's *Subjection of Woman* [1869]" (cited in Degler, 1966). It went through nine printings between 1898 and 1920, was translated into German, Dutch, Russian, Danish, Italian, Hungarian, and Japanese, and was praised by Susan B. Anthony, Jane Addams and Florence Kelley.

Gilman was in love, with Houghton and with her work, and felt she could combine the two: "I do love work. And the power grows and grows. I feel very sure that loving you—being loved—being happy—is a great gain in it" (Gilman, 1995:240). They married on June 12, 1900. The marriage provided Gilman with a background against which she would do some of her best thinking. Perhaps what Houghton gave was a deep acceptance and a lasting admiration. When Gilman felt like domesticity, they were domestic; when she did not, they were not. For many years they lived happily in apartments, eating their meals out. Equally important to Gilman's happiness was the fact that she was reaching a wider and more appreciative audience than even before. From about 1898 to 1912, she was hailed as an extraordinary intellect and lecturer. A *St. Louis Post Dispatch* review of 1899 suggests her general reception: " 'It is not the least exaggeration to say that there has never been a public speaker in St. Louis, male or female, who cast as complete a spell over an audience . . . [with] the combination of strong mind, radical views and marked sprightliness of manner'" (Gilman, 1995:205). Her letters to Houghton are full of stories of the admiration women audience members showered on her.

Confident that she had found her work, she produced four major books of social theory between 1900 and 1911: *Concerning Children* (1900), a discussion of socialization; *The Home* (1903), a critical analysis of the home as a site of production; *Human Work* (1904), her most formal sociological statement of the relationship between work and consciousness, and *The Man-Made World, or Our Androcentric Culture* (1911), an exploration of patriarchal culture. She founded *The Forerunner,* a monthly magazine that she wrote and edited between 1909 and 1916, publishing the equivalent of six serialized books within its pages—including *The Man-Made World.* Beginning in 1907, she became more organizationally identified as a sociologist, publishing in the *American Journal of Sociology,* attending and presenting at meetings of the American Sociological Society.

Decline   American writer Willa Cather observed, " 'The world broke in two in 1922 or thereabouts'" (Leuchtenberg, 1958:272–273). By 1923, Gilman, like so many of her generation, was at a very different place than she has been in the heady years of 1898–1916. She had moved from being a pacifist to a war supporter who became almost fanatically anti-German. She also became more racist in her attitudes. In earlier years her focus had been on ways to bring all races to what she saw as the same point of evolutionary progress. Now she seemed to move toward a sense of "Americans" as superior, and by "Americans" she seemed to mean people like herself—above all, a Beecher. She had—as she acknowledged, her daughter lamented, and her writings reveal—never been good at taking the point of view of the other sympathetically. She could take it melodramatically, she could take it cognitively in order to carry the argument; but she lacked the quality she had so accurately labeled in Jane Addams—the ability to set an idea down and walk all around it, seeing everyone's point of view. Her tremendous success had occurred when she had found and held an audience who did not wish to hear every point of view, who wished to hear their own point of view, the point of view of upper-middle-class women who wanted freedom. After World War I, Gilman's voice ceased to speak to a large audience. The Nineteenth Amendment had settled women's rights for many; the war had destroyed Progressive idealism; reform darwinist faith in human evolution had yielded to Freudian determinism.

The changes in the world, the knowledge of her own aging and of the limits of her power (for she had been very influential) left her bitter. And the bitterness perhaps touched that part of her that was still the poor relation, the bright undervalued square peg in a round hole. Houghton died of a massive cerebral hemorrhage a year before Gilman herself. She spent her last days living two doors from her daughter Katharine in Pasadena—with her longtime friend, Katharine's other mother, Walter Stetson's second wife, Grace Channing.

GENERAL SOCIAL THEORY

Assumptions

Gilman was influenced by three configurations of thought popularly expressed in her era: (1) reform social darwinism; (2) Progressivism, particularly those strands of its reform ideology that drew on non-Marxian or utopian socialism; and (3) feminism, the growing mobilization by women for rights, including the right to vote and the right to economic independence.

The major formal influence on Gilman's thought was evolutionary social theory, the theoretical formalism of which may have attracted the system-builder in her. She was not a conservative, laissez-faire social darwinist like Herbert Spencer, but a reform social darwinist like Lester Ward (to whom she dedicated her 1911 study *Our Man-Made World*). Reform social darwinism argued that the evolution of human consciousness gave humans the capacity to construct their social environment and thus to direct the course of any further evolution.[2] Gilman was particularly attracted to Ward's "Gynaecocentric Theory" which argued that the female, the producer of life, is the original human type and that the progress of the species depends on her development; that the male evolved only to help in procreation but had, through a series of complex environmental accidents, become woman's master; and that this imbalance between male and female was the cause of many social problems. Gilman's acceptance of evolutionary thought led her to seek to explain any existing social condition in terms of a prehistoric first cause.

Reform social darwinism helped give intellectual legitimacy to Progressivism, itself the convergence of a vast number of intellectual, moral, and religious movements that argued for greater equalization of human prosperity. Progressives both mirrored and shaped a literature of social criticism: Lincoln Steffens's *The Shame of the Cities* (1904), Jacob Riis's *How the Other Half Lives* (1890), William Stead's *If Christ Came to Chicago* (1894), Ida Tarbell's *The History of Standard Oil* (1904). A popular novel in this literature was Edward Bellamy's utopian *Looking Backward* (1888), which preached socialism in a form acceptable to middle-class Americans. In *Looking Backward,* the hero falls into a dream in 1887 and wakes in the year 2000 to find the United States transformed: business corporations now constitute "The Great Trust," a form of state capitalism; every worker is both an employee and an owner; this collective organization of production has eliminated poverty, crime, slums; and people embrace an ethic of social responsibility. Women play a significant part in this new society; no longer economically dependent on men, they can choose the best husbands and, thus, make happier marriages and healthier children. The novel sparked the organization of "Nationalist" clubs, on whose circuit Gilman began her career as a lecturer. She did not like *Looking Backward* as a novel, but did agree with its ideas about shared wealth, shared production, and equal rights for men and women. Its socialism was reinforced for her by her subsequent relationship to Fabianism (see Chapter 8).

Women's activity in the Nationalist Clubs was only one part of their general mobilization for reform through a vast variety of clubs and associations. The women's club movement was Gilman's most vital connection to feminism—to its claim for rights for equal access to the male-dominated public sphere and to its affirmation of a distinctive female social ethic essential to public discourse. It is important not to underestimate the strength of the women's club movement; in its varied forms it was the grassroots base for women's participation in Progressivism (see Chapters 3 and 7). European-American women formed clubs of every sort for government reform, suffrage, women's education, pro-labor legislation, responsible consumerism, world peace, and "social purity," which spoke to real concerns about sexuality and marriage, the double standard, and prostitution (e.g., Scott, 1992; Blair, 1981; Skocpol, 1992; Gordon, 1994). African-American women formed their own clubs and associations to promote education and to fight the mounting undeclared race war against their people (see Caraway, 1991; Giddings, 1984; Gordon, 1994; Scott, 1992; and Chapter 5 in this text). Gilman was active in all these women's groups—save, apparently, the black women's organizations. An uncomfortable point for any student of Gilman is her failure to deal with differences among women (see "Gilman and the Tradition of Feminist Sociology," following).

Major Themes

Gilman was a theorist who genuinely believed in the critical and ameliorative possibilities of theory. With this faith, she constructed a systematic social theory that explains human life as characterized both by a fundamental sociality and by unnecessary, socially produced human pain. Central to Gilman's dual vision of society—what it is and what it might be—is the dynamic relation between gender and social structure. This section presents Gilman's sociological theory in terms of four themes—her model of collective life, her theoretical method, and her concepts of the two crucial relations between gender and social structure, the *sexuo-economic relation* and *androcentric culture.*

1. Gilman's model of social life links three analytically distinct but interdependent aspects of social relations: work, common consciousness (or culture), and excessive sex-distinction (or gender). For Gilman the subject of sociology is "human social relation," a phrase she uses to describe the process of reciprocal action and inter-psychic orientation among individuals within the context of a shared collective membership. Human social life is fundamentally a complex of such relations: "Our whole social structure, together with social progress and social action, rests in reality on social relationship" (1903:21). Gilman does not make macro and micro distinctions but, instead, traces relational flows from interactions between typified actors through the complexities of institutional and societal existence and back to typified individual interactions. She sees society as "an organization of human beings, alive, complex, exquisitely developed in co-ordinate inter-service" (1900:278–279). She presents the home or the economy as people relating in ways distinctive to and typical of specific interactional sites. Thus, a characteristic relationship of the home is socialization, which Gilman describes as action and orientation between mother and child; the characteristic relationship of the industrial economy is mutual dependence among specialists within the division of labor. In their movement between sites, people link institutions like home and economy. She portrays individuals not as unique characters but as typified actors expressive of social relations: the young girl waiting for a husband; the man burdened by the need to support his family; the child trying to figure out right and wrong; as well as those filling more obvious and specialized roles, such as teacher and dentist, which arise from and have meaning only within the context of a complex society.

Although Gilman often uses a vocabulary associated with functionalism—"social system," "structure and function," "organic" unity, and "social pathology"—her sociological project begins not in the functionalist problematic of order but in the critical problematic of human pain: "So unbearable is the amount of human pain that we alone among all animals manifest the remarkable phenomenon of suicide—a deliberate effort of a form of life to stop living because living hurts so much" (1904:8).* Sociology becomes a key instrument in her critical quest to reduce this pain, because "society feels first and most what hurts it, . . . our study of sociology is prefaced by social pathology. . . . We must know the mechanics of a thing if we are to mend it" (1904:15–16). To know and mend society, Gilman presents a model of the interactions among three fundamental arrangements of social relation: work; "common consciousness" or culture; and "excessive sex-distinction" or gender. Each relational pattern originates in human biological capacity, is modified by the distinctive qualities of human sociality, and assumes its present form through interaction with the other two.

---

*An asterisk following a citation in the text means that the passage quoted is given in fuller context in the readings at the end of the chapter.

All life-forms work to get from the physical environment the necessities for sustaining life. Human work is distinguished by its degree of sociality. More than the members of any other species, humans can work collectively and refine task specialization. Thus, "[m]an alone has permanently mastered his food supply; instead of an endless chase it is a closed circle—he makes that which makes him" (1904:86–87). Human task specialization produces a division of labor that refines itself into greater and greater functional complexity and, concomitantly, greater interdependence. Over history, this specialization and interdependence have evolved into a complex collective economy, the mark of full sociality in human life. In this economy, people experience sociality as an organic unity of mutual service and mutual exchange.

Because she assigns so much weight to work, Gilman is concerned to establish the relation between individual and economy. The economy shapes individual personality; "the individual is still inexorably modified by his means of livelihood" (1898:3). It is through participation in an interdependent economic relation that the individual can achieve economic independence—an essential social good for Gilman. Economic independence exists for the individual when she or he is assured a fair and predictable livelihood in return for her or his work. Further, the human being in the social relation works not just to earn a living but to express the self. Individual creativity is not a distinguishing trait of individual human beings but arises out of the social relation. Gilman illustrates the social source of creative energy with a typified neolithic woman worker who "in her already growing social consciousness . . . has more stimulus coming in than her body can sit quiet under. . . . So [she] is moved to transmit her press of feeling; . . . and she does so in some decoration of her jar or basket. This decoration is an embodied joy, and, being fixed in visible form, it then transmits joy to as many as behold it. It is a little fountain of social energy" (1904:106–107).

But work, which should be the source of humanity's greatest joy, is distorted in its interaction with culture, which Gilman defines as the "common consciousness through which coordinate action may take place" (1898:124)—a definition important in its linkage of society, action, and mind. Culture has its basis in the biological potential of the human brain to form ideas, or concepts. Human social relations are mediated by concepts, by communication, and by culture: "Society is a psychic condition; all social relationships exist and grow in the human mind" (1904:38–39).* Individual human consciousness, in turn, is a social product developed through socialization, language, and interaction. Culture is vital in Gilman's social theory because she sees concepts having a power of facticity—people come to know the world not directly but through their idea of it. One major cause of human pain is that people think wrongly. In each of the books of her middle period—*Concerning Children* (1900), *The Home* (1903), and *Human Work* (1904)—Gilman traces the maladjustments she sees to an area of human work produced by wrong ideas. *Concerning Children* describes how the valuing of obedience, punishment, and control transforms socialization from a process which should produce confident, creative, self-willing individuals to a process which reproduces timidity and authoritarianism in each generation. *The Home* contrasts the inefficiency and ignorance permeating domestic work (cooking, cleaning, home crafts, home management, child care, adult care) with people's collective mythology of the home as protective, private, beautiful, mother-reverencing, and economically sensible. *Human Work*, arguably her most ambitious sociological statement, presents a detailed critique of the misconceptions in economic thinking that create fundamental dysfunctions in industrial capitalism. Gilman offers several explanations for the origin and persistence of wrong ideas: archaic carryovers from earlier times; the cognitive/emotional drive for conceptual consistency; the tendency to generalize from personal experience and to personalize general concerns; and credulity towards those who clothe themselves in the magic of authority, whether the chanting shaman or the posturing economist.

But Gilman's key explanation for wrong ideas in the social relation is "excessive sex-distinction," her phrase for what we call gender. Gender is for Gilman what class is for Marx: the source of her passionate condemnation of the world in place; the lens that focuses her sociological critique; the concept that, though analytically derived from the concepts of work and consciousness, assumes dynamic centrality in her theory. Lacking the word "gender," Gilman uses instead the word "sex," and she uses it in three distinct but interrelated ways: sex as a function in biological reproduction, sex as a role and cultural arrangement in society, and sex as sexuality. Human beings share with other animal species the male-female sex-distinction in biological reproduction. Biological reproduction requires sexual attraction, achieved through secondary sex-distinctions, that is, qualities distinguishing male and female and attracting them to each other. It is here that human sex-distinction ceases being wholly biological. Human beings, because of their conceptual capacities, magnify secondary sex-distinctions and create through the cultural construction of gender an "excessive sex-distinction." This excessive sex-distinction focuses cultural attention on differences between males and females rather than on the common qualities of humanity as a species.

For Gilman, excessive sex-distinction corrupts sociality by gendering the social world far beyond anything required for biological reproduction. In her general theoretical model, Gilman emphasizes the relation between gender and work, which she calls *the sexuo-economic relation,* and that between gender and culture, or *the androcentric culture* (see Themes 3 and 4, following).

2. Gilman's method of doing sociology is the construction of a critical sociological theory. Gilman's choice of theory, rather than of application or research, was consistent with her intellectual preference for ideas over facts and for ideas which were intensely theoretical. Theory conformed with her conviction about the relation between mind and conduct: "A concept is stronger than a fact" (1923:4). Theoretical work allowed her to synthesize a variety of disciplines—biology, ethics, history, literature, and sociology—in order to understand the meaning of "humanness" as a quality transcending the conflicting elements of femininity and masculinity she could locate in her character, her biography, and the social world. For Gilman, theoretical work was a form of critical praxis, a means to correct the major cause of socially produced human pain—people's false concepts about reality.

Gilman's methods for doing theory are guided by a set of easily discernible rules. She typically opens by stating explicitly that her purpose is to explain and also to show how to ameliorate. She then offers some general rules for thinking theoretically: the principle of cause and effect, the need to rethink familiar "facts," the importance of studying the human species in relation to other species. Typically, she introduces her thesis in her first chapter and develops it in a variety of directions through the work. Her development shows the origins of the problem stated in the thesis, its various consequences—for social relations and human happiness—and what must be done to alleviate it.

Gilman's persona in her theory is that of a person in an argument with the prevailing common sense but false concepts of her day, and in agreement with the avant-garde discoveries of science and social science. The opponent she creates in this work is not usually a particular individual, but an ideal-typical "every person" whose taken-for-grantedness is based in false ideas. Her intended audience is an educated reading public, ideally, perhaps, people just beginning to think through the issues she takes on—most especially, issues of women's rights and economic justice. This sense of audience means that she, like most of the women theorists discussed in this book, has a deep commitment to accessibility.

Gilman succeeds in the difficult project of creating formal yet accessible theory primarily by her use of examples drawn from the commonplace understandings of her time. She uses four major types of evidence: cross-species comparisons; cross-cultural comparisons; selections from a broad range of popular culture, literature, language, folk sayings, and oral tradition; and details from the minutiae of everyday life. She relates this evidence with tongue-in-cheek drollery, so that the false concept is debunked as the reader laughs. Essentially she uses evidence to *illustrate,* to show that cases exist that fit the general proposition she is describing. It is, as she states, up to the reader to take the theory further in "study and discussion as shall prove its error or establish its truth" (1898:xxxix).

Above all, theory gave Gilman a way to unite her analytic and aesthetic sensibilities to present a social world in which micro and macro, dailiness and historic forces, individual emotion and social structure constantly interpenetrate: the mother cooking, the bric-a-brac on the shelf, the meat packer adulterating the product, the destruction of forests, the language with which people communicate and think. Gilman achieves a style of theorizing that might be characterized as "metaphysical," which seeks "the relations [that] . . . constantly connect the abstract with the concrete, the remote with the near, and the sublime with the commonplace" (Bennett, 1957:2–3, 10).

3. Gilman's central thesis is that human sociality has been systematically distorted by the sexuo-economic relation. "The sexuo-economic relation," the conceptual framework of *Women and Economics* (1898), Gilman's best-known work in social theory, is, for Gilman, the basic arrangement of inequality in society. It results from the confounding in human social relations of work, biological sex-distinction, and socially constructed excessive sex-distinction, or gender. Gilman's analysis of the sexuo-economic relation can be divided into four parts—its definition, its origins and maintenance, its negative effects on human life, and strategies for its elimination.

Definition   The sexuo-economic relation is a condition, existing only among human beings, in which one sex, the female, is economically dependent on the other sex, the male: "We are the only animal species in which the female depends on the male for food, the only animal species in which the sex-relation is also an economic relation" (1898:5, 22).* Gilman's first move in advancing this thesis is to show that women are denied the basic activity that gives human beings economic independence (see Theme 1, preceding): they are placed in a situation in which there is no direct relation between their work efforts and their realization of livelihood. Women do work—serving other people through housework and child care, enabling those others to be productive. But for Gilman "the salient fact in this discussion is that whatever the economic value of the domestic industry of women is, they do not get it. . . . The women who do the most work get the least money and the women who have the most money do the least work" (1898:14).* To argue that motherhood is women's economic contribution is to make the obscene claim that women exchange mothering for food and shelter (1898:15). If motherwork were the issue, women would be waited upon by men who did all the other work so that women could devote themselves fully to mothering. The fact that this is not so points to the real issue: women work not for their children alone but "for men; . . . It is not motherhood that keeps the housewife on her feet from dawn till dark; it is house service, not child service" (1898:20). In the sexuo-economic relation, women as a class are denied economic independence and are restricted to serving men as a class. Their condition is that of subordination in a relationship of domination. "Their labor is the property of another. They work under another's will; and what they receive depends not on their labor, but on the power and will of another" (1898:7).*

Origins and Maintenance   Gilman locates the origin of the sexuo-economic relation in human prehistory and explains its continuation over time through her concept of excessive sex-distinction. The turn to a mythic moment in prehistory to explain the origins of the sex classes is similar to Marx's strategy in explaining the origins of economic classes; there is also an embedded psychological thesis in Gilman's explanation. Gilman first describes a moment when the quality that is to distinguish human beings as a species—the mental capacity to think of new forms of social relation—begins to complicate biological sex attraction and procreation. Before this moment of relational inventiveness, she pictures the human male, like other animals, competing with other males for the right to mate with the female, and the human female, when not mating with the male, foraging in the forest as freely and successfully as the male. Then came the moment "when it occurred to the dawning intelligence of this amiable savage that it was cheaper and easier to fight a little female, and have done with, than to fight a big male every time. So he instituted the custom of enslaving the female; and she losing freedom, could no longer get her own food nor that of her young" (1898:60).

In addition to male desire for sexual control of women, Gilman claims that man's domination of woman also springs from his need for sociability, or recognition by an Other. The invention of female enslavement by males is psychologically fueled by the male need to appropriate for himself the primary moment of human intersubjectivity, that between mother and child. Gilman sees human beings defined by "the imperative demand for the establishment of a common consciousness between . . . hitherto irreconcilable individuals." The relation between mother and child—"the overlapping of personality, the mutual need . . . that holds together these interacting personalities"—is the first achievement of common consciousness in human prehistory. The male, in enslaving the female, ensures his own place in this common consciousness, the "common interest, existing now not only between mother and child, but between father, mother and child" (1898:124–125). Gilman argues that this wish by the male to command both the woman's sexuality and her capacity to recognize his subjectivity, or personhood, is sentimentalized as a positive and noble passion—love. In Gilman's account, "love" begins in domination. From this original moment of bonding by enslavement has come the cultural construction of gender, or excessive sex-distinction, which continues to reproduce male dominance and female subordination. Gender is a product of the human capacity for conscious, planful, conceptually mediated orientation to each other. Human beings have effectively gendered work, the psyche, the world: "We have differentiated our industries, our responsibilities, our very virtues along sex lines" (1898:41).*

Negative Effects: The Corruption of Sociality   Sociality is a human-species potential, the capacity to realize self and joy by working together. The sexuo-economic relation corrupts this possibility by assigning individuals to work not on the basis of ability but by sex; shaping personality not for humanness but for maleness or femaleness; arranging marriage not between equals but between master and subordinate, and providing homes not to meet individual need but to reward conformity to the sexuo-economic relation. And all this is reproduced through the child in the home.

The sex relation, or sexuality, tends to lead people to think in personal, or private, rather than social terms. This emphasis on the personal becomes pathological in the sexuo-economic relation, which forces people to divide the world into separate, contrasting realms of "public" and "private." Gilman sees this division as a false concept; there is no purely private world, no public world unaffected—and uncorrupted—by the failures of the private.

The sexuo-economic relation compels men to put the public good second to the private good: "We are so used to considering it the first duty of a man to support his family that it takes a very glaring instance of bribery and corruption in their interests to shake our conviction; but, as a sociological law, every phase of the prostitution of public service to private gain . . . marks a diseased social action" (1898:106–107).* The burden of the economic dependency of others makes it much harder for the married man to organize for collective action, as in labor unions, than for the single man. The married man in the sexuo-economic relation may be a wage slave or an exploiter of other men, an employer of wage slaves. All is justified in terms of the ultimate rationale, the need to support his family. At home the man, whether wage slave or exploiter, is allowed, to the detriment of his character, to be a petty tyrant. Having "a whole human creature consecrated to his direct personal service" leads the man to an exaggerated sense of desire, agency, and entitlement in both the so-called public and private spheres (1898:338). His sense of his sexual needs is exaggerated because sexuality becomes connected with economic and creative potency.[3]

The woman in the sexuo-economic relation is socialized to suppress and distort her desire and agency, focusing them on obtaining a male mate. She must conform to the principle of sexual attraction by becoming the weaker sex, a social construct, not a biological destiny. She is taught to separate wanting from acting, as exemplified in what Gilman describes as "the ingenious cruelty of the arrangement" of courtship (1898:89): "Marriage is the woman's proper sphere, her divinely ordered place, her natural end . . . *But*—she must not even look as if she wanted it! . . . Think of the strain on a highly sensitive nervous organism to have so much hang on one thing, . . . and to be forbidden to take any step toward securing it!" (1898:87–88).* Denied the human species-trait of production in a full social environment, the woman redoubles her efforts to establish the sanctity of the home, the rightness of the little world that has been allowed her. But her efforts are restricted to a ministry to narrow bodily needs and the activity of consumption becomes her economic function. Thus, the sexuo-economic relation develops in the woman the personality of the subordinate. Living with her actions always subject to another's will, she learns not to spend strength in planning what she may not be allowed to execute. She comes, on the one hand, to act only under pressure and, on the other, to develop "a perverse capricious wilfulness in little things,—the reaction from a forced submission" (1898:333–334).

The modern home is almost a prehistoric relic, unspecialized, disorganized, and unrewarding, which corrupts not only the character and life of the woman but the sanctity of marriage, the health and economy of the nation, and the reproduction in the young of appropriate social virtues. Married love collides with the sexuo-economic relation that separates the lovers permanently into two classes, two spheres of activity, his public and progressive, hers private and belated. Gilman takes the preparation of food—the task by which humans advanced beyond all other species—as a prime example of the negative effects of the modern home on the national economy and health. The adulteration of food becomes a ready source of profit for large businesses because the isolated housewife in her individual purchases lacks both the knowledge and the power to affect the global production and distribution of food. The child growing up in this environment is socialized to see his mother as a servant, his father as a wage-slave for the family, and himself in whatever proportions the family chooses to give him.

> We may all preach to our children as we will of the great duty of loving and serving one's neighbor; but what . . . the child grows up to see and feel, is the concentration of one entire life—his mother's—upon the personal aggrandizement of one family, and the human service of another entire life—his father's—so warped . . . by the necessity of "supporting his family" that treason to society is the common price of comfort in the home . . . and is unblamed by the moral sense of the dependent woman (1898:278, 279).

The mother, restricted to the private world, does not know how to tell the daughter to break free, the son how to value his work not for wage but for joy, nor can she tell either how to meet the social claim, "the great duty of . . . serving one's neighbor."

Strategies for Elimination   Gilman does not call for the abolition of the home, but for its redefinition. People must expand their sense of love and commitment to reach beyond the present private family home. Gilman argues that all people need a place they can consider home, that that right must not be linked to the sexuo-economic relation, and that a variety of living spaces can be designed to provide such homes. One step in this expansion must be the liberation of women—and men—from the sexuo-economic relation. But this step must be concomitant with a redesign of the home, a project to which Gilman devotes a significant amount of her sociology, detailing changes in the home's architecture, work, childrearing, and provisioning arrangements, so that it becomes a site for the equal empowerment of all its members. (See "Gilman and the Tradition of Feminist Sociology," following.)

4. Gilman's second thesis is that human sociality has been subverted by the development of an androcentric culture rather than a human one. In *The Man-Made World, or Our Androcentric Culture,* Gilman completes a shift in her theory of gender and social structure; she moves from an emphasis on gender stratification, the sexuo-economic relation, to an emphasis on patriarchy, or the androcentric culture. By the "androcentric culture" Gilman means a common consciousness in society—a system of concepts—patterned not by human understandings but by masculine interests and experience, by "the effect on our human life of the unbridled dominance of one sex" (1911:19).

A consistent theme in Gilman's sociology is that collective concepts are powerful social forces; "the power to form and retain concepts, and act under their influence precisely as if they were facts, is what gives the element of special progress and also special perversity to human conduct" (1904:39).* Much of the "perversity" in human relations results from collective adherence to systems of false concepts. The theme of false concepts, present if not directly named in all Gilman's sociology, is most fully developed in *Human Work* (1904). There, Gilman explicates seven "false concepts" about human life and work that have persisted because of the human desire for consistency (see Figure 4-1). This desire for consistency originates in the wish for a steady flow of energy, unimpeded by conceptual contradictions. The pressure for consistency intensifies when concepts are collectively held as common consciousness, or culture.

FIGURE 4-1   Gilman's Analysis of Major False Concepts in *Human Work*

Concept	Erroneous content	Correction
Ego Concept	That consciousness is a purely separate and personal experience	Human consciousness is collectively developed, and ego must be balanced by a sense of the social
Pleasure-in-Impression Concept	That people receive joy from what they get rather than what they do	Joy is in doing, in coordinating individual activity with that of others
Pay Concept	That people work only for reward	People work because energy demands expression—and human energy increases through sociality
Want Theory	That people will not work unless they have some ungratified want	People work because they find self-actualization in work
Self-Interest Theory	(Akin to Want) that people work only to preserve self	Species preservation is the first law of nature and of human work
Pain Concept	That pain is good in that it motivates people to work, that slums, etc., develop strength	People confuse occasional anecdotes with cause; systematic evidence shows that adversity does not make people better; no one says "Let life be hard for me so that it will build my character"
Law of Supply and Demand	That everyone will get the economic goods they need because supply will respond to demand	People are starving right now; all this "law" means is that if one has cash and can pay and if there is anything to be had, one can perhaps get it

By 1911, in *The Man-Made World,* Gilman has clarified her critique, seeing these false concepts as the product of an androcentric culture: "We have, so far, lived and suffered and died in a man-made world . . . If a given idea has been held in the human mind for many generations . . . ; and if it is one of the oldest we have in stock, one of the big, common, unquestioned world ideas, vast is the labor of those who seek to change it" (1911:17).* Gilman's purpose is this vast labor: to make problematic what has been taken for granted, the androcentric or patriarchal patterning of society's ideas and institutions. She argues that while sex-distinctive traits of maleness and femaleness are common to nearly all species, each species also has species-distinctive traits. In humans, however, this is altered because excessive sex-distinction has led people to concentrate on masculinity and femininity and to ignore common human traits. The masculine traits, which human males share with males of other species, are "desire, combat, self-expression" (1911:28). "Desire" means not only sexuality but an extraordinary capacity for wanting, for wishing to have and possess; "combat" means aggressiveness, the need for an antagonist in order to complete the meaning of an action; and "self-expression" is the sense of one's entitlement as an individuated agent. Gilman's critique of androcentric culture is constructed around two basic themes: that it is founded on male dominance of women and society and that it is patterned by qualities inherent to masculinity without countervailing feminine or human themes.

Male dominance in the sexuo-economic relation lets males define themselves as "human," "as the race type," women as, at best, *other,* "a strange, diverse creature, quite disharmonious in the accepted scheme of things . . . 'the sex' . . . set apart for special services peculiar to femininity" (1911:18).* Man needs this cultural definition of women so that he may keep "the whole world," eliminating any competition by relegating woman to "the home; because she was female" (1911:23). Gilman shows how male cultural domination extends to language, the vehicle of concept formation, shaping and distorting thought about family, health and beauty, art, literature, games and sports, ethics and religion, education, 'society' and 'fashion,' law and government, crime and punishment, politics and warfare, and industry and economics. For example, in the chapter titled "Games and Sports," she contrasts the socially "unpardonable sin" of "'unsportsmanlike conduct'" with the culturally irrelevant charge of "not good housewifery"—an illustration of how male interests conceptualize the standard for judging both the significance and the correctness of behavior (1911:116–117).

Masculine traits infuse social relationships with a configuration of dominance in which one actor expresses his individuated will and desire by reducing another actor to the status of subordinate. Gilman sees this desire for obedience to arbitrary will persisting in present laws, as in the case where "a man breaks a law of which he never heard [and] is not excused therefor; the penalty rolls on the same" (1911:182). Androcentric culture defines such arbitrariness as the majesty of the law—the expression of the will of the dominant who does not have to negotiate with subordinates. Domination produces hierarchy, a society based in order-givers and order-takers, and has transformed the human family into what Gilman calls the "proprietary family," an institution modified to serve not the child but the man. Within this distorted construction of the family, the man chooses as his mate not a strong, willful partner but the one who has most shaped herself to please, that is, to submit as a subordinate to domination.

The other major configuration of masculine traits in androcentric culture is combativeness which makes an oppositional schema basic to all aspects of social life—government, law, politics, religion, education, economics. In economics and industry, the male mind can only conceive of effort born out of opposition: "we find always and everywhere the antagonist; the necessity for somebody or something to be overcome" (1911:236).* This heritage of combat has created an attitude that despises labor as the task assigned to the defeated and enslaved. This schema of combat also distorts the practices of government. The American political party system is nothing but "the technical arrangement to carry on a fight" (1911:221).* Gilman suggests that political parties, and their accompanying definition of the political process as a war, are not inevitable; that it would be possible to have a democracy without parties, with representatives and policies selected on their merits. She recognizes that the androcentric mind would answer back, "'There has never been a democracy without factions and parties,'" to which Gilman replies, "There has never been a democracy, so far,—only an androcracy" (1911:222).*

In seeking an alternative to the man-made world, Gilman looks first to women, reversing her principal stance in *Women and Economics* (1898) that women as housewives are the non-progressive faction in society. By 1911, she presents a concept of "Economic Woman" as an alternative to the economists' concept of "Economic Man." Woman is the archetypical worker, working not out of fear of punishment or desire for gain, but because of love and the need for expression. Women, out of their experience of household management, bring the right concepts to work and economy and government: "the maintenance of peace, health, order, and morality; the care and nourishment of children as far as done at home; . . . How best to spend! time, strength, love, care, labor, knowledge, and money" (1911:228–229).*

Yet even in *The Man-Made World,* Gilman continues to argue that what is needed is not female triumph but human triumph. She takes the position that a *human* government would be founded and administered so that its laws and principles serve as clear guides to conduct, not weapons of combat. In such a system, "law ceases to be authority and becomes co-ordination" in the same way that the rules of a game like checkers are designed not to punish but to let people play together (1911:185–186). A *human* political order may begin with the experience of "public parenting," in which people understand that care of other people's children does not mean neglect of their own—indeed, quite to the contrary: "[O]ur children suffer individually from bad social conditions, but cannot be saved individually" (1900: 288). The principle of collective solutions to individual suffering confronts the human being with the most "serious sociological question"—how to use the state to achieve the collective social will (1900:290).

GILMAN'S RELEVANCE FOR THE HISTORY AND PRESENT PRACTICE OF SOCIOLOGY

Gilman and the Canon of Sociology

Unlike Martineau and Addams, for whom theory was an extension of other sociological work, Gilman believed in the ameliorative possibility of social theory. In her quest to create a general social theory, she has much in common with male sociologists of both the founding and classic generations. The addition of her theory to the canon offers us a unique angle of vision on the major paradigms of mainstream sociology—functionalism, Marxian conflict theory, and interpretive theory.

General Commonalities: The Theoretical Voice Gilman, like Spencer, Karl Marx, Emile Durkheim, Max Weber, Georg Simmel, and George Herbert Mead, writes in the voice of the grand theorist. She writes with the confidence—even the bravado, as Marx does—of someone who can stand outside the social frame and see, describe, analyze, and prescribe changes in social arrangements. Her tone is recognizably that of the sociological theorist, and her theory is not implicit in writings with another purpose; it is her project. In her framing, we find ideas which are now familiar to us as markers of foundational and classical sociological theory—comparison with other species (Spencer, Park, Mead); an assumption of human societal development (Spencer, Durkheim, Mead, Park); conditioning social facts (Marx, Durkheim) and interactions (Simmel, Mead, Park); the centrality of economic life (Marx, Weber); and the significance of collective ideas (Durkheim, Weber, Mead).

Her arrangement of these arguments is both sufficiently familiar and sufficiently innovative to mark Gilman's work as a distinctive body of theory. Although social evolutionary vocabulary permeates many of her statements, and these referents have fallen out of favor, contemporary sociologists can screen these referents out, as they have in reaching for what is perceived as valuable in the theories of Spencer, Marx, Durkheim, Mead, and Park. Unlike the men, she makes her theory accessible through vivid references to daily life and popular culture. Also unlike the men, she does not make a distinction between micro and macro experience; her concept of social relation weaves its way through all forms of human life, from the typified interactions she uses to ground her theory to her transinstitutional analyses.

Commonalities and Differences: Functionalism At first reading, Gilman's vocabulary and understandings seem to be functionalist, making use of such terms as "organic social relations," "institutions," "the social system," "function," "interdependence," "the division of labor," "increased task specialization," "pathology," and "social evolution." When Gilman writes about society, she assumes certain systemic qualities: an institutional order, understood as patterns of action and behavior in which humans collectively meet basic needs. Those institutions include family, economy, religion, education, law and government. Each performs certain particular functions—family, the care of the young; economy, the production of material necessities; religion, the production and promulgation of ethical codes; law and government, the production of agreement about the use of social resources to solve social problems. Gilman's functionalism is more like that of Spencer and Talcott Parsons than that of Durkheim; its focus is on interdependencies in a social system rather than the maintenance of social order through collective representations. Gilman differs from Spencer and Parsons in that she presents institutions less as macro normative structures than as interactional patterns maintained by people in actual life sites.

But these commonalities are outweighed by her differences from functionalism. In her theory, human sociality, social relation, and social union are human-species potentials; her problematic, then, is not to explain how sociality, relation, and union come to be, but to explain how they are corrupted. Her concern is not with how to produce order but with how to promote progress toward fairness. Fairness exists when all people are able to participate fully in the interdependence of social life—that is, able to work and do "mutual service"—in a way that both pleases the individual and promotes the good of the society. Gilman's inclusion in the canon raises the possibility of a genuinely *critical functionalism*. Her inclusion leads one to ask, what happened to that possibility; this question returns us to the work of the sociologist she most admired, Lester Ward, who has also been written out of the canon.

Commonalities and Differences: Marxian Conflict Sociology   Despite a vocabulary of functionalism—or what is now associated with functionalism—Gilman's writing has a tone much more like that of Marxian conflict theory. She is in an argument, and the issue at stake is the way to organize a just society. Gilman shares the essential Marxian positions that the existential quality of the human being is work, that contemporary society is corrupt because it distorts the nature of human work, and that the two key distortions are alienation from work and maldistribution of socially produced goods and services. She agrees that the cause of these distortions is in stratificational practices that do not allow people to participate equally in the interdependent functions of social production.

But for Gilman, the essential cause of social inequality is not class but gender. It is gender that produces a distorted division of labor and false concepts about work. Gilman, like Marx, imagines a mythic beginning point for humanness—a point he locates at the moment people begin to control the production of material life, and she, through the lens of gender, locates at the moment when the species begins to control its food supply. She emphasizes, in a way Marx does not, the gender component in this movement. Marx traces man's movement from that first moment to the creation of the family and then to the making of history, a history in which women have no place. Gilman focuses on women's enslavement by men; on women's loss of the ability to participate in the social organization of production, save as slaves; and on the corruption of the human attitude towards work because of this enslavement. Work becomes associated with the activities of those who are held by force—women and slaves. Class stratification arises out of gender stratification. The enslaving male both makes women a separate class and at the same time begins to set himself against his fellows in competing for social goods in order to protect and feed this female he now owns.

Gilman sees the desire for property and possession as extensions of male qualities of desire, combat, and individuation that determine the organization of social life around struggle and domination. These cross-species male qualities, which Gilman asserts to be all right in their place as sources of energy, become pathological in human society as gender interacts with consciousness and people transform a biological fact into an ideology and a stratificational system.

Commonalities and Differences: Interpretive Theory   For Gilman, as for the interpretive theorists, mind and meaning are major and independent forces in society. She fits with the interpretive tradition developed by Max Weber, Alfred Schutz, and the social constructionist school of Peter Berger and Thomas Luckmann rather than the interactionist school of Simmel, Mead, and Herbert Blumer. Her interest is less in how people interact through symbols than in the concepts, the common stock of knowledge, that people come to hold about reality. Unlike the interpretive theorists, she does not see shared meanings as necessarily producing human happiness. She is distinctive among interpretive theorists in that a major part of her theoretical work is to explain the origin of wrong typifications, or constructions, of reality and to suggest right ones. Though agreeing that people's reality is socially constructed, she emphasizes that that construction occurs in and is laid upon fundamentally inequitable arrangements of production. The production of concepts, like all other forms of production, has been corrupted by the fundamental false concept of excessive sex-distinction. False concepts persist because consistency in concepts gives human beings a steady flow of energy, while inconsistency produces the uncomfortable state later to be called "cognitive dissonance" (Festinger 1957).

Exclusion from the Canon   Gilman's exclusion from the canon should be a major source of cognitive dissonance for the profession of sociology, especially considering the renaissance she has enjoyed over the last ten years in literature and women's studies. Although she did everything that one might expect of a significant sociological theorist, and in a language, English, that means she has always been accessible to American sociologists, she has been systematically written out of American sociology's construction of its own sociological and theoretical past. Her six books of sociological theory develop—in the coherent, authoritative, systematic, and accessible style already noted—as comprehensive an analysis of society as any offered by her male contemporaries. Her writings appeared in the *American Journal of Sociology,* the *Annals of the American Academy of Political and Social Science,* and the *Publications of the American Sociological Society.* She maintained membership in the American Sociological Society from its foundation in 1895 to her death in 1935 (Keith, 1991) and presented before its annual convention in 1908 and 1909. Her writing is replete with the awareness that she is bringing a sociological consciousness to her work. Only a complex process of anti-woman and anti-feminist bias really explains Gilman's disappearance from the record of sociology and sociological theory. As with the other women discussed in this text, Gilman's gender diminished her authority as a sociological spokesperson in an increasingly male-dominated profession. So, too, did her development of a general theory out of women's lived experiences of home, children, sexuality, housework, gender identity, femininity, and masculinity. Moreover, her activist and feminist stance, for radical reform of both gender and class relations, for the systematic restructuring of home life, education, work, culture, and religion, would make her seem too political and valuational to a field moving rapidly towards a value-neutral stance. Without a large population of women in the profession or a strong feminist movement in society after 1920, Gilman was allowed to disappear. Only now, with the reversal of both these trends, is the moment ripe for her rediscovery in sociology.

Gilman and the Tradition of Feminist Sociology

Of all the women we designate as founders of feminist sociology, it is Gilman who most places gender per se at the center of her analysis. Gilman's contribution to the feminist paradigm is to identify four concepts crucial to feminist analysis (though her labels vary slightly from those we use here): (1) gender as social construct and as social structure, (2) compulsory heterosexuality, (3) capitalist patriarchy, and (4) domination as a mode of relationship. Like all feminist theorists, she seeks not simply to theorize the world but to change it. But unlike the other women treated in this text, Gilman is insensitive to the feminist concern with differences among women.

Gender as the Stratificational Structure For Gilman, humanity through its collective consciousness participates in its own making; one of the things it has made is gender, and gender has become the pervasive stratificational structure in social organization. Gender has "not only an immediate effect on individuals through sex-action, and through the sex-affected individuals upon society, but also an effect upon society through economic action, and through the economically affected society upon the individual" (1898:99). Gender stratification explains class and economic conflict, the maldistribution of goods and services, the distortion of human work, an overemphasis on sexuality, the hyper-masculinity of men, the frustrated agency of women, political ineffectiveness, domestic inefficiency and unhappiness, and intergenerational, or parent–child, tensions. A sociological analysis, for Gilman, always starts with an investigation of the patterning of gender in the situation being investigated. Not until the 1970s do we again witness in sociology such a systematic theorizing of the significance of gender.

Compulsory Heterosexuality Gilman sees that the mode of control in the sexuo-economic relation for both men and women is compulsory heterosexuality. The sexuo-economic relation rests on every woman's having to be connected to a man for her food supply, that is, her livelihood. An unmarried woman without a man has no place to be—"[t]he scorn of male and female alike falls on this sexless thing: she is a human failure" (1898: 90). Even if she becomes "a human failure," in an ideal patriarchy the woman is still dependent on attachment to some male relative. Compulsory heterosexuality forces the woman to be available to the man as body servant, serf, and instrument for the fulfillment of his sexual desire, leading humans to a morbid sexual obsession which far exceeds the needs of procreation, love, and intimacy. For the man, compulsory heterosexuality becomes training in domination through the experience of having his wife and, by extension, his family as the instruments of his will. If he is of the ruling class, this experience trains him further for the domination of his workers; if he is of the worker class, it both compensates him for the lack of larger areas to dominate and ensures that he will stay docile in order to maintain his small kingdom. In her last book, *His Religion and Hers* (1923), Gilman finds in Freud's theories proof of the intertwining of patriarchal culture, morbid sexuality, and domination, part of the male backlash against women's gains in legal and economic independence: "[T]he perverted sex-philosophy of Freud . . . seems to embody the last effort on the part of man to maintain his misuse of the female. . . . Not since the phallic religions of antiquity has sex-worship so strongly appeared" (1923:165–166).

Capitalist Patriarchy For Gilman, patriarchy drives capitalism. Humans cannot form concepts, or think, without being implicated in patriarchal culture. At the base of the modern economy is an androcentric culture, a masculine conceptual system, that takes male qualities—most especially desire and aggression—and makes them qualities of an unchangeable human nature. The working out of the complex economy of capitalism has its root in unbridled desire, in a constant need for expansion; in the exploitation of the other, be he competitor or employee; and in the sense of individual entitlement that repeatedly asserts, "All's fair in love and war," and then proceeds to define everything as war. The gender system allows the invention of cultural justifications like "to support his family" as a way of making selfishness and greed acceptable and good.

Under patriarchy, woman is excluded from participation in the public world and the larger economy. Her potential for mutual service and giving is redirected from the child and the community to body service to the individual male who is her food supply. She is both a victim of and an accomplice in the rule of capitalist patriarchy, which creates a vast mythology of the home in order to romanticize the woman's imprisonment there. Gilman devotes much of her study *The Home* to the task of debunking this mythology. For instance, she deconstructs the myth of domestic privacy, showing the bickering and power struggles among a motley group of family members crowded together—the children oversupervised, the father fleeing to a work space away from the family, the invasive presence of domestic servants, tradespeople, salespeople, and visitors: "The mother—poor invaded soul—finds even the bathroom door no bar to hammering little hands. From parlour to kitchen, from cellar to garret, she is at the mercy of children, servants, tradesmen and callers. So chased and trodden is she that the very idea of privacy is lost to her mind; she has never had any, she doesn't know what it is" (1903:40).

Domination   Gilman defines domination as the situation in which one person is subjected to the will of another and traces its origins to two forces—the sexuo-economic relation and patriarchal culture. The sexuo-economic relation places the man in the position of master, the woman in the position of subordinate. Patriarchal culture legitimizes in consciousness what the sexuo-economic relation has made a practical necessity, reproducing domination through the development of the individual personalities of the male as master and the female as subordinate. When the man goes into the public world and meets others like himself, he is thrown into an endless process of conflict and combat over who shall be master and who shall serve. This is the pattern of our politics and our economy.

Change   To change the world-in-place, Gilman says, the sex-classes must be broken up. The first step in achieving this is the economic emancipation of women, who must move into the public sphere to claim status as human beings rather than as a sex. This movement requires fundamental changes in gender socialization and education; the physical development of women to their full size and strength; and a rethinking and renegotiation of the personal, relational, and sexual expectations between women and men. But most basically it requires the rational dismantling and reconstruction of the institution of the household, so that women can have freedom to do the work they choose and society may be enriched by their labor. In this last strategy, we have Gilman's most novel and problematic approach to a revolution in gender relations. In extraordinary detail she sets herself the project of redesigning domestic space and domestic activity. In her transformed world of the home, each person will have a room of their own and space for association with the family of their choice and construction. Child care, food service, laundry, and household cleaning will be handled professionally, in humane work spaces, by enlightened, well-paid workers, who find their calling and their dignity in such work. Surrounding them all—those working in the newly designed domestic spaces, those being reared there, and those coming home from work elsewhere—will be cultural, intellectual, recreational, and health facilities for the new communal lifestyle, paid for by the saving realized from the elimination of earlier wasteful domestic drudgery and earlier wasteful marketplace drudgery. It is Gilman's utopia, as communism was Marx's utopia. The recognition of women as people rather than as females will lead to a reorientation of society toward individuals generally: "What the human race requires is permanent provision for the needs of individuals, disconnected from the sex-relation. . . . Every human being needs a home,—bachelor, husband, or widowers, girl, wife, or widow, young or old. They need it from cradle to grave and without regard to sex-connections" (1898:298).

An Indifference to Difference   Gilman's theory does not explore the issue of differences among women. This neglect is probably due to the absence of a concern with vantage point in her sociology. Unlike most of the other women in this volume, Gilman's theoretical voice is less the first-person "I, a woman" and more the third-person editorial—or grand theorist's—"we." Since she does not as an ongoing practice situate herself as a woman in the world she theoretically describes, she is not led to the understanding that others in that world also speak from specific situated embodiments. Her focus is on women as a class and she assumes that class to be women like herself. Lane notes that Gilman, near the end of her life, in her summing up of the year 1932, "gave herself the ultimate comfort . . . for a life well lived. She wrote: 'One girl. / One girl reads this and takes fire! / Her life is changed. She becomes a power—a mover of others— / I write for her'" (Lane, 1990:346). Gilman would have deserved that comfort more if she had been able truly to see that "one girl" as *any* girl. She was sometimes disrespectful of working-class women, and she indulged in racist stereotyping. These prejudices are more visible in her personal writings than in her theoretical work. While her theoretical writings are occasionally marred by an example couched in racist or classist language, it is important to recognize that the theory itself does not have racism or classism as a foundational element. The question before any feminist attempting to use this otherwise brilliant theory is how to draw a circle to take her in.

ENDNOTES

1. Years later, Gilman would write to Martha: " 'Those years with you, that blessed summer of eighty-one—I doubt if most people have as much happiness in all their lives as I had then'" (cited in Hill, 1980:68).
2. The evolutionary arguments of reform social darwinism were enhanced by the now discredited belief that acquired traits could be inherited—the so-called Lamarckian theory. The textbook exemplar of this argument is that giraffes' necks get longer as they reach for higher, tastier leaves on a tree

and the acquired long neck is passed on to the next generation. The claim tremendously enhanced "scientific" arguments for social reform: if humans modified their social environment and their behaviors, they would improve their offspring and future generations through the genetic inheritance of improved acquired characteristics. This thesis runs through Gilman's sociology, but it is not essential to it. Her basic argument for human control of the social environment is that improved social conditions will produce better people.

3. Gilman writes at length on prostitution as "the full-flower of the sexuo-economic relation" (1898: 171). She argues, "In no other animal species is the female economically dependent on the male. In no other animal species is the sex-relation for sale. A coincidence" (1898: 95). She sees the woman as prostitute and the male as consumer engaged in a transaction that only the sexuo-economic relation can explain; she sees the "virtuous" women who condemn the prostitute as really objecting to unfair trading practices since the prostitute is selling cheaper what they feel obliged to sell dear. Gilman wonders if greater damage is not done to the female and male characters by marriages made in order to gain a livelihood.

Excerpts from *Women and Economics*

EXCERPT FROM CHAPTER I

This selection is excerpted from pages 1–22. It gives an explanation of the sexuo-economic relation in human society, that is, gender stratification with women as a subordinate and dependent class. The reader should remember that when Gilman uses "race" or "racial," she is referring to the human race and using "race" as synonymous with "species."

In spite of the power of the individual will to struggle against conditions, to resist them for a while, and sometimes to overcome them, it remains true that the human creature is affected by his environment, as is every other living thing. The power of the individual will to resist natural law is well proven by the life and death of the ascetic. In any one of those suicidal martyrs may be seen the will, misdirected by the ill-informed intelligence, forcing the body to defy every natural impulse,—even to the door of death, and through it.

But, while these exceptions show what the human will can do, the general course of life shows the inexorable effect of conditions upon humanity. Of these conditions we share with other living things the environment of the material universe. We are affected by climate and locality, by physical, chemical, electrical forces, as are all animals and plants. With the animals, we farther share the effect of our own activity, the reactionary force of exercise. What we do, as well as what is done to us, makes us what we are. But, beyond these forces, we come under the effect of a third set of conditions peculiar to our human status; namely, social conditions. In the organic inter-

changes which constitute social life, we are affected by each other to a degree beyond what is found even among the gregarious animals. This third factor, the social environment, is an enormous force as a modifier of human life. Throughout all these environing conditions, those which affect us through our economic necessities are most marked in their influence.

Without touching yet upon the influence of the social factors, treating the human being merely as an individual animal, we see that he is modified most by his economic conditions, as is every other animal. Differ as they may in color and size, in strength and speed, in minor adaptation to minor conditions, all animals that live on grass have distinctive traits in common, and all animals that eat flesh have distinctive traits in common,—so distinctive and so common that it is by teeth, by nutritive apparatus in general, that they are classified, rather than by means of defence or locomotion. The food supply of the animal is the largest passive factor in his development; the processes by which he obtains his food supply, the largest active factor in his development. It is these activities, the incessant repetition of the exertions by which he is fed, which most modify his structure and develop his functions. . . .

The human animal is no exception to this rule. Climate affects him, weather affects him, enemies affect him; but most of all he is affected, like every other living creature, by what he does for his living. Under all the influences of his later and wider life, all the reactive effect of social institutions, the individual is still inexorably modified by his means of livelihood: "the hand of the dyer is subdued to what he works in.". . .

. . . On the clear line of argument that functions and organs are developed by use, that what we use most is developed most, and that the daily processes of supplying economic needs are the processes that we most use, it follows that, when we find special economic conditions affecting any special class of people, we may look for special results, and find them.

Source: Charlotte Perkins Gilman, *Women and Economics* (New York: Small and Maynard, 1898).

In view of these facts, attention is now called to certain marked and peculiar economic conditions affecting the human race, and unparalleled in the organic world. We are the only animal species in which the female depends on the male for food, the only animal species in which the sex-relation is also an economic relation. With us an entire sex lives in a relation of economic dependence upon the other sex, and the economic relation is combined with the sex-relation. The economic status of the human female is relative to the sex-relation.

It is commonly assumed that this condition also obtains among other animals, but such is not the case. There are many birds among which, during the nesting season, the male helps the female feed the young, and partially feeds her; and, with certain of the higher carnivora, the male helps the female feed the young, and partially feeds her. In no case does she depend on him absolutely, even during this season. . . . In no case is the female throughout her life supported by the male.

In the human species the condition is permanent and general, though there are exceptions. . . .

To many this view will not seem clear at first; and the case of working peasant women or females of savage tribes, and the general household industry of women, will be instanced against it. Some careful and honest discrimination is needed to make plain to ourselves the essential facts of the relation, even in these cases. The horse, in his free natural condition is economically independent. He gets his living by his own exertions, irrespective of any other creature. The horse, in his present condition of slavery, is economically dependent. He gets his living at the hands of his master; and his exertions, though strenuous, bear no direct relation to his living. In fact, the horses who are the best fed and cared for and the horses who work the hardest are quite different animals. The horse works, it is true; but what he gets to eat depends on the power and will of his master. His living comes through another. He is economically dependent. So with the hard-working savage or peasant women. Their labor is the property of another: they work under another will; and what they receive depends not on their labor, but on the power and will of another. They are economically dependent. This is true of the human female both individually and collectively.

In studying the economic position of the sexes collectively, the difference is most marked. As a social animal, the economic status of man rests on the combined and exchanged service of vast numbers of progressively specialized individuals. The economic progress of the race, its maintenance at any period, its continued advance, involve the collective activities of all the trades, crafts, arts, manufactures, inventions, discoveries, and all the civil and military institutions that go to maintain them. . . . Economic progress, however, is almost exclusively masculine. Such economic processes as women have been allowed to exercise are of the earliest and most primitive kind. Were men to perform no economic services save such as are still performed by women, our racial status in economics would be reduced to its most painful limitations. . . .

This is not owing to lack of the essential human faculties necessary to such achievements nor to any inherent disability of sex, but to the present condition of women, forbidding the development of this degree of economic ability. . . . Speaking collectively, men produce and distribute wealth; and women receive it at their hands. . . .

Studied individually, the facts are even more plainly visible, more open and familiar. From the day laborer to the millionaire, the wife's worn dress or flashing jewels, her low roof or her lordly one, her weary feet or her rich equipage,—these speak of the economic ability of the husband. The comfort, the luxury, the necessities of life itself, which the woman receives, are obtained by the husband, and given her by him. And, when the woman, left alone with no man to "support" her, tries to meet her own economic necessities, the difficulties which confront her prove conclusively what the general economic status of women is. . . . But we are instantly confronted by the commonly received opinion that, although it must be admitted that men make and distribute the wealth of the world, yet women earn their share as wives. This assumes either that the husband is in the position of employer and the wife as employee, or that marriage is a "partnership," and the wife an equal factor with the husband in producing wealth.

Economic independence is a relative condition at best. In the broadest sense, all living things are economically dependent upon others,—the animals upon the vegetables, and man upon both. In a narrower sense, all social life is economically interdependent, man producing collectively what he could by no possibility produce separately. But, in the closest interpretation, individual economic independence among human beings means that the individual pays for what he gets, works for what he gets, gives to the other an equivalent for what the other gives him. I depend on the shoemaker for shoes, and the tailor for coats; but, if I give the shoemaker and the tailor enough of my own labor as a house-builder to pay for the shoes and coats they give me, I retain my personal independence. I have not taken of their product, and given nothing of mine. As long as what I get is obtained by what I give, I am economically independent.

Women consume economic goods. What economic product do they give in exchange for what they consume? The claim that marriage is a partnership, in which the two persons married produced wealth which neither of them, separately, could produce, will not bear examination. . . .

. . . Man and wife are partners truly in their mutual obligation to children,—their common love, duty, and service. But a manufacturer who marries, or a doctor, or a lawyer, does not take a partner in his business, when he takes a partner in parenthood, unless his wife is also a manufacturer, a doctor, or a lawyer. . . . She is in no sense a business partner, unless she contributes capital or experience or labor, as a man would in like relation. Most men would hesitate very seriously before entering a business partnership with any woman, wife or not.

If the wife is not, then, truly a business partner, in what way does she earn from her husband the food, clothing, and shelter she receives at his hands? By house service, it will be instantly replied. . . .

For a certain percentage of persons to serve other persons, in order that the ones so served may produce more, is a contribution not to be overlooked. The labor of women in the house, certainly, enables men to produce more wealth than they otherwise could; and in this way women are economic factors in society. But so are horses. The labor of horses enables men to produce more wealth than they otherwise could. But the horse is not economically independent nor is the woman.

The labor which the wife performs in the household is given as part of her functional duty, not as employment. . . .

But the salient fact in this discussion is that, whatever the economic value of the domestic industry of women is, they do not get it. The women who do the most work get the least money, and the women who have the most money do the least work. Their labor is neither given nor taken as a factor in economic exchange. It is held to be their duty as women to do this work; and their economic status bears no relation to their domestic labors, unless an inverse one. Moreover, if they were thus fairly paid,—given what they earned, and no more,—all women working in this way could be reduced to the economic status of the house servant. Few women—or men either—care to face this condition. The ground that women earn their living by domestic labor is instantly forsaken, and we are told that they obtain their livelihood as mothers. . . .

If this is so, if motherhood is an exchangeable commodity given by women in payment for clothes and food, then we must of course find some relation between the quantity or quality of the motherhood and the quantity and quality of the pay. This being true, then the women who are not mothers have no economic status at all; and the economic status of those who are must be shown to be relative to their motherhood. This is obviously absurd. . . . Visibly, and upon the face of it, women are not maintained in economic prosperity proportioned to their motherhood. Motherhood bears no relation to their economic status. . . . The claim of motherhood as a factor in economic exchange is false to-day. But suppose it were true. Are we willing to hold this ground, even in theory? Are we willing to consider motherhood as a business, a form of commercial exchange? Are the cares and duties of the mother, her travail and her love, commodities to be exchanged for bread?

It is revolting so to consider them. . . . [W]hat remains to those who deny that women are supported by men? This (and a most amusing position it is),—that the function of maternity unfits a woman for economic production, and, therefore, it is right that she should be supported by her husband. . . .

Because of her maternal duties, the human female is said to be unable to get her own living. . . .

Is this the condition of human motherhood? Does the human mother, by her motherhood, thereby lose control of brain and body, lose power and skill and desire for any other work? Do we see before us the human race, with all its females segregated entirely to the uses of motherhood, consecrated, set apart, specially developed, spending every power of their nature on the service of their children?

We do not. We see the human mother worked far harder than a mare, laboring her life long in the service, not of her children only, but of men; husbands, brothers, fathers, whatever male relatives she has; for mother and sister also; for the church a little, if she is allowed. . . .

It is not motherhood that keeps the housewife on her feet from dawn till dark; it is house service, not child service. Women work longer and harder than most men, and not solely in maternal duties. . . .

In spite of her supposed segregation to maternal duties, the human female, the world over, works at extra-maternal duties for hours enough to provide her with an independent living, and then is denied independence on the ground that motherhood prevents her working!

If this ground were tenable, we should find a world full of women who never lifted a finger save in the service of their children, and of men who did *all* the work besides, and waited on the women whom motherhood prevented from waiting on themselves. The ground is not tenable. A human female, healthy, sound, has twenty-five years of life before she is a mother, and should have twenty-five years more after the period of such maternal service as is expected of her has been given. The duties of grandmotherhood are surely not alleged as preventing economic independence.

The working power of the mother has always been a prominent factor in human life. She is the worker *par excellence,* but her work is not such as to affect her economic status. Her living, all that she gets,—food, clothing, ornaments, amusements, luxuries,—these bear no relation to her services in the house, or to her motherhood. These things bear relation only to the man she marries, the man she depends on,—to how much he has and how much he is willing to give her. The women whose splendid extravagance dazzles the world, whose economic goods are the greatest, are often neither houseworkers nor mothers, but simply the women who hold most power over the men who have the most money. The female of genus homo is economically dependent on the male. He is her food supply.

EXCERPT FROM CHAPTER II

This selection is excerpted from pages 23–38. It introduces the theme of gender, or excessive sex-distinction, as a pathological consequence of the sexuo-economic relation.

Knowing how important a factor in the evolution of the species is the economic relation, and finding in the human species an economic relation so peculiar, we may naturally look to find effects peculiar to our race. We may expect to find phenomena in the sex-relation and in the economic relation of humanity of a unique character,—phenomena not traceable to human superiority, but singularly derogatory to that superiority; phenomena so marked, so morbid, as to give rise to much speculation as to their cause. Are these natural inferences fulfilled? Are these peculiarities in the sex-relation and in the economic relation manifested in human life? Indisputably. . . .

As the racial distinction of humanity lies in its social relation, so we find the distinctive gains and losses of humanity to lie also in its social relation. We are more affected by our relation to each other than by our physical environment. . . .

Rudely classifying the principal fields of human difficulty, we find one large proportion lies in the sex-relation, and another in the economic relation between the individual constituents of society. To speak broadly, the troubles of life as we find them are mainly traceable to the heart or the purse. . . .

Every other animal works out the kind of sex-union best adapted to the reproduction of his species, and peacefully practises it. We have worked out the kind that is best for us,—best for the individuals concerned, for the young resultant, and for society as a whole; but we do not peacefully practise it. So palpable is this fact that we have commonly accepted it, and taken it for granted that this relation must be a continuous source of trouble to humanity. "Marriage is a lottery," is a common saying among us. "The course of true love never did run smooth." And we quote with unction *Punch's* advice to those about to marry,—"Don't!" That peculiar sub-relation which has dragged along with us all the time monogamous marriage has been growing to be the accepted form of sex-union—prostitution—we have accepted, and called a "social necessity." We also call it "the social evil." We have tacitly admitted that this relation in the human race must be more or less uncomfortable and wrong, that it is part of our nature to have it so.

Now let us examine the case fairly and calmly, and see whether it is as inscrutable and immutable as hitherto believed. What are the conditions? What are the natural and what the unnatural features of the case? To distinguish these involves a little study of the evolution of the processes of reproduction.

Very early in the development of species it was ascertained by nature's slow but sure experiments that the establishment of two sexes in separate organisms, and their differentiation, was to the advantage of the species. Therefore, out of the mere protoplasmic masses, the floating cells, the amorphous early forms of life, grew into use the distinction of the sexes,—the gradual development of masculine and feminine organs and functions in two distinct organisms. . . . As the distinction increased, the attraction increased, until we have in all the higher races two markedly different sexes, strongly drawn together by the attraction of sex, and fulfilling their use in the reproduction of species. These are the natural features of sex-distinction and sex-union, and they are found in the human species as in others. The unnatural feature by which our race holds an unenviable distinction consists mainly in this,—a morbid excess in the exercise of this function. . . .

. . . Nothing could be more inevitable, however, under our sexuo-economic relation. By the economic dependence of the human female upon the male, the balance of forces is altered. Natural selection no longer checks the action of sex-selection, but co-operates with it. Where both sexes obtain their food through the same exertions, from the same sources, under the same conditions, both sexes are acted upon alike, and developed alike by their environment. Where the two sexes obtain their food under different conditions, and where that difference consists in one of them being fed by the other, then the feeding sex becomes the environment of the fed. Man, in supporting woman, has become her economic environment. Under natural selection, every creature is modified to its environment, developing perforce the qualities needed to obtain its livelihood under that environment. Man, as the feeder of woman, becomes the strongest modifying force in her economic condition. Under sexual selection the human creature is of course modified to its mate, as with all creatures. When the mate becomes also the master, when economic necessity is added to sex-attraction, we have the two great evolutionary forces acting together to the same end; namely, to develop sex-distinction in the human female. For, in her position of economic dependence in the sex-relation sex-distinction is with her not only a means of attracting a mate, as with all creatures, but a means of getting her livelihood, as is the case with no other creature under heaven. Because of the economic dependence of the human female on her mate, she is modified to sex in an excessive degree.

EXCERPT FROM CHAPTER III

This selection is excerpted from pages 40–49. It provides more detail on the meaning of "excessive sex-distinction" and an explanation of how it has a much more negative impact on the female than on the male.

In establishing the claim of excessive sex-distinction in the human race, much needs to be said to make clear to the general reader what is meant by the term. To the popular mind, both the coarsely familiar and the over-refined, "sexual" is thought to mean "sensual"; and the charge of excessive sex-distinction seems a reproach. This should be at once dismissed, as merely showing ignorance of the terms used. A man does not object to being called "masculine," nor a woman to being called "feminine." Yet whatever is masculine or feminine is sexual. To be distinguished by femininity is to be distinguished by sex. To be over-feminine is to be over-sexed. To manifest in excess any of the distinctions of sex, primary or secondary, is to be over-sexed. . . .

The primary sex-distinctions in our race as in others consist merely in the essential organs and functions of reproduction. The secondary

distinctions, and this is where we are to look for largest excess—consist in all those differences in organ and function, in look and action, in habit, manner, method, occupation, behavior, which distinguish men from women. . . . Certain psychic attributes are manifested by either sex. . . . The tendency to fight is a sex-distinction of males in general: the tendency to protect and provide for, is a sex-distinction of females in general.

With the human race, whose chief activities are social, the initial tendency to sex-distinction is carried out in many varied functions. We have differentiated our industries, our responsibilities, our very virtues, along sex lines. It will therefore be clear that the claim of excessive sex-distinction in humanity, and especially in woman, does not carry with it any specific "moral" reproach, though it does in the larger sense prove a decided evil in its effects on human progress.

In primary distinctions our excess is not so marked as in the farther and subtler development; yet, even here, we have plain proof of it. Sex-energy in its primal manifestation is exhibited in the male of the human species to a degree far greater than is necessary for the processes of reproduction,—enough, indeed, to subvert and injure those processes. . . . This inordinate demand in the human male is an excessive sex-distinction. In this, in a certain over-coarseness and hardness, a too great belligerence and pride, a too great subservience to the power of sex-attraction, we find the main marks of excessive sex-distinction in men. It has been always checked and offset in them by the healthful activities of racial life. Their energies have been called out and their faculties developed along all the lines of human progress. In the growth of industry, commerce, science, manufacture, government, art, religion, the male of our species has become human, far more than male. Strong as this passion is in him, inordinate as is his indulgence, he is a far more normal animal than the female of his species,—far less over-sexed. To him this field of special activity is but part of life,—an incident. The whole world remains besides. To her it is the world. This has been well stated in the familiar epigram of Madame de Staël,—"love with man is an episode, with woman a history." It is in woman that we find most fully expressed the excessive sex-distinction of the human species,—physical, psychical, social. . . .

Women's femininity—and "the eternal feminine" means simply the eternal sexual—is more apparent in proportion to her humanity than the femininity of other animals in proportion to their caninity or felinity or equinity. "A feminine hand" or "a feminine foot" is distinguishable anywhere. We do not hear of "a feminine paw" or "a feminine hoof." A hand is an organ of prehension, a foot an organ of locomotion: they are not secondary sexual characteristics. The comparative smallness and feebleness of woman is a sex-distinction. We have carried it to such an excess that women are commonly known as "the weaker sex." There is no such glaring difference between male and female in other advanced species. . . .

In its psychic manifestations this intense sex-distinction is equally apparent. The primal instinct of sex-attraction has developed under social forces into a conscious passion of enormous power, a deep and lifelong devotion, overwhelming in its force. This is excessive in both sexes, but more so in women than in men,—not so commonly in its simple physical form, but in the unreasoning intensity of emotion that refuses all guidance, and drives those possessed by it to risk every other good for this one end. . . .

It is good for the individual and for the race to have developed such a degree of passionate and permanent love as shall best promote the happiness of individuals and the reproduction of species. It is not good for the race or for the individual that this feeling should have become so intense as to override all other human faculties, to make a mock of the accumulated wisdom of the ages, . . .

. . . And, while in men the immediate dominating force of the passion may be more conspicuous, it is in women that it holds more universal sway. For the man has other powers and faculties in full use, whereby to break loose from the force of this; and the woman, specially modified to sex and denied racial activity, pours her whole life into her love, and if injured here, she is injured irretrievably. . . . It is maintained in her in the face of a lifetime of neglect and abuse. The common instance of the police court trials—the woman cruelly abused who will not testify against her husband—shows this. . . .

But it is in our common social relations that the predominance of sex-distinction in women is made most manifest. . . . So utterly has the status of woman been accepted as a sexual one that it has remained for the woman's movement of the nineteenth century to devote much contention to the claim that women are persons! That women are persons as well as females,—an unheard of proposition!

EXCERPT FROM CHAPTER V

This selection is excerpted from pages 76–90. It explains how the sexuo-economic relation, manifest as excessive sex-distinction, not only hurts individual development but shapes and distorts all human relations, human society, and the human experience of work.

The sex relation is intensely personal. All the functions and relations ensuing are intensely personal. The spirit of "me and my wife, my son John and his wife, us four and no more," is the natural spirit of this phase of life. By confining half the world to this one set of functions, we have confined it absolutely to the personal. And the man that is born of woman is reared by her in this same atmosphere of concentrated personality, and afterward spends a large part of his life in it. This condition tends to magnify the personal and minimize the general in our minds, with results that are familiar to us all. The difficulty of enforcing sanitary laws, where personal convenience must be sacrificed to general safety, the size of the personal grievance as against the general, the need of "having it brought home to us," which hinders every step of public advancement, and our eager response when it is "brought home to us"—these are truisms. . . . This is natural enough, inevitable enough, and only mentioned here as partly explaining why people do not see the general facts as to our over-sexed condition. Yet they are patent everywhere, not only patent, but painful. Being used to them, we do not notice them, or, forced to notice them, we attribute the pain we feel to the evil behavior of some individual, and never think of it as being the result of a condition common to us all. . . . [L]et us, in spite of these hindrances, see if the visible results among us are not such as must follow such a cause, and let us seek them merely in the phenomena of every-day life as we know it, not in the deeper sexual or social results. . . .

[An] instance of so grossly unjust, so palpable, so general an evil that it has occasionally aroused some protest even from our dull consciousness is this: the enforced attitude of the woman towards marriage. To the young girl, as has been previously stated, marriage is the one road to fortune, to life. She is born highly specialized as a female: she is carefully educated and trained to realize in all ways her sex-limitations and her sex-advantages. What she has to gain even as a child is largely gained by feminine tricks and charms. Her reading, both in history and fiction, treats of the same position for women; and romance and poetry give it absolute predominance. Pictorial art, music, the drama, society, everything, tells her that she is *she* and that all depends on whom she marries. Where young boys plan for what they will achieve and attain, young girls plan for whom they will achieve and attain . . . "he" is the coming world.

With such a prospect as this before her; with an organization specially developed to this end; with an education adding every weight of precept and example, of wisdom and virtue, to the natural instincts; with a social environment the whole machinery of which is planned to give the girl a chance to be seen, to provide her with "opportunities" and with all the pressure of personal advantage and self-interest added to the sex-instinct,—what one would logically expect is a society full of desperate and eager husband-hunters, regarded with popular approval.

Not at all! Marriage is the woman's proper sphere, her divinely ordered place, her natural end. It is what she is born for, what she is trained for, what she is exhibited for. It is, moreover, her means of an honorable livelihood and advancement. *But*—she must not even look as if she wanted it! She must not turn her hand over to get it. She must sit passive as the seasons go by, and her "chances" lessen with each year. Think of the strain on a highly sensitive nervous organism to have so much hang on one thing, to see the possibility of attaining it grow less and less yearly, and to be forbidden to take any step toward securing it! This she must bear with dignity and grace to the end. . . .

The cruel and absurd injustice of blaming the girl for not getting what she is allowed no effort to obtain seems unaccountable; but it becomes clear when viewed in connection with the sexuo-economic relation. Although marriage is a means of livelihood, it is not honest employment where one can offer one's labor without shame, but a relation where the support is given outright, and enforced by law in return for the functional service of the woman, the "duties of wife and mother." Therefore no honorable woman can ask for it. It is not only that the natural feminine instinct is to retire, but that, because marriage means support, a woman must not ask a man to support her. It is economic beggary as well as a false attitude from a sex point of view.

Observe the ingenious cruelty of the arrangement. It is just as humanly natural for a woman as for a man to want wealth. But, when her wealth is made to come through the same channels as her love, she is forbidden to ask for it by her own sex-nature and by business honor. . . .

Since women are viewed wholly as creatures of sex even by one another, and since everything is done to add to their young powers of sex attraction;

since they are marriageable solely on this ground, unless, indeed, "a fortune" has been added to their charms,—failure to marry is held a clear proof of failure to attract, a lack of sex-value. And, since, they have no other value, save in a low order of domestic service, they are quite naturally despised. What else is the creature good for, failing in the functions for which she is created? The scorn of male and female alike falls on this sexless thing: she is a human failure.

EXCERPT FROM CHAPTER VI

This selection is excerpted from pages 106–113. It explains how the sexuo-economic relation corrupts and distorts work and collective production.

[T]he sex-relation itself is totally personal. Our economic relation, on the contrary, though originally individual, becomes through social evolution increasingly collective. By combining the human sex-relation with the human economic relation, we have combined a permanently individual process with a progressively collective one. . . . This . . . has affected the economic relation of society by bringing into it a tendency to individualism with sex-advantage, best exhibited in the frequent practice of sacrificing the public good to personal gain, that the individual may thereby "support his family." We are so used to considering it the first duty of a man to support his family that it takes a very glaring instance of bribery and corruption in their interests to shake our conviction; but as a sociological law, every phase of the prostitution of public service to private gain, from the degradation of the artist to the exploitation of the helpless unskilled laborer, marks a diseased social action. . . .

. . . The tendency to individualism with sex-advantage is developed in man by an opposite process to that operating on the woman. She gets her living by getting a husband. He gets his wife by getting a living. It is to her individual advantage to secure a mate. It is to his individual sex-advantage to secure economic gain. The sex-functions to her

have become economic functions. Economic functions to him have become sex-functions. This has confounded our natural economic co-operation, with the element of sex-competition,—an entirely different force. . . .

. . . [T]o make the sexual gain of the male rest on his purchasing power puts the immense force of sex-competition into the field of social economics, not only as an incentive to labor and achievement, which is good, but as an incentive to individual gain, however obtained which is bad; thus, accounting for our multiplied and intensified desire to get,—the inordinate greed of our industrial world. . . .

The contest in every good man's heart to-day between the "ought to" and the "must," between his best work and the "potboiler," is his personal share of this incessant struggle between social interest and self-interest. For himself and by himself he would be glad to do his best work, to be true to his ideals, to be brave in meeting loss for that truth's sake. But . . . "Marriage makes a mouse of a man." To the young business man who falls into evil courses in the sex-relation the open greed of his fair dependant is a menace to his honesty, to his business prospects. On the same man married the needs of his wife often operate in the same way. The sense of the dependence of the helpless creature whose food must come through him does not stimulate courage, but compels submission.

READING 4-2

Excerpts from *Human Work*

Gilman calls for a general and critical sociology addressing human pain and beginning, analytically, with a study of economy, work, and false concepts.

Source: Charlotte Perkins Gilman, *Human Work* (New York: McClure and Phillips, 1904).

EXCERPT FROM CHAPTER I, "INTRODUCTORY"

This selection is excerpted from pages 5–16.

Social phenomena have been going on about us since we began to be human; they are as familiar as physical or physiological phenomena, but even less understood. Yet the interaction of social forces and social conditions form increasingly prominent factors in human life.

Primitive man was most affected by physical conditions, he had to adjust himself to the exigencies of climate, of the soil, of animal competitors. Modern man has to adjust himself mainly to social conditions, he is most affected by governments, religions, economic systems, general customs. Yet the study of this especially pressing and important environment is but little advanced. The smooth-worn commonplace facts slip through our fingers, and we fail to see the meaning of our most important surroundings simply because we have always had them. Also we allow ourselves to be discouraged by the extent and complexity of social conditions. This is quite needless. . . .

Moreover, early writers on this subject have frightened us with technicalities. Mention some patent fact about our social composition, show a relation, suggest a law, and your alarmed hearer cries, "Oh, that is Political Economy! I cannot understand that, it is too difficult!" It is really a pity that such awe should be felt in the contemplation of our social processes; as though a man were afraid to learn anything about his digestion on the ground that it was "physiology."

The statement, "Hens lay eggs," expresses a fact in Ornithology, Zoology, and Biology—but it is none the more difficult to grasp. The special student may, if he so desires, amass enough knowledge in these lapping sciences to appall the uninitiated; but a mere practical farmer can learn enough of the nature and habits of hens to insure a profitable supply of eggs, without overtaxing his brain. There may be fields of sociological science quite beyond the average mind, and rightly left to the learned specialist; but that is no reason why we should not learn enough of the nature and habits of society to insure a more profitable and pleasant life. . . .

For many an age the pain of human life has formed so conspicuous a fact that we have called the earth "The Star of Suffering." Our common illustrations of happiness are drawn from the lower animals: "as happy as a clam," we say; "as gay as a lark"; "as merry as a cricket."

The world's greatest religions have rested on a conception of general human unhappiness. . . .

So unbearable is the amount of human pain that we alone among all animals manifest the remarkable phenomenon of suicide—a deliberate effort of a form of life to stop living because living hurts so much. Social evolution does not proportionately abate social suffering; it improves external conditions and insures physical existence more and more reliably; but it does not make us commensurately happier. We die of different diseases, and we do not die so soon, but we continue to suffer while alive, we continue to refer to "the sea of human misery," we continue to kill ourselves because we cannot bear the pain of being alive. . . .

Society has long since mastered the difficulties of adjustment with physical conditions, but cannot arrange its own intersocial conditions on a satisfactory basis. "Man's inhumanity to man makes countless thousands mourn"—not nature's. From the Arctic Circle to the Tropics man gets along contentedly enough with natural obstacles; he may be checked and modified in development, but he is not unhappy; he strikes a balance with nature and is comparatively at rest. But in his progressive social development he has not yet been able to strike a balance; his interhuman relations are uncertain and mischievous. . . .

Are these disadvantages of human life essential, as heretofore supposed; or are they merely pathological phenomena and quite unnecessary? We are now beginning to take the latter view, and a most cheerful one it is. . . .

[W]e in our present stage of civilisation, are partly retarded by natural conditions of environment. . . .But meanwhile our progress is retarded far more by conditions of social pathology—by ignorance, poverty, and crime; and these conditions are no part of our essential environment, but are due to economic errors and superstitions. . . .

Now, since we can easily see in history how we have at given times suffered from certain popular mistakes, and how on better knowledge we have outgrown those errors and their painful consequences, why is it not reasonable to assume that we may outgrow our present mistakes and superstitions and their painful consequences? Is it not possible that the persistence in society of certain morbid phenomena is due to an equal persistence of certain false ideas? and that the one may be removed by removing the other? . . .

Our most conspicuous troubles to-day are economic. . . . [I]n economic development we find that whereas there is a great extension and multiplication of wealth, yet there is a mighty product of evil which seems to keep pace with the advance of civilisation. . . .

Now, knowing more of the nature of society, we can begin to classify and analyse its difficulties more intelligently and find them somewhat in this order. Let us call poverty in-nutrition—a large part of our social tissues are insufficiently nourished. Let us call wealth over-nutrition, or repletion, or congestion, or fatty degeneration—a small part of our social tissues are gorged and inflamed with too much nourishment. Then let us call our large supply of poor, false, bad things: adulterated articles of food, shoddy clothes, paper shoes,—all the flood of worthless stuff society produces and consumes,—mal-nutrition; the blood is bad and does not nourish. Back of the phenomena we find still more important conditions, having to do not with the nourishment of the body politic, but with its activities. There is wrong action in the social organism; it does not work properly. Hence this local congestion of wealth, this peculiar arrest of

distribution which makes both rich and poor dissatisfied in the widest field of life—work.

Work is the most conspicuous feature of human life. In the conditions of work, in our ideas and feelings about work, in our habits, methods, and systems of work, lies the subject-matter of this book. It is held that our difficulties are to be found, not in any essential traits of human nature, and not in any essential conditions of human life, but merely in the preservation in our minds of certain ancient and erroneous ideas and feelings which act continually upon the normal processes of social economics, preventing the process and poisoning the product. . . . It is here asserted that we have still in the popular mind certain traditions—superstitions, falsehoods—about work, and that to them is traceable the economic distresses so conspicuous among us. . . .

. . . [S]ociety feels first and most what hurts it, and our study of sociology is prefaced by social pathology. . . .

We need the patient, scientific study of the social body, its structure and functions, anatomy, physiology, and pathology, as we have had it for the physical body; we need careful recorded observation of the results of previous remedies, and of new ones as well, and all this in a new field of science. We have plenty of facts at hand; all history lies behind us with its glaring records; all life is before us to-day in every stage of development; but we have only begun to arrange and study those facts from the point of view of the sociologist. If a watch goes wrong, we examine its "works" for fracture, loss, misplacement, or some "foreign body"; but to do this successfully involves knowledge of what a watch is, what it is for, how it is made, and how it works. We must know the mechanics of the thing if we are to mend it. So if Society goes wrong we must examine its works, and we cannot tell if they are wrong, nor set them right, unless we have some knowledge of what Society is, what it is for, how it was made, and, above all, how it works.

EXCERPT FROM CHAPTER III, "CONCEPT AND CONDUCT"

This selection is excerpted from pages 37–40.

A given society, in any age, possesses certain dominant ideas and feelings proper to it; and the individuals manifesting most of those ideas and feelings are most beneficial to that society and so to themselves. But if members of a given society persist in maintaining and acting upon social ideals of a previous age, they are injurious to their society and so to themselves. . . .

Society is a psychic condition; all social relations exist and grow in the human mind. That one despot can rule over a million other men rests absolutely on their state of mind. They believe that he does; let them change their minds, and he does not. As a human animal the despot is of such size, weight, colour—he is a physical fact. As a Despot—he is but a psychical fact—he exists as a Despot only in the minds of men. (This is not Christian Science, but sociological science.) He is a concept, a common concept, acting under which all men do thus and thus; outgrowing which, they discard their Despot and adopt some other political belief. . . .

. . . Man reacts to external conditions as do other animals, but also he acts according to those special inner conditions—his ideas. The power to form and retain concepts, and act under their influence precisely as if they were facts, is what gives the element of special progress and also of perversity to human conduct. This internal environment, the general furnishing of a man's brain, and more particularly his basic concepts, do more to determine his action than does external environment. His reaction to external conditions is modified by these internal conditions; unless you know them you cannot predict the result; unless you change them you cannot change the result. . . .

This power of directing action by concepts is at once our great advantage and disadvantage. If the concepts are true, if they are founded on fact and in accordance with law, they promote advantageous conduct; if they are false, they promote disadvantageous conduct. Even if once true, that is, as true as the brains of a given period, acting on the knowledge of that period, could comprehend, they become mischievous if not changed to suit the . . . larger knowledge of a later time.

EXCERPT FROM CHAPTER VI, "THE NATURE OF SOCIETY (II)"

This selection is excerpted from pages 79–94.

The proposition is that Society is the whole and we are the parts: that the degree of organic development known as human life is never found in isolated individuals, and that it progresses to higher development in proportion to the evolution of the social relation; that a man is individually, a complete animal, with sufficient ability to attain the necessities of an animal existence: but that as a human being he is but a minute fraction of a great entity, the necessities of whose existence are only to be attained by the complex interdependent activities of many men.

That this relation is strictly organic, involving the high specialisation of the individual man to the social service in activities which are of no possible benefit to his separate animal life—(as the activities of a dentist or a teacher); but which are of visible benefit to his community, his community in turn supporting him.

That these common and composite activities have developed a life-form quite above and beyond that of its constituent men; with a structure and functions outside of and including theirs. That whereas the life-processes of the constituent individuals must of course be insured and improved by the higher life inclosing them; yet that a greater or less sacrifice of individual interests may at any time be necessary—and is naturally made—the greater including the less.

That this Social Organisation tends to make safe and happy its constituent organisms in their separate animal lives, yet their greatest happiness lies in their recognition and fulfilment of the social life.

That an increasing social consciousness and social activity is the most healthful and happy growth for the human race; and further, that "the riddle of human life" is made quite simple by this purely natural and evolutionary position.

In proof and illustration let us consider certain facts, most of them commonly known to us all, but not commonly considered in this connection. We will observe in turn the organic nature of Society as shown in its nutritive processes, in its high and personally sacrificial specialisations, and in its patently collective mental life. . . .

. . . Among facts suitable for nursery education is the glaring one that in plainest economic relation "no man liveth to himself nor dieth to himself."

. . . The daily necessities of one man are met by the activities of countless other men. If they were gone, the one man could not supply himself with any of these things; but would, if he lived, sink to the level of the savage hunter,—who is indeed "self-supporting." We have, it is true, a system of exchange in which it is endeavoured to make each man's share in the common product proportionate to his personal efforts; but even if this system worked successfully it would not alter the fact that the supplies are really made by the others—and the one—alone—could not make them.

. . . The life of any creature is primarily dependent on the regular renewal of its constituent particles. . . . [T]o postpone the dying the structure is continually supplied with fresh materials. This continuous supply of fresh material we call nutrition. It is an increasingly elaborate process. . . .

Whatever form the dinner took, wherever the dinner went, there followed the fluent, ever-changing animal organism, producing tooth or claw, tongue or proboscis, seven stomachs or a private fish-pole— whatever was necessary to lure, catch, hold, inclose, and assimilate, this ever-receding and sometimes actively resisting, but always indispensable dinner. The evolution of animal organisms is conditioned mainly upon the food supply.

How does humanity figure in this transformation scene?

Man alone, of the whole animal kingdom, has attained a complete new stage in this imperative process of nutrition. Where the most primitive ameboid cell can but receive food; where the whole machinery of later organisms can but seize food; man, and man alone, produces food. Through all the ages, through every conceivable modification of structure and function, the animal has pursued its dinner. Man has caught it.

Man alone has permanently mastered his food supply; instead of an endless chase it is a closed circle—he makes that which makes him. That is why physical evolution stops with man—and psychical evolution begins. . . . By what strange new power is this immense step taken, which has enabled this one out of all created forms to apply productive force, instead of mere destructive force, to his food supply? By the power of organisation. By entering upon that new life, the social life, which raises us above all lower forms.

. . . A second field of proof of our organic relation, and one as patent as the first, is the complex specialisation of humanity. . . .

. . . Society consists of numbers of interrelated and highly specialised functions, the functionaries being individual human animals. Society develops them—they could never have been evolved in solitude. As easily conceive of independent eyes, rolling around and doing business by themselves as of independent teachers, carpenters, dentists. Society maintains them, as the body does the eye. . . .

We now come to a third, and in itself a fully sufficient proof of the organic nature of society. . . .

. . . That degree of brain development which we call "human" is only found in creatures socially related; it is not individual brain power, but social. The human brain, for health and usefulness, for its normal life, requires a number of human beings with whom to feel, think, and act. We can, it is true, physically isolate a human animal, and maintain his animal life; but his human life—*i.e.*, the social life; his "feelings" and "thoughts," the whole field of brain activity—is injured.

It is the compelling functional necessity of the brain to discharge into other brains, as well as to seek from them its vast and varied stimulus.

In more immediate and commonplace instances we see the same law. The difficulty of "keeping a secret," *i.e.,* of voluntarily retaining stimulus; the necessity of "relieving one's mind"—a perfectly fit phrase, as much so as its familiar physiological analogue; the value of the confessional; and, commonest of all, the vivid interest of each human brain in the affairs of the others; all these show the collective nature of that organ.

The most ordinary woman, gossiping with her neighbours, manifests this social necessity for contact and exchange, however low. "Mind your own business!" we cry, and cry in vain. No brain advanced enough to be called human can possibly find full use and exercise in contemplation of one person's business. It must concern itself in the business of others, their common business.

The human brain is a social organ. Human thought is a social function.

<hr>

READING 4-3

Excerpts from *The Man-Made World, or Our Androcentric Culture*

In the excerpts here, Gilman explains what she means by "androcentric culture" and discusses the consequences of androcentric culture for politics and economy.

EXCERPT FROM CHAPTER I, "AS TO HUMANNESS"

This selection is excerpted from pages 9–23.

<hr>

Source: Charlotte Perkins Gilman, *The Man-Made World, or Our Androcentric Culture* (New York: Charlton Company, 1911).

Let us begin, inoffensively, with sheep. The sheep is a beast with which we are all familiar, being much used in religious imagery; the common stock of painters; a staple article of diet; one of our main sources of clothing, and an everyday symbol of bashfulness and stupidity. . . .

All these things, and many that are similar, occur to us when we think of sheep. They are also ewes and rams. Yes, truly; but what of it? All that has been said was said of sheep, *genus ovis,* that bland beast, compound of mutton, wool, and foolishness, so widely known. In regard to mutton, to wool, to general character, we think only of their sheepishness, not at all of their ramishness or eweishness. . . .

Returning to our muttons, let us consider the ram, and wherein his character differs from the sheep. We find he has a more quarrelsome disposition. He paws the earth and makes a noise. He has a tendency to butt. So has a goat—Mr. Goat. So has Mr. Buffalo. . . .

The ewe, on the other hand, exhibits love and care for her little ones, gives them milk and tries to guard them. But so does a goat—Mrs. Goat. So does Mrs. Buffalo and the rest. This mother instinct is no peculiarity of *genus ovis,* but of any female creature. . . .

We may now generalize and clearly state: That is masculine which belongs to the male—to any or all males, irrespective of species. That is feminine which belongs to the female, to any or all females, irrespective of species. That is ovine, bovine, feline, canine, equinine or asinine which belongs to that species, irrespective of sex.

In our own species all this is changed. We have been so taken up with the phenomena of masculinity and femininity, that our common humanity has largely escaped notice. We know we are human, naturally, and are very proud of it; but we do not consider in what our humanness consists; nor how men and women may fall short of it, or overstep its bounds, in continual insistence upon their special differences. It is "manly" to do this; it is "womanly" to do that;

but what a human being should do under the circumstances is not thought of. . . .

. . . What then are true human characteristics? In what way is the human species distinguished from all other species?

Our human-ness is seen most clearly in three main lines: it is mechanical, psychical and social. Our power to make and use things is essentially human; we alone have extra-physical tools. . . .

That degree of brain development which gives us the human mind is a clear distinction of race. The savage who can count a hundred is more human [than] the savage who can count ten.

More prominent than either of these is the social nature of humanity. We are by no means the only group-animal; that ancient type of industry the ant, and even the well-worn bee, are social creatures. But insects of their kind are found living alone. Human beings never. Our human-ness begins with some low form of social relation and increases as that relation develops.

Human life of any sort is dependent upon what Kropotkin calls "mutual aid," and human progress keeps step absolutely with that interchange of specialized services which makes society organic. . . .

Humanity, thus considered, is not a thing made at once and unchangeable, but a stage of development; and is still, as Wells describes it, "in the making." Our human-ness is seen to lie not so much in what we are individually, as in our relations to one another; and even that individuality is but the result of our relations to one another. . . .

Taken separately and physically, we are animals, *genus homo;* taken socially and psychically, we are, in varying degree, human; and our real history lies in the development of this human-ness.

Our historic period is not very long. Real written history only goes back a few thousand years, beginning with the stone records of ancient Egypt. During this period we have had almost universally what is here called an Androcentric Culture. The history, such as it was, was made and written by men.

The mental, the mechanical, the social development was almost wholly theirs. We have, so far, lived and suffered and died in a man-made world. So general, so unbroken, has been this condition, that to mention it arouses no more remark than the statement of a natural law. We have taken it for granted, since the dawn of civilization, that "mankind" meant men-kind, and the world was theirs.

Women we have sharply delimited. Women were a sex; "the sex," according to chivalrous toast; they were set apart for special services peculiar to femininity. . . .

. . . The man was accepted as the race type without one dissentient voice; and the woman—a strange, diverse creature, quite disharmonious in the accepted scheme of things—was excused and explained only as a female.

She has needed volumes of such excuse and explanation; also, apparently, volumes of abuse and condemnation. In any library catalogue we may find books upon books about women. . . .

This is a book about men—as such. It differentiates between the human nature and the sex nature. It will not go so far as to allege man's masculine traits to be all that excuse or explain his existence; but it will point out what are masculine traits as distinct from human ones, and what has been the effect on our human life of the unbridled dominance of one sex.

We can see at once, glaringly, what would have been the result of giving all human affairs into female hands. Such an extraordinary and deplorable situation would have "feminized" the world. We should have all become effeminate.

See how in our use of language the case is clearly shown. The adjectives and derivatives based on woman's distinctions are alien and derogatory when applied to human affairs; "effeminate"—too female, connotes contempt, but has no masculine analogue; whereas "emasculate"—not enough male, is a term of reproach, and has no feminine analogue. . . .

. . . [A]ll our human scheme of things rests on the same tacit assumption; man being held the human type; woman a sort of accompaniment and subordinate assistant, merely essential to the making of people.

She has held always the place of a preposition in relation to man. She has been considered above him or below him, before him, behind him, beside him, a wholly relative existence—"Sydney's sister," "Pembroke's mother"—but never by any chance Sydney or Pembroke herself.

Acting on this assumption, all human standards have been based on male characteristics, and when we wish to praise the work of a woman, we say she has "a masculine mind.". . .

If a given idea has been held in the human mind for many generations, as almost all our common ideas have, it takes sincere and continued effort to remove it; and if it is one of the oldest we have in stock, one of the big, common, unquestioned world ideas, vast is the labor of those who seek to change it. . . .

The task here undertaken is of this sort. It seeks to show that what we have all this time called "human nature" and deprecated, was in great part only male nature, and good enough in its place; that what we have called "masculine" and admired as such, was in large part human, and should be applied to both sexes; that what we have called "feminine" and condemned, was also largely human and applicable to both. Our androcentric culture is so shown to have been, and still to be, a masculine culture in excess, and therefore undesirable. . . .

To the man, the whole world was his world; his because he was male; and the whole world of woman was the home; because she was female. She had her prescribed sphere, strictly limited to her feminine occupations and interests; he had all the rest of life; and not only so, but, having it, insisted on calling it male.

EXCERPT FROM CHAPTER XII, "POLITICS AND WARFARE"

This selection is excerpted from pages 220–225.

In politics the military ideal, the military processes, are so predominant as to almost monopolize "that part of ethics."

The science of government, the plain wholesome business of managing a community for its own good; doing its work, advancing its prosperity, improving its morals—this is frankly understood and accepted as A Fight from start to finish. Marshall your forces and try to get in, this is the political campaign. When you are in, fight to stay in, and to keep the other fellow out. Fight for your own hand, like an animal; fight for your master like any hired bravo; fight always for some desired "victory"—and "to the victors belong the spoils.". . .

Life, to the "male mind" (we have heard enough of the "female mind" to use the analogue!) *is* a fight, and his ancient military institutions and processes keep up the delusion. . . .

What do we find, here in America, in the field of "politics?"

We find first a party system which is the technical arrangement to carry on a fight. It is perfectly conceivable that a flourishing democratic government be carried on *without any parties at all;* public functionaries being elected on their merits, and each proposed measure judged on its merits; though this sounds impossible to the androcentric mind.

"There has never been a democracy without factions and parties!" is protested.

There has never been a democracy, so far,—only an androcracy. . . .

In other words men have made a human institution into an ultra-masculine performance; and, quite rightly, feel that women could not take part in politics *as men do.* That it is not necessary to fulfill this human custom in so masculine a way does not occur to them. . . .

Anyone will admit that a government wholly in the hands of women would be helped by the assistance of men; that a gynaecocracy must, of its own nature, be one-sided. Yet it is hard to win reluctant admission of the opposite fact; that an androcracy must of its own nature be one-sided also, and would be greatly improved by the participation of the other sex.

The inextricable confusion of politics and warfare is part of the stumbling block in the minds of men. As they see it, a nation is primarily a fighting organization; and its principal business is offensive and defensive warfare; therefore the ultimatum with which they oppose the demand for political equality—"women cannot fight, therefore they cannot vote."

EXCERPT FROM CHAPTER XIII, "INDUSTRY AND ECONOMICS"

This selection is excerpted from pages 227–243.

The Forest of Truth, on the subject of industry and economics, is difficult to see on account of the trees. . . .

Possibly the present treatment of the subject will appeal most to the minds of those who know least about it; such as the Average Woman. To her, industry is a daylong and lifelong duty, as well as a natural impulse; and economics means going without things. To such untrained but also unprejudiced minds it would be easy to show the main facts on these lines.

Let us dispose of Economics first, as having a solemn scientific appearance. . . .

Domestic Economics covers the whole care and government of the household; the maintenance of peace, health, order, and morality; the care and nourishment of children as far as done at home; the entire management of the home, as well as the spending and saving of money; are included in it. Saving is the least and poorest part of it; especially as in mere abstinence from needed things; most especially when this abstinence is mainly "Mother's." How best to spend! time, strength, love, care, labor, knowledge, and money—this should be the main study in Domestic Economics.

Social, or as they are used to call it, Political Economics, covers a larger, but not essentially different field. A family consists of people, and the Mother is their natural manager. Society consists of people—*the same people*—only more of them. All the people who are members of Society are also members of families—except some incubated orphans maybe. Social Economics covers the whole care and management of the people, the maintenance of peace and order and morality; the care of children, as far as done out of the home; as well as the spending and saving of the public money—all these are included in it.

This great business of Social Economics is at present little understood and most poorly managed, for this reason. . . .

In our present study the principal fact to be exhibited is the influence of a male culture upon Social Economics and Industry.

Industry, as a department of Social Economics, is little understood. Heretofore, we have viewed this field from several wholly erroneous positions. From the Hebrew (and wholly androcentric) religious teaching, we have regarded labor as a curse.

Nothing could be more absurdly false. Labor is not merely a means of supporting human life—it *is* human life. Imagine a race of beings living without labor! They must be the rudest savages.

Human work consists in specialized industry and exchange of its products. . . .

. . . Following that pitiful conception of labor as a curse, comes the very old and androcentric habit of despising it as belonging to women, and then to slaves.

As a matter of fact industry is in its origin feminine; that is, maternal. It is the overflowing fountain of mother-love and mother-power which first prompts the human race to labor; and for long ages men performed no productive industry at all; being merely hunters and fighters.

It is this lack of natural instinct for labor in the male of our species, together with the ideas and opinions based on that lack, and voiced by him in his many writings, religious and other, which have given to the world its false estimate of this great function, human work. That which is our very life, our greatest joy, our road to all advancement, we have scorned and oppressed; so that "working people," the "working classes," "having to work," etc. are to this day spoken of with contempt. Perhaps drones speak so among themselves of the "working bees!"

Normally, widening out from the mother's careful and generous service in the world, we should find labor freely given, with love and pride.

Abnormally, crushed under the burden of androcentric scorn and prejudice, we have labor grudgingly produced under pressure of necessity; labor of slaves under fear of the whip, or of wage-slaves, one step higher, under fear of want. . . . [T]he malign features of our industrial life are distinctly androcentric: the desire to get, of the hunter; interfering with the desire to give, of the mother; the desire to overcome an antagonist—originally masculine, interfering with the desire to serve and benefit—originally feminine.

Let the reader keep in mind that as human beings, men are able to over-live their masculine natures and do noble service to the world; also that as human beings they are to-day far more highly developed than woman, and doing far more for the world. The point here brought out is that *as males* their unchecked supremacy has resulted in an abnormal predominance of masculine impulses in our human processes; and that this predominance has been largely injurious.

As it happens, the distinctly feminine or maternal impulses are far more nearly in line with human progress than are those of the male; which makes her exclusion from human functions the more mischievous.

Our current teachings in the infant science of Political Economy are naively masculine. They assume as unquestionable that "the economic man" will never do anything unless he has to; will only do it to escape pain or attain pleasure; and will, inevitably, take all he can get, and do all he can to outwit, overcome, and if necessary destroy his antagonist.

Always the antagonist; to the male mind an antagonist is essential to progress, to all achievement. . . .

Therefore in industry and economics we find always and everywhere the antagonist; the necessity for somebody or something to be overcome—else why make an effort? If you have not the incentive of reward, or the incentive of combat, why work? "Competition is the life of trade."

Thus the Economic Man.

But how about the Economic Woman?

To the androcentric mind she does not exist—women are females, and that's all; their working abilities are limited to personal service.

That it would be possible to develop industry to far greater heights, and to find in social economics a simple and beneficial process for the promotion of human life and prosperity, under any other impulse than these two, Desire and Combat, is hard indeed to recognize—for the "male mind."

So absolutely interwoven are our existing concepts of maleness and humanness, so sure are we that men are people and women only females, that the claim of equal weight and dignity in human affairs of the feminine instincts and methods is scouted as absurd. . . .

Union, organization, complex interservice, are the essential processes of a growing society; in them, in the ever-increasing discharge of power along widening lines of action, is the joy and health of social life. But so far men combine in order to better combat; the mutual service held incidental to the common end of conquest and plunder.

CHAPTER 5

Anna Julia Cooper (1858–1964) and Ida B. Wells-Barnett (1862–1931)— The Foundations of Black Feminist Sociology

BIOGRAPHICAL BACKGROUND

Anna Julia Cooper was born on August 10, 1858,[1] in Raleigh, North Carolina, and died on February 27, 1964, at her home in Washington, D.C. at the age of 105. Ida B. Wells-Barnett was on born July 16, 1862, in Holly Springs, Mississippi, and died on March 25, 1931, in Chicago, Illinois. As African American women in the post–Civil War period, Cooper and Wells-Barnett created social theory under conditions of radical social change which they experienced biographically and understood historically and sociologically. While they were not intellectual intimates, that is, they did not "feed" each other ideas, they responded to the same critical experiences in African American history; and in the early 1890s, each published significant social analyses—Cooper, the book-length collection of essays *A Voice from the South* (1892), and Wells-Barnett, two major research pamphlets, *Southern Horrors* (1892) and *A Red Record* (1895). We place them together in this chapter for three main reasons: (1) save for Cooper's extraordinarily long life, they were almost exact contemporaries and shared a common regional heritage; (2) each brought a sociological consciousness to her response to African American experience, and (3) there are thematic commonalities in their social analyses which form part of the tradition of black feminist thought (see Collins, 1990; Giddings, 1984, and "General Social Theory" and "Cooper and Wells-Barnett and the Tradition of Feminist Sociology" later in this chapter).

To understand the biographical experiences that propelled them to social analysis, we have to look at the challenge posed to African Americans in the period between 1865 and 1900. The gulf separating Cooper and Wells-Barnett from their white contemporaries is illustrated by the fact that for Addams (Chapter 3), Gilman (Chapter 4), and the Chicago Women (Chapter 7), the Civil War was a date, not a life event; their lives can be told without a mention of Reconstruction. But for Cooper and Wells-Barnett, the Civil War and Reconstruction are major life-patterning experiences. Some of the white women we have studied chose to go into situations of hardship, but they knew they could always retreat to the safety of upper-middle-class material security. Cooper and Wells-Barnett could duck or fight, but they could not escape American racism. In their lifetimes, the African American was freed from slavery (1865); plunged back into it almost immediately in the Southern Black Codes (1865–1867); "liberated" anew with opportunities for education and political participation under the policies of radical Reconstruction (1867–1875); abandoned by the North with the withdrawal of federal troops from the South (1877); and left to struggle against disenfranchisement, mob violence and organized terrorism, and the steady encroachment of legal segregation in the South, and against pervasive racism and de facto segregation in the North.

But African Americans refused to be defeated, mobilizing both organizationally and intellectually for collective self-protection and self-advancement. They started businesses, founded newspapers and schools, enrolled in white schools, patented inventions, and became teachers, lawyers, dentists, doctors, ministers, journalists, skilled craftspersons, small entrepreneurs, and laborers in every walk of life they were permitted. They protested against attempts to exclude them from opportunities, organizing at the local level into teachers' groups, settlement houses, and women's and men's clubs, and at the national level into the National Association of Colored Women's Clubs (which had its own paper, *Woman's Era*), the National Association of Colored Men, the Colored National League, the National Afro-American Council, the American Negro Academy, the Invincible Sons and Daughters of Commerce (a secret society pledged to buy from black merchants and shopkeepers), the Negro Business League—and by 1910, the National Association for the Advancement of Colored People. At every step, while they had some white support, they met with a much greater white opposition.

Intellectually, the 1890s were an open moment for African Americans; they were still inspired by the hope of the post-Emancipation period, and no one, black or white, could foresee with certainty how quickly and rigidly the United States would become a segregated society. In this context of opportunity and oppression, African Americans created a rich discourse of social and political analysis in which women were active participants. Henry Louis Gates suggests that "literary historians could well call [the period 1890–1910] the 'Black Woman's Era,'" so extraordinary was the productivity of black women in fiction (Gates, 1988:xvi)—a productivity paralleled in essays of literary criticism and social analysis. It was within this discourse that Cooper and Wells-Barnett created their sociology.

In the two sections that follow, we trace how Wells-Barnett's and Cooper's personal biographies interface with this history, focusing especially on the events that turned them toward social analysis.

Ida B. Wells-Barnett

The best introduction to Wells-Barnett's life is her autobiography, *Crusade for Justice* (1970), which although unfinished at her death, has been admirably edited by her

Ida B. Wells-Barnett, age about 25

daughter, Alfreda M. Duster. Useful overview biographical essays are Thomas Holt's "The Lonely Warrior: Ida B. Wells-Barnett and the Struggle for Black Leadership" (1982) and Trudier Harris's introduction to the Schomburg Library edition of Wells-Barnett's selected works (1991). Emilie Townes studies the religious and philosophic underpinnings of Wells-Barnett's activism in *Womanist Justice, Womanist Hope* (1993). Paula Giddings is working on a major biography.

Wells-Barnett was born to slave parents who after the Civil War used their new-won freedom for themselves and their children. Her mother, Elizabeth Warrenton Wells, enrolled to learn to read her Bible at what is now Rust College, an institution started by white Northerners for the education of freedmen. Her father, Jim Wells, continued to work as a skilled carpenter for the white builder to whom his slave master had apprenticed him; her mother cooked for the builder, and the family lived on his property. In her autobiography, Wells-Barnett credits her parents with giving her the interest in politics, the clear sense of justice, and the confidence for independent thought which are hallmarks of her sociology. She remembers proudly that when the white builder tried to dictate her father's vote—a common practice of coercion by white employers toward black employees—Jim Wells resisted, promptly moving his family off the builder's property, buying his own tools, and opening his own carpentry shop. Wells-Barnett attended school at Rust College until 1876, when a yellow fever epidemic killed her parents and left her, the oldest of five children, determined to keep the family together.

She cut short her formal education and became a teacher, responding to the desperate need for anyone with literacy to teach in the schools that were being formed throughout the South. A quick study, she found herself in demand as a teacher and worked to qualify to teach in Memphis, where salaries were higher than in the rural districts. In Memphis, Wells-Barnett joined a circle of other black schoolteachers who shared writing and discussion on Friday evenings, producing a newspaper covering the week's events and gossip. Wells-Barnett became its editor and was encouraged by the popularity of her work to submit columns, under the pen name Iola, to black Baptist papers. Her career as a journalist starts in these efforts, and it is as a journalist that she comes to social analysis.

Her first major personal act of resistance to discrimination occurred in this period, beginning on May 4, 1884, when, traveling back to Memphis and sitting as usual in what was called the "ladies car," she was ordered by the conductor to move to the "smoker." This order, though Wells-Barnett did not realize it at the time, was one consequence of the U.S. Supreme Court ruling in 1883 that the Congressional Civil Rights Act of 1875 was unconstitutional. This decision allowed Southern states to begin the practice of racial segregation—of which segregated railway cars were a part. Smoker cars were partitioned, and black men and women were put in one half, which Wells-Barnett describes as "filthy [and] stifling" (1892/1969:13). On that day in 1884, Wells-Barnett resisted strenuously, and on her return to Memphis began a complicated legal proceeding against the Chesapeake and Ohio railroad. She made headlines when she won her case in the circuit court—"DARKY DAMSEL GETS DAMAGES" (Wells-Barnett, 1970:19). She lost the case on appeal to the Tennessee Supreme Court and had to pay court costs of some $200, having resisted on principle the railroad lawyer's attempt to get her to settle out of court. The incident became famous in the African American community, and Cooper makes indirect reference to it.

But the event that led Wells-Barnett to her "crusade for justice" was the lynching of three black men in Memphis in 1892. By 1889, Wells-Barnett had embarked full-fledged on her career as a journalist and, following a practice she held to wherever possible, was part owner of the paper for which she wrote, *The Free Speech and Headlight of Memphis.* The lynching of 1892 took the lives of three men—Thomas Moss, Calvin McDowell, and Henry Stuart—who were making a success of an enterprise called the People's Grocery Company. One of them, Moss, was a close friend of Wells-Barnett, someone she identified as "believ[ing], with me, that we should defend the cause of right and fight wrong where we saw it" (1970:47–48). Their success led them to a quarrel with a white grocer across the street and to a confrontation in the dark in which three white men were injured. Wells-Barnett reports in her first anti-lynching pamphlet, *Southern Horrors,* "There was no law on the statute books which would execute an Afro-American for wounding a white man, but the 'unwritten law' did. Three of these men, the president, the manager and clerk of the grocery—'the leaders of the conspiracy' [according to white papers]—were secretly taken from jail and lynched in a shockingly brutal manner" (1892/1969:19).

Witnessing the way the white newspapers distorted the event, Wells-Barnett began a campaign against lynching through the pages of the *Free Speech.* Part of this campaign urged blacks to follow Moss's last words—"'tell my people to go West—there is no justice for them here'"—and Wells-Barnett reported a heavy black exodus from the city, with a resulting financial loss to white business (1970:53–54). But the lynchings did not stop in the South, and in the May 21, 1892 *Free Speech,* Wells-Barnett wrote the editorial that was to banish her from Memphis and to begin the analysis of the complex ties among gender, race, class, and geopolitical location that forms the theoretical core of her sociology. She directly confronted what had become the South's new excuse for lynching—the allegations that black men were raping white women: "Eight Negroes lynched since the last issue of the 'Free Speech' . . . and five on the same old racket—the new alarm about raping white women. . . . Nobody in this section of the country believes the old thread bare lie that Negro men rape white women" (Wells-Barnett, 1892/1969:4). She suggested that all the publicity may have pointed to an alternate reality—that white women were attracted to black men. White citizens of Memphis burned the *Free Speech* offices to the ground. Fortunately, Wells-Barnett was already out of town, keeping a prearranged engagement to report on a conference of the African Methodist Episcopal

Church in Philadelphia. Unable to return to Memphis, she accepted an offer from black publisher Thomas Fortune to write for his paper the *New York Age,* and her first article was a statement of what had happened in Memphis.

Her *New York Age* articles led to other opportunities. She met Frederick Douglass, the leading spokesperson in the African American community. Black women in New York and Brooklyn organized a testimonial in her honor at which she spoke to a large audience for the first time about what she knew about lynchings. The testimonial gave Wells-Barnett the money to publish her first pamphlet on lynching, *Southern Horrors,*[2] and began her public speaking career. Speaking in Philadelphia, she met Catherine Impey, a British reformer who offered to help Wells-Barnett take her anti-lynching campaign to Britain. Wells-Barnett launched an international anti-lynching campaign with two sets of lectures in Britain, in April 1893 and in March–June 1894. These British lectures got her enormous attention in the US white press—attention that was often abusive but which kept the issue of lynching before both the US and British publics.

Before her departure for her first British tour, Wells-Barnett was active in another struggle to shape public opinion, this time about the blatantly discriminatory exclusion of African American achievements from the Columbian World Exposition hosted in Chicago in 1892, a media event of proportions rivaling those of today's Olympic Games. This exclusion was particularly galling to African Americans because in the brief quarter century since Emancipation they had made enormous gains, having taken advantage of every opportunity remotely given or begrudged them. To expose this gross discrimination to both American and foreign visitors to the Exposition, Wells-Barnett and others decided to put out a pamphlet, *The Reason Why the Colored American Is Not in the World's Columbian Exposition* (1893).[3] They planned to have it printed in English, French, and German, but a shortage of funds let them do only the introduction in all three languages. Along with her own contribution on lynching, the pamphlet included papers by Frederick Douglass, J. Garland Penn of the Negro Press Association, and F. L. Barnett, the Chicago lawyer whom Wells would marry in 1895. Ten thousand copies were distributed to Fair visitors. Wells-Barnett's social analyses reflect an understanding of the power that a growing mass media would have in shaping public opinion and of the relation between that opinion and the enforcement or nonenforcement of the law. In 1895, she produced her second major analysis of lynching, *A Red Record,* in which she used white newspapers' statistics on and coverage of lynchings, saying, "Out of their own mouths shall the murderers be condemned" (1895:15).

Many feared that after her marriage Wells-Barnett would cease to be an effective social activist—she herself speaks of the problems of "a divided duty." But her activism continued unabated to the end of her life. She was so effective a speaker that African American women's clubs begged her to tour Illinois, promising her room, board, and childcare for her firstborn: "I have often referred to it in my meeting with the pioneer suffragists, as I honestly believe that I am the only woman in the United States who ever traveled throughout the country with a nursing baby to make political speeches" (1970:244). She was part of black protest delegations that called on Presidents McKinley and Wilson. She helped organize numerous black women's clubs; she tried to build bridges to white women's groups, with varying success; she started her own small but highly effective settlement, the Negro Fellowship League; she worked constantly to create a unified organization for

African Americans, beginning with the Afro-American League and ultimately contributing to the founding of the NAACP. And she continued to fight injustice wherever she found it—in single instances of young black men harassed by white police, organized race riots by whites, attempts by the *Chicago Tribune* to lobby for segregated schools, the continued practice of lynching, and what she and her husband (along with many others) saw as the attempts of Booker T. Washington to control black political power in the United States. Thomas Holt (1982) suggests that this last battle cost both Barnetts dearly, for Washington was an implacable enemy.

Wells-Barnett is described by Holt as "a lonely warrior" and by Townes, in a well-crafted distinction, as "not unusual in her inability to work in coalitions" (1994:173). This inability Wells-Barnett herself perceived, reporting her husband's remark "that I had to learn to take my friends as I found them, making allowances for their shortcomings, and still hold on to friendships" (1970:285). But this inability was a result of her greatest strength: an absolute fearlessness when standing for what she knew was right. She could be hurt and she could feel the pain of insult, but she could not be made to flinch in speaking her mind. She kept the determination that came to her after the lynching of Thomas Moss: "I felt that one had better die fighting against injustice than to die like a dog or a rat in a trap. I had already determined to sell my life as dearly as possible if attacked. I felt if I could take one lyncher with me, this would even up the score a little bit" (1970:62).

Anna Julia Cooper

Although Cooper's life still awaits a major biography, she has received several feminist treatments. Chief among these are Leona C. Gabel's short but well-reasoned *From Slavery to the Sorbonne and Beyond: The Life and Writing of Anna Julia Cooper* (1982); Louise Daniel Hutchinson's panoramic *Anna J. Cooper: A Voice from the South* (1981); Mary Helen Washington's able introduction to the Schomburg Library edition of *A Voice from the South* (1988), and Karen Baker-Fletcher's stimulating study of Cooper's theology and philosophy, *A Singing Something: Womanist Reflections on Anna Julia Cooper* (1994). Many of Cooper's privately printed manuscripts will be available with the publication of *The Voice of Anna Julia Cooper,* edited by Charles Lemert and Esme Bahn (1998).

In Cooper's life, unlike that of Wells-Barnett, the biographer does not find a crystallizing moment that explains her turn to social theory. Instead, Cooper's life is the story of an extraordinary intellect, with a genuine love for learning and for aesthetic experience, reflecting on a world that put up barriers of race, gender, and class to her pursuit of that love. In the years leading to *A Voice from the South,* Cooper showed remarkable ability and daring in her determination to find a life she could at first build only in imagination out of the slenderest of fragments.

Cooper was born Anna Julia Hayworth to Hannah Stanley, a slave of Fabius Hayworth, Cooper's probable father. Cooper's handwritten memories of her early years show a love of learning and an appreciation of the strengths of her mother (as well as a contempt for her father): "My mother was a slave & the finest woman I have ever known. Tho untutored she could read her Bible & write a little. It is one of my happiest childhood memories explaining for her the subtle differences between q's and g's or between b's and l's. Presumably my father was her master, if so I owe him not a sou. She was always too modest . . . ever to mention him" (reproduced in Hutchinson, 1981:4). Although her mother and brothers were only marginally literate, Cooper by age seven seems to have learned to read and write, despite living in the midst of a civil war and in a society that prohibited teaching slaves to read.

However acquired, her literacy gave Cooper her first opportunity to reach for a world beyond her home. When she was about eight, she became one of the few girls admitted to the newly founded Episcopal freedmen's school, St. Augustine Normal School and Collegiate Institute, where she received a stipend for tutoring other students, often adult men, in reading and writing. At St. Augustine's, Cooper formed

Anna Julia Cooper, age 34

a lifelong attachment to the Episcopal faith. An extraordinarily able student, she describes herself as being "like Oliver Twist," devouring everything set before her and begging for more to study (1892:76). In this quest, she had her first personal encounters with gender discrimination in education; the school gave aid to male students and left her and the other girls, no matter how able, to struggle to earn their way; she had to plead with the school president to be allowed to take the first class in Greek. Her love of learning and her devotion to Episcopalianism came together in the Greek class, which was taught by George A. C. Cooper, a native of the British West Indies, who became the second black ordained in the Episcopal Church in North Carolina, and whom she married in 1877. After his death in 1879, she never remarried; and years later she showed her continuing allegiance to a host of values and experiences—education, her faith, the marriage to Cooper, and the greatness of the African American people—in the donation to the school chapel of a stained-glass window in her husband's memory, telling the story of Simon of Cyrene, the black man whom legend has carrying the Cross part of the way on Jesus' march to crucifixion.

After her husband's death, Cooper made the daring decision to try to leave St. Augustine's, where she had been teaching, and go North for more education. With no role models, proceeding on what she knew by reputation and rumor, she wrote to Oberlin College in Ohio, known as a pioneering institution in the admission of women and African American students. Cooper sought admission to Oberlin's rigorous bachelor's curriculum, not its teaching certificate program. Only one black woman, Mary Jane Patterson in the class of 1862, had completed the bachelor's program before Cooper's admission. Writing directly to the president of Oberlin, Cooper introduced herself as what we would today term a non-traditional student—"the widow of an Episcopal clergyman (Colored)"—and stressed the tightness of her economic situation, the seriousness with which she took her education, and the thoroughness of her preparation (listing an impressive transcript of courses in Latin, Greek, and mathematics) (Hutchinson, 1981:32). She concluded by asking for free tuition.

Cooper entered Oberlin in the autumn of 1881, the same year as two other African American women, Mary Church (Terrell) and Ida Gibbs, both younger and from affluent families. At Oberlin, she lived with the large, comfortably situated Churchill family—Professor Charles H. Churchill, his wife, Henrietta Vance Churchill, their four children, and "Granma Vance" and she remained close friends with the Churchills all her life. The Churchill household made real the culturally rich life Cooper had imagined. Hutchinson suggests, "The Churchills had shown her another lifestyle, and the fierce determination of her mother and the cultured environment of the Churchills were to become role models that she would [always] remember" (1981:37).

Cooper graduated from Oberlin in 1884 and for the next three years experimented with making a life—first teaching mathematics and modern languages at Wilberforce University, a black school in Xenia, Ohio, and then, in 1885, in response to her mother's concerns, returning to Raleigh, as a teacher at St. Augustine's. She helped her mother and her brother's widow and six children and worked as a member of the North Carolina Teachers' Association (a black group). In 1886, she traveled to Washington, D.C., to address a meeting of the African American Episcopal clergy on the topic "Womanhood: A Vital Element in the Regeneration and Progress of a Race"; the address became a chapter in *A Voice from the South*.

By 1887 Cooper was seeking a life wider than Raleigh afforded. Awarded an MA in mathematics from Oberlin, she received through her Oberlin connections an offer to teach mathematics and science in the only black high school in Washington, D.C. The Washington Colored High School (known locally as "the 'M' Street School") admitted students by qualifying exam, drew from a mix of economic classes, and offered both industrial training and liberal arts courses. By 1891, Cooper was teaching the final year of Latin as well as the math and science courses.

In Washington, Cooper achieved the culturally rich life she wanted. She formed her most meaningful personal relationship, a friendship with the Reverend Francis J. Grimké and his sophisticated and artistic wife, Charlotte Forten Grimké. Until Charlotte Grimké's death in 1914, they maintained, with selected friends, a weekend pattern in which on Fridays they met at the Grimkés' and on Sundays at Cooper's for discussion, study, and music. In those early years in Washington, Cooper began to be in demand as a public speaker, and she used her talks to build a writing portfolio that in 1892 she would turn into *A Voice from the South*. We learn from that book, that in the years preceding its publication, Cooper developed a systematic social analysis to explain events in her personal life, the African American community, the women's movement, American literature and popular culture, and US society. She spoke at Howard University on the national importance of higher education for women; went to an exchange meeting with black teachers in Toronto, which afforded her an opportunity for cross-cultural comparison of race relations; listened to white suffragist Anna Shaw's talk, "Woman versus Indian," at the National Woman's Council in Washington, D.C., and took issue with its basic premise; responded immediately to the publication of the white racist poem "A Voodoo Prophecy," which had angered the African American community; followed critically the reports of the 1890 census; and offered one of the first reviews of William Dean Howells's novel of race relations, *An Imperative Duty* (1892). These events formed the empirical foundation for her social theory.

In 1892 Cooper published her great work of social analysis, *A Voice from the South,* claiming for the black woman a distinctive angle of vision on the social world: "from her peculiar coigne of vantage as a quiet observer . . . the colored woman . . . is watching . . . to weigh and judge and advise" (1892:138) (see "General Social Theory"). The book received superlative reviews from black and white publications alike, many of which are summarized in Monroe Majors's *Noted Negro Women: Their Triumphs and Activities* (1893); the Boston *Transcript,* the Chicago *Inter-Ocean,* the Detroit *Plaindealer,* the *Philadelphia Public Ledger,* the *Kingsley Times* (Iowa), and *Public Opinion* all gave it laudatory reviews. The *New York Independent* suggests the flavor of the book's general reception: "'It is an open secret that the author of this volume is Mrs. A. J. Cooper. She puts a voice in her book . . . which it is impossible to shake off. She writes with a strong but controlled passion, on a basis of strong facts'" (Majors, 1893:284–285).

The decade from 1892 to 1902 was one of heady achievement for Cooper. In 1893, she and two other African American women, Fannie Barrier Williams, a Chicago civic leader, and Fannie Jackson Coppin, a respected authority on education, were invited to speak at a special meeting of the (white) Women's Congress held in Chicago to coincide with the Columbian Exposition. In 1894, the Colored Women's League of Washington, D.C., which she had helped organize, officially incorporated and began offering a host of services—homemaking classes, kindergarten training for teachers, aid for poor blacks who had immigrated from the rural South. In 1895, Cooper addressed the first National Conference of Colored Women in Boston. In 1896, she attended the first Annual Convention of the National Federation of Afro-American Women—an event made momentous by the presence of Harriet Tubman. Cooper was one of the few women to participate in the American Negro Academy. In 1900, she attended the first Pan-African Conference in London, delivering the speech on "The Negro Problem in America."

This productivity came to an end in 1902 when Cooper became principal of the M Street School. Her workload as principal and her commitment to service in the black community left less time for writing, and her administration was complicated by a highly political debate on black education. Many people, in the black and white communities, for a mix of reasons, supported the plan of Booker T. Washington of Tuskegee Institute which called for rigorous training in industrial arts as the best way to guarantee black people a place in US society; others were equally committed to W. E. B. DuBois's call for a liberal arts education to prepare "the talented tenth" as a core leadership for the race. Cooper tried to walk a middle ground in this debate, acknowledging the worth of industrial training and yet believing that black students who had a love of classical learning should be allowed that too—that the mind knew no color line. But despite her best efforts, she became embroiled in what was known as "the M Street School Controversy." This battle is still being dissected, but in broad outline we can trace its main elements: white racism, black dissension, and sexism. Cooper's own statement is a good summary:

> "During my principalship of M St. H.S. the colored prin.[cipal] was under the white Director of High Schools. At a meeting of Principals she [Cooper is referring to herself] was told when the question of scholarships in colleges came up, that her graduates were not eligible to try for them. The Director at the same time recommended to Congress that a different curriculum be granted to the Colored High School, whose pupils he said were not capable of doing the regular work. Insubordination was charged and effectively pressed when the principal sent to Harvard, Yale, Brown and Oberlin students directly from the M St. classes who passed successfully their entrance exams . . . For which unpardonable 'sin' against racial supremacy said principal suffers to this day the punishment of the damned from both the white masters and the colored understrappers." (cited in Gabel, 1982:54)

Cooper's fitness as principal was questioned and she was slurred with typical sexist charges that she could not maintain discipline, that she was too sympathetic with poorly prepared students, and that she herself engaged in immoral behavior with her foster son (she had adopted John and Lula Love of North Carolina when their parents died in the 1890s). In 1906, the board canceled the contracts of all teachers, rehiring each teacher individually, and Cooper was not rehired. She spent the next four years teaching at Lincoln University in Jefferson City, Missouri—a period she regarded as exile. In 1910 a new superintendent invited her back to teach Latin at the M Street School.

Demoted but not broken, Cooper returned to Washington determined to vindicate herself by earning her doctorate, a project made difficult by the continuing politics of the District school system and by her own decision in 1915 to assume the guardianship of her deceased brother's five grandchildren. Prior to this adoption, she had studied intermittently during summers in Paris—she was a gifted linguist—and had moved towards a doctorate at Columbia with the preparation of an edition of a French medieval epic. But her guardianship made meeting the residency requirements at Columbia impossible. Not until 1922, when the children were older, did she try again for the doctorate—this time at the Sorbonne. Cooper, in her mid-sixties transferred her credits from Columbia and wrote her dissertation, *Slavery and the French Revolutionists, 1788–1805,* in French (1925/1988), receiving her doctorate in 1925.

Cooper lived another active forty years. After her retirement from the D.C. school system, she took the leadership of an adult education program known as Frelinghuysen University designed for working black men and women. Cooper ran the university out of her home until 1940, when she retired again. In 1951, at the age of 93, she published privately a two-volume work, *Personal Recollections of the Grimké Family and the Life and Writings of Charlotte Forten Grimké.*

Evaluating Cooper's life, Baker-Fletcher suggests that Cooper perhaps "failed to question the class ideology she grew into as she moved up the socio-economic ladder" (1994:173). To a degree this may be true, but in Cooper's defense it must be noted that she may have found in the world of ideas a place where she was absolutely at home. In her educational philosophy and her social service, Cooper seems to have balanced respect for the manual arts with her genuine love of the life of the mind. Cooper's social theory is, in part, a response to a world which on the basis of race, class, and gender, denies people that "sense of freedom in mind . . . necessary to the . . . inspiring pursuit of the beautiful. A bird cannot warble out his fullest and most joyous notes while the wires of his cage are pricking and cramping him at every heart beat" (1892:223).

GENERAL SOCIAL THEORY

Assumptions

Cooper's and Wells-Barnett's ideas were shaped by the discourse within the African American community (Collins, 1990; Giddings, 1984) that was working to define itself under the new conditions seemingly made possible by emancipation and to relate to white discourse, much of it racist. This community of intellectuals and activists, many of them women, included free blacks active in abolitionist activities before the Civil War, older blacks who had lived under slavery for a significant part of their lives, and members of the generation to which Cooper and Wells-Barnett belonged, the first generation to grow up after Emancipation.[4]

This community took as one assumption that white domination and its accompanying doctrine of white supremacy had to be confronted. American social darwinists were giving intellectual legitimacy to white, which at this time meant Anglo-Saxon, imperialism abroad and supremacy at home, producing dogma such as that in James K. Hosmer's *Short History of Anglo-Saxon Freedom:* "'Though Anglo-Saxon freedom in a more or less partial form has been . . . imitated. . . . By that race alone it has been preserved amidst a thousand perils; to that race alone is it thoroughly congenial'" (in Hofstadter, 1955:174). This same racism came to infect and corrupt the white women's movement for suffrage, beginning perhaps with the fierce debates surrounding the Fifteenth Amendment, which gave black men the right to vote while still denying that right to all women. O'Neill summarizes the racism in the white women's movement as follows:

> By the 1890's the growth of racist feelings through the country and the emergence of a Southern suffrage movement combined to make, as Aileen Kraditor puts it, a "pact between woman suffrage and white supremacy" both natural and expedient. It was sealed at the NAWSA convention in New Orleans in 1903. On that occasion Anna Howard Shaw [argued that white men] "have put the vote into the hands of your black men, thus making them the political superiors of your white women. Never before in the history of the world have men made former slaves political superiors of their former mistresses. . . ." When Dr. Shaw, who grew up in Michigan, took so crude a line, no one would expect Southern women to be less candid. (1971:70)

The situation was confused by the fact that women like Shaw and Susan B. Anthony often acted in personally liberal ways—ways reported by both Cooper and Wells-Barnett. Caraway, in *Segregated Sisterhood,* points out that this double standard in behavior "should serve as a warning about the limitation of personal commitments to decency; those private goals yield easily to other perceived interests" (1991:154).

Amidst this growing racism, African American women spoke in a double and sometimes triple context—as blacks and as women to white Americans, as women to black men, and as individuals of particular class backgrounds to and for themselves. They defined themselves to white America as American black citizens and as Christians, emphasizing the ties that they shared with white Americans and the failure of white Americans to keep their own principles. In 1891, Frances Ellen Watkins Harper, lecturer, poet, and novelist, in an address to the National Council of Women of the United States, in Philadelphia, presented the African American case:

> I deem it a privilege to present the negro, not as a mere dependent asking for Northern sympathy or Southern compassion, but as a member of the body politic who has a claim upon the nation for justice, simple justice, which is the right of every race, upon the government for protection, which is the rightful claim of every citizen, and upon our common Christianity for the best influences which can be exerted for peace on earth and good-will to men. . . .
>
> A government which can protect and defend its citizens from wrong and outrage and does not is vicious. A government which would do it and cannot is weak; and where human life is insecure through either weakness or viciousness in the administration of law, there must be a lack of justice. (1891/1976:247–248)

Further, black women had to address the ever present, rarely publicly spoken charge of sexual immorality. Addressing the Women's Congress in Chicago in the year of the Columbian Exposition, on the same speaker's platform as Cooper, Chicago civic leader Fannie Barrier Williams detailed the extraordinary accomplishments of African American women, then laid the blame for sexual immorality on the white institution of chattel slavery and white men, and alluded subtly to the continuing sexual exploitation of black women by white men by praising the "chivalric sentiment" of African American men in protecting the women of their race—"I do not wish to disturb the serenity of this conference by suggesting why this protection is needed or the kind of men against whom it is needed" (1893/1976:274–275).

In situations which pitted the identity of race against the identity of gender, black women tended to agree with Harper's analysis: "that when it was a question of race she let the lesser question of sex go. But the white women all go for sex, letting race occupy a minor position" (Lerner, 1972:245). Giddings notes, however, that while there was a strong and vocal movement of white anti-suffragists, "one would be hard pressed to find any Black woman who did not advocate getting the vote" as a way to stop sexual exploitation, increase education, and improve working conditions (1984:120).

Mary Church Terrell voiced the concerns of black women among themselves about class differences and about the duties of those empowered through class position toward those disempowered. Terrell, a leading figure in the black women's club movement, argued that "'Self-preservation demands that [Black women] go among the lowly . . . to whom they are bound by ties of race and sex . . . to reclaim them'" (cited in Giddings, 1984:97). Black women recognized that class differences among them were largely unperceived in a white world in which race was the first identifier imposed on them and gender the second. Class and individual attainment could go all but unnoticed and never count enough to overmaster the other two identities.

Finally, as part of their assumptions, Cooper and Wells-Barnett were engaged in dialogues about progress and history. Like other African Americans, they saw themselves as lucky to be alive at this moment of dawning opportunities. In their treatment of history,

Cooper and Wells-Barnett assume that their reader will know U.S. history and current events—most especially slavery and Reconstruction—and at the same time that that reader may have a white sense of that history and those events. Their writings show that an alternative interpretation of Reconstruction was already in place in the black community, as suggested in Cooper's description of it as the period of "alleged corruption of Negro supremacy, more properly termed the period of white sullenness and desertion of duty" (1892:192).

Major Themes

Cooper and Wells-Barnett construct a sociological analysis of society as a dynamic of power and difference, a theory as complete and critical as any achieved in American sociology—a radical, non-Marxian conflict theory. Their focus is on a pathological interaction between difference and power in U.S. society, a condition they variously label as "repression," "domination," "suppression," "despotism," "subordination," "subjugation," "tyranny," "our American conflict." Looking at society through the dual lenses of race and gender, they come also to class, and help to create a black feminist sociology. This section presents their sociology in terms of four themes: their sense of the project of social analysis and of a method appropriate to that project, their model of the social world, their theory of domination, and their alternative to domination.

1. Cooper and Wells-Barnett create sociology from the standpoint of the oppressed; for them, the project of social analysis is justice and the method appropriate to the project is cross-examination. Cooper and Wells-Barnett undertook social analysis as part of their morally propelled resistance to oppression. Standing in the situation of the oppressed, they use social analysis to *witness* to what is happening, as a means of empowering the African American community, exposing the oppressors, and appealing to the conscience of potentially supportive publics. Wells-Barnett (1892/1969) begins her analysis of lynching with this claim: "Somebody must show that the African-American race is more sinned against than sinning, and it seems to have fallen upon me to do so. . . . If this work can . . . arouse the conscience of the American people to a demand for justice . . . I shall feel I have done my race a service" (1892/1969:Preface). Cooper offers essentially the same justification for her theoretical project, which she defines as part "of our American Conflict" over race, saying that she speaks "because I believe the American people to be conscientiously committed to a fair trial and ungarbled evidence, and because I feel it essential to a perfect understanding and an equitable verdict that truth from *each* standpoint be presented at the bar" (1892:II).*

Cooper explicitly contrasts this orientation to sociology with that of scientific objectivity, a contrast she typifies as that between "faith" and "skepticism" (and among her representatives of the skeptical, or "unimpassioned," scientist are Auguste Comte and Herbert Spencer). Faith is essential for the individual, race, or nation to meet "the great,

---

*An asterisk following a citation in the text means that the passage quoted is given in fuller context in the readings at the end of the chapter.

the fundamental need . . . for heroism, devotion, sacrifice"—qualities incompatible with "a primarily skeptical spirit." She defines faith as *"treating the truth as true"* (1892:297). People, including the social analyst, will not always agree on truth; but people as moral agents must openly declare and publicly practice what they believe to be true. Wells-Barnett shares Cooper's sense that moral agency begins in a willingness to live what you profess to believe.

In bringing a moral standard to bear in their analysis of society, Cooper and Wells-Barnett use two principles: (1) whether the actors in the situation are true to their professed principles and, (2) whether the actors in the situation conform to the analyst's own principles of just behavior. For Cooper the fundamental source of truth is in religion. Applying that standard to American society in her time, and especially to the African American's situation, she analyzes that situation as the direct result of the Anglo-Saxon's confusion of faith: "[T]he problematical position at present occupied by descendants of Africans in the American social polity . . . grow[s] . . . out of the continued indecision in the mind of the more powerful descendants of the Saxons as to whether it is expedient to apply the maxims of their religion to their civil and political relationships" (1892:185). Wells-Barnett's moral stance is in the principles of American democracy. Her critique of the United States is for its failure to abide by its laws. In her analysis, she calls to account those people who stand as hypocrites—by practicing action contrary to their enacted laws, by lying about the connection between their actions and their laws, or by failing to speak out against practices they absolutely know to be in contradiction of those laws.

Cooper and Wells-Barnett must invent a strategy for doing research from the position of the subordinate with some cultural capital but without the resources that dominants command to produce and disseminate knowledge for the whole society. They choose to use the imagery of the courtroom in framing their method of social analysis. They "cross-examine": they establish their own standpoint; from that standpoint on the margin of power, they challenge dominants' claims about the facts, using the dominants' own words as evidence; they give their own eyewitness accounts and "subpoena" into the record the eyewitness accounts of other subordinates. They, thus, create a critical and forensic empiricism.

Speaking as witnesses, Cooper and Wells-Barnett present data from their direct observations of situations and events, for example, of Jim Crow laws and mores in public transportation, of their travels in other countries where race was not an instrument of oppressive practice, of conditions in Memphis before and after the lynching of Thomas Moss (Wells-Barnett), of barriers to the education of African American women (Cooper). Both try to collect data themselves. Cooper sends out a questionnaire to colleges admitting women, asking about their record in the education of black women (1892:73–74) and heads the Committee to Study the Georgia Convict Lease System set up by the National Association of Colored Women's Clubs (Hutchinson, 1981:96). Wells-Barnett initiates her own investigation by correspondence following the New Orleans race riots of 1900 (1900/1991:311–314). In her autobiography covering her years in Chicago, she recounts her personal attempts to work as a participant observer in situations in which riots or lynchings were imminent or abating.

But by and large, power differentials in the society mean that Cooper and Wells-Barnett must use the "defendant," that is, the white oppressor, as their chief source of data, interpreting the texts produced by dominants who control the production of knowledge. Wells-Barnett announces her intention in *A Red Record* (1895) to use white newspaper accounts of lynchings as her main data base:

> The purpose of the pages which follow shall be to give the record which has been made, not by colored men, but that which is the result of the compilations made by white men, of reports sent over the civilized world by white men in the South. Out of their own mouths shall the murderers be condemned. . . . [T]he incidents hereinafter reported have been confined to those vouched for by the [Chicago] Tribune. (1895:15)*

Cooper and Wells-Barnett show how the dominant sees the situation, and they assess that viewpoint by the standards they have established as a moral basis for critique: (1) how does the situation as described fit the principles the dominant professes; (2) how do the principles professed within the particular situation fit the more general principles of the rule of law, the ethics of the Judeo-Christian tradition, and the logic of human reason.

One strategy is simply to let the dominants' own texts convict them. Cooper, for example, presents French historian Hippolyte Taine's description of Anglo-Saxon hordes of the fifth century—"'Huge white bodies, cool-blooded, with fierce blue eyes, reddish flaxen hair. . . . Brutal drunken pirates and robbers, they . . . , landed anywhere, killed everything'" (1892:157)—to establish her depiction of an Anglo-Saxon heritage of unbridled aggression. Wells-Barnett shows the same traits among white Americans of her own day by presenting white press accounts of black lynchings; for instance, she reproduces the New York *Sun's* account of the torture killing of a mentally disabled Negro named Henry Smith, accused of murdering and violating a four-year-old white girl—a charge never proved:

> "Words to describe the awful torture inflicted upon Smith cannot be found. . . . The child's father, her brother, and two uncles . . . gathered about the Negro as he lay fastened to the torture platform and thrust hot irons into his quivering flesh. . . . Every groan from the fiend, every contortion of his body was cheered by the thickly packed crowd of 10,000 persons. . . . After burning the feet and legs, the hot irons—plenty of fresh ones being at hand—were rolled up and down Smith's stomach, back, and arms. Then the eyes were burned out and irons were thrust down his throat." (1895:27)*

Wells-Barnett reprints the account in full in *A Red Record.*

A second strategy is to critique and rework the data produced by those in power. Using lynching reports as produced in the *Chicago Tribune,* Wells-Barnett develops statistics showing the exact nature of the alleged crime of the victim, the state where the lynching occurred, the sex and age of the victim, and the race. She notes anomalies in context like the time of the lynching in one report: "In Brooks County, GA., Dec. 23rd [1894], while this Christian country was preparing for Christmas celebration, seven Negroes were lynched in twenty-four hours because they refused, or were unable to tell the whereabouts of a colored man named Pike, who killed a white man" (1895:91). And she examines various conclusions that can be drawn from the data: most importantly, that despite the repeated excuse that the black man had raped a white woman, only one-third of the black victims of lynching were so charged. Cooper also critiques white data. She points out the covert racism of census data:

> One would like to be able to give reliable statistics of the agricultural and mechanical products of the colored laborer, but so far I have not been able to obtain them. . . . Our efficient and capable census enumerators never draw the color line on labor products. You have no trouble in turning to the page that shows exactly what percentage of colored people are illiterate, or just how many have been condemned by the courts; no use taking the trouble to specify whether it was for the larceny of a ginger cake, or for robbing a bank of a cool half million and skipping off to Canada: it's all crime of course, and crime statistics and illiteracy statistics must be accurately detailed—and colored. (1892:268–269)

Analyzing the depiction of the African American in white American literature, Cooper first notes the general absence of such depiction, and then criticizes the portraits whites do give as often created in ignorance of their subject or even out of a desire to do harm. As a particularly egregious example of ignorance, she takes William Dean Howells's novel *An Imperative Duty* (1892), which treats shallowly of miscegenation. Howells was an American Realist, a school that espoused giving a truthful portrait of life, yet his picture of black experience is inaccurate and hastily drawn. Howells, in Cooper's view, fails by his own standard: "Mr. Howells fails . . . because he gives only a half truth, and that a partisan half truth. One feels that he had no business to attempt a subject of which he knew so little, or for which he cared so little. . . . [I]t is an insult to humanity and a sin against God to publish any such sweeping generalizations of a race on such meager and superficial information" (1892:203). Wells-Barnett, citing the work of Frederick Douglass, offers an extended critique of the various excuses Southern whites have used over history for their wholesale attacks on African Americans—fear of insurrection, the need to maintain a white man's government against the threat of black male enfranchisement, and rape. She places each excuse in its historic context and concludes: "If the Southern people in defense of their lawlessness, would tell the truth and admit that colored men and women are lynched for almost any offense, from murder to a misdemeanor, there would not now be the necessity for this [research]" (1895:11).*

2. Cooper and Wells-Barnett analyze any situation-at-hand in terms of the degree to which difference and power interact pathologically, as domination, or justly, as equilibrium. Cooper and Wells-Barnett present a model of social life in which the outcomes for individuals and for groups turn on the ways power is exercised and difference is organized—by race, class, gender, and geopolitical location. They extrapolate this model from and apply it to specific situations-at-hand. Many of the specific situations-at-hand they confronted were identical: Jim Crow segregation laws, exclusion of African Americans from the Columbian Exposition, white denial of the African American contribution to the building of the United States, the abuse of the African American by the political and legal systems, the misrepresentation of the African American in white media and culture, the work of building the black woman's movement and of trying to build bridges to the white woman's movement. But their most personal and compelling situations-at-hand differed. Wells-Barnett's direct experience with lynching led her to the lifelong crusade for justice that was then and is now the basis of her reputation. Cooper's position as an educator and an intellectual led her to concentrate on discrimination against blacks in education and white denial of black intelligence, and to a special concern with the denial of educational opportunities to black women—a denial in which black men were often complicitous.

American society, in Cooper's and Wells-Barnett's models, teeters between two possible configurations of difference: domination or equilibrium. Domination's project is absolute control, and found its fullest expression in slavery, which Cooper describes as the effort of the Southerner to make the Negro "absolutely his own in body, mind, and sensibility" (1892:102). In America, racial domination distorts "difference" to mean both departure from and subordination to the norm of Anglo-Saxon whiteness: "as if to become white is the sole panacea . . .—the universal solvent for all America's irritation" (Cooper, 1892:172). For Wells-Barnett, domination is epitomized in lynching, a practice "in which might makes right . . . done to a people because of race and color" (1895:7; 1892/1969:10). Both see that class and gender are implicated in the so-called "race problem." Wells-Barnett (1970) argues that "Lynching was an excuse to get rid of negroes who were acquiring wealth and property"(1970:64). Cooper especially focuses on the problem of sexism confronting women generally and the black woman in particular.

In their model, the intersection of difference and power does not inevitably produce domination. The alternative to domination is equilibrium. Equilibrium is not conflict free but is domination free. In equilibrium no one interest, class, race, society, or individual is able to dominate and conflicts are resolved by negotiation. Equilibrium requires balance in group access to material resources as well as the will to mobilize those resources. Much of Cooper's and Wells-Barnett's writings are devoted to advancing the project of gaining this necessary balance for subordinated groups.

Neither woman presented these two configurations as morally neutral. Wells-Barnett's critique of domination is a basic moral claim: domination is wrong because justice is right. If people believe in justice—and she believes that there is a potential in human conscience, a moral sense, that does support justice—then they cannot support domination. Her method and her work are to appeal to this moral sense. Cooper in particular is absorbed with making a theoretical argument against domination. In an extended presentation, she makes the case that domination is wrong because it denies the principles of the physical universe, the record of history, the commandments of religion, and the human psychological need for a sense of progress. In all these instances, harmony and progress are "the unvarying result of the equilibrium of opposing forces" (1892:150). Drawing on the theory of eighteenth-century French historian Francois Guizot, she argues that in America the contending races, classes, principles, and interests are the "conditions in embryo" for progress and liberty. Thus, America does have a race problem, but that problem is a potential source of strength and growth.

3. For Cooper and Wells-Barnett, domination is a system of oppression and privilege patterned by five factors—history, ideology, material resources, manners, and passion. The central issue in their theory is the nature of domination. This is not just a theoretical but a practical problem, for understanding domination is a prerequisite to undermining a system bent on destroying the African American.

History   Cooper and Wells-Barnett concentrate their explorations of domination in the historically specific situation of the United States in the nineteenth century, understood as falling into four periods: pre–Civil War, Civil War, Reconstruction, and post-Reconstruction. The pre–Civil War period presents a case of absolute domination. In comparison, Reconstruction and post-Reconstruction demonstrate the conflict between domination and equilibrium. Their choice of the United States race problem was made because it was for them overwhelmingly the situation-at-hand; but this is also their method of analysis—a case must be historically specific to be analyzable, domination does not exist outside of history. Cooper returns to the study of the historically specific setting of domination in her 1925 dissertation, analyzing the interplay between the practice of slavery in the French colony of Haiti and the ideals articulated in the French Revolution.

Ideology   Criteria of division and distinction are essential to domination and are created through ideologies that distort and exaggerate selected differences between people. Wells-Barnett recognizes the power of ideology which in lynch law effectively "closed the heart, stifled the conscience, warped the judgment and hushed the voice of press and pulpit" (1892/1969:14). The ideology of white supremacy in the American case construes difference as a distinction between the deserving strong and the weak who are undeserving because of their weakness. Cooper critically confronts Spencerian social darwinism, especially its popularized notion of "survival of the fittest," which she satirizes as "the survival of the bullies" (1892:118). She traces the ideological transformation of African American virtue into African American weakness, describing how during the Civil War: "when the homes and helpless ones of this country were absolutely at the black man's mercy and not a town laid waste, not a building burned, and *not a woman insulted*—it is no argument, I say, for you to retort, *'He was a coward; he didn't dare!'* The facts simply do not show this to have been the case" (1892:198).

The label of weakness is one step in the ideological movement of domination to legitimize the definition of the subordinate as the "Other"—the being so unlike oneself that the rules one applies to oneself do not apply to this other. Cooper describes the white Southerner persuading the visitor that the African American is Other, one beyond the pale of normal human responses, "giv[ing] object lessons with his choicest specimens of Negro depravity and worthlessness; taking [the visitor] through what, in New York would be called 'the slums,' [and naming] our terrible problem, which people of the North so little understand" (1892:108). Wells-Barnett analyzes how this ideological portrayal of the subordinate as Other is then pushed further by the strategy Adolf Hitler will later recommend as "the big lie" which through repetition transforms that other into a monster who deserves tyrannical subjugation: "Humanity abhors the assailant of womanhood, and this charge upon the Negro at once placed him beyond the pale of human sympathy. With such unanimity, earnestness and apparent candor was this charge made and reiterated that the world has accepted the story that the Negro is a monster" (1895:10).*

The ideological practice of using difference to create Otherness employs several criteria for the subordination of others—most notably, race, gender, and class—creating a "matrix of domination" that both oppresses and privileges (Collins, 1990). Cooper's analysis repeatedly traces the complex intersection of race, class, and gender in individual experience under conditions of domination. Taking as a specific situation-at-hand her ride on Southern trains under Jim Crow conditions, she first notes the nexus of race/class/gender oppression in the plight of young, poor black men she sees from the train window: "working on private estates, convicts from the state penitentiary, among them squads of boys fourteen to eighteen years of age in a chain-gang, their feet chained together and heavy blocks attached—not in 1850, but in 1890, '91, and '92" (1892:96). She then points to the impossible fragmentation of self this same nexus produces for women of color: "[A]t a dilapidated station . . . I see two dingy little rooms with 'FOR LADIES' swinging over one and 'FOR COLORED PEOPLE' over the other; while wondering under which head I come" (1892:96). The matrix of domination on the one hand produces fragmentation and confusion for a lady (gender, class) of color (race), while on the other hand in the chain gang, these criteria (race, gender, class) intersect to reproduce the conditions of slavery.

Wells-Barnett began her analysis of race/class/gender dynamics with the lynching of Thomas Moss and his partners, established businessmen who had "believed the [race] problem was to be solved by eschewing politics and putting money in the purse." The white newspapers described them as "Negro desperadoes who kept a low dive" (1892/1969:18–19). Class, then, is the lie offered as an explanation for the lynching—the victims were dangerous lower-class blacks—and class indeed is much of the reason for the lynching, which started with white resentment of Moss's business success. She concludes that "white citizens are wedded to any method however revolting, any measure however extreme, for the subjugation of the young manhood of the race. They have cheated him out of his ballot, deprived him of his civil rights of redress therefor in civil courts, robbed him of the fruits of his labor, and are still murdering, burning, and lynching him" (1892/1969:37). She also explores the distortion of intimacy between individuals produced by the race/gender nexus. Race stratification corrupts the relation between white men and black women, entitling the former to unregulated desire, and creating a centuries-long sexual oppression of the latter: "no one who reads the record, as it is written in the faces of the million mulattoes in the South, will for a minute conceive that the southern white man had a very chivalrous regard for the honor due the woman [that] circumstances placed in his power" (1895:13).* Relationships between white women and black men are also corrupted. White women, terrified of discovery and social disgrace, will lie, betray, even help lynch their lovers—though not always; Wells-Barnett's cases also show white women offering desperate resistance in an effort to save black lovers. The ultimate victim of this situation is the black man "lynched for an assault upon women when the facts were plain that the relation between the victim lynched and the alleged victim of his assault was voluntary" (1895:81).* For in the logic of the oppressor, the white man, "it is impossible for a voluntary alliance to exist between a white woman and a colored man, and therefore, the fact of an alliance is a proof of force" (1895:11).*

Material Resources Domination turns not only on ideological and relational exaggerations of difference but on the marshaling of material resources—violence, production, the knowledge that makes production possible, and communication. Wells-Barnett's case studies make clear the amount of material resources expended in lynching: guns, rope, kerosene, hot brands, nails, and human labor. Both women describe the ways whites control basic means of production—capital, commerce, transportation, and technical skill. Cooper is concerned about the marginalization of the skilled black worker: "The white engineer holds a tight monopoly both of the labor market and of the science of his craft. Nothing would induce him to take a colored apprentice or even to work beside a colored workman" (1892: 255). Wells-Barnett focuses on white control of communication, which means that "the race which holds Negro life cheap [is the same race] which owns the telegraph wires, newspapers and all other communications with the outside world. They write the reports which justify lynching by painting the Negro as black as possible, and those reports are accepted by the press associations and the world without question or investigation" (1893/1991:75).

Cooper and Wells-Barnett argue, however, that material interest is an insufficient explanation of domination. Cooper shows that many actions taken by the dominant are not in his real material self-interest. For instance, reflecting on the experience of travel in segregated railroad cars, she can but "wonder at the expensive arrangements of the company and of the state in providing special and separate accommodations for the transportation of the various hues of humanity" (1892:94). Wells-Barnett points out as a lesson in the history of race relations that since Reconstruction no concession by blacks to whites' supposed material self-interest has stemmed violence against blacks.

Manners   One explanation of the persistence of domination is its routinization and reproduction in everyday interactions between racial dominants and subordinates. Cooper and Wells-Barnett sketch the daily practices in Southern society of "doing race" in the context of differential power. To the dominant in the taken-for-granted stance, the issue, as Cooper portrays it, is one of manners, of the prescribed norms for routine relations, within and across lines of racial distinction. Expectations of reciprocal civility, in the dominant's view, extend only to those one regards as one's social equals—that is, to those of the white race (framed by understandings of class and gender). In interactions across race, deferential civility is expected only of the subordinate; the expectation of dominants in this situation is that they will enact distance to subordinates as a sign of their superiority, occasional suspensions of this expectation in specific cases serving only to prove the general rule. As Cooper puts it, "[T]here is hardly a man of them [white Southerners] but knows, and has known from childhood, some black fellow whom he loves as dearly as if he were white. . . . He would die for A or B, but suddenly becomes utterly impervious to every principle of logic when you ask for the simple golden rule to be applied to the class of which A or B is one" (1892:218). Wells-Barnett traces the fatal consequences that flow from the subordinate's suspension of this relational rule, reporting on numerous instances of lynching in which African Americans were charged with being saucy and, in her autobiography, on numerous instances of white persons—from President Wilson to a Chicago society matron—taking offense when a black person simply held firm, stated the truth, or contradicted a white statement.

Manners, thus, matter to racism, to domination. Through the pervasive patterning of daily relationships the subordinate is spiritually drained, while the superordinate reproduces an allegiance to an oppressive system by a multitude of taken-for-granted practices. And manners, if even mildly nudged in the direction of civility, can begin systematically to undermine domination.

Passion   But above all, domination rests on emotion, a desire for absolute control, which is a self-feeding, ever expanding passion. Wells-Barnett sees the violent emotion in lynching as "the inevitable result of unbri[d]led power exercised for two and a half centuries, by the white man over the Negro" (1892/1969:7). This passion is intensified by any threat to itself, any manifestation of autonomy by the subordinate, for within the emotional framing of the caste system of race, the subordinate's autonomy triggers the dominant's self-induced terror of pollution and defilement. Exploring this point, Cooper analyzes a powerful propaganda poem by a white man, "A Voodoo Prophecy" by Maurice Thompson, published in the white New York *Independent.* The speaker in the poem is supposed to be a black man.

> Within my loins an inky curse is pent,
>   To flood
>   Your blood
> And stain your skin and crisp your golden hair.
>
> As you have done by me, so will I do
>   By all the generations of your race;
>   Your snowy limbs, your blood's patrician blue
>   Shall be
>   Tainted by me,
> And I will set my seal upon your face. (cited in Cooper, 1892:215)

Cooper's argument is that "Maurice Thompson in penning this portrait of the Negro, has, unconsciously it may be, laid bare, his own soul—its secret dread and horrible fear" (1892:217).* White guilt creates this terror of reprisal. The lie about black rape of white women and the brutal cruelty which meets any such charge are responses of a collective memory of white rape of black women. The dominant is afraid that the situation may be reversed—that the subordinate will assume dominance over him. Wells-Barnett traces this in the brutal resistance to black enfranchisement: "'No Negro domination' became the new legend on the sanguinary banner of the sunny South, and under it rode the Ku Klux Klan, the Regulators, and the lawless mobs, which for any purpose chose to murder one man or a dozen as suited their purpose best" (1895:9).*

Cooper and Wells-Barnett make passion neither a secondary nor a derivative factor in domination, but its self-renewing energy; in this analysis, they make a significant contribution to critical sociological theories of power—both neo-Marxian and feminist. This thesis challenges the easy claim of the possibility of rational discourse and helps us understand the violence and recalcitrant determination to triumph through injustice that are part of our present as well as our past.

4. Cooper and Wells-Barnett argue for a society patterned by coexistence, or equilibrium, rather than domination. Cooper's and Wells-Barnett's alternative to domination is neither a melting pot of assimilation nor a functional complementarity of institutions. Rather, they foresee a society characterized by ongoing conflict between the competing interests and contrasting ideals of opposing groups who are sufficiently equal in power resources to prevent domination by one faction: "Progressive peace in a nation is the result of conflict; and conflict, such as is healthy, stimulating, and progressive, is produced through the co-existence of radically opposing or radically different elements" (Cooper, 1892:151). This conflict swirls around a space that it itself generates—a space in which practices of civility and reciprocity, as well as the processes of liberty and progress, are dynamically produced and reproduced. The facts of difference, framed by norms of inclusion, infuse the practice of power in this alternative to domination, which Cooper calls "equilibrium" or "coexistence."

Wells-Barnett advocates a series of strategies for subordinate groups to achieve equal empowerment. They must use whatever economic resources they can effect to force the dominant into capitulation: boycotts, withdrawal of labor, publicity to drive away capital investment. They must be willing to meet force with force: "When the white man who is always the aggressor knows he runs as great a risk of biting the dust every time his Afro-American victim does, he will have greater respect for Afro-American life" (1892/1969:23). They must mobilize public opinion. For Wells-Barnett the problem of domination, as manifest in lynching, is to be met in two courts—that of law and that of public opinion; and these two she sees as linked: "The strong arm of the law must be brought to bear upon lynchers in severe punishment, but this cannot and will not be done unless a healthy public sentiment demands and sustains such action" (1892/1969:21). Her methods are to create a black media, to use the white press against itself, and to take her case to an audience that will listen—Northern blacks, Northern whites, and the world community.

Cooper adds to this the case for coalition between subordinates, especially women and people of color. Domination exists in the United States, she argues, because of two fundamental forms of *dis*equilibrium in the current social system: one, the Anglo-Saxon race exercises a disproportionate influence in the national discussion, and that race bears a tradition of excessive aggression as its way of being; two, the woman's voice has been largely excluded, and the civilization is based on the masculine cultural ethic. Cooper connects these two imbalances by placing the current civilization in a historical context: "Since the idea of order . . . succumbed to barbarian brawn and brutality in the fifth century, the civilized world has been like a child brought up by its father. It has needed the great mother heart to teach it to be pitiful, to love mercy, to succor the weak and care for the lowly" (1892:51). She makes the case for a heritage of Anglo-Saxon aggression, using Taine's description of the barbarian of the fifth century as the quintessential Anglo-Saxon (see Theme 1, preceding). Her manifest message is of an Anglo-Saxon heritage that is contemptuous of weakness, proclaiming, "Verily we are the people, and after us there is none other. Our God is power; strength, our standard of excellence" (1892:53). But the description also presents a hidden message—that of the white man as brute.

Against this, she contrasts her own heritage as an African American and the heritage of female culture. Cooper praises the African American's desire "for law and order, his inborn respect for authority, his inaptitude for rioting and anarchy, his gentleness and cheerfulness as a laborer" (1892:173). In her discussion of masculine and feminine cultures, she argues that the presence of the feminine principle in the public arena will radically transform the world culture:

> You will not find theology consigning infants to lakes of unquenchable fire long after women have had a chance to grasp, master, and wield its dogmas. . . . [Y]ou will not find jurisprudence formulating as an axiom the absurdity that man and wife are one, and that one the man . . . ; you will not find political economists declaring that the only possible adjustment between laborers and capitalists is that of selfishness and rapacity—that each must get all he can and keep all that he gets. (1892:58)

But, Cooper warns, for the female ethic to triumph, woman must not, in her own quest for her rights, trample on the rights of others, or be drawn into a masculine engagement in which what matters is to conquer. Looking at the growing racism in the white women's rights movement, Cooper is dismayed that some women seem willing to claim their right to vote by arguing the unworthiness of already enfranchised men of color, men of races they hold inferior to the Anglo-Saxon woman. For Cooper the woman's duty is absolutely clear: "Woman should not, even by inference, or for the sake of argument, seem to disparage what is weak. For woman's cause is the cause of the weak; and when all the weak shall have received their due consideration, then woman will have her 'rights'" (1892:117).

For Cooper, the role of the black woman in building the coalition among women and people of color is essential. The black woman represents the voice of the weakest and yet the most enduring; she is the inexterminable element most abused among all the contending forces—and she has been too long silent. Equilibrium in the individual, in the race, in the nation, and in the world now depends on her voice.

THE RELEVANCE OF COOPER AND WELLS-BARNETT FOR THE HISTORY AND PRESENT PRACTICE OF SOCIOLOGY

Cooper and Wells-Barnett and the Canon of Sociology

Cooper and Wells-Barnett did their most important and creative sociological work in the early 1890s; their work predates or is contemporaneous with the now canonized contributions of white male thinkers like Emile Durkheim, Max Weber, Georg Simmel, and George Herbert Mead, as well as the contributions of white women sociologists like Addams, Gilman, Marianne Weber, Webb, and the Chicago Women.

Four claims can be made about their contribution. First, as a general social theory created through the lens of race relations, it is without precedent in mainstream sociological theory and should be viewed as an essential statement in the context of the present need for a more multi-cultural understanding of the discipline. Second, Cooper and Wells-Barnett were not lone voices, but part of an enormous, segregated tradition of social analysis by African Americans—including a rich discourse by African American women (Collins, 1990; Giddings, 1984) and the towering but shamefully neglected achievement of W. E. B. DuBois. Third, Cooper and Wells-Barnett create a social theory morally and passionately centered in a standard of justice derived from Judeo-Christian religion and

American democratic and republican claims. They strengthen the claim that sociology is a science of morality, a claim that runs from Comte and Martineau to Addams but vanishes in the discipline's scramble for professional modernity and detachment. And fourth, Cooper and Wells-Barnett produce a theory of the intersection of race, class, and gender which adds a vital strand to the feminist tradition of sociology. In this section, we assess the relationship of Cooper and Wells-Barnett to three paradigms—functionalism, Marxian conflict theory, and interpretive theory. In the next section, we assess their significance for the feminist paradigm.

Functionalism   Cooper and Wells-Barnett both reject the social darwinist ideology of "the survival of the fittest" which permeates early American functionalism. Yet both seek order, which Cooper calls "equilibrium," as a social good. Unlike white male functionalists, however, Cooper and Wells-Barnett believe that equilibrium is achieved out of contention between distinct cultural groups rather than through assimilation. To use the later language of Talcott Parsons, they locate equilibrium in the processes of two functional areas—integration and latent pattern maintenance. Wells-Barnett focuses on the legal system as the source of order but adds the important corollary that the legal system will work only if public opinion supports its working. She is one of the first sociologists—perhaps only Harriet Martineau predates her—to recognize the role of the mass media as a force in social structure. Cooper is concerned with the role of the home and the role of the woman in socializing children, civilizing adults, and reinforcing group mores. One of her chief emphases is that the mores of civility in a highly diverse society function to "lubricate the joints and minimize the frictions of society" and that women have a major part to play in shaping these mores (Cooper, 1892:121). Thus, Cooper sees women's expressive function as patterning not only the private but the public sphere (an argument later made in Johnson 1988, 1989, 1993). Cooper and Wells-Barnett would reject the functionalist project of objectivity; their project is not to show what is, but to produce what is just. Given the inequities in society, the analyst must privilege the least-heard voices.

Marxian Conflict Theory   Cooper and Wells-Barnett acknowledge the role of material resources in conflict; but they do not see ideas or ideology as a superstructure resting on a material substructure. Central to their analysis is the sense that ideas, though sometimes influenced by material conditions, can in turn pattern the way a society organizes its material conditions. Wells-Barnett, urging African Americans to act to protect themselves, names as an immediate step: "help disseminate the facts . . . to the end that public sentiment may be revolutionized" (1892/1969:97). Cooper and Wells-Barnett differ significantly from Marxian conflict theory in that they do not see class as the primary relation of inequality but argue that unequal arrangements of race, gender, color, class, and geopolitical location all affect individual biography and social structure. They also see a difference between class practices of exploitation and color and race practices of prejudice, tracking the horizontal hostility between white and black workers in the United States. Nor do they see conflict being resolved by a classless society. For them, difference and opposition are permanent facts of social life; the challenge to a society is to find equitable ways to manage conflict.

Interpretive Theory   Cooper and Wells-Barnett have much in common with the interpretive paradigm: belief in symbolic interaction, in socially constructed typifications, and in interactional practice as a shaping force in society. But they differ sharply with mainstream interpretive theory in that they see meaning and interaction occurring across lines of difference and power. They recognize that symbolic meanings are constructed within a historical context and that issues of power, domination, and subordination are always present in that construction. Cooper argues that a frictionless interaction does not arise naturally out of association or as the result of a sympathetic understanding of the other as an individual. Rather, civility across lines of difference depends on a typified impersonal generalization of the other as *any other,* who deserves the politeness one accords to *all* others. In societies organized by domination, one is never simply "any other"; one is always an other in a complex power relation. The dominant cannot relate to the subordinate as any other, but only as a "less-than" other; the closer the subordinate becomes to the dominant in status, which would seem to bring the possibility of more sympathetic understanding, the more the dominant responds by seeking to re-establish difference—through rudeness, incivility, and coercion.

Cooper and Wells-Barnett and the Tradition of Feminist Sociology

Adding Cooper and Wells-Barnett to the tradition of feminist sociology challenges and expands that tradition in ways that are more significant than the consequences of their addition to the male canon. For the white women sociologists in this text, "race" meant diverse ethnic groupings in which the African American experience was one of many; none of them in life experience or intellectual endeavor focused on the black/white schema central to Cooper and Wells-Barnett and to much of the history and politics of the United States. The white women's personal identity might be challenged in terms of how much authority or freedom a woman should exercise, but their bodily safety was not at issue. In contrast, Cooper and Wells-Barnett had personal and wide experience with the arbitrary exercise of power as domination and the manipulation of difference into radical caste inferiority. Given these differences in life situation, it is remarkable first to note how much there is a feminist sociological tradition shared by all the women in this text. Second, it is important to add to this tradition Cooper's and Wells-Barnett's distinctive theoretical understandings. Third, we must not, in presenting Cooper and Wells-Barnett together, homogenize them so that important differences between them are obscured.

Commonalities of a Feminist Tradition   Like nearly all the women in this text, Cooper and Wells-Barnett have a faith in the moral appeal and in the human being as a moral agent. They recognize that moral agent as an embodied actor, having physical needs and weaknesses, vulnerable to intimidation, and capable of failure through bodily exhaustion or violation. They believe in the moral duty of women to speak out (and that society should educate women so they can speak out), not just on women's issues, but on all the critical political, economic, social, and religious issues facing the country and the world. They share with Martineau, Gilman, and Weber a willingness to confront sexuality as part of human experience. And, like Martineau, they confront the relation between race and sexuality. They share with the Chicago Women a confidence in research and in empirical data—although they bring a more critical edge to their use of that data, always considering its source. Like Addams and Martineau most especially, each follows the methodological practice of keeping herself present in her social science accounts as a woman with a particular biography and vantage point shaped by race, class, nationality, religion, and history.

Distinctive Contributions of a Black Feminist Tradition

Diversity Cooper and Wells-Barnett place diversity—differences between individuals and between groups of individuals—squarely at the center of the feminist problematic. They accept the fact that diversity makes collisions of interests and beliefs a permanent feature of social life. To think of a moment when conflict ceases is really to imagine the erasure of diversity, possible only under practices of monstrous tyranny. The issue is how to equally empower all parties in a conflict to allow for a dynamic negotiation of interests and claims.

Domination as Pathology All the feminists considered in this book understand the theoretical essence of domination: the project by one party to reduce other parties to nonexistence as independent subjectivities. Cooper and Wells-Barnett understand this fundamentally, its ideal-type being their community's recollection of slavery. What they add to this theoretical understanding of domination is, first, an analysis of how domination operates if challenged. They describe in detail the physical coercion the dominant will use—not only material deprivation, but brutality, torture, killing, and terrorism. This thesis is essential to a feminist understanding of domination; without it, the interconnections among media reports of disparate but continuous violent moments in world events may go theoretically unremarked. Second, Cooper and Wells-Barnett show us that domination is not only a calculus of will, but an enactment of passion. Dominants enjoy the experience of their power and do not yield it in response to reasonable appeals. Domination must be understood as a pathology which even when momentarily dismantled, will—without constant countervailing vigilance—erupt again.

The Matrix of Privilege and Oppression Cooper and Wells-Barnett describe a situation of domination as one in which social diversity is organized in terms of a matrix of oppression and privilege in which race, class, gender, color, and geopolitical location intersect in individual lives and societal configurations. They describe the effects of this oppressive complex in their own lives, through self-reflective accounts; in the lives of their community, through anecdotes (Cooper) and case studies (Wells-Barnett); and in US history and politics. They see that this matrix works not only to oppress but also to privilege. They look at the white male's sense of entitlement toward black women, at the Southern white woman's attempt to divide the women's movement in terms of race, and at the Northern white feminist's prioritizing of her interest, gender, over other dimensions of oppression such as race and class.

Differences between Women For Cooper and Wells-Barnett, the experience of gender subordination does not necessarily lead women to transcend differences produced by race and class. They write frequently on the white woman's blindness to the plight of poor black women, on stereotypical thinking by white women about black women and men, and on the betrayal by white feminists of people of color. Cooper captures the anomaly of the black woman's situation, appealed to on the grounds of gender and class injustice and ignored in terms of racial injustice:

> One often hears in the North an earnest plea from some lecturer for "our working girls" (of course this means white working girls). . . . I am always glad to hear of the establishment of reading rooms and social entertainments to brighten the lot of any women who are toiling for bread. . . . But how many have ever given a thought to the pinched and down-trodden colored women bending over wash-tubs and ironing boards—with children to feed and house rent to pay, wood to buy, soap and starch to furnish—lugging home weekly great baskets of clothes for families who pay them for a month's laundrying barely enough to purchase a substantial pair of shoes! (1892:254–255)

Wells-Barnett portrays white women's stereotypical ideas of race in her account of her protracted fight with Frances Willard of the Women's Christian Temperance Union (WCTU) over the specific issue of voluntary sexual relations between white women and black men—a relation Willard called "an imputation upon half the white race"—and over the policy issue that the WCTU refused to come out firmly against lynching. Cooper bitterly portrays Southern white women's racism in women's organizations and sharply criticizes the willingness of white women to use racism as a tool in their struggle for suffrage. To Cooper and Wells-Barnett, progressive whites are potential allies in the struggle against domination—theirs is the conscience that can be reached; but societal racism makes them unreliable allies.

Differences between Cooper and Wells-Barnett   Our intention in presenting Cooper and Wells-Barnett together has been to suggest some of the elements of a black feminist tradition in sociology. We have therefore focused on their similarities. We do not, however, wish to so blend them that the reader sees only "two black women sociologists"; there are important differences between them. The primary difference may be that Wells-Barnett was above all an activist, a researcher, and a crusading journalist, while Cooper was essentially an intellectual and theorist. But these two styles of doing sociology are distinguished from each other only in our present configuration of the sociological enterprise, a configuration that arises out of a gender, race, and class politics within the profession. In the tradition of black sociology, one has to understand that the roles of activist and theorist are linked responsibilities of the social analyst. Wells-Barnett had strong theoretical interests, and Cooper was active in fighting for black rights all her life.

Additionally, Wells-Barnett may be most theoretically excited by the ways knowledge and public opinion are socially constructed and act back upon the society that has constructed them, while Cooper may be most fascinated by the logical connection or disconnection between what people claim to believe and what they are capable of doing. Both women define the human being in terms of moral agency, but Cooper develops this position out of her own religious faith and locates the source of that agency in the "infinite possibilities of the individual human soul" (1892:298); Wells-Barnett develops her position from a belief in democratic legal processes and locates the essence of the individual's moral agency in the potential for accountability. In exploring issues of sexuality and race, Wells-Barnett insists that unions between blacks and whites are a natural outcome of close contact. Cooper prefers to see these as exceptions to the rule, since her desire is to calm what she has defined as one of the white Southerner's worst fears. Cooper and Wells-Barnett both look to black empowerment through education and economic mobilization, but Wells-Barnett is comfortable in a way Cooper is not with the possibility that a part of empowerment must be through violent resistance. Cooper's faith restrains her here, while Wells-Barnett's commitment to law inspired by public sentiment urges her on. Wells-Barnett believes that public opinion can be shaped by both appeals to conscience and appeals to self-interest, of which the most basic is the knowledge that one will get hit back.

Wells-Barnett expresses a feminist consciousness first by a championing of the weak; she is willing to fight for the very weakest member of society, as she shows in the case of Henry Smith, the poor, black, mentally impaired man accused of murder (a charge Wells-Barnett seems to accept). Further, she makes the paradigm of gender and race central to her analysis of American society. Cooper's feminist consciousness is most present in her critique of masculine culture and her eloquent description of what she sees as the nature of the balancing feminine principle: "Let her try to teach her country that every interest in this world is entitled at least to a respectful hearing, that every sentiency is worthy of its own gratification, that a helpless cause should not be trampled down, nor a bruised reed broken" (1892:124).

ENDNOTES

1. There is debate about this date, but it is the one Cooper herself used in filling out "A Survey of racial attitudes of Negro students" in 1930 for a study by Dr. Charles S. Johnson (1932), a sociologist who was president of Fisk University.
2. Her method of distribution was, in part, always to have copies of the pamphlet with her and to urge her listeners and readers to pass it or the facts in it on to other persons—to spread the word.
3. The pamphlet was not late, the Fair was; the management could not get the buildings ready until 1893.
4. On the basis of whether the formative years were primarily slave or free, Cooper (1858–1964), Wells-Barnett (1862–1931), Booker T. Washington (1856–1915), W. E. B. DuBois (1868–1963), and Mary Church Terrell (1863–1954) belong to this first generation after emancipation; Frederick Douglass (ca. 1817–95), Harriet Tubman (ca. 1820–1913), and Sojourner Truth (ca. 1797–1883) belong to those who had lived part of their lives as slaves; and Fannie Barrier Williams (1855–1930), Charlotte Forten Grimké (1837–1914), and Frances Ellen Watkins Harper (1825–1911) are examples of those born into free black families before emancipation.

Excerpts from Wells-Barnett's *A Red Record*

These selections are excerpted from pages 1–98. They show the main points in Wells-Barnett's theory and method: that domination results from the interaction of history, ideology, material resources, and emotion; that justice needs the mobilization of public opinion and a legal system that protects the weak; that sexual attraction across race happens frequently, but the ideology of domination tries to hide this; and that the oppressed must turn the oppressors' own words against them, using the white media to convict white people by cross-examination of the data they present. The reader should note Wells-Barnett's careful construction of lynching statistics, of which only a sample is given here.

EXCERPT FROM CHAPTER I, THE CASE STATED

The student of American sociology will find the year 1894 marked by a pronounced awakening of the public conscience to a system of anarchy and outlawry which had grown during a series of ten years. . . .

Beginning with the emancipation of the Negro, the inevitable result of unbri[d]led power exercised for two and half centuries, by the white man over the Negro, began to show itself in acts of conscienceless outlawry. During the slave regime, the Southern white man owned the Negro body and soul. It was to his interest to dwarf the soul and preserve the body. Vested with unlimited power over his slave, to subject him to any and all kinds of physical punishment, . . . the white owner rarely permitted his anger to go so far as to take a life, which would entail upon him a loss of several hundred dollars. . . .

Source: Ida B. Wells-Barnett, *A Red Record* (Chicago: Donohue and Henneberry, 1895).

But Emancipation came and the . . . white man had no right to scourge the emancipated Negro, still less has he a right to kill him. But the Southern white people had been educated so long in the school of practice in which might makes right, that they disdained to draw strict lines of action in dealing with the Negro. . . . [A] new system of intimidation came into vogue; the Negro was not only whipped and scourged; he was killed.

Not all nor nearly all of the murders done by white men during the past thirty years in the South have come to light, but the statistics as gathered and preserved by white men, and which have not been questioned, show that during these years more than ten thousand Negroes have been killed in cold blood, without the formality of judicial trial and legal execution. And yet, as evidence of the absolute impunity with which the white man dares to kill a Negro, the same record shows that during all these years, and for all these murders only three white men have been tried, convicted, and executed. . . .

Naturally enough the commission of these crimes began to tell upon the public conscience, and the Southern white man, as a tribute to the nineteenth century civilization, was in a manner compelled to give excuses for his barbarism. . . . That greatest of all Negroes, Frederick Douglass, in an article of recent date . . . shows that there have been three distinct eras of Southern barbarism, to account for which three distinct excuses have been made.

The first [excuse] given to the civilized world for the murder of unoffending Negroes was the necessity of the white man to repress and stamp out alleged "race riots." . . . It was always a remarkable feature in these insurrections and riots that only Negroes were killed during the rioting, and that all the white men escaped unharmed. . . .

. . . But this story at last wore itself out. No insurrection ever materialized; no Negro rioter was ever apprehended and proven guilty, and no dynamite ever recorded the black man's protest against oppression and wrong. . . .

Then came the second excuse, which had its birth during the turbulent times of reconstruction. By an amendment to the Constitution the Negro was given the right of franchise, and, theoretically at least his ballot became his invaluable emblem of citizenship. . . . "No Negro domination" became the new legend on the sanguinary banner of the sunny South, and under it rode the Ku Klux Klan, the Regulators, and the lawless mobs, which for any cause chose to murder one man or a dozen as suited their purpose best. It was a long, gory campaign; the blood chills and the heart almost loses faith in Christianity when one thinks of Yazoo, Hamburg, Edgefield, Copiah, and the countless massacres of defenseless Negroes whose only crime was the attempt to exercise their right to vote.

. . . Scourged from his home; hunted through the swamps; hung by midnight raiders, and openly murdered in the light of day, the Negro clung to his right of franchise with a heroism which would have wrung admiration from the hearts of savages. He believed that in that small ballot there was a subtle something which stood for manhood as well as citizenship, and thousands of brave black men went to their graves, exemplifying the one by dying for the other.

The white man's victory soon became complete. . . . With no longer the fear of "Negro Domination" before their eyes, the white man's second excuse became valueless. . . .

Brutality still continued: Negroes were whipped, scourged, exiled, shot and hung whenever and wherever it pleased the white man so to treat them, and . . . the murderers invented the third excuse—that Negroes had to be killed to avenge their assaults upon women. . . .

Humanity abhors the assailant of womanhood, and this charge upon the Negro at once placed him beyond the pale of human sympathy. With such unanimity, earnestness and apparent candor was this charge made and reiterated that the world has accepted the story that the Negro is a monster. . . .

The Negro has suffered much and is willing to suffer more. . . . But there comes a time when the veriest worm will turn, and the Negro feels today that [he must] . . . defend his name and manhood from this vile accusation. . . .

. . . [T]he Negro must give the world his side of the awful story. . . .

. . . The question must be asked, what the white man means when he charges the black man with rape. Does he mean the crime which the statutes of civilized states describe as such? Not by any means. With the Southern white man, any mesalliance existing between a white women and a colored man is a sufficient foundation for the charge of rape. The Southern white man says that it is impossible for a voluntary alliance to exist between a white woman and a colored man, and therefore, the fact of an alliance is a proof of force. In numerous instances where colored men have been lynched on the charge of rape, it was positively proven after the victim's death, that the relationship sustained between the man and woman was voluntary. . . .

It was for the assertion of this fact, in the defense of her own race, that the writer hereof became an exile; her property destroyed and her return to her home forbidden under penalty of death. . . .

But threats cannot suppress the truth.

During all the years of slavery, no such charge was ever made. . . . While the master was away fighting to forge the fetters upon the slave, he left his wife and children with no protectors save the Negroes themselves. And yet during those years of trust and peril, no Negro proved recreant to his trust and no white man returned to a home that had been dispoiled.

Likewise during the period of alleged "insurrection" . . . in the Reconstruction era, when the hue and cry was against "Negro Domination." . . . It must appear strange indeed, to every thoughtful and candid man, that more than a quarter of a century elapsed before the Negro began to show signs of such infamous degeneration.

. . . To justify their own barbarism [Southern white men] assume a chivalry which they do not possess. True chivalry respects all womanhood, and no one who reads the record, as it is written in the faces of the millions of mulattoes in the South, will for a minute conceive that the southern white man had a very chivalrous regard . . . for the womanhood which circumstances placed in his power. . . . Virtue knows no color line, and the chivalry which depends upon complexion of skin and texture of hair can command no honest respect.

When emancipation came . . . [f]rom every nook and corner of the North, brave young white women answered that call and left their cultured homes, their happy associations and their lives of ease, and with heroic determination went to the South to carry light and truth to the benighted blacks. . . . [T]hese young women . . . became social outlaws in the South. . . . "Nigger teachers"—unpardonable offenders in the social ethics of the South, and were insulted, persecuted and ostracised, not by Negroes, but by the white manhood which boasts of its chivalry toward women.

And yet . . . thrown at all times and in all places among the unfortunate and lowly Negroes, whom they had come to find and to serve, these northern women . . . went about their work, fearing no assault and suffering none. . . .

The Negro . . . faithful to his trust in both of these instances . . . should now have the impartial ear of the civilized world. . . .

. . . [H]e must disclose to the world that degree of dehumanizing brutality which fixes upon America the blot of a national crime. . . . It becomes a painful duty of the Negro to reproduce a record which shows that a large portion of the American people avow anarchy, condone murder and defy the contempt of civilization. . . .

The purpose of the pages which follow shall be to give the record which has been made, not by colored men, but that which is the result of compilations made by white men, of reports sent over the civilized world by white men in the South. Out of their own mouths shall the murderers be condemned. For a number of years the Chicago Tribune, admittedly one of the leading journals of America, has made a specialty of the compilation of statistics touching upon lynching. The data compiled by that journal and published to the world January 1st, 1894, up to the present time has not been disputed. In order to be safe from the charges of exaggeration, the incidents hereinafter reported have been confined to those vouched for by the Tribune.

EXCERPT FROM CHAPTER II, "LYNCH LAW STATISTICS"

From the record published in the Chicago Tribune, January 1, 1894, the following computation of lynching statistics is made referring only to the colored victims of Lynch Law during the year 1893:

ARSON

Sept. 15, Paul Hill, Carrollton, Ala.; Sept. 15, Paul Archer, Carrollton, Ala.; Sept. 15, William Archer, Carrollton, Ala.; Sept. 15, Emma Fair, Carrollton, Ala.

SUSPECTED ROBBERY

Dec. 23, unknown negro, Fannin, Miss.

ASSAULT

Dec. 25, Calvin Thomas, near Bainbridge, Ga.

ATTEMPTED ASSAULT

Dec. 28, Tillman Green, Columbia, La.

INCENDIARISM

Jan 28, Patrick Wells, Quincy, Fla.; Feb. 9, Frank Harrell, Dickery, Miss.; Feb. 9, William Fielder, Dickery, Miss. . . .

BURGLARY

Feb. 17, Richard Forman, Granada, Miss.

WIFE BEATING

Oct. 14, David Jackson, Covington, La. . . .

OFFENSES CHARGED ARE AS FOLLOWS

Rape, 39; attempted rape, 8; alleged rape, 4; suspicion of rape, 1; murder, 44; alleged murder, 6; alleged complicity in murder, 4; murderous assault, 1; attempted murder, 1; attempted robbery, 4; arson, 4; incendiarism, 3; alleged stock poisoning, 1; poisoning wells, 2; alleged poisoning wells, 5; burglary, 1; wife beating, 1; self defense, 1; suspected robbery, 1; assault with battery, 1; insulting whites, 2; malpractice, 1; alleged barn burning, 4; stealing, 2; unknown offense, 4; no offense, 1; race prejudice, 4; total, 159.

LYNCHINGS BY STATE

Alabama, 25; Arkansas, 7; Florida, 7; Georgia, 24; Indian Territory, 1; Illinois, 3; Kansas, 2; Kentucky, 8; Louisiana, 28; Mississippi, 17; Missouri, 3; New York, 1; South Carolina, 15; Tennessee, 10; Texas, 8; Virginia, 10. . . .

While it is intended that the record here presented shall include specially the lynchings of 1893, it will not be amiss to give the record for the year preceding. The facts contended for will always appear manifest—that not one-third of the victims lynched were charged with rape, and further that the charges made embraced a range of offenses from murders to misdemeanors.

In 1892 there were 241 persons lynched. . . .

Of this number 160 were of Negro descent. Four of them were lynched in New York, Ohio, and Kansas; the remainder were murdered in the South. Five of this number were females. The charges for which they were lynched cover a wide range. They are as follows:

Rape, 46; murder, 58; rioting, 3; race prejudice, 6; no cause given, 4; incendiarism, 6; robbery, 6; assault and battery, 1; insulting women, 2; desperadoes, 6; fraud, 1; attempted murder, 2; no offense stated, boy and girl, 2.

In the case of the boy and girl above referred to, their father, named Hastings, was accused of the murder of a white man; his fourteen-year-old daughter and the sixteen-year-old son were hanged and their bodies filled with bullets, then the father was also lynched. This was in November, 1892, at Jonesville, Louisiana.

EXCERPT FROM CHAPTER III, "LYNCHING IMBECILES" TORTURED AND BURNED IN TEXAS

Never in the history of civilization has any Christian people stooped to such shocking brutality and indescribable barbarism as that which characterized the people of Paris, Texas, and adjacent communities on the 1st of February, 1893. The cause of this awful outbreak of human passion was the murder of a four year old child, daughter of a man named Vance . . . a police officer in Paris for years . . . known to be a man of bad temper, overbearing manner and given to harshly treating the prisoners under his care. . . .

In the same town there lived a Negro, named Henry Smith, a well known character, a kind of roustabout, who was generally considered a harmless, weak-minded fellow. . . . Smith . . . was accused of murdering Myrtle Vance. The crime of murder was of itself bad enough . . . but . . . the father and his friends . . . shamefully exaggerated the facts and declared that the babe had been ruthlessly assaulted and then killed. . . . As a matter of fact, . . . [p]ersons who saw the child after its death, have stated, under the most solemn pledge to truth, that there was no evidence of such an assault. . . .

Lest it might be charged that any description of the deeds of that day [of Smith's lynching] are exaggerated, a white man's description which was published in the white journals of this country is used. The New York Sun of February 2d, 1893, contains an account, from which we make the following excerpt:

["]PARIS. Tex., Feb. 1, 1893.—Henry Smith, the negro ravisher of 4-year-old Myrtle Vance, has expiated in part his awful crime by death at the stake. . . . When the news came last night that he had been captured at Hope, Ark. . . . the city was wild with joy. . . . Curious and sympathizing alike, they came on train and wagons, on horse, and on foot, . . . Whiskey shops were closed, unruly mobs were dispersed, schools were dismissed by a proclamation from the mayor, and everything was done in a business-like manner. . . .

Arriving here at 12 o'clock the train was met by a surging mass of humanity 10,000 strong. The negro was placed upon a carnival float . . . and, followed by an immense crowd, was escorted through the city. . . .

. . . [W]hen he was told that he must die by slow torture he begged for protection. . . . He pleaded and writhed in bodily and mental pain. . . . His clothes were torn off piecemeal and scattered in the crowd, people catching the shreds and putting them away as mementos. The child's father, her brother, and two uncles then gathered about the Negro as he lay fastened to the torture platform and thrust hot irons into his quivering flesh. . . . Every groan from the fiend, every contortion of his body was cheered by the thickly packed crowd of 10,000 persons. . . . After burning the feet and legs, the hot irons—plenty of fresh ones being at hand—were rolled up and down Smith's stomach, back, and arms. Then the eyes were burned out and irons were thrust down his throat.

The men of the Vance family having wreaked vengeance, the crowd piled all kinds of combustible stuff around the scaffold, poured oil on it and set it afire. The Negro rolled and tossed out of the mass, only to be pushed back by the people nearest to him. . . . Hundreds of people turned away, but the vast crowd still looked calmly on. . . .["]

It may not be amiss in connection with this awful affair, in proof of our assertion that Smith was an imbecile, to give the testimony of a well known colored minister, who lived at Paris, Texas, at the time of the lynching. He was a witness of the awful scenes there enacted, and attempted in the name of God and humanity, to interfere in the programme. He barely escaped with his life, was driven out of the city and became an exile because of his actions. . . . [W]e quote his account as an eye witness of the affair. . . .

"I had known Smith for years, and there were times when Smith was out of his head for weeks. Two years ago I made an effort to have him put in an asylum. . . . For days before the murder of the little Vance girl, Smith was out of his head and dangerous. He had just undergone an attack of delirium tremens and was in no condition to be allowed at large."

EXCERPT FROM CHAPTER V, "LYNCHED FOR ANYTHING OR NOTHING"

Details are very meagre of a lynching which occurred near Knox Point, La., on the 24th of October, 1893. Upon one point, however, there was no uncertainty, and that is, that the persons lynched were Negroes. It was claimed that they had been stealing hogs, but even this claim had not been subjected to the investigation of a court. That matter was not considered necessary. A few of the neighbors who had lost hogs suspected these men were responsible for their loss, and made up their minds to furnish an example for others to be warned by. The two men were secured by a mob and hanged.

Perhaps the most characteristic feature of this record of lynch law for the year 1893, is the remarkable fact that five human beings were lynched and that the matter was considered of so little importance that the powerful press bureaus of this country did not consider the matter of enough importance to ascertain the causes for which they were hanged. It tells the world, with perhaps greater emphasis than any other feature of the record, that Lynch Law has become so common in the United States that the finding of the dead body of a Negro, suspended between heaven and earth to the limb of a tree, is of so slight importance that neither the civil authorities nor press agencies consider the matter worth investigating. . . .

. . . John Hughes, of Moberly, and Isaac Lincoln, of Fort Madison, and Will Lewis in Tullahoma, Tenn., suffered death for no more serious charge than that they "were saucy to white people." In the days of slavery it was held to be a very serious matter for a colored person to fail to yield the sidewalk at the demand of a white person, and it will not be surprising to find some evidence of this intolerance existing in the days of freedom. But the most that could be expected as a penalty for acting or speaking saucily to a white person would be a slight physical chastisement, to make the Negro "know his place" or an arrest and fine. But Missouri, Tennessee and South Carolina chose to make precedents in their cases and as a result both men, after being charged with their offense and apprehended, were taken by a mob and lynched. The civil authorities . . . did not feel it their duty to make any investigation after the Negroes were killed. They were dead and out of the way and as no one would be called upon to render account for their taking off, the matter was dismissed from the public mind.

EXCERPT FROM CHAPTER VI, "HISTORY OF SOME CASES OF RAPE"

It has been claimed that . . . all colored men, who are lynched, only pay penalty for assaulting women. It is certain that lynching mobs have not only refused to give the Negro a chance to defend himself, but have killed their victim with a full knowledge that the relationship of the alleged assailant with the white woman who accused him, was voluntary and clandestine. . . . This [Wells-Barnett's] defense has been necessary because the apologists for outlawry insist that in no case has the accusing woman been a willing consort of her paramour, who is lynched because overtaken in wrong. It is well known, however, that such is the case. . . . Such cases [of mutual consent] are not rare, but the press and people conversant with the facts, almost invariably suppress them.

The Cleveland, Ohio, Gazette, January 16, 1892, gives an account of one of these cases of "rape."

Mrs. J. C. Underwood, the wife of a minister of Elyria, Ohio, accused an Afro-American of rape . . . during [her husband's] absence in 1888, stumping the state for the Prohibition Party. . . . She subsequently pointed out William Offett, a married man, who was arrested, and, being in Ohio, was granted a trial.

The prisoner vehemently denied the charge of rape, but confessed he went to Mrs. Underwood's residence at her invitation and was . . . intimate with her at her request. This availed him nothing against the sworn testimony of a minister's wife, a lady of the highest respectability. He was found guilty, and entered the penitentiary, December 14, 1888, for fifteen years. Sometime afterwards the woman's remorse led her to confess to her husband that the man was innocent. These are her words: "I met Offett at the postoffice. It was raining. He was polite to me, and as I had several bundles in my arms he offered to carry them home for me, which he did. He had a strange fascination for me, and I invited him to call on me. He called, bringing chestnuts and candy for the children. By this means we got them to leave us alone in the room. Then I sat on his lap. He made a proposal to me and I readily consented. Why I did so I do not know, but that I did is true. He visited me several times after that and each time I was indiscreet. I did not care after the first time. In fact I could not have resisted, and had no desire to resist."

When asked by her husband why she told him she had been outraged, she said: "I had several reasons for telling you. One was the neighbors saw the fellow here, another was, I was afraid I had contracted a loathsome disease, and still another was that I feared I might give birth to a Negro baby. I hoped to save my reputation by telling you a deliberate lie." Her husband, horrified by the confession, had Offett, who had already served four years, released and secured a divorce.

There have been many such cases throughout the South, with the difference that Southern white men in insensate fury wreak their vengeance without intervention of law upon the Negro who consorts with their women.

The Memphis (Tenn.) Ledger, of June 8, 1892, has the following: "If Lillie Bailey, a rather pretty white girl, seventeen years of age, who is now at the city hospital would be somewhat less reserved about her disgrace there would be some very nauseating details in the story of her life. She is the mother of a little coon. The truth might reveal a fearful story of depravity or evidence of a rank outrage. She will not divulge the name of the man who has left such black evidence of her disgrace, and in fact says it is a matter in which there can be no interest to the outside world. She came to Memphis nearly three months ago, and was taken in at the Woman's Refuge. . . . She remained there until a few weeks ago when the child was born. The ladies in charge of the Refuge were horrified. The girl was at once sent to the city hospital. . . . When the child was born an attempt was made to get the girl to reveal the name of the Negro who had disgraced her, she obstinately refused and it was impossible to elicit any information from her on the subject."

Note the wording: "The truth might reveal a fearful story of depravity or evidence of a rank outrage." If it had been a white child, or if Lillie Bailey had told a pitiful story of Negro outrage, it would have been a case of a woman's weakness or assault and she could have remained at the Woman's Refuge. But a Negro child and to withhold its father's name and thus prevent the killing of another Negro "rapist" was a case of "fearful depravity."

EXCERPT FROM CHAPTER X, "THE REMEDY"

It is a well established principle of law that every wrong has a remedy. Herein rests our respect for law. The Negro does not claim that all of the one thousand black men, women, and children, who have been hanged, shot, and burned alive during the past ten years, were innocent of the charges made against them. We have associated too long

with the white man not to have copied his vices as well as his virtues. But we do insist that the punishment is not the same for both classes of criminals. In lynching, opportunity is not given the Negro to defend himself against the unsupported accusations of white men and women. . . . No evidence he can offer will satisfy the mob: he is bound hand and foot and swung into eternity. Then to excuse its infamy, the mob almost invariably reports the monstrous falsehood that its victim made a full confession before he was hanged. . . .

What can you do, reader, to prevent lynching, to thwart anarchy, and promote law and order throughout our land?

1st. You can help disseminate the facts contained in this book by bringing them to the knowledge of every one with whom you come in contact, to the end that public sentiment may be revolutionized. Let the facts speak for themselves, with you as a medium.

2d. You can be instrumental in having churches, missionary societies, Y.M.C.A.'s, W.C.T.U.'s and all Christian and moral forces in connection with your religious and social life, pass resolutions of condemnation and protest every time a lynching takes place; and see that they are sent to the place where these outrages occur.

3d. Bring to the intelligent consideration of Southern people the refusal of capital to invest where lawlessness and mob violence hold sway. Many labor organizations have declared by resolution that they would avoid lynch infected localities as they would the pestilence when seeking new homes. If the South wishes to build up its waste places quickly, there is no better way than to uphold the majesty of the law by enforcing obedience to the same, and meting out the same punishment to all classes of criminals, white as well as black. "Equality before the law," must become a fact as well as a theory before America is truly the "land of the free and the home of the brave."

4th. Think and act on independent lines in this behalf, remembering that after all, it is the white man's civilization and the white man's government which are on trial. This crusade will determine whether . . . this Nation shall write itself down a success at self government, or in deepest humiliation admit its failure complete; whether the precepts and theories of Christianity are professed and practiced by American white people as Golden Rules of thought and action, or adopted as a system of morals to be preached to heathen until they attain to the intelligence which needs the system of Lynch Law.

5th. Congressman Blair offered a resolution in the House . . . The organized life of the country can speedily make this a law by sending resolutions to Congress indorsing Mr. Blair's bill.

ungarbled evidence, and because I feel it essential to a perfect understanding and an equitable verdict that truth from *each* standpoint be presented at the bar,—that this . . . Voice has been added to the already full chorus. The "other side" has not been represented by one who "lives there.". . .

. . . [A]s our Caucasian barristers are not to blame if they cannot *quite* put themselves in the dark man's place, neither should the dark man be wholly expected fully and adequately to reproduce the exact Voice of the Black Woman. . . .

. . . If these . . . utterances can in any way help to a clearer vision and a truer pulse-beat in studying our Nation's problem, this Voice by a Black Woman of the South will not have been raised in vain.

READING 5·2

Excerpts from Cooper's *A Voice from the South*

EXCERPT FROM "OUR RAISON D'ÊTRE."

This selection is excerpted from pages i–iii. In this preface, Cooper invokes the image of the courtroom for her social analysis, arguing that all viewpoints need to be represented in the discussion of American race relations, and that the black woman's vantage point is distinctive and important.

. . . The colored man's inheritance and apportionment is still the sombre crux, the perplexing *cul de sac* of the nation. . . . One important witness has not yet been heard from. The summing up of the evidence deposed, and the charge to the jury have been made—but no word from the Black Woman.

It is because I believe the American people to be conscientiously committed to a fair trial and

EXCERPT FROM "WOMAN VERSUS THE INDIAN"

This selection is excerpted from pages 80–126. Cooper responds here to a speech by a leading white feminist who argues that it is unjust for men of color (including Native American men) to have the vote denied to white women. Cooper offers a sociological analysis of the importance of manners (or mores) in social life and thus in affecting relations between races; an historical analysis of the power of the white South in influencing politics and manners in the United States; a feminist analysis of the corruption of the white women's movement by Southern racism; and her own vision of feminist values as promoting inclusivity and opposing domination.

In the National Woman's Council convened at Washington, February 1891, among a number of thoughtful and suggestive papers read by eminent women, was one by the Rev. Anna Shaw, bearing the above title. . . .

Susan B. Anthony and Anna Shaw . . . [a]s leaders in the woman's movement of today . . . have need of clearness of vision as well as firmness of soul in adjusting recalcitrant forces, and wheeling into line the thousand and one none-such,

Source: Anna Julia Cooper, *A Voice from the South* (Xenia, OH: Aldine Press, 1892).

never-to-be-modified, won't-be-dictated-to banners of their somewhat mottled array.

The black woman and the southern woman, I imagine, often get them into the predicament of the befuddled man who had to take singly across a stream a bag of corn, a fox, and a goose. . . .

The black woman appreciates the situation and can even sympathize with the actors in the serio-comic dilemma.

But, may it not be that, as women, the very lessons which seem hardest to master now, are possibly the ones most essential for our promotion to a higher grade of work? . . .

The American woman of to-day not only gives tone directly to her immediate world, but . . . the deepest layers of society feel the vibrations. It is pre-eminently an age of organizations. The "leading woman," the preacher, the reformer, the organizer "enthuses" her lieutenants and captains, the literary women, the thinking women; these in turn touch their myriads of church clubs, social clubs, culture clubs, pleasure clubs and charitable clubs, till the same lecture has been duly administered to every married man in the land (not to speak of sons and brothers). . . .

The American woman then is responsible for American manners. . . . The atmosphere of street cars and parks and boulevards, of cafes and hotels and steamboats is charged and surcharged with her sentiments and restrictions. Shop girls and serving maids, . . . wage earner, salaried toiler, or propri-etress . . . are . . . bound together by a system. . . . The one talismanic word that plays along the wires from palace to cook-shop, from imperial Congress to the distant plain, is *Caste.* With all her vaunted independence, the American woman of to-day is as fearful of losing caste as a Brahmin in India. That is the law under which she lives, . . . the lesson which she instills into her children with their first baby breakfasts, the injunction she lays upon husband and lover with direst penalties attached. . . .

It was the good fortune of the Black Woman of the South to spend some weeks, not long since, in a land over which floated the Union Jack. The Stars and Stripes were not the only familiar experiences missed. A uniform, matter-of-fact courtesy, a genial kindliness, quick perception of opportunities for rendering any little manly assistance . . . in shops and waiting rooms, in cars and in the streets seemed to her chilled . . . soul to transform the commonest boor in the service of the public into one of nature's noblemen, and when the old whipped-cur feeling was taken up and analyzed she could hardly tell whether it consisted mostly of self pity for her own wounded sensibilities, or of shame that her country-men offered such an unfavorable contrast.

. . . The Black Woman of the South has to do considerable travelling in this country, often unattended. . . .

I purposely forbear to mention instances of personal violence to colored women travelling in less civilized sections of our country, where women have been forcibly ejected from cars, thrown out of seats, their garments rudely torn, their persons wantonly and cruelly injured. America is large . . . There are murderers and thieves and villains in both London and Paris. Humanity from the first has had its vultures and sharks, and representatives of the fraternity who prey upon mankind may be expected no less in America than elsewhere. That this virulence breaks out most readily and commonly against colored persons in this country, is due of course to the fact that they are, generally speaking, weak and can be imposed upon with impunity. Bullies are always cowards at heart and may be credited with a pretty safe instinct in scenting their prey. Besides, society, where it has not exactly said to its dogs "s-s-sik him!" has at least engaged to be looking in another direction or studying the rivers of Mars. It is not of the dogs and their doings, but of society holding the leash that I shall speak. . . .

There can be no true test of national courtesy without travel. . . . Moreover the weaker and less influential the experiment, the more exact and scientific the deductions. . . . [T]he Black Woman holds that her femininity linked with the impossibility of popular affinity or unexpected attraction through position and influence in her case makes her a touchstone of American courtesy. . . .

I would eliminate also from discussion all uncharitable reflections upon the orderly execution of laws existing in certain states of this Union, requiring persons known to be colored to ride in one car, and persons supposed to be white in another. A good citizen may use his influence to have existing laws and statutes changed or modified, but a public servant must not be blamed for obeying orders. A railroad conductor is not asked to dictate measures, nor to make and pass laws. His bread and butter are conditioned on his managing his part of the machinery as he is told to do. If, therefore, I found myself in that compartment of a train designated by the sovereign law of the state for presumable Caucasians, and for colored persons only when traveling in the capacity of nurses and maids, should a conductor inform me, as a gentleman might, that I had make a mistake, and offer to show me the proper car for black ladies; I might wonder at the expensive arrangements of the company and of the state in providing special and separate accommodations for the transportation of the various hues of humanity, but I certainly would not take it as a want of courtesy on the conductor's part. . . . But when a great burly six feet of masculinity with sloping shoulders and unkempt beard swaggers in, and . . . growls out at me over the paper I am reading, "Here gurl," (I am past thirty) "you better git out 'n dis kyar 'f yer don't, I'll put yer out,"— my mental annotation is *Here's an American citizen who has been badly trained . . .* ; and when in the same section of our enlightened and progressive country, I see from the car window, working on private estates, convicts from the state penitentiary, among them squads of boys from fourteen to eighteen years of age in a chain-gang, their feet chained together and heavy blocks attached—not in 1850, but in 1890, '91 and '92, I make a note . . . *The women in this section should organize a Society for the Prevention of Cruelty to Human Beings, and disseminate civilizing tracts and send*

throughout the region apostles of anti-barbarism. . . . And when farther on in the same section our train stops at a dilapidated station, rendered yet more unsightly by dozens of loafers . . . ; and when, looking a little more closely, I see two dingy little rooms with "FOR LADIES" swinging over one and "FOR COLORED PEOPLE" over the other; while wondering under which head I come, . . . I know that if by any fatality I should be obliged to lie over at that station, and driven by hunger, should be compelled to seek refreshments or the bare necessaries of life at the only public accommodation in the town, that [some] stick-whittler would coolly inform me, without looking up from his pine splinter, "We doan uccommodate no niggers hyur.". . .

. . . I have determined to plead with women . . . to institute reform by placing immediately in our national curricula a department for teaching GOOD MANNERS.

Now, am I right in holding the American woman responsible? Is it true that the exponents of women's advancement . . . can teach this nation to be courteous, to be pitiful, having compassion, one of the other . . . ?

I think so. . . .

One of the most singular facts about the unwritten history of this country is the consummate ability with which Southern influences, Southern ideas and Southern ideals, have from the very beginning even up to the present day, dictated to and domineered over the brain and sinew of this nation. Without the wealth, without education, without inventions, arts, sciences, or industries, without well-nigh every one of the progressive ideas and impulses which made this country, prosperous and happy, personally indolent and practically stupid, poor in everything but bluster and self-esteem, the Southerner has nevertheless with Italian finesse and exquisite skill, uniformly and invariably . . . manipulated Northern sentiment. . . . Indeed, the Southerner is a magnificent manager of men, a born educator. For two hundred years he trained to his hand a people whom he made absolutely his own, in body, mind, and sensibility. He so insinuated differences and distinctions among them, that their personal attachment for him was stronger than for their own brethren and fellow sufferers. He made it a crime for two or three of them to be gathered together in Christ's name without a white man's supervision, and a felony for one to teach them to read even the Word of Life; and yet they would defend his interest with their life blood; his smile was their happiness, a pat on the shoulder from him their reward. . . .

And he not only managed the black man, he also hoodwinked the white man, the tourist and investigator who visited his lordly estates. The slaves were doing well, in fact couldn't be happier,—plenty to eat, plenty to drink, comfortably housed and clothed—they wouldn't be free if they could. . . .

In politics the two great forces, commerce and empire, which would otherwise have shaped the destiny of the country, have been made to pander and cater to Southern notions. . . . Every statesman from 1830 to 1860 exhausted his genius in persuasion and compromises to smooth out her ruffled temper and gratify her petulant demands. But like a sullen younger sister, the South has pouted and sulked and cried: "I won't play with you now; so there!" and the big brother at the North has coaxed and compromised and given in, and—ended by letting her have her way. Until 1860 she had as her pet an institution which it was death by law to say anything about, except that it was divinely instituted, inaugurated by Noah, sanctioned by Abraham, approved by Paul, and just ideally perfect in every way. And when, to preserve the autonomy of the family arrangements, in '61, '62 and '63, it became necessary for the big brother to administer a little wholesome correction . . . she assumed such an air of injured innocence, . . . the big brother has done nothing since but try to sweeten and pacify and laugh her back into a companionable frame of mind. . . .

. . . Still Arabella sulked,—till the rest of the family decided she might just keep her pets, and manage her own affairs and nobody would interfere.

So now, if one intimates that some clauses of the Constitution are a dead letter at the South and that only the name and support of that pet institution are changed while the fact and essence, minus the expense and responsibility, remains, he is quickly told to mind his own business and informed that he is waving the bloody shirt.

. . . Not even the chance traveller from England or Scotland escapes. The arch-manipulator takes him under his special watchcare and training, uses of his stock arguments and gives object lessons with his choicest specimens of Negro depravity and worthlessness; takes him through what, in New York, would be called "the slums" . . . but in Georgia is denominated "our terrible problem, which people of the North so little understand.". . . [A]nd not long after the inoculation begins to work, you hear this old-time friend of the oppressed delivering himself something after this fashion: "Ah, well, the South must be left to manage the Negro. . . . The Negro is not worth a feud between brothers and sisters."

Lately a great national and international movement characteristic of this age and country . . . the movement making for Woman's full, free, and complete emancipation, has, after much courting, obtained the gracious smile of the Southern woman—I beg her pardon—the Southern *lady*. . . .

Now the Southern woman (I may be pardoned, being one myself) was never renowned for her reasoning powers. . . .

. . . [S]he imagines that because her grandfather had slaves who were black, all the blacks in the world of every shade and tint were once in the position of slaves [and that] . . . [c]ivility to the Negro implies social equality. . . .

When I seek food in a public café or apply for first-class accommodations on a railway train, I do so because my physical necessities are identical with those of other human beings of like constitution and temperament, and crave satisfaction . . . ; and I can see no more "social equality" in buying lunch at the same restaurant, or riding in a common car, than there is in paying for dry goods at the same counter or walking on the same street.

The social equality which means forced or unbidden association would be as much deprecated and as strenuously opposed by the circle in which I move as by the most hide-bound Southerner in the land. Indeed I have been more than once annoyed by the inquisitive white interviewer, who, with spectacles on nose and pencil and note-book in hand, comes to get some "points" about "*your people.*" My "people" are just like other people—indeed, too like for their own good. . . .

What the dark man wants then is merely to live his own life, in his own world, with his own chosen companions, in whatever of comfort, luxury, or emoluments his talent or his money can in an impartial market secure. Has he wealth, he does not want to be forced into inconvenient or unsanitary sections of cities to buy a home and rear his family. Has he art, . . . [h]is talent aspires to study without proscription all the masters of the ages. . . .

Has he religion, he does not want to be made to feel that there is a white Christ and a black Christ, a white Heaven and a black Heaven, a white Gospel and a black Gospel,—but the one ideal of perfect manhood and womanhood, the one universal longing for development and growth. . . .

This . . . is why I conceive the subject to have been unfortunately worded which was chosen by Miss Shaw at the Women's Council and which stands at the head of this chapter.

Miss Shaw is one of the most powerful of our leaders, and we feel her voice should give no uncertain note. Woman should not, even by inference, or for the sake of argument seem to disparage what is weak. For woman's cause is the cause of the weak. . . .

The cause of freedom is not the cause of race or a sect, a party or a class,—it is the cause of human kind . . . [T]he reform of our day, known as the Woman's Movement, is essentially such an embodiment. . . . And specially important is it that there be no confusion of ideas among its leaders as to its

scope and universality. All mists must be cleared from the eyes of woman if she is to be a teacher of morals and manners. . . . [I]t is important and fundamental that there be no chromatic or other aberration when the teacher is settling the point, "Who is my neighbor?"

. . . Woman in stepping from the pedestal of statue-like inactivity in the domestic shrine . . . is merely completing the circle of the world's vision. . . .

. . . The world has had to limp along with the wobbling gait and one-sided hesitancy of a man with one eye. Suddenly the bandage is removed from the other eye and the whole body is filled with light. It sees a circle where before it saw a segment. The darkened eye restored, every member rejoices with it. . . .

. . . Why [then] should woman become plaintiff in a suit versus the Indian, or the Negro or any other race, or class who have been crushed under the iron heel of Anglo Saxon power and selfishness? If the Indian has been wronged and cheated by the puissance of this American government, it is woman's mission to plead with her country to cease to do evil and to pay its honest debts. If the Negro has been deceitfully cajoled . . . , let it be woman's mission to plead that he be met as a man and honestly given half the road. . . . [L]et her rest her plea, not on Indian inferiority, nor on Negro depravity, but on the obligation of legislators to do for her as they would have others do for them were relations reversed. Let her try to teach her country that every interest in this world is entitled at least to a respectful hearing, that every sentiency is worthy of its own gratification, that a helpless cause should not be trampled down, nor a bruised reed broken; and when the right of the individual is made sacred, when the image of God in human form, whether in marble or clay, whether in alabaster or ebony, is consecrated and inviolable, . . . when race, color, sex, condition, are realized to be the accidents, not the substance of life, . . . then is mastered the science of politeness, the art of courteous contact, which is naught but the practical application of the principal of benevolence, the back bone and marrow of all religion; then woman's lesson is taught and woman's cause is won—not the white woman nor the black woman nor the red woman, but the cause of every man or woman who has writhed silently under a mighty wrong. . . . Her wrongs are thus indissolubly linked with all undefended woe, all helpless suffering, and the plenitude of her "rights" will mean the final triumph of all right over might.

EXCERPT FROM "HAS AMERICA A RACE PROBLEM; IF SO, HOW CAN IT BEST BE SOLVED?"

This selection is excerpted from pages 149–174. It presents Cooper's sociological theory of the interconnections among conflict, diversity, equilibrium and progress; and her argument that racial diversity and multi-culturalism are essential.

There are two kinds of peace in this world. The one produced by suppression, which is the passivity of death; the other brought about by a proper adjustment of living, acting forces. . . .

Now I need not say that peace produced by suppression is neither natural nor desirable. Despotism is not one of the ideas that man has copied from nature. All through God's universe we see eternal harmony and symmetry as the unvarying result of the equilibrium of opposing forces. Fair play in an equal fight is the law written in Nature's book. And the solitary bully with his foot on the breast of his last antagonist has no warrant in any fact of God. . . .

. . . Progressive peace in a nation is the result of conflict; and conflict, such as is healthy, stimulating, and progressive, is produced through the co-existence of radically opposing or racially different elements. Bellamy's ox-like men pictured in *Looking Backward* . . . are nice folks to read about; but they are not natural; they are not progressive. God's world is not governed that way. The child can never gain strength save by resis-

tance, and there can be no resistance if all movement is in one direction. . . .

I confess I can see no deeper reason than this for the specializing of racial types in the world. . . .

Each race has its badge, its exponent, its message, branded in its forehead by the great Master's hand which is its own peculiar keynote, and its contribution to the harmony of nations.

Left entirely alone,—out of contact, that is with other races . . . there is unity without variety, . . . a monotonous dullness which means stagnation,—death.

It is this of which M. Guizot complains in Asiatic types of civilization; and in each case he mentions I note that there was but one race, one free force predominating. . . .

Now I beg you to note that in none of these [ancient civilizations that died] was a RACE PROBLEM possible. . . .

But the course of empire moves one degree westward. Europe becomes the theater of the leading exponents of civilization, and here we have a *Race Problem,*—if indeed, the confused jumble of races, the clash and conflict, the din and devastation of those stormy years can be referred to by so quiet and so dignified a term as "problem." Complex and appalling it surely was. Goths and Huns, Vandals and Danes, Angles, Saxons, Jutes. . . .

Taine describes them as follows:

"Huge, white bodies, cool-blooded, with fierce blue eyes, reddish flaxen hair; ravenous stomachs, filled with meat and cheese, heated by strong drinks. Brutal drunken pirates and robbers, they dashed to sea in their two-sailed barks, landed anywhere, killed everything; . . ."

What could civilization hope to do with such a swarm of sensuous, bloodthirsty vipers? . . .

Once more let us go to Guizot. . . . "European civilization has within it the promise of *perpetual progress.* It has now endured more than fifteen centuries and in all that time has been in a state of progression. . . . While in other civilizations the exclusive domination of a principle (*or race*) led to tyranny, in Europe the diversity of social elements (*growing out of the contact of different races*) the incapability of any one to exclude the rest, gave birth to the LIBERTY which now prevails. . . ."

There is no need to quote further. This is enough to show that the law holds good in sociology as in the world of matter, *that equilibrium, not repression among conflicting forces is the condition of natural harmony, of permanent progress, and of universal freedom.* . . .

But European civilization, rich as it was . . . was still not the consummation of human possibilities. . . . It is not . . . till the scene changes and America is made the theater of action, that the interplay of forces narrowed down to a single platform.

Hither came Cavalier and Roundhead, Baptist and Papist, . . . conservative Tory, the liberal Whig, and the radical Independent, . . . the Englishman, . . . the Chinaman, the African, . . . Irish, Jews. Here surely was a seething caldron of conflicting elements. . . .

Conflict, conflict, conflict.

America for Americans! . . . shrieks the exclusionist. Exclude the Italians! Colonize the blacks in Mexico or deport them to Africa. Lynch, suppress, drive out, kill out! America for Americans!

"Who are Americans?" . . .

The red men used to be owners of the soil,—but they are about to be pushed over into the Pacific Ocean. . . . If early settlers from abroad merely are meant and it is only a question of squatters' rights—why, the Mayflower, a pretty venerable institution, landed in the year of Grace 1620, and the first delegation from Africa, just one year ahead of that,—in 1[6]19. . . .

The fact is this nation was foreordained to conflict from its incipiency. Its elements were predestined from their birth to an irrepressible clash followed by the stable equilibrium of opposition. . . . Compromise and concession, liberty and toleration were the conditions of the nation's birth and are the *sine qua non* of its continued existence. . . .

The supremacy of one race,—the despotism of a class or the tyranny of an individual can not ultimately prevail on a continent held in equilibrium by such conflicting forces and by so many and such strong fibred races as there are struggling on this soil. . . .

Has America a Race Problem?

Yes.

What are you going to do about it?

Let it alone. . . .

God and time will work the problem. . . .

. . . And we think that men have a part to play in this great drama no less than gods, and so if a few are determined to be white—amen, so be it; but don't let them argue as if there were no part to be played in life by black men and black women, and as if to become white were the sole specific and panacea for all the ills the flesh is heir to—the universal solvent for all America's irritations. . . .

. . . Let us not disparage the factor which the Negro is appointed to contribute to that problem. America needs the Negro. . . . [H]is instinct for law and order, his inborn respect for authority, his inaptitude for rioting and anarchy, his gentleness and cheerfulness as a laborer, and his deep-rooted faith in God. . . .

. . . [T]he historians of American civilization will yet congratulate this country that she has had a Race Problem and that descendants of the black race furnished one of its largest factors.

EXCERPT FROM "ONE PHASE OF AMERICAN LITERATURE"

This selection is excerpted from pages 173–237. Here, Cooper uses white American literary texts about the African American as her data for exploring American black–white relations, exposing white racism and presenting her own portrait of the African American contribution to American society. She also ventures into a sociology of literature in her explorations of the relations between society and artistic product. Albion Tourgee is a now relatively forgotten white author who had served in the Union army and been a judge during Reconstruction.

By a rough classification, authors may be separated into two groups: first, those in whom the artistic or poetic instinct is uppermost—those who write to please—or rather write because *they* please. . . .

In the second group belong the preachers,—whether of righteousness or unrighteousness, . . . all those writers with a purpose or a lesson. . . .

Now owing to the problematical position at present occupied by descendants of Africans in the American social polity,—growing, I presume, out of the continued indecision in the mind of the more powerful descendants of the Saxons as to whether it is expedient to apply the maxims of their religion to their civil and political relationships,—most of the writers who have hitherto attempted a portrayal of life and customs among the darker race have belonged to our class II: they have all, more or less, had a point to prove . . . and through sheer ignorance ofttimes, as well as from design occasionally, have not been able to put themselves in the darker man's place. The art of "thinking one's self imaginatively into the experiences of others" is not given to all, and it is impossible to acquire it without a background and a substratum of sympathetic knowledge. . . .

This criticism is not altered by our grateful remembrance of those who have heroically taken their pens to champion the black man's cause. . . .

. . . In presenting truth from the colored American's standpoint Mr. Tourgee excels, we think, in fervency and frequency of utterance any living writer, white or colored. . . . Not many colored men would have attempted Tourgee's brave defense of Reconstruction and the alleged corruption of Negro supremacy, more properly termed the period of white sullenness and desertion of duty. Not many would have dared, fearlessly as he did, to arraign the country for an enormous pecuniary debt to the colored man for the two hundred and forty-seven years of unpaid labor of his ancestors. . . . We appreciate the incongruity and the indignity of having to stand forever hat in hand as beggars or

be shoved aside as intruders in a country whose resources have been opened by the unrequited toil of our forefathers. We know that our bill is a true one—that the debt is as real as to any pensioners of our government. But the principles of patience and forebearance, of meekness and charity, have become so ingrained in the Negro character that there is hardly enough self-assertion left to ask as our right that a part of the country's surplus wealth be *loaned* for the education of our children; even though we know that our present poverty is due to the fact that the toil of the last quarter century enriched these coffers, but left us the heirs of . . . empty handed mothers and fathers. Oh, the shame of it! . . .

In [his novel] Pactolus Prime Mr. Tourgee has succeeded incomparably, we think, in photographing and vocalizing the feelings of the colored American in regard to the Christian profession and the pagan practice of the dominant forces in the American government. And as an impassioned denunciation of the heartless and godless spirit of caste founded upon color, as a scathing rebuke to weak-eyed Christians who cannot read the golden rule across the color line, . . . the book is destined to live. . . .

Among our artists for art's sweet sake, Mr. Howells has recently tried his hand also at painting the Negro, . . . and I think the unanimous verdict of the subject is that, in this single department at least, Mr. Howells does not know what he is talking about. . . . [In] *An Imperative Duty.* . . . Mr. Howells merely meant to press the button and give one picture from American life involving racial complications. The kodak does no more; it cannot preach sermons or solve problems.

. . . [In portraying black characters, however] Mr. Howells fails—and fails because he gives only a half truth, and that a partisan half truth. One feels that he had no business to attempt a subject of which he knew so little, or for which he cared so little. There is one thing I would like to say to my white fellow countrymen, and especially to those who dabble in ink and affect to discuss the

Negro; . . . namely that it is an insult to humanity and a sin against God to publish any such sweeping generalizations of a race on such meager and superficial information. We meet it at every turn—this obtrusive and offensive vulgarity, this gratuitous sizing up of the Negro and conclusively writing down his equation, sometimes even among his ardent friends and bravest defenders. Were I not afraid of falling myself into the same error that I am condemning, I would say it seems an *Anglo Saxon characteristic* to have such overweening confidence in his own power of induction that there is no equation which he would acknowledge to be indeterminate, however many unknown quantities it may possess. . . .

. . . What I hope to see before I die is a black man honestly and appreciatively portraying both the Negro as he is, and the white man, occasionally, as seen from the Negro's standpoint.

There is an old proverb "The devil is always painted *black*—by white painters." And what is needed, perhaps, to reverse the picture of the lordly man slaying the lion, is for the lion to turn painter.

CHAPTER 6

Marianne Weber (1870–1954)— A Woman-Centered Sociology

BIOGRAPHICAL BACKGROUND

Marianne Schnitger Weber was born on August 2, 1870, in Oerlinghausen in the principality of Lippe, Germany; she died on March 12, 1954, in Heidelberg. She is remembered today, if at all, as the wife of Max Weber, one of the towering figures in the history of sociology. That he is so—and that she is so remembered—is part of her life story; for in her own time she was as notable a public figure as he, recognized as a feminist intellectual, a social theorist, a sociologist of law, and the author of some eight books of social analysis, of which, prior to the translations in this text, only *Max Weber: A Biography* (1926/1975) had been translated into English. There are only four sources about Marianne Weber's life available in English: Harry Zohn's admirable translation of her biography of Max, which can reveal much to the careful reader-between-the-lines; Anne Camden Britton's 1979 master's thesis, "The Life and Thought of Marianne Weber"; and two short articles (Roth, 1990; Tijssen, 1991). Available in German and drawn on in the Britton thesis is Weber's own autobiography, *Lebenserinnerungen* ("Memoirs of a Life") (1948).

The biographical sketch that follows is a first step toward establishing Marianne Weber's career as a social theorist and sociologist in her own right. In order to focus on her, and to resolve a terminological problem, in this chapter (as much as clarity of presentation permits), we refer to her simply as Weber and to her husband as Max. We suggest that the key to Weber's career may lie in certain qualities of character, acquired in childhood and shaped in adulthood: a determination to survive, a determination to survive as someone of note, and a determination to strike that note in social thought and policy. We trace her career chronologically through three life periods— Girlhood: 1870–1893; Marriage: 1893–1920; and Widowhood: 1920–1954. This pattern follows the one she suggests for herself in her biography of Max. It unfolds against the background of a series of dramatic changes in German history, which we describe in the course of the chronology.

Girlhood: 1870–1893

In January 1871, a few months after Weber's birth, Germany, hitherto a conglomerate of self-governing political entities, was unified into a nation-state under the monarchy of autocratic Prussia and its tyrannical "Iron Chancellor," Otto von Bismarck. The new nation was shaped by Bismarck's anti-democratic, militaristic political leadership (1871–1890), by rapid industrialization that made Germany one of the world's most powerful economies (1870–1900), and by the social upheaval resulting from this industrialization. In Germany, as elsewhere, these changes produced an expanded middle class and new educational opportunities for middle-class women, conditions that both framed Weber's life and became a focus of her social analysis.

But these conditions did not immediately affect Weber's early life, which was marked by economic and psychic stress and status inconsistency. She was linked on her mother's side to the prestigious Weber family, which included her grandfather Karl, a leading businessman in the provincial town of Oerlinghausen, and the politically and intellectually influential Berlin family of Karl's brother, Max Weber, Sr., the father of Marianne's future husband, Max, Jr. But her mother, Anna, had married a man the Webers considered beneath them—Eduard Schnitger, a country doctor at a time when the career of doctor carried little prestige. Marianne was born within the first year of this marriage and two years later Anna died after the birth of a second child.

Thus, Marianne spent her early life outside the comfort of the Weber circle, cared for by Eduard Schnitger's mother and sister in circumstances of hardship and genteel poverty. Her Aunt Flora struggled to earn a little income as the village schoolteacher, and Weber received a basic education and many lessons in piety in the Schnitger home. The austerity of this childhood deepened into experiences of terror with the collapse into insanity of her father and his two brothers. Her father lived away and she saw him only on visits, but her uncles went insane at her grandmother's home. Weber recounts "hidden horrors and terrible sounds and visions" and running as a child to the mental asylum on more than one occasion to have an uncle taken away (Britton, 1979; Weber, 1926/1975:173).

From Weber's own account and from the evidence of her life, she appears to have developed a combination of coping strategies in this situation of childhood stress that would evolve into the pattern of her adult personality. First, it was important to her that she be defined to herself and by others as typical and normal, rather than eccentric or different. She affirms her own normality by remembering herself as "from the ground up a happy child" (Britton, 1979:10). Second, Weber taught herself to distance from the experience of her father's insanity, "distracting herself by drawing. . . . 'Inside me nothing was changed'" (Britton, 1979:9). Third, she focused on the happy, if occasional, occurrences in her life—a magical garden, a close friend, a special Christmas. She repaired to this strategy in later life, drawing travel pictures during Max's mental illness and, in the massive insanity of Hitler's regime, focusing on the details of a birthday party. Fourth, she formed an absolute determination to escape to a better place. She clung to the magic key to escape, her Weber family: "And in the background there was her . . . grandfather who was . . . rich and through whom she was part of a respected family. One day she would have access to a wider, brighter, existence" (Weber, 1926/1975:173). And the Weber connection did provide her a series of opportunities to that wider life.

The first opportunity occurred when her grandfather Karl Weber agreed to send her away, at age sixteen, to a fashionable finishing school in Hanover. Here she again experienced status inconsistency: no longer the special student of the village school, countrified and serious about her studies, she was uneasy with her classmates who emphasized social refinement. But Weber was a quick study, honing the skill of keeping an inner core of determination hidden beneath a facade of fitting in. She allowed herself to be "finished," learning to dance, to speak French and English, to appreciate music and art, while inwardly resolving "to become someone of note . . . [with] a 'burning ambition' to achieve" something that would make her "first in importance" (Britton, 1979:9–10).

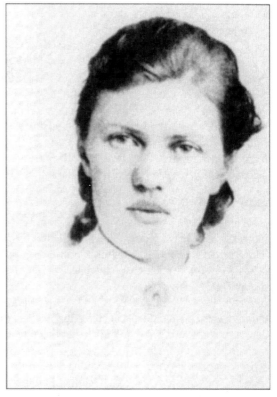

Marianne Weber, age 23

After three years in Hanover, in 1889, Weber returned "home" to live with her mother's married sister, Alwine, who offered a comfortable provincial middle-class home, although Weber's duties were very much those of the poor relation. Weber's unhappiness and boredom in a setting that "offered nothing to her aspiring intellect" unsettled the family, and Weber found herself invited to spend a few weeks, in 1891, in Berlin, with the family of Max Weber, Sr., his wife, Helene, and Marianne's second cousin Max, Jr. In that affluent and sophisticated family, Marianne at last caught a glimpse of the life she wanted. She could hardly "get her fill of the intellectual atmosphere of their home and the cultural treasures of the big city . . . *this at last was living*" (1926/1975:174–175, her italics). In 1892, a year after this first visit, Weber managed to return to live with her Berlin cousins, for further training of "her modest artistic talent" (1926/1975: 175–176). Here she formed the two critical emotional relations of her adult life—with her aunt Helene and her cousin Max. Helene's life was one of high-minded and stoic unhappiness in a demanding and destructive marriage (see "Assumptions" later in this chapter). Marianne, by her account, became Helene's confidante and loving solace, and Helene, for her, the mother she had never had; their closeness continued until Helene's death in 1919.

Max, his mother's favorite child and other confidante, was already widely recognized as a brilliant young scholar, with doctoral degrees in law and history, a reputation as a social science researcher, and a visiting lecturership at the University of Berlin. At age 28, he was in a five-year-long romantic relation with his cousin Emmy, a relationship much approved by Helene, although Emmy had a long history of nervous illness and was frequently in sanatoriums. Marianne Weber gives no account of the course of her own courtship with Max, or of her role in promoting it; but by the end of 1892, Max had broken his engagement to Emmy, overcome Helene's misgivings, and proposed marriage to Marianne. Amidst the ritual domestic flurry of their engagement, Marianne notes that she regarded herself as "at the beginning of her intellectual development" (1926/1975:186). Max and Marianne Weber married in the fall of 1893.

Marriage: 1893–1920

Marianne and Max's marriage was lived in the context of a continuing patriarchal military-industrial state under Kaiser Wilhelm II and a growing opposition from liberals, socialists, and feminists. In 1914, Wilhelm's militaristic politics helped precipitate World War I (1914–1919), which left Germany defeated, humiliated, and burdened with punitive reparation payments. We have two primary sources of information about Weber's life during her marriage, her biography of Max and her social theory. Weber's project in her 700-page biography is to portray Max as the towering intellect of his age; she appears in the margins of her narrative, a foil for his agency. In her theoretical writings up to 1920, however, she portrays marriage for the woman as a quest for two forms of fulfillment, for autonomy in her self-determined projects and for intimacy with the husband in a partnership of expanding interests, satisfactions, and mutual caring. In this section we focus on Weber's development as a social theorist as a way she realized autonomy and intimacy within her marriage.

Three general qualities characterize Marianne Weber's patterning of her life in marriage.[1] First, she accepted Max's relatively progressive views on women's role, which acknowledged her right to an intellectual life, in any space she could open up separate from the traditional duties he expected of his wife—managing his emotions, his household, and their social life (including relations with family). Second, in opening this space, she was resourceful and fortunate in being able to call out devoted service from the women she hired to be her housekeepers—over the 61 years from her marriage in 1893 to her death in 1954, she was served by and in her turn cared for three women, Berta, Lina and Lisbeth. Third, Weber worked to share Max's sociological life.

The first stage of the marriage, 1893 to 1898, was marked by Max's demanding pursuit of a life combining academic activity, intellectual production, and left-of-center politics. He taught first at Berlin; then, in 1894, as Professor of Economics at Freiburg; and in 1896 as Professor of Political Science at Heidelberg, the leading university in Germany. In this phase, Weber pursued her own higher education and began to establish a place of her own in feminism. At Freiburg between 1894 and 1895, she followed her "own mood. . . . and . . . occupied herself with . . . scholarship"—a course of action which raised questions "about what a woman could, should, and was allowed to do" (1926/1975:203–204). The demands of a university job meant that Max had less time for philosophic research, but Weber began studying seriously with neo-Kantian philosopher

Heinrich Rickert, Jr. She was also soon exploring feminist thought, after attending an 1895 political congress that included prominent feminist speakers. At Heidelberg in 1896, she became the leader in a newly organized society for the dissemination of feminist ideas while remaining busy with her own studies—attending Max's lectures in political economy, sitting in on other lectures in philosophy, and beginning to do her own writing. The Webers together worked to open Heidelberg to women students, who came in only small numbers at that time.

But in 1897, a crisis occurred that brought this phase to a sudden halt. In front of Marianne and his mother, Helene, Max berated his father for his years of tyrannical abuse of Helene; his father died shortly thereafter without being reconciled to either Helene or Max. This event has been used in psychological studies of Max to explain the stage that followed (e.g., Kandal, 1988; Mitzman, 1970; Weber, 1926/1975). That second stage of the marriage, 1898 to 1904, was marked by Max's nervous collapse into deep depression; his withdrawal from academic, political, and intellectual life; his movement in and out of mental sanatoriums; his constant need to travel; his resignation from his prestigious Heidelberg professorship; and his stumbling recovery of mental health. Weber's own career was sidetracked by Max's breakdown. She presents the attempt to help him endure his illness and work for recovery as her first concern for years. But even in the dark days of 1900, she worked on the publication of *Fichte's Sozialismus und sein Verhältnis zur Marx'schen Doktrin* ("Fichte's Socialism and Its Relation to Marxist Doctrine") (1900) and "Politics and the Women's Movement" (1901) and left Max for a short time in order to attend a feminist convention. The period of the illness brought the couple very close, realizing Weber's other project, the quest for intimacy in her marriage. She describes herself as an effective caregiver who had "herself inherited weak nerves and from childhood was used to treating those who suffered in the same way with a special consideration" and remembers their life in this period as "filled with an affection and intimacy that even the patient experienced as a new happiness" (1926/1975:236–237). As life became semi-normal, Weber found herself in the role-reversed situation of becoming the public speaker in the marriage, often staying at political meetings late into the night while Max stayed silent and rested at home.

In the third stage of the marriage, 1904 to approximately 1914, Max maintained his mental health by a careful balance of renewed scholarship and leisure. The year 1904 was a turning point; in that year, the Webers toured America, Max accepted the editorship of a new journal in social science, *Archiv fur Socialwissenschaft und Socialpolitik,* and published in that journal his now famous monograph *The Protestant Ethic and the Spirit of Capitalism.* It appears that during this period of the marriage, while his affection for Marianne persisted, Max experimented sexually outside the marriage and fell in love with their mutual friend Else Jaffe (Britton, 1979; Green, 1974). As Max recovered, Weber, too, became more active in scholarship and public life. On the American tour, she met both Jane Addams (Chapter 3) and Florence Kelley (Chapter 7), and between 1904 and 1907 she published several papers on women's experience, engaging critically with the theories of Charlotte Perkins Gilman (Chapter 4). In 1907 she published her landmark work *Ehefrau und Mutter in der Rechtsentwicklung* ("Marriage, Motherhood, and the Law"). That year, also, Weber's grandfather Karl died, and his bequest to his granddaughter left her and Max, the "cast-off professor . . . freed from financial worries" (1926/1975:367). The Webers now lived in much greater comfort, and Weber began to build her intellectual salon, which included Max's colleagues Werner Sombart, Robert Michels, Georg Simmel, and Max's philosopher brother Alfred, as well as prominent feminists like Marie Baum, Gertrud Baumer, and Gertrud Simmel. Weber, by 1908, was well known in political and intellectual circles as a feminist. She writes that in late 1908, she and Max attended a political meeting at which he spoke unexpectedly and passionately, and one man asked another, "'Who's that Max Weber anyway?'" and was told "'Oh, he's Marianne's guy'" (1926/1975:407). We can detect something of this rise in Weber's status in a newly critical and confident tone in her writings, "The Question of Divorce" (1909), "Authority and Autonomy in Marriage" (1912),* "On the Valuation of Housework" (1912),* "Women and Objective Culture" (1913)—collected in *Frauenfragen und Frauengedanken* ("Reflections on Women and Women's Issues") (1919). From about 1910 on, her closeness with Max became problematic, though Weber herself was still deeply committed to the idea of her marriage to Max. In part, she and Max were caught up in their separate career paths; in part, Max was increasingly absorbed with Else Jaffe. Yet, in form, the marriage remained solid—the intellectual salon continued; Max fiercely defended Weber from anti-feminist attacks; the relation to Max's family, particularly to his mother, formed a close bond between them.

The last stage of the marriage, 1914 to 1920, had as backdrop World War I, political upheaval in Germany, and a devastating peace treaty that would leave the country in economic anarchy. In this period Max seems to have moved to regain a full regimen of activity; he published his multi-volume comparative study of religion, organized military hospitals, lectured, participated in the peace negotiations of 1918–1919 (he advised against signing the treaty, which he saw as disastrously unfair and rigged on all sides), and emerged as a candidate for high office in the newly created Weimar Republic. In the midst of the war, Weber continued to write—"The New Woman" (1914), "The Ideal of Marriage" (1914), "War as an Ethical Problem" (1916), "Changing Types of University Women" (1917), "The Forces Shaping Sexual Life" (1918a), and "Women's Special Cultural Tasks" (1918b).* In 1919 she collected these and other essays in *Reflections on Women and Women's Issues* and became the first German woman representative elected to a state assembly (Baden). In 1920 she was elected president of the Federation of German Women's Organizations. But her marriage was beleaguered on all sides—by Max's devotion to Else Jaffe, by the death of Helene Weber, by the suicide of Max's sister Lili, and by the emotions stirred by the bitter aftermath of a devastating war. Weber's move to adopt Lili's children may in part have been an attempt to save her marriage. But events overcame her struggle when Max Weber died unexpectedly of pneumonia on June 14, 1920.

Widowhood: 1920–1954

Weber's life and career after Max's death were determined by the tumultuous events of the Weimar Republic (1920–1933), the rise of Nazism (1933–1938), World War II

---

*An asterisk indicates that this paper is translated into English for the first time in the readings at the end of this chapter.

(1939–1945), and the post-war occupation and division of Germany into a communist eastern state and a democratic-capitalist western state (1945–1954). The Weimar Republic was marked by political and cultural freedom on the one hand and severe economic instability and inflation on the other. Weber's life in this period began with a major personal depression produced by Max's unexpected death. For four years, she withdrew from public and social life, so dramatically that her friends appealed to her to hold to her own feminist principles of autonomy. She worked out her grief in her project of constructing Max's fame for posterity. Between 1920 and 1922, she prepared ten volumes of Max's writings for publication, including the multi-volume major theoretical statement *Economy and Society,* as well as *Religion and Capitalism, Politics as a Vocation, Science as a Vocation, Collected Works* (a volume of his early and obscure writings), a volume of his political essays, and a collection of his correspondence (Britton, 1979). Between 1923 and 1926, she completed the famous biography. This editing and writing was a psychic strategy for coping with grief, and its consequences are enormously significant for Western sociology. As Max Weber scholar Guenther Roth admits, "It is . . . fair to say that without Marianne Weber, her husband's work might not have gained its later importance for the course of social science" (Roth, 1990:67). By the mid-1920s Weber had worked through the crisis of grieving and re-emerged into public life. In 1924, she accepted an honorary doctorate from Heidelberg—a singular honor for a woman—for both her own scholarship on women and her editing of Max's work. In 1926, she re-established her weekly intellectual salon, which she kept functioning, in one way or another, until the end of her life. She entered upon her most intense phase of public speaking on women's issues, often speaking to audiences of over 5,000 (Britton, 1979). She published *Die Idee der Ehe und die Ehescheidung* ("The Idea of Marriage and Divorce") (1929) and *Die Ideale der Geschlechtergemeinschaft* ("The Ideal of Community between Men and Women") (1930). Her domestic life in these years centered on juggling scarce funds in the hyper-inflation of Germany's economy, caring for and then adopting Lili's four children, and being in turn cared for by a loving circle of friends, including Else Jaffe.

The period of repression and terrorism that began in 1933 and continued until the Allied Occupation of Germany in 1945 marked the end of Weber's public career as a feminist speaker. Hitler dissolved the Federation of German Women's Organizations in 1935, and political discussion, even in private circles, became a dangerous activity. On Hitler's regime, Weber commented: " 'A people in need of honor, for whom the belief in an unseen God and His kingdom had vanished, quieted its longing vision in creating a god from an enslaver'" (cited in Britton, 1979:110). Despite her need to keep a low profile in these years, she maintained her intellectual circle, offered what succor she could to her Jewish friends and other dissidents, grieved herself into depression over their fate under Nazi oppression—and still kept writing. *Frauen und Liebe* ("Women and Love"), a curious compromise between official expectations and Weber's feminist views, was published in 1935, early in the Nazi regime; *Erfülltes Leben* ("The Fulfilled Life") was published by an underground press in 1942 and reissued after the occupation in 1946. Weber's seventieth and seventy-fifth birthdays were marked in subdued but loving ceremonies by her circle of friends, amidst the ravages of the war.

After Germany's defeat, as word of the full horror of the Nazi regime became public knowledge, she wrote of herself experiencing, "'[a]bove all, guilt, that I fall into again and again'" (cited in Britton, 1979:156). Yet she defended her role of silence and in-visibility during those years: "'How do you know the power of terror? Every open outcry was atoned for by a desperate death and a useless martyrdom. We have saved ourselves only by silence'" (cited in Britton, 1979: 154). Early in the Occupation, Weber was visited by two Harvard graduate students who told her that Max's theories were famous in America—a report that gave her the deepest satisfaction. Weber her-self remained busy writing—first her own memoirs in 1948 and then a revised edition of Max's biography in 1952. In her last years, she watched the construction of a pros-perous and democratic West Germany, many of whose elder statesmen were drawn from her old Heidelberg salon.

GENERAL SOCIAL THEORY

Assumptions

Weber's sociology in the period 1890–1920 is primarily framed by three strands of Ger-man social thought: (1) a gender ideology of aggressive and sensual masculinity and spir-itual, domesticated femininity, (2) the first major wave of feminist organization and thought, and (3) the neo-idealist formulation of social science by liberal male academics like Max Weber and Georg Simmel.

Traditional Gender Ideology   The German unification of 1871 was achieved by the authoritarian and militaristic regime of the monarchy of Prussia led by Bismarck. Huge, hard-drinking, coarse in speech, and a ruthless power-broker, Bismarck presented a model of unchallengeable male domination, allowing no competing personalities in his political inner circle, terrifying other politicians into almost childlike compliance. While many liberals, including Marianne and Max Weber, were critical of him, the Chancellor was an object of national devotion and deification. Men of all classes—including Max Weber's father—sought to emulate his power, his sensuality, his energy, his will to domi-nation (Kandal, 1988). Bismarck both helped to create and magnified a traditional ideal of manhood in late-nineteenth-century Germany.

In this cultural milieu, wives were expected to be subservient to their husbands, sexu-ally chaste except in response to their husbands, and restricted to the private sphere of *Kinder, Kirche, und Küche* (children, church, and kitchen). Men had to find their place in public life and were free to seek sexual gratification outside the home with mistresses and prostitutes. Confronting these expectations, women created an ideology of their own that subtley resisted the ideology of male dominance. They defined marriage, children, and religion as the means for expressing the traits of spirituality and ethereal goodness that defined femininity. In the face of a materialistic and militaristic public culture, they saw women's world as a place of peace, harmony, and spiritual uplift. These competing im-ages of maleness and femaleness were often a source of acute tension between the sexes—a tension bitterly enacted in the unhappiness of the marriage of Max's parents, Max, Sr. and Helene Weber (Weber, 1926/1975). Weber describes the grandmother and aunts who raised her, and her mother-in-law, Helene, as all embodying in some degree this image of pure womanhood. Even as she moved into the political discourse of feminism and the academic discourse of social science, Weber remained deeply affected by this image of womanhood, as well as by its critique of traditional maleness.

German Feminism Despite the centrality of Bismarckian politics, Germany was not a uniform and undifferentiated political landscape. The powerful academic community in its many university bases split between factions who conformed to the norms of the governing regime and factions intensely critical of that regime. The rapid industrialization of Germany between 1870 and 1900 created an affluent middle class, segments of which advanced a progressive liberal tradition. The expanding working class was politically mobilized by many forms of socialist thought, including that of German exiles Karl Marx and Friedrich Engels.

Against this background, "the woman question"—the debate over women's second-class social status—became an important political issue, and a series of women's organizations sprang up to claim better conditions for women (Kandal, 1988). One powerful sector advocated a liberal feminist agenda of equal rights: access to education and employment; equal wages for equal work; health and child care benefits; full political rights and suffrage; and changes in marriage laws to give women property rights, rights to their children, the possibility of divorce, and the possibility of partnership with rather than subordination to the husband. The most powerful organization of liberal feminists was the Federation of German Women's Organizations (*Bund deutscher Frauenvereine*), which between 1890 and 1920 would move into its most militant mode, led by theoretical critiques of patriarchal practices. Weber, after her monumental 1907 study *Marriage, Motherhood, and the Law,* was regarded as a leading intellectual of the liberal feminist movement and followed a demanding and remunerative lecture circuit as a spokeswoman for the federation (serving as president in 1920); she saw many of its projects realized—the admission of women to higher education and professional careers, enfranchisement, and the election of women representatives.

Weber was also affected in varying degrees by three alternative feminist positions. One such position was that of socialist feminists like Emma Ihrer, Ottilie Baader, Helene Grunberg, Gertrud Hanna, Clara Zetkin, Luise Zietz, Lily Braun, and Marie Jucharz (Fout, 1984:8–9), who were based in the socialist labor unions and the socialist political party, the Social Democrats. Despite the sexist and anti-feminist bias in these organizations, socialist feminists mounted a formidable critique of the linked exploitative arrangements of capitalism and patriarchy, arguing for the rights and interests of working-class women and for working-class solidarity as the means both to destroy capitalist-patriarchy and to emancipate women and men. Weber drew from socialist feminism an understanding of economically determined class relations as the primary variable creating differences among women in life experiences and needs. Her analyses are sensitive to class differences. But she never formally articulates a critique of capitalism, nor does she envisage its disappearance. Essentially, her position is that patriarchy is analytically separate from capitalism, and that changing the customary and legal practices of patriarchy would remove most of the abuses of power that socialist feminists linked to capitalism.

In part, this view was a result of her relation to a second feminist position, that of cultural feminism, which was itself an expansion of the older German belief in women's special spiritual and ethical qualities. Cultural feminism had been at the core of the original German feminist movement, though that movement shifted in the mid-1890s to the liberal agenda we described earlier. But even with this shift, many women, though loyal to the liberal agenda, still affirmed the value of what they saw as women's special qualities of spirituality and goodness. Weber rejected traditional essentialist claims about fundamental differences in male and female nature, yet held that the gender patterning of human work gave women, as a group, the primary responsibilities for producing, reproducing, and enriching human life at the level of ongoing dailiness (Kandal, 1988; Tijssen, 1991).

Third, Weber also responded to a feminist strand in the German configuration of critique known as "the erotic movement" (Green, 1974; Kandal, 1988). The erotic movement, which had its base in artistic and intellectual circles radiating out of Munich, called for the overturn of the traditional double standard of sexuality, and for a revolution in sexual mores for both women and men. This revolution would reconnect men and women with their essential human energy and free them from the repressions projected into human culture in all forms of sadomasochistic domination. Erotic feminism drew on the new insights of Freudian psychoanalytic thought, which in turn may be viewed as a response to the hyper-patriarchal family structure of traditional and Bismarckian Germany. Erotic feminism called for sexual experimentation, the dismantling of monogamy, the liberation of women and men through free love, and for a critique of heterosexuality through homoerotic exploration. Erotic feminist arguments were expounded by close friends and associates of Weber—most importantly, Else Jaffe—and thus affected her friendships and her marriage. Weber devotes a significant part of her theory to discussing issues of sexuality generally and the theses of erotic feminism in particular (see Theme 2, following).

Neo-Idealist Social Science   As Max's wife, Weber lived and wrote at the center of the circle of thinkers who shaped the classic German contribution to sociology typically termed the neo-idealist tradition, presented to sociologists today primarily through the theories of Max Weber and Simmel. In essence, the view of sociology in which Weber was immersed is marked by the following themes. Social science is not identical to natural and physical science because its subject matter, human beings, is a phenomenon unique in nature. Human beings act and relate on the bases of subjectively held meanings which in large measure reflect intra-psychic assimilation of the historical and cultural structures of their particular society. Social science thus requires a method that explores the historical and cultural uniqueness of societies, the meaningful actions of human beings in these societies, and the structured patterns of association and organization that they create. Social scientists, while themselves shaped by cultural meanings, which affect their selection and definition of research issues, should stand methodologically in the meaning systems of modern science and aspire to empirically rigorous, value-neutral investigation. Modern Western society is the primary subject for such investigation. The characteristic malaise of modern Western society comes from individuals' loss of meaningfulness in their activities. This loss of meaningfulness results from the growth of massive and impersonal bureaucratic structures, and from the spread of a culture emphasizing neither transcendent meaning nor a practical means–ends calculus as the motive for action, but rather the rote following of prescribed rules. Weber presents a clear summary of this theory in Chapter 10 of her biography of Max. One characteristic of Weber's sociology is her modification of this social science theory through feminist critique and through her method of standing in women's situation as the place from which to discover the social world.

Major Themes

Weber takes women's experience as the starting point for her sociological investigation, and she makes women the subjectivity through which social experience is seen and evaluated. Her sociology is thus woman-centered both in the issues it studies and in the angle of vision it takes. Her work stands as a reaction to what she saw developing within the male circles of social science she knew so intimately: the easy assumption that the statement made about the social actor either fit both men and women or that women were not significant enough to warrant a separate analysis. But her sociology is not merely reactive; it is a proactive feminist statement, affirming women's rights to moral autonomy, economic independence, and sexual fulfillment, and naming their distinctive contributions to society and culture. We present her theory in terms of four themes: a groundedness in women's experience, a focus on marriage as the paradigm for patriarchy, a use of women's work as a way to map the social world, and a sensitivity to differences among women.

1. Weber grounds her critical feminist sociology in her experience as a woman in a male-created world and in her response to the analysis of that world in the male-dominated discourse of sociology. Weber takes as her starting point the changing position of women in Germany at the beginning of the twentieth century and her own lived experience of that change. In this she is consistent with the neo-idealist belief that one cannot generalize beyond a historically specific situation and she anticipates the current feminist argument that analysis begins with one's personal lived experience. From this starting point, she describes the experience of women now seeking a life within and a life outside of marriage: "our time first knows the conflict between marriage and profession, between the special . . . tasks of the woman and her . . . need to build with others the suprapersonal cultural world" (1912a/1919/1997:40).[†] Thus, she begins by defining the age—"our time"— not in terms of political events made by men but in terms of women's experience. For women, the key feature of the age is that they both continue to work in the home and now go out to work because of the capitalist reorganization of society: "the new life-style forces of the machine age broke open the circle of her [woman's] gender-determined tasks and led her out of the protection of the house, and thereby out of the realm of her husband's control" (1912a/1997:33).[†]

Weber's analysis of social organization from the standpoint of women shows that society attempts to produce a harmonious communal life through the gender socialization of its members. But this gender socialization is patterned by patriarchy, a transinstitutional arrangement that subordinates women and privileges men. Weber focuses her critique of

---

†A dagger following a citation in the text means that the passage quoted is given in fuller context in the readings at the end of the chapter.

patriarchy on two primary and interconnected areas of women's experience—marriage and work—and on the way societal harmony is bought at the expense of women's autonomy. She analyzes marriage as an intricate relation of power and intimacy, and women's work as a complex of experiences encompassing both work done at home and work done in the public sphere. Weber shows how women's lives are framed by the male-dominated institutions of law, religion, and economy; by an historical context that is a series of male-made events; and by male-dominated analyses of these institutions and events.

In working out her sociology, Weber is aware that she not only describes woman's place in a male-dominated world, but that she does so using the analytic frameworks of male-dominated discourses, most particularly sociology. Thus, her sociology engages explicitly with the theories of Simmel and implicitly with the theories of her husband Max. In dialogue with Simmel, she reworks his idea of the gender division of labor in the production of a meaningful human world and she brings the lens of gender to bear on his theme of human alienation. In dialogue with Max, she does a feminist reworking of his theory of power as authority. She writes not from a position of value-neutrality but as an open advocate of change toward greater equality between the sexes. Drawing on women's lived experience, she develops a model of the social actor that emphasizes not only the quest for meaning (as in Max's model) or the desire for sociability (as in Simmel's) but the embodied practical need for material existence; the embodied sensual need for erotic and sexual gratification; the psychic need for agency, or self-directed action; the emotional need for intimacy; and the ethical needs for moral autonomy and harmony with others. For Weber, these needs are essential human needs, the species demands of both women and men. Under patriarchy, men are granted psychic and relational entitlement to fulfil their human needs, while women are defined and relationally situated to sublimate these human needs into service as the enablers of men's will.

2. Weber treats marriage as paradigmic of the patriarchal distortion of human life. Weber's analysis begins with her understanding that for women in her day the expectation of marriage is the shaping fact of existence. She traces the consequences of this basic principle—that woman understands herself and is understood by men and by the society as a being destined for marriage—across the institutions of law, work, religion, government, philosophy, and education.[2] But her study of the position of women begins with marriage itself. Much of her work, including her major work *Marriage, Motherhood, and the Law* (1907), is devoted to a historical/structural analysis of marriage. The cutting edge of her analysis, however, is her formulation of the microsocial dynamics of marriage as a complex and ongoing negotiation over power and intimacy, in which money, women's work, and sexuality are key issues.

History and Structure   Weber introduces her historical account of Western marriage with the premise that "whoever wants to thoroughly understand and correctly judge the inner structure of marriage, the relationship between the sexes, must cast at least a brief glance over the history of its development, and above all over the leading ideas through which it has been defined" (1912a/1919/1997:27).[†] Analyzing texts of law, religion, politics, and philosophy, she begins a history of marriage with what she calls "primitive patriarchy" in which "the wife was the husband's property" and "the sole formal formative principle of the relationship" was "simply the right of the stronger" (1912a/1919/1997:27).[†] She shows that Greek, Roman, Jewish, and early Christian law incrementally restricted the husband's power by establishing that the wife had some legitimate claims on the husband and in the society because of the marriage relation. Early Christian doctrines designed to restrict sexuality, while challenged by the modern age, nevertheless introjected into the marriage the possibility of a "spiritual and moral relation between husband and wife" (1912a/1919/1997:30).[†] For Weber the significance of the Protestant ethic lies not in the spirit of capitalism but in women's claim to autonomy through its assertion that each person, male or female, is an independent moral agent accountable to God alone.[3] "Within the religious communities of the New World that were sustained by the Puritan spirit, the idea of the religious equality of woman first came to be taken seriously. . . . Freedom of conscience, the mother of all personal rights of the individual, stood, across the ocean, at the cradle of women's rights as well" (1912a/1919/1997:31).[†]

Weber then shows how this doctrine of freedom of conscience became the basic moral claim in both the political revolutions of the eighteenth century and the philosophic achievement of German idealism. German idealism argued that the capacity for reason means that each individual has the responsibility to be self-actualizing and morally self-directing. The ethical basis for social relations, thus, must be that each person respect these capacities in every other person and that "no person may regard a fellow human being as *simply* the means to his/her own personal ends" (1912a/1919/1997:32).[†] This principle of ethical social life, Weber claims, must be applied to the marriage relation. But she shows that in looking at the marriage relation, the philosophers let the male desire for domination override the philosophic imperative for consistency. Rather than protesting woman's subordination within marriage, these philosophers argued that the woman in entering into marriage willingly agrees as part of that contract to relinquish her autonomy to the husband.

Weber's historical review concludes that women's recent acquisition of a degree of autonomy in marriage came about not through the evolution of ideas but through new industrial conditions that removed her from her husband's control, thrusting her as a worker for wages into the public sphere. With irony Weber notes that these new industrial conditions forced an important concession from the German legal system—"the independently earned wages of the wife remain reserved to her as her property" (1912a/1919/1997:35). Yet Weber emphasizes that most contemporary marriage laws reinforce a patriarchal patterning of marriage and household.

Interaction and Negotiation   After this macrosocial framing of marriage, Weber shifts her analysis to the microsocial dynamics of the marital relation. She shows how patriarchy, which gives the man the authority to make decisions so that the married couple may present "an external appearance of unanimity" (1912a/1919/1997:36),[†] erodes the integrity of the marriage relationship itself. For a marriage based in such "authority," that is, in enforced super- and subordination, destroys the possibility of intimacy. In marriage, only recognition of the other's autonomy can produce free exchange, shared growth, and continued interest in the other: Enforced subordination must finally destroy the presence of the other, that is, of the wife to the husband. The wife may come to practice "a simply hypocritical submission" or experience "a wasting-away of her whole intellectual/spiritual development" or suddenly introject autonomy as a "hostile element" in the marriage (1912a/1997:36).[†] Further, ensured superordination arouses in the husband "unrealistic and unrealizable desires" so that "he cannot rest when he does not know himself to be continuously the master of her totally personal inner life, as well" (1912a/1919/1997: 37).[†] Weber sees the worst fate of patriarchal marriage as that condition in which "the spouses live together without further effort," preserving the appearance of unanimity, although the husband is left without anyone with whom he can share as an equal, and the wife, without anyone to whom she may speak her mind (1912a/1919/1997:40).[†]

Money   In most marriages, Weber argues, the wife is an economic dependent of her husband. Even in cases where she works, full- or part-time, her income typically is only a fraction of his. This relation of economic super- and subordination permeates the marital relation as an ongoing irritant and erodes the woman's sense of moral adulthood.

> [T]he wife must come pleading and coaxing to her husband on matters of her personal needs. . . . As someone held in dependency . . . she adopts the weapons of the weak and tries to reach her goal by all sorts of roundabout ways . . . How disfiguring are all these various slave tricks that our sex still adheres to because we must obtain so many of the things we need for our lives by stealth from a "lord and master." (1912b/1919/1997:43–44)[†]

A predictable source of money for her autonomous use, in household management and for personal expenses, is essential for a woman's freedom, agency, and moral maturity.

Weber explores many possible routes by which the wife might have economic independence. She criticizes Gilman's proposal that all women go out into the workforce, showing, through census data, that only a tiny minority of upper-class, educated women will attain fulfilling, well-paid jobs. The majority of wage-earning women, she points out, do hard, underpaid work out of necessity, not choice. She considers the possibility of the government's paying women for the very valuable domestic work they all do. Such a payment would require a *meaningful* allowance from the state—not a token contribution—and would in total exceed the whole state budget. She weighs the proposal that the husband pay the wife for her housework and considers how a money value might be set. Like Gilman, she sees that the hardest-working wives, the wives of poor men, would get insignificant payments, while the wives of wealthy men, if paid the going rate for housework, often would be near destitution. In place of these proposals, Weber suggests a change in law and custom—a new requirement in all families that a budget be developed to cover household and personal expenditures, contributed to regularly by the wage earners in the home, in amounts proportional to their earnings, and arbitrated by the state in case of conflict. This proposal suggests a state policy that endorses women's autonomy by requiring a budget negotiation between husband and wife as beings equally materially entitled.

Sexuality   One of the immediate ways in which people try to achieve intimacy in marriage—and outside of it—is through sexuality and erotic experience. Weber distinguishes between sex and eros: pure physical sexuality she sees as impulsive, ultimately unfulfilling, and ethically questionable; erotic love, on the other hand, uses sexual pleasure as a means to achieving the interpersonal intimacy Weber views as both an essential human need and a social good. She argues that erotic intimacy should be a project for both women and men, and that it can better be achieved by more open discussion, sex education, and where necessary, contraception. She rejects the radical stance of free love, because erotic love is of itself transient and, if separated from the more long-term project of male/female intimacy, destined to wither away. She argues that because intimate closeness is the more general value, the partners in a sexual relation need to build a complex of mutual interests, projects, and pleasures around the first flame of erotic intimacy so that the closeness can grow even if the erotic link weakens. "Feeling," she writes, "does not always remain at the heights, we change, we return to the everyday. . . . To set love no laws is to surrender to impermanence, and to turn one's back on the Other to whom one owes such happiness . . . One has to bring the life materials of the day too, the inexhaustible abundance of the world into the partnership" (1918a/1919/1997:62). Weber's explicit discussion of sexual negotiation springs in part from her theoretical focus on marriage as the ideal-typical site of male/female relations, in part from her principles that autonomy and intimacy are essential human needs—and above all, from her project of standing where women stand and from that place naming and exploring the issues of daily life that confront them as moments of moral decision making.

3. Weber uses women's work to map and explain the construction and reproduction of the social person and the social world.

Weber's theory of women's work starts with the idea that all culture is the result of human work: "We understand as culture all intellectually determined, purposeful working on and shaping of material given by nature" (1918b/1919/1997:1).[†] Human work creates a range of cultural products from the most abstract and massively reified cultural phenomena, such as philosophy or language, to the most personal and reflective efforts at self-development, such as personal honesty or cleanliness as values. Between these two poles, Weber argues, lies a vast unexplored cultural territory: "the middle ground of immediate daily life" which is essential to our understanding of society, culture, the gendered division of work, and women's contribution to social life (1918b/1919/1997:2).

But before turning to exploring this middle ground of culture, Weber makes the claim that all human beings, women and men, potentially share the same species traits for work, that is, for cultural production. Woman

> as *human being* . . . shares with the man an abundance of talents and abilities that direct her towards the same tasks and forms of activity as they do him . . . woman is called, on principle, to participate in every kind of cultural *work* for which her individual talents fit her. . . . There is absolutely no realm of activity, be it technology, law and custom, or art, science, philosophy and religion from which she may be justifiably excluded. (1918b/1919/1997:2 [her italics])[†]

Yet woman is assigned in the gender division of work to the tasks of producing daily existence. In exploring the work of immediate daily existence, Weber gives a woman-centered portrait of society and human work that moves to the center of analytic attention issues overlooked in male-dominated sociology. Among the activities she recognizes in the cultural production of dailiness are: caregiving for "spouse, the aging parent, . . . the coming generation"; housekeeping which "depends materially upon . . . how all the various items . . . bought as market wares . . . will be arranged, used, and cared for"; strategic consumerism to "exert an influence over production"; child-care, both practical provisioning and socialization, "the forming of their natures through certain precepts and ideals"; the emotional and physical restoration of adults by creating "a home, a place of recovery . . . in which human beings . . . fragmented by jobs . . . can continually restore themselves"; the production and reproduction in home and community of "what we may term a *culture of expression* [which] shapes the behavior of the individual towards the surrounding others"; and finally, morality itself, "the ability to, as the phrase goes, 'transpose oneself into the soul of another'" (1918b/1919/1997:3–8).[†] In sum, it is within this everyday environment that the human being produces the self who will affect other people through actions in the world.

Weber generates this analysis of women's work as part of a dialogue with Simmel, who responded to the debate on women's place in society by introducing a sociology of gender into the classic canon, where it would remain unremarked by historians of the discipline until the ferment of late-twentieth-century feminism sent male scholars back to classical male scholarship in search of the missing "woman question" (see Coser,1977; Kandal, 1988; Oakes,1984). Simmel superimposes his theory of gender on his more fundamental, now classic distinction between objective and personal culture. "Objective culture" is his term for all the supra-personal objects and texts that transcend and shape individual social existence—tools, technology, science, art, language, academic knowledge, religion, law, money, moral systems, and so on. "Personal culture" is his term for the individual's psychic achievement of a sense of the meaningfulness of existence. Simmel argues that men create objective culture out of their gender-specific capacities for specialization, detachment, depersonalization, symbolic mediation, and action in pursuit of long-term goals (Oakes, 1984:23–25). Objective culture, however, according to Simmel, is a reified and alienating milieu that attracts male effort, consumes male energy, and separates men from the wholeness of a personal culture. On the other hand, women's gender-specific traits, which are typically the opposite of men's, give them little propensity for creating objective culture but a heightened capacity for achieving "the beautiful soul" of personal culture, the most fundamental project of humankind. Women are in this respect superior to men. They remain, however, secondary and skeptical participants in objective culture, which is masculine in essence. Simmel sees man's capacity for achieving personal culture, a sense of the meaningfulness of existence, as threatened by the runaway expansion of objective culture in modern Western societies.

Weber first answers Simmel's theory of gender with her argument that women and men have equal capacities for work. Objective culture, she says, is created and maintained by human work. But personal culture also takes work—"mastery" over "instinctive impulses" and "the realization of the intrinsic possibilities" of human nature (1918b/1919/1997:1).[†] In many of her essays in *Reflections on Women and Women's Issues* (1919/1997), she charts women's participation in objective culture: from women's age-old economic work in agriculture, to their more recent participation in industry, trade, and the professions, their experiences in and contributions to higher education, and their role in politics. Her purpose in all these accounts is to show the diversity of women's contributions to objective culture, the degree to which those contributions are like those of men, and also, on occasion, how these contributions are in contrast to the typical male model of cultural production. She also stresses the ways in which patriarchy affects women's experiences in these areas of work—by unequal treatment, unequal reward, and the demands and expectations of heterosexuality in the sites of production. But she also claims that when women come to objective culture, as when they pursue a university education or a governmental office, they bring to that objective culture a special knowledge drawn from their gender-specific work in the middle ground of immediate daily existence.

More significantly, she claims that women's cultural work encompasses not only the personal culture and the objective culture, but also the crucial third sphere of work—the production of immediate daily life—which brings those two poles together in ways essential both to societal continuity and to individual self-development. Thus women work with immediate practical concerns, on an ongoing daily basis, to mediate and translate the texts and products of objective culture into a usable environment for individuals in daily life. This women's work is not trivial or marginal, as male sociology represents it. It is work that calls for practical judgment, physical exertion, relational skill, aesthetic sensibility, and ethical and moral groundedness—that is, for all the qualities of humanness.

This great middle ground of culture, an undiscovered continent of women's work, is the bridge—and, to a degree, the solution to the tension Simmel sketches—between objective and personal culture. It is the space in which one cultural form is translated into the other, in either direction; and optimally, the action of translation—connecting objective culture to the personal through dailiness, and vice versa—leads to morality, or ethical meaningfulness, in action and understanding.

4. Weber's sociology is framed by an understanding of differences among women resulting from class, education, age, and ideology. In her analysis of women's experience, Weber consistently recognizes categorical differences among women produced by their various locations in social structure, of which location in the class structure seems to her the most important. She understands the profound differences between rural and urban women in the Germany of her day, and the distinctions between rural women themselves: "The life patterns of these [agricultural] classes, for the most part still structured around traditional farm labor, are . . . so different from the life patterns of all other classes . . . that it would be senseless to look . . . for . . . a general formulation. . . . Besides . . . [it] contains within itself such diverse existences as those of the peasant landholder . . . the resident farm worker, the seasonal worker and the day laborer" (1912b/1919/1997:46).[†] Within urban society, women are distinguished by the occupation and earnings of their husbands and by their own employment, whether full- or part-time; in industry, sales, commerce, hotels, restaurants; as domestics, laborers, or free professionals. Weber points out that the free professionals are themselves distinguished by whether they work in the traditional women's professions of midwifery and teaching or belong to a tiny elite of academics, artists, writers, and so on.

These differences in class location produce material differences which translate in daily living into enormous differences in lifestyle, needs, and perceptions. Weber is insistent that the leaders of the women's movement not generalize from their own elite class experiences to advocate any one policy or strategy for the relief of all women. She is particularly concerned about the argument by feminist spokeswomen—including Gilman—that all women can be emancipated and fulfilled through wage sector employment. Weber argues that within the realities of capitalist employment, most women's wage work, indeed, most people's wage work, is done out of necessity and is hard, "fragmenting" and unfulfilling. Bearing the double burden of wage work and housework, women of most class positions lead lives in which the solution of employment for all will not produce utopia.

Weber is aware of the particular privilege of women like herself—financially secure, educated, and living unencumbered by marriage or in marriages like her own with liberal-minded husbands. For her, this privilege brings specific responsibilities: to speak for women in male discourses, to permeate those discourses with the particular interests and sensibilities of women, and to undertake the work of linking objective culture to the cultural middle ground of daily life in order to morally uplift both the average, less-privileged woman's life, and the overspecialized, alienated understandings of privileged male culture. Weber's later work *Frauen und Liebe* ("Women and Love") (1935) is a deliberate effort at popularizing her theoretical ideas, and she reports in her autobiography (1948) her delight when ordinary women wrote to say how much they had learned from this work.

Weber discusses other lines of difference between women. In her 1917 essay "Types of Academic Women" (1917/1919/1997), she looks at differences between three generations of university-educated women. The first generation, the heroic type, had to fight their way alone into the academic halls of male privilege, often adopted masculine ways and dress in order to blend in, were typically older and single, and abandoned thoughts of marriage because that quest seemed to betray the self they had invented. Yet these sacrifices led to a full life: they were happy, thankful, and triumphant in the sense that they were working not just for themselves but for all women. The second generation, guided by the first and a growing women's movement, felt much less pressure to express personhood at the expense of womanhood, seeing possibilities for love and marriage in relationships with male classmates. But they frequently found themselves assigned to academic drudgery rather than intellectually challenging projects and often felt isolated from the rich female experience of creating the ongoing immediacies of the everyday world. But it is the third—and in her day, current—generation, that Weber worries about: now admitted on the same conditions as males, they have no special sense of having won a prize just to be there; their attention is divided between studies and the wish to remain attractive to men, between a desire to be involved in the production of immediate existence and an attention to objective theoretical work. In other essays, Weber explores differences among types of feminists, differences between women created by the competing ideologies of "the cult of domesticity" and "the new woman," and differences between the genteel parochialism of provincial women and the avant-garde groups in the big cities.

Awareness of these many lines of diversity has several consequences for Weber's sociology. It draws her to a sympathetic and tolerant imagining, a practical *verstehen*, of the views of women very different from herself. It makes her a pragmatist in her choice of policy directions for women, seeking not necessarily the theoretically "most feminist" solutions but those that lend themselves most flexibly to the diverse circumstances under which women live. And it makes her reflectively aware of her own situated vantage point, which she affirms thoughtfully, modestly, and with conviction.

WEBER'S RELEVANCE FOR THE HISTORY AND PRESENT PRACTICE OF SOCIOLOGY

Weber and the Canon of Sociology

Weber's major relation to the canon is her significance for the German contribution to interpretive sociology. In this section we look at the ways in which she modifies our understanding of the theories of Max Weber and Georg Simmel. Until we have a more complete translation of her works, particularly until we have a translation of *Ehefrau und Mutter in der Rechtsentwicklung* (1907), it is impossible fully to assess her significance in the Max Weber–Georg Simmel discourse. At this point we would say that while she contributes a provocatively critical voice to that discourse, the scope of her sociology does not begin to approximate the monumental contributions of the two men. Moreover, it is apparent from her writings available in English that Weber worked within a framework of concepts and themes that we take as hallmarks of Max's and Simmel's thinking and which she herself attributes to them: concepts such as "social content," "social form," and "ideal type"; themes such as alienation as the product of the exponential growth of objective culture, economic classes as significant but not determinative social structures, the relation between law and society and between religion and meaning, and the importance of power relations in both interpersonal and macro-social arrangements. Also, Weber adopts the methodology of these men, a methodology of analyzing historically specific cases and of approaching human subjects with sympathetic understanding of their meanings.

Yet Weber inserts a critical and feminist wedge into this discourse by bringing to bear on it the subversive question of feminism: And what about the women? Standing in women's experience and generalizing from that experience, she quietly but effectively dismantles some of Max's and Simmel's most famous theoretical constructions. We have already described her feminist critique of Simmel's sociology of gender and his theory of how gender correlates with the two realms of objective and personal culture (see Theme 3, preceding). As part of this critique, Weber rejects Simmel's posture of despair over the consequences for meaningful human life of an autonomous, expanding, and reified objective culture. She presents many of his arguments as the situated concerns of a privileged-class male thinker. She makes clear, for example, in her analysis of the housewife and money, that philosophic despair over money as a culture reification is the luxury of those who have easy and non-problematic access to it; that for those who lack any direct route to fiscal independence, money, or the lack thereof, is a practical issue, and access to sufficient money is a prerequisite for free moral agency. She rejects the thesis that men by nature are less able than women to do the work of creating personal culture, that they are the tragic victims of their genius for creating objective, supra-personal cultural forms. Indeed, as she explores the vast middle continent of women's cultural work in producing immediate, daily life, one is led to conclude (though Weber does not push the point home, for that is not her style of argument) that privileged-class men can reflect on the tragedy of alienating objective culture because they can still think and feel meaningfully. That continuing capacity for feeling is the result of the daily cultural production by women, production which renews meaning and well-being, though it goes unremarked in male intellectual discussions of modern culture.

Weber's relation to Max's sociology is more elusively critical, for her presentation of herself, and her marriage, is of a partnership based in mutual loyalty. Yet when Weber poses the question, "And what about the women?" to Max's sociology, she in fact shows that Weber has no answer at all—no presence of women, either negatively or positively, in his sociology. Thus, the woman question is more marginal in Max Weber's thinking than in the classic but conservative texts of Emile Durkheim (Lehmann, 1996), or the equally classic, sentimentally liberal writings of Simmel (Coser, 1977; Oakes, 1984). This masculinist bias in Max Weber's thought, insightfully explored by Kandal (1988) and Bologh (1990), is there despite his personal respect for women, close bond to his mother, relatively egalitarian relationship to Marianne, support of her intellectual and political ambitions, and liberal support of other women students who studied with him. Introducing Marianne Weber to the canon shows us both the consequences and the reproduction of patriarchal assumptions in the work of even the best intentioned of male theorists. It may be of Max that she is thinking when she writes of "husbands, particularly from the intellectually leading classes, who are ready to value their own wife as an individual and to renounce . . . the exercise of their gender privilege" but who are not "willing to fundamentally resign their rights of authority over the whole female sex" (1912a/1919/1997:33–34).[†]

In her stunningly critical essay "Authority and Autonomy in Marriage" (1912a/1919/1997), Weber makes a series of feminist critiques of Max's sociology. First, she argues that only from the perspective of a superordinate is the problematic of power primarily a question of whether it is exercised coercively or authoritatively. The subordinate experiences the exercise of power as control over her or his own will. Max's typology of coercion versus authority addresses only the degree of overtness and explicitness in the tyranny exercised in the relations of domination. It leaves unexplored the ethical issues of subordinating the will of the less powerful actor and of the subordinate's equal right to individual autonomy. Second, in this and other essays, Weber describes the subordinate as not necessarily complying with authoritative domination. For from the subordinate's viewpoint, the superordinate makes the rules that say that the relationship of domination is one of legitimate authority. The subordinate has to find ways in which to survive as a willful subjectivity under domination by using the powers of the weak: secrecy, manipulation, lies, silence, childishness, coquetry, and sexuality. Third, Weber's analyses of the religious history of Western society reveal that Max's sociology of religion, including his exploration of Protestantism and the Puritan sects, is conducted with a concern only for the consequences of those massive, culture-forming institutions for male lives; that their profound consequences for women in particular and human relations in general are left unexplored. Fourth, Weber shows that the preservation of patriarchal domination between the sexes in the most intimate and daily of human relations, marriage, is the skeleton at the feast in the philosophic and social science celebrations of expanding democratic rights in Western societies, which are taken for granted in Max's sociology. Finally, Weber is not value-neutral in her theoretical stance. She is partisan for women, calling for state policies that will liberate them from patriarchy. In her autobiography she reports that Max would read her essays and urge her not to be "emotional," but that, despite her wish for his approbation, she was unwilling to write theory in a value-neutral voice (Kirchen, 1997).

Weber's gendered and personalized voice, then, lets us see that the writings of Max Weber and Georg Simmel, though presented in the universal and abstract voice of "pure theory," are also statements by particular people with gender, class, and biographical distinctiveness (see Bologh, 1990). One example of this is found in their very different senses of human work (see Theme 3, preceding). A second example is found in the understanding of the human actor. Max shows us individuated human beings, pursuing personal projects with a consciousness of others as a "social environment." Simmel shows us individuated human beings linked by a web of association across physical and social space. Marianne Weber shows us the social actor engaged in a complex juggling act— moving from responsive activity towards others, to goal-oriented production, to acts of communication with others, to absorption in associational procedures, and then to reflective self-monitoring. This was the reality of Marianne Weber's own experience of agency. Here, as elsewhere, by speaking consciously from a particular gendered viewpoint rather than from a universal stance, she achieves the broader rather than the narrower understanding of a key social science concept.

Weber and the Tradition of Feminist Sociology

Since our entire presentation of Weber's theory begins with the claim that it is a critical *feminist* sociology, to develop that argument here would be repetitive and redundant; this section, then, is simply a concluding statement. As an actively avowed feminist leader, Weber represents in her very person an important bridge between contending loyalties faced by many women in academia, a loyalty to the women's movement and feminist theory and practice, and a loyalty to one's discipline. Weber reports the tensions this caused her in her own career, especially in her refusal to do value-free sociology, despite Max's urgings. She represents in her work the feminist sociological commitment that one's work should be grounded in improving women's lives. *Ehefrau und Mutter in der Rechtsentwicklung* (1907) is a comprehensive study of woman's position as it has been defined through her most formal relationship with men, the institution of marriage. In offering this history, Weber shows women how to critique the male-created texts which frame and permeate the relationships in which they live. She brings to light an invisible (because taken for granted) area of women's work: the production that women do to create and sustain the milieux in which individuals can develop characters that let them relate ethically and intimately to others. She connects the dailiness of household work—the arrangement of furniture, the timing of meals, the appropriateness of manners in eating, the carefulness in dress so as not to cause distress to others—with an individual's total effect on others in the world. And she names that work descriptively "the shaping of immediate existence," drawing the connections—as do Anna Julia Cooper, Gilman, and Harriet Martineau—among the practice of manners, the substance of morals, and the maintenance of the home. While giving us one of the purest theoretical statements we have of what is generally called "housework" or "homemaking," she also offers a balanced assessment of the practical policy problem of how women should be monetarily compensated for housework. She connects the issue of wages for housework to the more fundamental proposition of the need for money as a requisite for autonomy in a capitalist society. Finally, Weber raises her voice in a male-dominated sociological discourse. She introduces into this discourse, which has largely assumed the male experience as the experience of the neutral social actor, the possibility of woman as the social actor. From this woman-centered vantage point, she proceeds to develop both a sociology and a critique of existing sociologies.

ENDNOTES

1. The claim has been made in several sources (Britton, 1979; Mitzman, 1970; Roth, 1990) that the marriage was unconsummated. We have found no evidence in the accounts by Marianne thus far available to us to support this.
2. In a later work, *Women and Love* (1935), Weber appears to explore a variety of possibilities besides traditional heterosexual marriage as ways of achieving meaningful human intimacy; but at the time of the essays we are examining, marriage was, for the vast majority of German women, the fact of life with which to come to terms.
3. Weber focuses especially on the Quaker doctrine of the inner light, which demands obedience to God as revealed to one in individual meditation and communion rather than through texts or authorities. She sees in that doctrine the most extreme statement in all of the Protestant ethic of the duty of the individual soul to act as an autonomous moral agent. The doctrine of the inner light does not allow one to retreat to some authority in the form either of text or priest-as-interpreter; it says, as Weber chooses to represent it, that the individual male or female must come directly into contact with God and be guided by this essentially autonomous experience of God.

READING 6-1

Excerpts from "Selections from Marianne Weber's *Reflections on Women and Women's Issues*"

All references to pages are to the manuscript pages of the Kirchen translation. The analysis of Weber's theory presented in this chapter draws primarily on this volume of her feminist and sociological essays on women's experiences of sexuality, marriage, divorce, housework, wage work, education, scholarship, law, and politics. These essays were written between approximately 1904 and 1919. They show Weber in discourse with Georg Simmel, Max Weber, Charlotte Perkins Gilman, Gertrud Simmel, and a large body of contemporary scholarship in Germany on women's lives and women's issues. The readings presented here mark the debut of Marianne Weber's theoretical writings for an English-speaking audience.

EXCERPT FROM "AUTHORITY AND AUTONOMY IN MARRIAGE"

This selection is excerpted from pages 27–41. In it, Weber explores the relation between women and men in patriarchy, focusing on the patriarchal patterning through history, by religion, philosophy, and law, of the most intimate of male–female relations, marriage. This essay gives Weber's feminist critique of domination and is a nuanced critique of Max Weber's themes of authority and power, as well as of his analytic emphases in his study of religion in general and Puritanism in particular. Marianne Weber looks at those aspects of Max's theory from a standpoint in women's experience.

Whoever wants to thoroughly understand and correctly judge the inner structure of marriage, the relationship between the sexes, must cast at least a

brief glance over the history of its development, and above all over the leading ideas through which it has been defined. So far as one can know, for all cultured European peoples, at the beginning of historical times the wife was the husband's property. Through purchase or exchange he acquired unlimited property rights over her and her children. He could therefore dispose of her as he wished—for example, sell her, repudiate her, set up rival women as her fellows, at any time—while in contrast to him she was without any rights, lastingly tied to him, and bound to fidelity and obedience. The sole formal formative principle of the relationship between husband and wife is therefore in the first instance simply the right of the stronger: primitive *patriarchy*. . . . The relationship between man and woman can be characterized as *marriage* in the true sense only when the absolute power of the husband finds its limits in certain duties toward the wife. Everywhere, this first occurs when the family of the wife no longer hands her over to the man without conditions, before everything not without endowing her with a dowry, which elevates the woman from concubine to wife. She thereby acquires the right that *her* children, before all other children of the man, must be counted as his "legitimate heirs." And so developed everywhere out of the purely natural power-relationship the oldest conscious form of sexual relationship, the so-called "legitimate marriage," as security for certain women and their children against the polygamous impulses of the man. For the rest, marriage at first retained the character of an ownership relation.[1]

Each great cultural epoch has formed and shaped this original structure, and along identical lines. Wherever morality increased, there increased also the effort to protect the wife in some way from barbaric arbitrariness on the part of the husband. On the other hand, lordship over her and the children remained everywhere assured to him.

Source: Marianne Weber, "Selections from Marianne Weber's *Reflections on Women and Women's Issues*," trans. Elizabeth Kirchen (Unpublished manuscript, 1997) (Originally published as *Frauenfragen und Frauengedanken*, Tübingen: J. C. B. Mohr, 1919). Used with permission of Elizabeth Kirchen.

---

[1]For the history of this transaction, see Marianne Weber, *Marriage, Motherhood, and the Law*, Tübingen, 1907.

He was directed toward a humane patriarchy, a gentler rule over the wife, but not to the recognition of her as his comrade.

The creation of monogamy as a legal institution was the work of the Greeks and Romans. That is to say, they created *statutory* monogamy, which certainly forbade the husband to take several women into the house and allowed him to have legitimate children from only one wife, but which hindered him neither legally nor indeed morally from possessing outside the house, without contractual obligation, as many other women as he wished. Here too the command of martial fidelity, with threat of severe punishment, remained imposed on the wife alone. . . .

In contrast to the Greeks and Romans, ancient Judaism still permitted polygamy. But it first surrounded marriage with a *religious* consecration of absolutely world-historical importance. Marriage was revealed to the prophets of the Old Dispensation as God's oldest institution and ordinance. . . . God Himself had, however, also defined the relationship of the spouses. He created a "helpmeet" for the husband and hung over her the command, "Your will shall be subject to your husband and he shall be your lord.". . . This sanctioning of patriarchy had the most wide-reaching consequences. Up into our own times it determined the structure of Christian marriage. For the noble Christian message of the religious equal status of woman was already, by the greatest apostle, diverted from its applicability to the husband. Paul, the Christian propagandist, who sought in all other areas to break through Judaic tradition, stayed, in reference to woman, completely within its territory. When questioned about the "law" he affirmed not only the wife's duty of obedience to the husband, but also her general placement in regard to man as a being of secondary status: "For man does not come from woman, but woman from man. And man is not created for the sake of woman, but woman for man." Solidified into dogma, this formulation makes its power felt up to today in those circles that believe in definitive revelation, and even beyond them. In a different direction, however,

Christianity created a great new cultural possession: intensification of the demand for legal monogamy into an indispensable religious/moral demand which was now aimed not only at the wife, but also, for the first time in history, emphatically at the husband. . . . Only when the husband, too, was directed to union with *one* woman could marriage . . . , out of the natural stuff of transitory sexual love, . . . grow the tenderest and deepest *soul*-relationship between husband and wife. . . .

To be sure, the perfection of the Christian ideal of marriage soon suffered damage through church teachings. In reaction against the sexual license of the late-antique cultural world, the church overemphasized the ideal of mastery of instinctive drives into contempt for everything natural and demanded their strongest possible suppression. The natural basis of the fellowship of husband and wife was relegated to the realm of the sinful, that was still admittedly allowed within marriage, but that was nevertheless even there worthy of no consecration. Remaining unmarried was esteemed the more perfect condition. Eve, the type of the physical-sensual woman, the mother of sin, the temptress to evil, was contrasted with the virginal Mary, the embodiment of non-sensual motherhood.

Protestantism did again elevate marriage, as "God's work," over celibacy as "the work of man," but it too left sexual love with the stain of being an "evil desire," stemming not from God but from the devil, which only within marriage was marginally tolerated by God . . . New arguments were sought out from the Bible for the subordination of the woman. In this way Luther most emphatically cited Eve's fall as its historical cause. . . .

But, from another angle, the Protestant spirit contributed to the deepening of the ideal of marriage and to the shaping of its everyday practice, namely through those currents outside the official Reformation churches that were characterized as "Puritanism." To be sure, Puritanism reached this goal by a roundabout route that is not immediately obvious. Namely, it carried the monastic ascetic ideals—discarding all the pleasures of living, suppression of all sensual pleasure—with inexorable harshness into the world and also into marriage. Luther's God did still, like the Catholic one, look on *marital* sensual pleasures, with magnanimous generosity, "through the fingers." The Puritan's God allowed them only for the purpose of procreation, to the greater glory of God.

However sharply we may today reject this demonizing and rationalizing of basic life forces, it is still not to be forgotten that . . . [o]nly when the restraint of the elementary, even within marriage, was taken seriously could the spiritual fusion of the spouses, the intimacy of their emotional relationship take center stage as the most important meaning of marriage.

What in such circles marriage could become is most beautifully expressed in a farewell letter, in the religiously colored speech of that time, from the Quaker W. Penn to his wife, as he left his motherland to found a new kind of state on the other side of the ocean. "Remember thou wast the love of my youth and much the joy of my life, the most belov'd as well as most worthy of all my earthly comforts. And the reason of that love was more thy inward, than thy outward excellencies (which yet were many) God knows and thou knowst it. I can say it was a match of Providence's making, and God's image in us both was the first thing, and the most amiable and engaging ornament in our eyes." What a world lies between *this* understanding of the relation between the sexes and that which comes to light in the well-known utterance of a Greek thinker: "We have courtesans, so that we can enjoy ourselves with them, then purchased women for the care of our bodies, and lastly wives, who are to give us legal offspring and whose responsibility it is to watch over all our household affairs."

Within the religious communities of the New World that were sustained by the Puritan spirit, the idea of the religious equality of woman first came to be taken seriously. For the Quakers, even the teachings of the Bible did not count as the definitive and only possible revelation, but rather as one part of the multitudinous forms in which the "inner light"

shone upon humans. They could therefore let drop the dogma of the God-willed subordination of woman. *"Obey God rather than men":* this saying, which confirmed the individual's *freedom of conscience* as an untouchable right in contrast to every earthly authority, was there for the first time also acknowledged for the wife in reference to the husband. Freedom of conscience, the mother of all personal rights of the individual, stood, across the ocean, at the cradle of women's rights, as well. . . .

That idea, that each person—precisely because he/she is a person—possesses certain inalienable rights in respect to all other people and every earthly authority, was then directed by the eighteenth century upon secular matters: upon the state, as the demand for full political recognition and equality under the law for its citizens; upon the community as the moral claim of the individual for a certain sphere of internal and external freedom. These ideas won their deepest meaning and their highest clarity in the ethical teachings concerning freedom of German Idealism, through our great thinkers Kant and Fichte. The aspects relevant to our present concerns can be summed up in a few sentences. The human being is ordained, as possessor of reason, to be his/her own director, that is, to act not more or less after the caprice of instinctive impulses, but rather in accordance with the dictates of conscience, obedient to moral laws. As the possessor of this capacity for *autonomy* the human takes on the specific value that distinguishes him/her as *an individual* from all other beings and may therefore lay claim to being "an end in one's self." There follows for the shaping of human relationships one simple and unshakable basic principle: that each one must heed the command in every other human to become an end in one's self, that no person may regard a fellow human being as *simply* the means to his/her own personal ends.

In practice there is hardly any conceivable human relationship that can disregard this principle, if it wishes to be ethically sufficient. Above all, the road from the recognition of this principle to a new formulation of the relationship between the sexes would seem to be short. For it follows from this principle that for the wife, too, the highest ethical aim of existence can be nothing other than development to morally autonomous personhood. It follows that for her, as well, it is *immoral* to bow to another's will contrary to her own conscience. It follows that she, too, may not be used simply as a means to her husband's ends.

But . . . [e]ven the greatest proclaimers of autonomy never considered touching the patriarchal system. Rather, they sought by skillful chess moves of reasoning to set woman's fundamental subordination in apparent harmony with the new ideals. . . . [M]arriage . . . was explained as a compact through which the woman voluntarily subjected herself to her husband. . . .

But what continued to be denied to the woman in the realm of ideas, was soon forced upon her in the realm of realities. The new life-style forces of the machine age broke open the circle of her gender-determined tasks and led her out of the protection of the house, and thereby out of the realm of her husband's control. The progressive shrinking of the scope of household work under the pressure of technical and economic forces compels an ever-increasing proportion of women outside, temporarily or permanently, to stand on their own two feet. . . . We are also experiencing, in our time, a comprehensive redefinition of morals and attitudes in relation to woman . . . [y]et with regard to marriage, where husband and wife are interdependent in the most immediate way, *statutorily protected male supremacy* still prevails as an indispensable formative principle. We certainly find an increasing number of husbands, particularly from the intellectually leading classes, who are ready to value their own wife as an individual and to renounce, in relationship to her, the exercise of their gender privileges. But only a very few men today are willing to fundamentally resign their rights of authority over the whole female sex.

This is revealingly documented in the judicial form of modern marriage that the German Parliament bestowed on us at the turn of the century. To

be sure, civil law now fundamentally recognizes women's ability to act and enter into liabilities and makes them fully responsible in business and other activities, as men are. But a married woman's freedom of action is everywhere restricted wherever the house-mastery of the husband is possibly threatened. So our marriage laws have developed a peculiarly convoluted profile, which exhibits all the lack of form that a compromise between irreconcilable basic premises implies. . . .

Modern women, who seek for their sex individual rights in the deepest sense, that is, responsibility and non-dependency, protest against these relics of the patriarchal system. . . . Modern women . . . raise the idea of the *comradeship of spouses,* as opposed to the authority of the husband, as a formative principle of marriage. They propose 1) putting aside the general right of the husband to make decisions; 2) a different division of parental rights, of the nature that in *irreconcilable* differences of opinion the father decides for the sons, the mother for the daughters. They work toward the time when 3) women of all classes will be assured of a sphere of economic independence, through more precise specification of the husband's duty to support the wife.

This is not the place to examine these legal questions more closely. Therefore we return to the basic ethical question: whether authority or autonomy should shape the relationship of the spouses.

How then does marriage look, when in accordance with its juridical formulation the authority *on principle* of the husband does *in fact* set the rules for the relationship of the spouses? . . . When opinions differ between the spouses, an external appearance of unanimity is thereby effortlessly produced—and for the sake of this extremely extrinsic purpose, the authoritarian principle is still defended today.

But is this purpose worth the sacrifice it costs? It is obvious that a continual subjugation of the wife's will, without her own inner agreement and conviction, can result either in a simply hypocritical submission that will be slyly shaken off again behind the husband's back or, on the other hand, that it will bring about a suppression of her own capacity to judge and thereby a wasting-away of her whole intellectual/spiritual development. . . .

. . . The patriarchally minded husband will certainly want to oversee and control the inner life, too, of the wife. . . . He cannot rest when he does not know himself to be continuously the master of her totally personal inner life, as well. He will feel the need to oversee her reading, her friendships, her outside-the-house interests. This half-unconscious tendency . . . is often simply suggested by tradition. . . . The inner protest of the patriarchally minded husband who does not, however, enjoy the full, naive absence of self-consciousness of earlier times most often then clothes itself in the concern that the wife may be neglecting her household duties and her children—an appeal that, naturally, seldom fails to be powerful with scrupulous, sensitive women. . . . Has it not, down the centuries, been made for her a religious duty and the preliminary condition of her happiness that she learn to "accommodate herself," in silent obedience? . . . This situation can change only when the husband learns to resign all claim to fundamental authoritarian privileges.

Does the ethical autonomy of the wife then forbid every subordination of her will, overall, to the will of the husband? Certainly not. *Free-willed* subordination, yielding, that is offered as a free gift of love is something different from enforced subordination. . . .

Out of such a conviction even the autonomous wife can of course make the will of her husband her own and place *her* wishes and interests behind *his*. But when that may occur can be decided only in the forum of her own conscience and only from case to case. . . . Only the free offerings of love to the life aims of a superior have beauty and worth. Also when brought by the husband to the wife, they do not dishonor.

When, however, instead of this free giving of oneself, the wife, simply for the sake of convenience, for the sake of outward peace, or to please the husband, is at the disposal of his needs and everyday aims, against her own inner voice, she then commits an *offense* against her own human worth; she then downgrades herself to a second-class being. And the consequences of such a relationship of the spouses recoil upon the husband, as well. She who is subordinated to him stays "subordinate" in the entirety of her nature: half a child, ignorant of the world, intellectually undemanding, closed within the circle of the household, her interests clinging to the purely personal and small. And that is the tragic irony of her fate: this woman who for the sake of being at her husband's disposal has not let her power of moral judgment and her intellectual qualities grow up fully is most often, over the extent of the years, left far behind in inner matters by the striving, active husband. . . . So we often experience that the much-praised German paragon of pure housewifeliness does indeed remain lastingly valuable to her husband as the mother of his children and the source of his comfort, but that he rarely thinks of sharing his higher spiritual/intellectual life with her. . . . [T]he thick dust of tedium covers the relationship and dulls to grey what was once bright and colorful. . . .

Or the other possibility: time and fate ripen the woman in spite of her authoritarian constraint. Then one day her will and judgment do indeed break through the restraints. . . . To the husband, the personal life of the wife, which has for so long been latent, appears then as an alien, hostile element, disturbing the happiness of the marriage. The unreserved trust dwindles, an often unhealable breach ruptures the married life, and this all only because the wife has first discovered herself so belatedly, while the husband has not learned to value the being at his side as, like himself, "ordained to self-determination."

Modern women . . . [l]ike women of all eras, . . . are ready to make to marriage those sacrifices which are necessarily demanded of them as sexual beings and which are today possibly much harder for many to make than in earlier times, because our time first knows the conflict between marriage and profession, between the special gender tasks of the woman and her inner need to build with others the suprapersonal cultural world. But they now also want to be regarded as adults and respected by the husband as the companion of his life. . . .

It is no small task to keep the marital relationship, through all the stages of a long life—from the time of everything-demanding youthful passion, over the high-point of life, where alongside love an abundance of other forces fight for mastery of the soul, to the declining days—free from the stifling ashes of the everyday and the habitual. Much more dangerous than all suffering and struggles that fate can impose from outside, more to be feared than those problems which arise from the wrestlings of the soul, is the unending chain of satiated, comfortable, struggle-*free* everyday, in which the spouses live together without further effort. Only when for husband and wife the holdings of the soul, the riches of the inner life remain constantly growing, can the holy fire of tender and deep feeling find ever-renewed nourishment. . . . For this, however, it is before all else essential that the wife, too, remains someone who strives and develops.

EXCERPT FROM "ON THE VALUATION OF HOUSEWORK"

This selection is excerpted from pages 42–58. Here, Weber argues for women's economic autonomy as a key step towards their acquisition of full emancipation. She does so, however, with an understanding that most women live in marriages, with responsibility for both housework and child care, and that their wage-earning capacities in capitalist-patriarchy cannot give them as much independently earned money as they require for economic autonomy. She explores the various proposed policies for enhancing the financial independence of the typical woman, including the possibility of wages for housework, showing her knowledge of key feminist arguments and her skill at using quantitative data.

The German woman's movement is not bound by one single creed. But complete unanimity of opinion prevails that the woman within marriage, as one outside it, must be regarded as being called upon to take responsibility for herself in her thinking and acting, and that therefore the concept of full fellowship between the marriage partners, instead of her subordination on principle, must be set up as the formative principle for the marriage relationship. Unanimity also prevails on what must follow from this principle, in regard to the formulation of marriage law and marital moral customs: the elimination of any male privileges that are not objectively necessary, such as the general right of the husband to make decisions, his monopoly of parental authority, and his rights over the use of the wife's property.

Here I will merely sound the fundamental notes of a general marriage reform and select out for detailed discussion a specialized problem, one which has not yet found unanimous agreement within our ranks. This is the question of a *new valuation for the work a housewife performs,* that arises, for the wife, directly out of her need for economic—to be precise, pecuniary—independence. We do agree that a wife, like every independent adult, requires her own sphere of control over money in order to feel herself to be, within marriage as well, a free individual person. She requires this control as much in her sphere of housewifely activity as in the shaping of her personal life. But as is well known, this condition is even today not guaranteed by law and has only recently, in very *narrow* strata of our people, been assured by custom. . . .

A typical consequence of this is that still, among broad strata of society, the husband—evidently on the assumption that he can thereby obtain greater economy from the wife and exercise a certain control over the distribution of expenditures—will part with even the requisite household money in only small installments. Equally widespread is the custom that the wife must come pleading and coaxing to the husband on matters of her personal needs: a new dress, a journey, gifts to friends, assistance to the poor, and the like. Undoubtedly such demands for money for trivial, everyday needs, whose costs the husband, for his part, cannot accurately estimate, often arouse considerable *unwillingness* in countless otherwise completely generous husbands—and naturally all the more, the more often he has to be approached for small sums. It is a very common psychological phenomenon that anyone, husband or wife, bears much more calmly the occasional major sacrifice or, too, regularly repeated, fixed exactions that are imposed with the apparent inevitability of a natural law, than when he has to be solicited over and over again for small amounts whose expenditure he cannot control. And under such circumstances this necessity of asking very often becomes for the wife, when she has a legal right and when the means are to hand, a wearisome psychological hardship. Whether the husband grants her requests and *how* he fulfills them—amiably or bad-temperedly, with or without remarks on her qualities as a housewife—depends not only on enduring psychological motivations, but also on completely accidental ones: the more or less favorable mood of the moment. Precisely this feeling of *dependency* upon the subjective responses of another person, however perfect he may be—to say nothing of however imperfect—, drags on the wife, and not only for the passing moment. On the contrary, it can heavily burden her general attitude toward life and her self-respect and be felt, even in otherwise happy marriages, as a demeaning condition.

Aside from this, far from gratifying effects upon the character of the wife are frequently the result. As someone held in dependency, she often does not find the courage to carry through her wishes in a straightforward way. So she adopts the weapons of the weak and tries to reach her goals by all sorts of roundabout ways and trickery. . . . How disfiguring are all these various slave-tricks that our sex still adheres to because we must obtain so many of the things we need for our lives by stealth from a "lord and master"!

We are agreed that this situation must change . . . It is only over the *ways* to realize our necessary pecuniary independence that differing opinions prevail among us. Three main lines of thinking can be identified. A sizeable minority among us, influenced by the socialist theories . . . and also the intellectu-

ally lively book of our American comrade-in-arms Ch. Perkins-Gilman, demand the economic emancipation of the wife through *independent earnings,* . . . from the increasing instance of long-term work for pay. . . .

This position has been presented so often that I do not need to expound it further here. The arguments on the other side are also well known. They hold that combining marriage and motherhood with suitable professional work, founded on special talents and tastes, is desirable and indeed, in countless cases, inwardly necessary. Nevertheless *full-time* paid employment for wives can in the unqualified masses be seen only as an inevitable Must for many, but cannot be regarded as a destiny to be aspired to for *all.* I . . . content myself with throwing light on the issue through several new facts.

According to the last professional census of 1907, out of 10.8 million married women, 2.8 million (about 26%) were employed full-time. . . . This is certainly an impressive number, which will probably rise still more in the future. If, however, we look at the distribution among the various groups of professions and then estimate their average earnings, it will be evident that the life patterns of those masses cannot assume the importance for a new configuration of marriage that one is inclined, at first, to attribute to them. Of that 2.8 million, over 2 million are *agricultural* workers. The life patterns of these classes, for the most part still structured around traditional farm labor, are in purely economic terms so different from the life patterns of all other classes of the population that it would be senseless to look to them for indications of a *general* formulation for the future. Besides, the position of this group of married women working for pay, which contains within itself such diverse existences as those of the peasant landholder and the resident farm worker, the seasonal worker and the day laborer, has not been sufficiently studied to permit general conclusions about their position vis-à-vis the husband. It is better, therefore, to leave them out of this discussion entirely.

Of the remaining approximately 795,000 fully employed women, 56% are in industrial work, 35%

in trade and commerce, 5% in domestic work or hired work of various kinds, and only 3.8% in the so-called "free professions," of whom by far the majority, namely 61%, are midwives, whose profession by its nature looks to married women. The distribution of these 795,000 married women over the statistically differentiated levels of the professional ladder reveals that the main contingent, 77%, belongs to the lowest level, that of so-called "hired help" or "day workers." The stratum of "independents," "salaried employees," and those working in the "free professions" encompasses, altogether, only 23%.

Let us now illuminate this problem from yet another angle. If we ask ourselves the question of whether the women who are employed full-time can, by their earnings, achieve actual pecuniary independence from the husband, we will be so bold as to affirm this for the 23%, those belonging to the group of independents or in the free professions. But we can in no way simply affirm this for the group of hired workers.

About the level of married women's earnings in the areas of urban paid work, too, not much reliable and comprehensive material exists as yet. According to the careful compilations of Dr. Rose Otto[1] the contribution to the family income in *working-class* families of married women who work full-time comes *predominantly* to between 20% and 30%. . . . [I]s it sufficient for her true economic emancipation from her husband? She can naturally cover her own personal living expenses, as long as her ability to work is little interrupted by pregnancies or she is helped by well-structured maternity insurance. . . .

. . . So let us simply establish . . . as the result of our statistical overview, that the majority of fully employed women in towns and cities are, at all events, recruited from the classes least likely to own property and presumably bear the double burden of motherhood and paid employment neither out of an

inclination toward their "profession" nor for the sake of pecuniary independence, but simply out of necessity and, further, that these women, too, as soon as they are mothers and want to fulfill the duties of motherhood, are anyhow in the overwhelming majority thrown economically upon the men.

All this is naturally even more true for married women who are employed only part-time, who spend only a small portion of their time in wage-earning. Their number has not, unfortunately, been established by statistics. [But] we are still left with over 5 million women who are housewives only.

It seems therefore *meaningless* and impossible, purely on the basis of the facts, to look to the circumstances of urban women working for pay, circumstances determined by cultural deprivation and often by sheer necessity, for guidelines to the shape of a woman's destiny among other classes. We also cannot do this in regard to the position of . . . married women who stand upon the higher rungs of the professional ladder. For they make up a mere 2% of *all* married women we are considering here. . . . And we must be clear about it that this group can certainly still increase substantially, but that it is nevertheless, purely on political-economic grounds, not *infinitely* expandable. If we orient our demands on the life styles and possibilities of these married women with high-quality work, we will again be bypassing, with a complete lack of realism, the typical lot of millions.

Recognition of these facts . . . has therefore engendered another proposal, that was, as far as I know, first formulated by Ellen Key. This was to gain pecuniary independence for the married woman by means of a general motherhood-subsidy that, through taxes levied on the general population, would assure to each mother, for every child, a specified sum of money with which to raise it. Were this subsidy to be calculated at a level high enough to make a contribution by the father to childrearing costs superfluous, then—but *only* then—would the economic tie, which under our form of marriage binds the child, and through the child the mother, to the husband, be in point of fact severed. The

---

[1]*The Factory Work of Married Women,* Stuttgart and Berlin, 1910.

requisite costs for this, for Germany—should a mere 300 marks fall to each child, up to age 16—would amount to more than 7 billion marks annually. The combined expenditures for army, navy, postal service, telegraph, national civil servants, and veterans' pensions amount to only 2.6 billion. Besides, with that sum of 300 marks per child, naturally only the women of the unpropertied classes, those with very modest cultural requirements, but not the women of other strata could be emancipated. In short, that proposal goes so far beyond any and all things achievable that here too we hardly need consider whether such a development could be regarded as desirable. Manifestly, the transfer of child-rearing costs onto the general public would indeed financially "emancipate," above all, the *husband* and father. . . .

. . . The question now is whether, for the millions, still another way is viable which might bring them closer to that goal . . . a new valuation of the *housewife's work*. . . . The activities of the mother in the house, that in most social strata embrace personal attention to feeding, clothing, good order, cleanliness, the comfort and well-being of household members, and the raising of the children, is to be valued as *professional* activity, just as much as the outside-the-house work of the husband, which would not be possible without this.

. . . But that demand is now . . . [that] the positive *economic* value of the housewife is to be codified and paid by the husband in the form of a salary. The demand for a new valuation of housework *in people's minds* is transformed into the catch phrase "compensation" or "pay" for a housewife's work, although without any suggestions one could take seriously being offered as to just how such compensation might be calculated. . . .

. . . Just try, for instance, to establish a fair basic salary for, say, the childless wife of a millionaire, who runs her household with the help of as many perfect servants as she wishes and, on the other hand, for the wife of a railway conductor earning 1500 to 1800 marks annually, who cares for her husband and her four children without outside help! . . .

So along this path, too, we get no further ahead, for of course the claims of the wife in any class must be aligned *not* with her contributions, but rather with the *family income*. . . . Consequently, what the wife can reasonably claim for herself will *vary* according to the level of income and the number of family members and is completely impossible to deduce from her own productivity. Whoever cannot come to terms with these conditions, rooted in the very nature of marriage and family, had simply better not get married.

That which we may, however, demand with complete justification for the married woman of whatever rank, is two-fold: that 1) the necessary and available moneys for the fulfillment of her domestic profession, that is for the management of the household, and 2) beside that, the money at her disposal to satisfy her own personal needs be secured to her in such a form as will, at least *in principle*, completely spare her the battle with the arbitrariness and subjectivity of the husband. In my opinion, this goal can for the foreseeable future, for the *general masses of women*, be reached only on the foundation of marriage *law* and only through a transformation of marriage *customs*. I have some very simple legal proposals to make on this point. . . .

. . . In the marriage laws, it would be specified *that the wife has a right to agreement over a fixed amount of money for household expenses and equally to an allotted sum for personal uses,* and in cases where the income of the wife must support the charges of the marriage, that is, when the husband is incapacitated from employment and is without means of support, the same right would be accorded to the husband. [F]or the masses of women without their own means, the "Just-Housewives," a portion of the husband's income would be earmarked for the purpose. The claim for agreement on a fixed *amount of money for household expenses, however, is of equal importance for all social strata.* . . . The fortunate necessity will thereby be created for the spouses to set out an annual budget, in accord with their annual income. A limit would be set upon the temptation for the husband to take from his earnings for his own use out of proportion to the needs of the family, to which, as is well known, he still often succumbs in proletarian circles. In addition, he would be spared a host of disagreeable feelings which the unexpected extortions commonly arouse in him. The wife, on the other hand, would be—in principle, at least—spared that demeaning petty warfare for something that is already legally owed her, and she would have won—in principle—some free scope for structuring her personal life.

[This negotiation] seems to me better left entirely to agreement between the spouses . . . and, in cases of dispute . . . to Surrogate's Court and the family council.

. . . When we will succeed in getting a hearing from the German lawmaker remains uncertain. We have already often experienced how much inertia he can display when the subject is the extension of women's rights. Under the current distribution of power in the state, we will still have a long wait. But even now we can draw closer to our goal. By steadily making known our desire for reform, we can develop the consciousness of our people about legal matters in that direction, and above all we can even now influence that transformation of marriage *custom* that is at least as important as the law. Here every modern woman can find a field of practical endeavor, not only in the public arena, but also person-to-person, and every marriage formed along model lines carries in itself the fertile seed of future formations. In the area of custom every single one of us can contribute silently to the ennobling of marriage and the elevation of women's lives. The new ways of living will then develop from the inside out and, of necessity, one day burst open the husk of past times.

EXCERPT FROM "WOMEN'S SPECIAL CULTURAL TASKS"

This selection is excerpted from pages 1–8 and 17–26. It presents Weber's debate with Georg Simmel's sociology of gender which assigns men and women to distinctive spheres of cultural production, men to the production of *objective culture and women to the creation of personal culture. Weber explores women's capacities for cultural production in both those areas, seeing both areas as work which women and men are equally capable of doing. She then introduces a third area of cultural production—"the middle ground of shaping immediate, daily existence"—and establishes its crucial importance for culture generally, and women's overwhelming significance to this area of work.*

We understand as "culture" any intellectually determined, purposeful working on and shaping of material given by nature. And whether we think of that which lies outside us, of the making of objects, classifications, and connections of ideas, or of the forming of the living human being, always in a process of becoming, we habitually distinguish between objective and subjective, between material and personal culture. These two directions of human striving—on the one hand toward lasting works and classifications that rise above the flux of events and the transitoriness of individual existence, on the other toward development of the individual personality—realize, when they come together in mutual interpenetration, the full content of the idea of culture. According to a profound philosophical interpretation,[1] culture in its deepest sense signifies *the perfecting of the soul through the development of all its inherent shoots and possibilities in the objective intellectual and spiritual works of humanity,* which as technology, law, and custom, as art, science, and religion stand in contrast to the individual as timeless values, forming and challenging him and compelling him into their service.

The soul can indeed achieve "the way to itself," i.e. the realization of its intrinsic possibilities, without the detour through that objective world of realities, as a pure, internal self-development "in religious fights of the soul, moral self-sacrifice, powerful intellectuality, harmony of communal life." But it will not yet have achieved that particular

---

[1]Georg Simmel, "The Concept and the Tragedy of Culture" in *Philosophical Culture,* p. 246ff.

value that culture means, because this form of completion requires self-permeation with objective structures, an internal connection, be it creating, be it making use of them. "Culture arises . . . when two elements come together, neither of which is in itself culture: the subjective soul and the objective intellectual product."

We will turn our attention later to this deepest sense of culture. First we will consider the distinction between personal and material, subjective and objective culture, in order to clarify for ourselves in that context cultural tasks that are perhaps especially significant for woman. To that end we must first remind ourselves yet again of the paradoxical fact that woman is a being simultaneously like and different from man. That is, as *human being* she shares with the man an abundance of talents and abilities that direct her toward the same tasks and forms of activity as they do him. And on the other hand, as *woman* important special tasks fall to her, as a result of her sexual identity, which hinder the realization of her universal human tasks. Regarded from the universal-human angle, woman is called, on principle, to participate in every kind of cultural work for which her individual talents fit her, and there is no question that her active participation in the realm of objective culture means necessary enlargement and valuable enrichment of our cultural store. There is absolutely no realm of activity, be it technology, law, and custom or art, science, philosophy and religion, from which she may justifiably be excluded. . . . Nature has [also] laid heavy gender duties upon the female organism, which are spared the male: "Twenty men together could not bear these burdens.". . . Beyond the gender responsibilities laid on her by nature there falls to her lot, because she is a woman, a special sphere of cultural tasks in which she is called upon to perform irreplaceable duties on the strength of her own special nature. This specifically female sphere of tasks, which are of course not her only ones or only hers, but for which she is most particularly equipped, we want to consider here.

There arises now before our view a unique middle ground between the structures of objective culture, separate from the individual, and the personal culture, inextricably bound to the individual, which we will name the shaping of immediate existence. In this personal/suprapersonal middle realm the world of objects, classifications, and ideas is divested of its character as an end in itself and consciously pressed into the service of development of the personality, individual existence, and immediate daily life. . . . [W]hen I speak of the shaping of immediate existence, I mean not merely the development and formation of the individual soul through culture, but also more: namely, the shaping of the intellectual and moral atmosphere that surrounds the individual, that flows out from the individual, that binds the individual with others into highly personal relationships of various kinds: companionship, friendship, love, marriage, family, etc. Furthermore, this includes the immediate environment of things and their arrangements within which our daily existence takes place. . . . [T]he *plain, uneventful everyday, too, is worthy in itself of being lived,* is a formative task that falls, first of all, to the woman. . . . The tending and fostering of this, the silent daily care for the people belonging to us, the chosen spouse, the aging parents, before all for the coming generation, lie within the special province of the woman. Along with caring for physical needs, the tasks of rearing the children are preeminent: the forming of their natures through certain precepts and ideals. So far as this takes place within the family, this work falls in great part to the mother. By means of the cultivation which the older generation accomplishes for the younger, not only are ever new ranks of individual beings formed, but also there simultaneously arise ever new forms of *morality,* which is a part of the living flow of immediate existence. . . .

What do we understand by this term "morality"? We call "morality" that forming power that cultivates immediate existence, with its prodigious diversity of emotional content and impulses, in that it restrains the instinctive appetites of the individual and regulates all the individual's conduct through certain unwritten laws and precepts, so that a harmonious communal life becomes possible. Morality shapes public life as well as private. But its most important seedbed is domesticity. Through the way in which the daily requirements of life are satisfied within the domestic circle, and through the way in which those united within that circle interact with one another, there comes into being a special quality of existence, which cannot develop without woman's form-giving power. . . . For only when the wife brings together all the small matters of the everyday into a meaningful texture and animates them with warmth and charm, is the house transfigured into a home, a place of recovery, of homecoming from the outside, in which human beings who have been fragmented by jobs and the struggle for a living can continually restore themselves to wholeness, to full humanity, and draw to themselves new powers for growth.

Admittedly, the great majority of the objects that are necessary for the construction of this domestic environment are, like the living-place itself, produced by men. But it depends materially upon the wife how all the various items, produced and brought in as market wares, will be arranged, used, and cared for. . . . [T]he educated consumer can still exert an influence over production through determined rejection of abominations against good taste. This is a power and a responsibility of which the educated woman is still far too unconscious. . . .

Far more important than the forming of the physical shell within which daily existence acts is the permeation of one's own being with morality and culture. . . . We will move from externals to internals and begin with what we may term *culture of expression,* so-called "good form," which is an important part of high morality. What does this signify? It shapes the behavior of the individual toward the surrounding others through those innumerable unwritten laws which we consciously transmit through education and which further we as examples involuntarily impress upon others through our own conduct. How we walk and stand, eat and clothe ourselves, our words and gestures, our deportment, i.e. the way in which we master our instinctive responses—greed, anger, hate, pain—, the entire How of our being: all this regulates itself according to the measure of our formal culture. The development of this should be begun as early as

possible with every young human being and is in the first instance the daily, painstaking task of the mother. Already at the awakening of consciousness she must set limits to the instinctive impulses of her child and lead the awakening reason, step by step, to mastery over the animal nature. According to widespread opinion, for formal morality a good nursery education is almost irreplaceable.

The particular and far-reaching importance of culture of expression is simply that every individual who possesses it has an immediate influence upon his or her surroundings, upon the entire environment with which he or she has contact. . . . That is to say, our actions, our conduct, and our current mood translate themselves immediately into the environment, exactly as we ourselves feel at all times influenced in the strongest way by the forms of our surroundings. . . .

I have up to now spoken of culture of expression, as the predominantly external form of character-building. High morality in the inner sense, which will be spoken of next, is not imprinted from outside; rather, it wells forth from the deeper levels of the soul. For the type of behavior that marks it—respect for the other person, kind and patient attention to the nature of others, the ability to, as the phrase so strikingly goes, "transpose oneself into the soul of another," and further, piety, humbleness before the good and great—all this cannot be achieved without overcoming natural egoism, which can only be accomplished through a pure will to goodness, welling up from the innermost depths. . . . The foundations for this are laid during youth. The awakening of the will toward ideal self-shaping arises primarily from the living model of the people around us who are further along this path than we are. The parents' house, therefore, bears the earliest and heaviest responsibility for the souls and characters of developing human beings, and whoever has dealings with children, whose tender adaptability responds to every impression, influences by every single personal expression how they thrive or how they are endangered. . . .

. . . But what we term cultural content in its most proper sense can only be acquired upon the by-path through the objective culture, through deep penetration into the world of the mind and spirit that crystallizes out of immediate existence, especially art, science, philosophy. Prerequisite for this is a certain level of intellectual development. To reach this, thoroughgoing intellectual or artistic schooling is necessary, such as remains reserved for only a thin stratum of people freed from mechanical work and the hard struggle for existence. This extraordinary privilege of acquiring such cultural content for oneself has up till now been far too little exercised by the women of the propertied classes. The earlier ideal of a specifically female education certainly did not point in this direction, either. Rather, it denied to women rigorous schooling of the intellect and serious search into the treasures of the mind, and we all still remember the fierce battles we had to wage for admission. Today, however, now that this has been achieved, every woman of the privileged class ought to strive zealously for those blessings. Only then will she have an impact as a bearer of culture in the fullest sense. . . .

. . . If the privileged woman wants to be the intermediary between the objective culture and immediate existence, if she wants to shape the content of that Everyday of which she is mistress, not merely to cultivate its forms, she must fill herself, by tireless effort, with deeper cultural content.

Now the question is, how does this task . . . relate to other goals it does not itself pursue? How, in the first place, to the truly national-German ideal of the perfect housewife? . . . This model, endowed with limitless readiness to serve her spouse and children and with all those domestic virtues which narrow circumstances prescribe for her, would be fostered and cared for as much by her education within the household as by the school for girls. But it nevertheless corresponded very well indeed with the specific gender interest of average husbands in selfless, able, undemanding, and submissive wives. . . .

The modern, intellectually awakened woman certainly does not need to remove the German ideal of the housewife from the temple in which she pays homage to the role-models of her own striving. It obviously should retain its validity and power for all coming generations, as well. But we have shattered its negative power as an absolute value and the *exclusive* developmental goal for the female sex because it has stifled our development as intellectual and spiritual beings and in general our common human powers and characteristics.

We must now further clarify to ourselves how the new substance of life and new forms of action that we modern women have ourselves sketched out are compatible with the goal set forth here: the unfolding of woman's soul in richer and deeper cultural content. For example, can the social, political, and administrative work, that we today expect from the women of privileged classes alongside their housewifely and mothering tasks, be combined with intellectual growth and the intensifying of existence? There is no question about the practical necessity of such service to the whole by those individuals fitted for it. . . . And just as unquestionably, social and political work as a *form of achievement* accomplishes for the woman herself the release of powers lying fallow, growth in capability, broadening of her intellectual and spiritual horizons, deepened understanding of everything human. . . . But there are limits, of course, to its fructifying power for the total personality, and it conceals, like all outwardly directed action, its own special dangers. Those who live out their natures *exclusively* in such forms of activity will never achieve cultural content in the real sense and also will hardly advance to deeper inward consciousness. For effective social and political work is by its nature work done in community with other people; it spins itself around us like an almost endless thread and entwines us in a whole network of relationships. In such work one is usually in company, constantly sees oneself placed before new tasks and possibilities; there is always something going on; one always feels usefully employed. Indeed, one is even pressed to sundry undertakings beyond what is in point of fact necessary, only because organizations and associations just happen to be there and must exercise influence and demonstrate their vitality. So this communal work sets life in pleasant, often-changing motion, satisfies, independent of its content, the need for fellowship, and releases the enterprising spirit, ambition, and striving for power. And the activity, when once it has been directed down this track, easily grows—if one leaves it to its own devices—into an unconquerable impulse toward continual busyness that counteracts self-forgetful immersion in the world of the spirit and the inward and indeed even dries up the capacity for collectedness and concentration. This danger is *slight* in real social work, when one undertakes concrete, practical individual tasks as a member of a social alliance for a specific purpose, e.g. care of the poor, of young people, etc. But it is not slight in organizational work of any kind. For this demands constant exchange with fellow workers, many-sided relationships, "association-forming" ["*Vergesellschaftung*"], i.e., the agglomeration of groups of people who must be held together for a specific purpose: in short, zealous activity and busyness. If one does not consciously counteract this danger, a new kind of spiritual shallowness arises, which does indeed have the advantage over the shallowness brought on by the usual social distractions, in that it serves a useful end, but which nevertheless also stifles the sense for the most essential: the animation and spiritualization of existence. . . . [N]o sort of prescription for the individual, to do this and to omit that, is required; the only necessity is watchfulness of oneself, listening to one's own inner voice, constant striving after the essential good things of life, after inner growth.

Finally, we still must ask how these highest and most inward goals of human personal development, which are exactly the same for man and woman, are compatible with professional activity, toward which we direct even the young women of the privileged classes, who do not need to earn their own livings and therefore would be able, alongside their special gender tasks, to dedicate themselves fully to thorough absorption of cultural content. Today it is a very real issue that the professional person and indeed also the infinitely privileged *intellectual* worker run great risks of stunting their personalities as a whole, because the demands of modern compartmentalized professional life are extraordinarily severe. Yet, at the same time, they can demand only a portion of an individual's powers in one-sided specialization and, as a result, can have a withering effect upon the many-sided susceptibility and liveliness of the soul. In this there is doubtless much that is accurate. Any activity that is tied on a daily basis to fixed hours of work and leaves insufficient leisure for flights of the mind and soul in other directions does contain this danger within itself. And we do encounter, in all professions that depend upon intellectual work, the type of the pure specialist, whose first-rate professional achievements fill us with admiration, but whose humanness seems to us somehow stunted and incomplete. This development is not necessary, however, if the individual consciously works against it. Whether or not this can be avoided depends perhaps less upon the structure of our professional life and its demands upon us than upon the inner attitude of the individual toward it, and most importantly upon the question of whether the earning of money, ambition, building a career, and striving for power—in general, the finite partial goals of existence—rule us totally, or whether behind these, other infinite, timeless values and ideals for the individual are recognized and striven for. . . . Systematic professional training and temporary professional activity, therefore, absolutely cannot be prized too highly for the development of the woman as a bearer of culture in the most comprehensive sense. . . . If she wishes in the future to become a bearer of culture in the full sense, it will require of her, as it does of the man, hard intellectual work in some direction or other, devotion to the thing for the thing's own sake, unfaltering struggle for deepened content of being, constant alignment of her existence upon timeless values and validities.

The Chicago Women's School of Sociology (1890–1920)— Research as Advocacy

BIOGRAPHICAL BACKGROUND

The "Chicago Women's School of Sociology" is our term for a network of women who worked collaboratively to produce a body of sociology linking social theory, sociological research, and social reform. Working primarily out of two bases, Hull-House and the University of Chicago, between 1889 and 1920, they created sociology in a shared context of ideas and action in which women supported women in the move into public life. They were influenced in varying degrees by Jane Addams's theory of civil society which called for an adjustment between the organization of production and the ethical content of social interaction (see Chapter 3). We focus here on eight members of this school—Edith Abbott, Grace Abbott, Sophonisba Breckinridge, Florence Kelley, Frances Kellor, Julia Lathrop, Annie Marion MacLean, and Marion Talbot.

In recognizing these women not simply as individuals but as a school of thought and a network for action and reform, we follow the insights of a distinguished body of feminist research: Dorothy Blumberg's *Florence Kelley: The Making of a Social Pioneer* (1966); Lela Costin's *Two Sisters for Social Justice: A Biography of Edith and Grace Abbott* (1983); Mary Jo Deegan's *Jane Addams and the Men of the Chicago School, 1892–1913* (1988) and *Women in Sociology: A Bio-Bibliographical Sourcebook* (1991); Virginia Kemp Fish's "Annie Marion MacLean: A Neglected Part of the Chicago School" (1981); Ellen Fitzpatrick's *Endless Crusade: Women Social Scientists and Progressive Reform* (1990); Linda Gordon's *Pitied but Not Entitled: Single Mothers and the History of Welfare* (1994); Robyn Muncy's *Creating a Female Dominion in American Reform, 1890–1935* (1991); Rosalind Rosenberg's *Beyond Separate Spheres: Intellectual Roots of Modern Feminism* (1982); Kathryn Kish Sklar's *Florence Kelley and the Nation's Work: The Rise of Women's Political Culture, 1830–1900* (1995); and Louise C. Wade's "Julia Lathrop" (1977).

229

Yet, ironically, it may be that the first notice of these women's interlocking careers begins not in feminist research but in conservative attacks. As early as 1923, the *Woman Patriot* newsletter declared that "'practically all the radicalism started among women in the United States centers about Hull-House, Chicago, and the Children's Bureau at Washington—with a dynasty of Hull-House graduates in charge of it since its creation'" (cited in Costin, 1983:143; see also Davis, 1973). Like Muncy (1991), we first read this claim with a certain amusement based in our own political beliefs. But we came to realize that the *Woman Patriot* and those who repeated its charges were perhaps not overstating the case. Working out of identifiable centers—Hull-House, the University of Chicago, the Chicago School of Civics and Philanthropy (later the University of Chicago School of Social Service Administration), the federal Children's Bureau, the National Consumers' League, and the Chicago Woman's Club—these women, connected in varying degrees of closeness, formed a genuine power base, and were not afraid, as Lathrop showed in her administration of the Children's Bureau, to use that power.

In the remainder of this section, we first present the women in the order in which they arrived in Chicago—for none, interestingly, were natives of the city;[1] we then focus on the various ways they interconnected in Chicago; and we conclude with a brief summation of their lives after 1921 (the year in which Julia Lathrop, the oldest of the group, resigned from the Children's Bureau).

Coming to Chicago

Julia Lathrop (1858–1932)   Julia Lathrop was born June 29, 1858, in Rockford, Illinois, where her father, William, was a lawyer, and her mother, Sarah Adeline Potter, a suffrage worker and cultural leader. She attended Rockford Seminary for one year, going on to graduate from Vassar in 1880. Unable to find a meaningful career after graduation—like so many educated women of her generation—she came home to Rockford and worked as her father's legal secretary, read law herself, and made some profitable investments. Lathrop did not discuss her internal struggles between 1880 and 1890; but Addams, in her biography *My Friend Julia Lathrop*, suggests that the Haymarket Massacre, a violent clash between labor and police in 1886, might have influenced Lathrop's thinking. Lathrop's introduction to the idea of Hull-House probably came in a speech Addams gave at Rockford in 1889 when she and Ellen Gates Starr were starting the settlement. A year later, in 1890, Julia Lathrop joined Hull-House. She would be for the rest of her life one of Addams's closest friends and most trusted colleagues—one of the two or three Hull-House residents to call her "Jane"—and a source of delightful humor (Hamilton, 1942).

Florence Kelley (1859–1932)   Florence Kelley was born on September 12, 1859, in Philadelphia. Her father, William Darrah Kelley, was a Republican congressman, an abolitionist, and an advocate of women's suffrage. Her mother, Caroline Bartram Bonsall, was an efficient household manager who bore eight children and with whom Kelley maintained an affectionate correspondence for much of her life. Kelley attended Cornell University, one of the first private universities to admit women to full status, and did her senior thesis on child labor—a subject which would be a lifelong concern. A rejection by the law school of the University of Pennsylvania, apparently on grounds of gender, and an older brother's illness took her to Europe. She studied at the University of Zurich and converted to the socialist ideas of Karl Marx and Friedrich Engels. In 1884, with Engels's consent, she translated from the German his 1845 classic, *The Condition of the Working Class in England in 1844;* she continued a correspondence with Engels until his death. In Zurich, she married a Russian doctor and fellow socialist, Lazare Wischnewetzky, with whom she had three children. Returning to America in 1886, Kelley and her husband attempted unsuccessfully to be active in the very complex and in-bred circles of the Socialist Labor Party in New York, finding themselves distrusted as "outsiders." The couple's first years in America were also marred by financial struggles. The marriage dissolved and Kelley rarely spoke of it; but one of her reasons for moving to Illinois was that divorce laws there gave her the best chance of getting custody of her children. Kelley arrived in Chicago with very limited means. Housing her children with a friend, she moved into Hull-House just after Christmas 1891.[2] She was a major intellectual force at Hull-House, and, like Lathrop, one of Addams's inner circle of friends.

Marion Talbot (1858–1947)   Marion Talbot was born on July 31, 1858, to a family with deep roots in Boston. Her father, Israel Tisdale Talbot, was a homeopathic doctor. Her mother, Emily Fairbanks Talbot, was a woman of considerable accomplishment. Marion's life as the eldest of the Talbots' six children is in part an interesting turn on Freud's observation that "A man who has been the indisputable favorite of his mother keeps for life . . . that confidence of success that often induces real success." To guarantee Marion an education equal to that accorded to young men, Emily Talbot fought a steady battle against a patriarchal ideology that maintained that higher education could destroy women's health, make them unable to reproduce, drive them to nervous disorders, and leave them hopelessly "masculinized" (Rosenberg, 1982:6–12). Over and against these male arguments, Emily presented a steady dose of feminism, and Marion persevered in her education, earning a bachelor of arts from Boston University in 1880 and in 1888 a bachelor of science from the Massachusetts Institute of Technology (MIT) in domestic science. In the years between 1880 and 1888, Marion worked with Emily Talbot, Alice Freeman Palmer (an early president of Wellesley), and Ellen H. Richards (a pioneer professor at MIT) to organize the Association of Collegiate Alumnae (ACA), which would become the American Association of University Women (AAUW). Palmer offered Talbot a position as an assistant professor of domestic science at Wellesley and was the prime mover in getting her to the newly established University of Chicago, where she was appointed assistant professor of sociology and assistant dean of women to Palmer in 1892. She became dean of women in 1893 and served as associate editor of the *American Journal of Sociology* from its foundation in 1895 until her retirement in 1925.

Sophonisba Breckinridge (1866–1948)   Sophonisba Breckinridge was born April 1, 1866, in Lexington, Kentucky; her father, William Cambell Breckinridge, came from an old political family in the state and continued the tradition as a congressman and lawyer; her mother, Issa Desha, also came from an elite Kentucky family but was an invalid for much of her life. Both parents seem to have supported her education. After her graduation from Wellesley in 1888, Breckinridge lived through a six-year period of crisis and indecision. She first taught in Washington, D.C. where her father was serving in Congress, then traveled in Europe, and then, on her mother's death in 1892, returned to Lexington, where she studied law in her father's office (with little paternal encouragement), and passed an oral exam admitting her, the first woman, to the Kentucky bar (Fitzpatrick, 1990). But her practice built slowly. Her father remarried in 1893. Then in 1894 he was defeated in his bid for re-election in a scandal-ridden campaign in which he was accused—apparently truthfully— of having an affair of nine years with a woman who had borne him three children and who sued him for breach of promise. His new wife took the whole event with difficulty. Breckinridge, depressed and shaken, accepted an invitation from a Wellesley classmate to visit Illinois in 1894, where she met Talbot who encouraged her to pursue a PhD in political science at the University of Chicago. Breckinridge moved to Chicago in 1894, earned her doctorate in political science in 1899, and became the first woman to earn a doctorate in law there in 1904. In 1908 she became a Hull-House resident and launched herself into numerous reform activities while working in various positions at the University of Chicago and the newly created Chicago School of Civics and Philanthropy.

Annie Marion MacLean (ca. 1870–1934) Annie Marion MacLean was born around 1870 in Prince Edward Island, Canada, to John and Christina MacLean; her father was a minister, and the family soon moved to Nova Scotia. Although she would later become a U.S. citizen, MacLean seems to have remained close to her Canadian family. Fish (1981) notes that three of MacLean's books are dedicated to family members. MacLean earned a bachelor's and a master's degree from Acadia College in Nova Scotia and then, perhaps because of Baptist connections between Acadia College and the University of Chicago, decided to attend graduate school at the university. She began graduate studies in sociology there in 1897, became the first woman to earn a master's degree in sociology, and earned her PhD in sociology in 1900, the second woman to do so. She taught in the Extension, or Home Study, Division of the university and kept up an active record of research and publication until her death in 1934.

Frances Kellor (1873–1952) Frances Kellor was born on October 20, 1873, in Columbus, Ohio. Her father, Daniel Kellor, deserted the family, and in 1875, her mother, Mary Sprague Kellor, moved the family to Coldwater, Michigan, where Kellor attended school and helped her mother who worked as a laundress and domestic servant. Finances forced Kellor to leave school in 1890. Taking a job on the local paper, she made the acquaintance of two sisters, Mary and Frances Eddy, and another wealthy woman, Celia Parker Woolley, who helped her attend Cornell University, from which she graduated in 1897 with an undergraduate degree in law. Woolley was now living in Chicago, and Kellor turned to the University of Chicago to pursue graduate work in criminology. She enrolled, with Woolley's aid and a scholarship from the Chicago Woman's Club, in the Department of Sociology in 1898. Between 1898 and 1905, Kellor was an intermittent resident of Hull-House (Fitzpatrick, 1990), and during her years at the University of Chicago she published extensively—especially in criminology and race relations. After moving to New York, she continued her Chicago contacts through her work on immigration, on race relations, and with the Progressive Party.

Edith Abbott (1876–1957) and Grace Abbott (1878–1939) Edith Abbott was born in Grand Island, Nebraska, on September 26, 1876; Grace Abbott was born there on

November 11, 1878. Their parents were homesteaders; their father, Othman Abbott, was a lawyer who became lieutenant governor of the state, and their mother, Elizabeth Griffin Abbott, was a worker for women's suffrage. Both parents cared about education for all their children, but their hopes were interrupted by a drought which hit Nebraska beginning in 1890, ruining farmers and the Grand Island Bank of which Othman Abbott was a director. He refused to go into bankruptcy, and the whole family readjusted plans in order to help pay off their indebtedness. Edith began teaching high school and took correspondence courses through the University of Nebraska, completing her BA in 1901. Grace studied at the newly founded Grand Island College, earned a PhB in 1898, and began high school teaching. In 1902, Edith Abbott took summer courses at the University of Chicago and met Sophonisba Breckinridge; by 1903, she had begun studying for a PhD in economics at the university. Grace Abbott studied intermittently at the University of Chicago from 1904 to 1907 when she moved to Chicago to study for a master's degree in political science. Grace Abbott began to reside at Hull-House in 1908. Edith Abbott taught briefly at Wellesley and studied at the London School of Economics under Beatrice and Sydney Webb between 1906 and 1908, but she returned to Chicago for good in 1908, joining her sister at Hull-House.

Interlocking Lives—The Emergence of a School

The Chicago Women's School of Sociology developed out of the interaction among several factors: the women's confrontation with the problems of a shared environment—Chicago; their work out of shared bases; their wish to create, despite patriarchal restrictions, a career in social science; their determination to use social science to achieve social change; and their creation of networks to achieve these ends.

Shared Space   The world the women came to in Chicago has been described elsewhere in this book (Chapter 3) as paradigmic of an America in transition to modern industrial capitalism. It was marked by extremes—of affluence and poverty, of privilege and oppression, of rapid expansion in material possibility and the multiplication of social problems, of ideological defenses of capitalism and of class, race, and gender privilege, and anarchist, socialist, and feminist critiques of these inequalities. The women discovered in Chicago dirt, disease, exhaustion, crowding, confusion, hopelessness, overwork, pain, and the overwhelming fact of difference introduced by the multitudes of nationalities who came as immigrants to work in the burgeoning industries. They came to know Chicago out of one of two bases, Hull-House and the University of Chicago. Talbot, the Abbotts, Breckinridge, Kellor, and MacLean were all originally drawn to Chicago by the university and all worked, taught, or studied there. Lathrop and Kelley were early and long-term residents of Hull-House; the Abbotts, Breckinridge, and Kellor all lived there at various points in their careers. The two bases were closely tied; Addams and Kelley taught at the University of Chicago on occasion (see Sklar, 1995:295–296 for a lively account); Talbot used her position as dean to get women students fieldwork at Hull-House. As graduate students, the Abbotts, Breckinridge, Kellor, and MacLean "worked in the city for better sanitation, public health, labor legislation, prison and criminal court reform, building codes and better schools" (Rosenberg, 1982:34).

The Chicago Women's School shared and patterned their experiences with each other and with many other women through various social networks. They shared informal friendship

FIGURE 7-1   **Shared Experiences**

	Publication in *AJS*	Hull-House residency	Educational bases in Chicago	Professional associations
Edith Abbot (1876–1957)	from 1908	1908–20	PhD U of C 1905; taught social statistics U of C 1913–20; CSCP 1907–20; SSA 1920–49	ASSA, NCCC, AASW
Grace Abbott (1878–1939)	from 1908	1908–17	MA U of C 1909; CSCP faculty 1914; SSA faculty 1939	NCSW, president 1923–24
Sophonisba Breckinridge (1866–1948)	from 1901	1907–20	PhD U of C 1901; assistant dean to Talbot; CSCP 1913–20; SSA 1920–49	AASW, NCSW, ASSA
Florence Kelley (1859–1932)	from 1896	1891–99	taught U of C 1899; law degree from Northwestern	ASS, ASSA, NCCC, chaired Committee on Standards of Living and Labor of NCCC
Frances Kellor (1873–1952)	from 1899	intermittent 1898–1905	graduate study in sociology U of C, 1898–1900	ASS, ASSA
Julia Lathrop (1858–1932)	1912	1890–1912	helped found CSCP, taught at, got E. Abbott and Breckinridge research there	NCCC; NCSW, president 1918
Annie Marion MacLean (ca. 1870–1934)	from 1899	visits	PhD sociology U of C 1900; home study faculty U of C 1903–34	ASS, ASSA
Marion Talbot (1858–1947)	from 1895	visits	Dean of women U of C 1892–1925	ASS, ASSA, American Public Health Association

Abbreviations: AASW = American Association of Social Workers; ACA = Association of Collegiate Alumnae (later AAUW); ASS = American Sociological Society (later ASA); ASSA = American Social Science Association; CB = Children's Bureau; CL = Consumer's League; CSCP = Chicago School of Civics and Philanthropy (later SSA); IPL = Immigrants' Protective League;

groups and lively discussions at Hull-House breakfasts and dinners. They all published in the *American Journal of Sociology* and also wrote for social service journals like *Charities, Survey,* and the *Proceedings of the National Conference of Charities and Corrections;* other academic journals, most especially the *Journal of Political Economy;* and more general intellectual publications like *Arena* and the *New England Quarterly.* They participated in women's voluntary associations such as the Chicago Woman's Club (which helped sponsor Kellor's research on Southern prisons' treatment of African Americans), the General Federation of Women's Clubs (which Lathrop used repeatedly in lobbying for support—first for a juvenile court system and then for the Children's Bureau), the ACA (which often met at

Government service	Progressive memberships and activities	Research on age, class, race, gender
through CSCP and SSA wrote reports for CB	NAWSA, pamphleteer for suffrage; ACA; WTUL; NAACP; UL; Chicago Women's Club	major works on women in industry, child labor, immigration
CB 1917–19; Illinois Immigration Commission 1919–21; replaced Lathrop as head of CB 1921–34	IPL, assistant director, then director 1908–17; International Congress of Women at The Hague 1915; Chicago Women's Club	major works on immigration
through CSCP and SSA wrote reports for CB	CL; IPL; NAWSA, vice president 1911; Progressive Party activist; NAACP; ACA; WTUL; Chicago Women's Club	housing, immigration, African Americans, women's work, equal wages
US Bureau of Labor study in Chicago 1893; Illinois State Inspector of Factories 1893	CL, national secretary 1900–1932; NAACP; NCLC; NAWSA; Chicago Women's Club	*Hull-House Maps and Papers; Some Ethical Gains Through Legislation;* labor studies of all sorts
New York Bureau of Industries and Immigration, head 1910	founded League for Protection of Colored Women 1906, which became UL 1911; American Arbitration Association 1926; Progressive Party activist for suffrage	social causes of crime; African Americans; employment agencies; immigration
Illinois Board of Charities 1893; first chief of CB 1912–20	charter member National Committee on Mental Hygiene 1909; Juvenile Court Committee; NCLC; active in women's clubs, which she used to lobby for CB	analyses of charities; reports of CB; *Hull-House Maps and Papers*
New York State Tenement House Commission	CL, publicized in *AJS* articles; YMCA, did research in coal fields for	work, especially women's work and wages
	ACA, charter member 1881, president 1895–97; National Federation of Women's Clubs; NAWSA	women's education; household management

NAACP = National Association for the Advancement of Colored People; NAWSA = National American Woman Suffrage Association; NCCC = National Conference of Charities and Corrections (later NCSW); NCLC = National Child Labor Committee; NCSW = National Conference of Social Work; WTUL = Women's Trade Union League; U of C = University of Chicago; UL = Urban League

Hull-House and which helped found the Illinois Consumers' League), and the National American Woman Suffrage Association (NAWSA). They were also active in mixed-gender groups, most notably the American Sociological Association, the American Social Science Association, the National Child Labor Committee (an organization which eventually grew to over 8,000 members), the National Conference of Charities and Corrections (later the National Conference of Social Work), the National Federation of Settlements, and the National Association for the Advancement of Colored People—as well as the Immigrants' Protective League (IPL). The complex professional and personal relational networks linking these women is summarized in Figures 7-1 and 7-2.

FIGURE 7-2 Relationships with Each Other

Edith Abbott–Grace Abbott sisters; shared professional interests; Edith more academic, Grace more political; very close	EA–Sophonisba Breckinridge met when EA did first summer course U of C 1904; taught together CSCP; founded SSA; co-authors; devoted friends	EA—Florence Kelley knew each other well; used each other's research on labor conditions; frequently cited each other; colleagues; members NCCC, ASS, NAACP	EA–Frances Kellor would have known each other through Hull-House; both worked on immigration studies
	Grace Abbott–Sophonisba Breckinridge Breckinridge founded IPL, which GA would later direct; would have been close acquaintances through Breckinridge's relation to E. Abbott	GA–Florence Kelley worked together on many child labor causes, GA paid Kelley special tribute at NCSW dinner in GA's honor, Kelley much admired by GA	GA–Frances Kellor shared concerns about immigrants
		Sophonisba Breckinridge–Florence Kelley SB supported CL; both participated in NAACP	SB–Frances Kellor shared concerns about immigrants and about discrimination against African Americans; at U of C during overlapping period
			Florence Kelley–Frances Kellor knew each other in New York, where Kellor recruited FK to Inter- Municipal League designed to protect domestic workers

Abbreviations: AASW = American Association of Social Workers; ACA = Association of Collegiate Alumnae (later AAUW); ASS = American Sociological Society (later ASA); ASSA = American Social Science Association; CB = Children's Bureau; CL = Consumer's League; CSCP = Chicago School of Civics and Philanthropy (later SSA); IPL = Immigrants' Protective League;

EA–Julia Lathrop Lathrop helped found CSCP and get EA and Breckinridge research appointments; EA did research for CB	**EA–Annie Marion MacLean** both wrote on women in industry, both studied U of C; though MacLean slightly earlier	**EA–Marion Talbot** longtime colleagues at U of C; Talbot helped EA get, keep various positions there
GA–Julia Lathrop very close; GA was Lathrop's choice to succeed her at CB, as she was Addams's choice for Hull-House; Lathrop spotted GA's potential early	**GA–Annie Marion MacLean** unclear how close; shared CL membership; both wrote on immigration	**GA–Marion Talbot** would have known each other well through E. Abbott; Talbot dean when GA was student U of C
SB–Julia Lathrop close relation through CSCP (see above) and research for CB	**SB–Annie Marion MacLean** both at U of C same time, different departments; shared interest in women's wages	**SB–Marion Talbot** Talbot got SB fellowship to make it possible for her to stay in Chicago, secured her many U of C positions; coauthors; loving friends, deeply attached
FK–Julia Lathrop longtime friends from Hull-House; fought smallpox battle together; idea for CB may have begun with FK and Lillian Wald; FK lobbied through NCLC for CB	**FK–Annie Marion MacLean** both members CL; both wrote on CL issues—same year, *AJS;* MacLean cited FK	**FK–Marion Talbot** ACA activities; NAWSA; Talbot CL supporter
Frances Kellor–Julia Lathrop FK occasional Hull-House resident; Progressive Party activist in position to support CB; would have shared Kelley as mutual contact	**FK-Annie Marion MacLean** both did pioneering participants-observation studies; in U of C graduate sociology program at same time	**FK–Marion Talbot** Chicago Women's Club; ACA; Talbot dean while FK at U of C
	Julia Lathrop–Annie Marion MacLean both members of ACA, both supporters of CL, both concerned with immigrants	**JL–Marion Talbot** both members of ACA, active in its Chicago chapter
		Annie Marion MacLean–Marion Talbot Talbot dean while AMM at U of C as student and teacher in Home Study; ACA; CL stalwarts

NAACP = National Association for the Advancement of Colored People; NAWSA = National American Woman Suffrage Association; NCCC = National Conference of Charities and Corrections (later NCSW); NCLC = National Child Labor Committee; NCSW = National Conference of Social Work; WTUL = Women's Trade Union League; U of C = University of Chicago; UL = Urban League

Activism and Research Out of this sharing, the Chicago Women developed a style of collaborative work which combined social science research and social activism to advance the rights of workers (especially of working women and children) and of immigrants, women, the poor, the elderly, and the sick. We offer selected illustrations of this collaboration.

In 1892 Hull-House residents responded to the poverty produced in their neighborhood by the "sweating system." In this system, manufacturers contracted out work to individuals to be done at "home" in tenement apartment-workshops, where family members and other temporary helpers labored to offer the contractor the most work for the least pay. Sparked by Kelley's instinct for the key point of leverage in a system, the Hull-House residents joined trades unions in lobbying for factory legislation that would regulate hours and working conditions, especially for women and children. Kelley got Addams and Lathrop to try to help sell the most unpopular aspect of the bill, the restrictions on child labor, on which many parents depended to complete family income. One result of their successful effort was that reform governor John P. Altgeld appointed Kelley the first Illinois State Inspector of Factories in 1893. Kelley in turn chose her deputies carefully, recruiting from Hull-House residents and neighbors and contacts she had in the unions.[3] In the midst of Kelley's work as a factory inspector, which involved patrolling sweatshops, there was an outbreak of smallpox, and Kelley and her inspectors argued that garments made in smallpox-infected tenements should be burned to prevent the spread of disease. Hull-House residents entered apartments to bring aid to the sick and to seize infected garments. One judge remembered Kelley and Lathrop during this epidemic: "'I saw those two women do that which the health department of the great city of Chicago could not do. The authorities were afraid not only of personal contagion but of damage suits if they destroyed the infected garments. They therefore said that there was no smallpox in Chicago. . . . [But] Kelley . . . and . . . Lathrop were risking their lives in the sweatshop districts . . . entering the rooms . . . of the sick'" (cited in Gordon, 1994:69). Kelley repeatedly turned her experience as inspector of factories to social science use—in two papers on the sweating industry in *Hull-House Maps and Papers* (1895), her *AJS* article "Aims and Principles of the Consumers' League" (1899), and her study *Some Ethical Gains Through Legislation* (1905).

In 1898, inspired by the work of the newly formed Chicago branch of the Consumers' League, which began out of efforts by the local ACA and held its organizational meeting at Hull-House, MacLean did a participant observation study of life as a woman worker in a department store, which she published in the *AJS* in 1899. She also pursued the ongoing issue of sweatshop labor in another participant observation study in 1903.

In 1900, Kellor got support from the Chicago Woman's Club to travel through the South comparing the criminal justice system there with that in the North. This research led Kellor to challenge the then-popular theories of Cesare Lombroso which saw criminality as the result of a genetic defect reflected in the criminal's physiognomy. Kellor's research led to a major study in criminology, *Experimental Sociology* (1901), the foreward of which was written by Charles R. Henderson, who had also advised MacLean on her dissertation.

In 1903, Talbot, in her continuing battle against sexism at the University of Chicago, fought a move to segregate men and women in introductory classes. Surveying the university's first ten years, she presented statistics showing how well women were doing generally in classes: of the 1,164 students to earn bachelor's degrees, 53 percent had been men and 48 percent women; but 199 women had earned the degree with honors, compared with 145 men; and 73 women had earned special honors, compared with 44 men. The university responded by deciding, following the logic of Albion Small, that women matured earlier and their presence in many introductory classes was discouraging the men; practices of sex segregation in classes were instituted (Deegan, 1988:195–199). Talbot, in turn, responded by trying to find ways to build female departments and programs. Talbot collaborated with Breckinridge in much of this work. In 1907, Breckinridge, working as an assistant dean to Talbot, confronted direct racism when an African American woman student sought accommodation in the dormitories and some southern women threatened to move out. Breckinridge held firm on behalf of the African American student and offered to help the white students move. But within days she was called into President Henry Pratt Judson's office and told that the residence halls were for white students only. Breckinridge, in her autobiographical notes, reports that she had at least managed to get it on record that the dean of women's office was in favor of open admission of all students to resident halls (Fitzpatrick, 1990:182). Breckinridge would go on to study housing discrimination against African Americans and to be active in the Chicago NAACP.

In 1903–1904, Lathrop worked with Graham Taylor, founder of the Chicago Commons Settlement House, to start a series of courses to produce persons qualified to work in various state charities and thus to strike a blow against the patronage system which Lathrop so opposed. By 1908, this program had become the Chicago School of Civics and Philanthropy. Lathrop lectured at the school, helped to organize one of its landmark courses in occupational therapy for the mentally ill (Wade, 1977), developed the school's research department, and secured appointments there for Edith Abbott and Breckinridge, who were struggling with various piecemeal positions at the University of Chicago. In 1920, Edith Abbott and Breckinridge succeeded in moving the financially pressed school into the University of Chicago as the School of Social Service Administration (SSA) (Fitzpatrick, 1990; Muncy, 1991).

The 1910 Garment Workers Strike in Chicago engaged the Abbott sisters as academics and reformers. The strike began in September when a group of women workers at Hart, Schaffner and Marx walked off the job to protest a reduction in the rate they were paid for piecework. The strike grew, and after about seven weeks involved 40,000 garment workers. Hull-House, where the Abbotts were residing, became a center for comfort and, as the winter came, for warmth and food. Grace Abbott went with Addams, Ellen Gates Starr, and other Hull-House residents to collect money for food and fuel; then she joined the picket lines and began to speak at strikers' meetings. Edith Abbott assigned her students at the Chicago School of Civics and Philanthropy to study the strike, record workers' grievances, and describe the character of garment manufacturing.

In 1912, this remarkable network of women achieved the creation of the federal Children's Bureau which, with the appointment of Lathrop as its head, became a key place for women reformers. The idea for the Children's Bureau supposedly originated over a breakfast conversation in 1903 between Kelley, then Secretary of the National Consumers' League and living at the Henry Street Settlement in New York City, and Lillian

Wald, the settlement founder and an old friend of Addams through settlement associations. Through the National Child Labor Committee, Kelley and Wald lobbied for the formation of the bureau from 1903 through 1912, when the enabling legislation was finally passed. On the day of its passage, Addams wrote to Wald and Kelley that it would be good to have a woman appointed as the first head; she then lobbied adroitly to get Lathrop appointed. Lathrop turned repeatedly to Hull-House and to Kelley and Wald for help in staffing the Bureau, used her position to secure research contracts for Breckinridge and Abbott at the CSCP (Muncy, 1991:87), and upon her retirement was able to secure the position of Bureau chief for Grace Abbott.

Similar patterns of activism, support, and sociological activity could be traced in several other settings—perhaps most notably for the rights of immigrants, a cause for which they all lobbied and worked. Breckinridge helped found the Immigrants' Protective League in 1907 and wrote on the immigrant experience, offering in one work, *New Homes for Old* (1921), a sympathetic case for the preservation of immigrant values in the new world. At Breckinridge's urging, Grace Abbott became head of the IPL in 1908 and also wrote extensively on the immigrant experience. Edith Abbott and Breckinridge's housing studies in Chicago focus especially on the problems of immigrant housing, and Abbott wrote casebooks on immigration. Kelley's pioneering work in *Hull-House Maps and Papers* depicts the complexity of ethnic relations in an immigrant neighborhood. Kellor looks at immigrant employment experiences in her study *Out of Work;* she was appointed secretary of the New York State Immigration Commission and became director and chief investigator of the New York Bureau of Industries and Immigration in 1910; in 1920 she wrote *Immigration and the Future.* Lathrop was a founder and trustee of the Illinois IPL, focused on the problems of immigrants in the charity systems of Chicago (1895), and was named by Coolidge to investigate conditions at Ellis Island in 1924. MacLean, an immigrant herself (from Canada), wrote "The Significance of the Canadian Migration" (1905), *Modern Immigration* (1925), and about her own naturalization in 1932. Talbot gives some attention to the special needs of immigrant children in *The Education of Women* (1910).

Motivation   The Chicago Women were, like the women Addams described repeatedly in her writing, educated for service and then denied opportunities to serve. Muncy (1991) argues persuasively that part of their drive for reform was their desire to create what she terms "a female dominion," a place where women could exercise power—a sense of power which was an unconscious mingling of the desire for agency with the more acceptable and traditional feminine role of service to others. We concur with Muncy and emphasize that this mingling may have been accomplished more easily for what we would term the "first generation"—Addams, Lathrop, Kelley, and Talbot—who, as pioneers, set out primarily with an ideal of service and gradually formed a career. By the second generation—MacLean, Kellor, the Abbotts, and to a degree, Breckinridge—women generally were receiving mixed signals: the schools which needed them as students and the success of the first generation of women reformers seemed to promise that they could make careers parallel to or intertwined with the careers made by men.[4] But Muncy's argument that personal ambition was a significant motivation is not a definition of self that the Chicago Women would easily have accepted. Talbot (1910) saw that "[t]he little band of leaders who did pioneer work in the last century in claiming and making new opportunities did brave service: in no respect did they do better service than in showing the value of ideals as a positive social force" (1910:3). Addams wrote on the question of motivation in her biography of Lathrop: "[T]hroughout Julia Lathrop's entire life one estimate of her character never changed and I could dip in anywhere to illustrate her disinterested virtue . . . , her unfailing sense of moral obligation and unforced sympathy. It is that sort of disinterested virtue which has been designated as 'the refusal to nurse a private destiny'" (1935:49). It is possible, as Gordon (1994) has documented, to see these women as clannish and in-bred, an early "old-girls' network"; but it is also possible, as Costin (1983:100) and Gordon (1994:70) have both noted, to see the entire network as possessing what Supreme Court Justice Felix Frankfurter described as "a rare degree of disinterestedness and indifference to the share of her own ego in the cosmos." What we argue here is that these women functioned as a group to become "prolific social innovators" (Scott, 1964:xxxvi) and to develop in interaction a sociological theory.

After the Progressive Era

The great age of the Chicago Women's School of Sociology coincided with the Progressive Era of reform. When that era ended, the women's extraordinary moment of glory was transformed. Much of what they had worked for anticipated the concerns and policies of the modern welfare state and was embodied in New Deal legislation in the 1930s, which Grace Abbott helped to draft. But much of that legislation fell far short of the actions both she and her sister Edith knew to be necessary for meeting the goals that had emerged out of the Progressive Era experiments in which the Chicago Women's School played a large part. Most especially the Chicago Women had attempted to establish the goals for a welfare state by defining a national standard of quality of life and setting minimums below which *no* citizen would be allowed to fall (see Chapter 3 and "The Chicago Women and the Canon" later in this chapter). The 1930s saw the deaths of Lathrop, Grace Abbott, Kelley, and MacLean. Edith Abbott and Breckinridge continued the good fight at the School of Social Service Administration into the 1940s. Talbot resigned as dean of women in 1925, with a parting shot to the University of Chicago Board of Trustees that women faculty were being treated abominably—a shot that may have found its mark, since Breckinridge, for instance, was appointed full professor in 1925 and became Samuel Deutch Professor of Public Welfare Administration in 1929. Talbot served from 1927 to 1930 as acting president of the Women's College in Constantinople, Turkey. Returning to the United States in 1930, she wrote a history of the ACA and her memoirs, *More Than Lore*. She died in 1947, and her close friend Breckinridge died a few months later, early in 1948. Kellor spent her life after 1926 writing on arbitration, producing several texts that are still classics of jurisprudence, and serving as president of the American Arbitration Association; she died in 1952. Edith Abbott was the last survivor of this group, spending her last years at Hull-House and returning to Nebraska to die in 1957. In one of her last major public addresses, in 1951, accepting the Survey Award from the National Conference of Social Work, she showed herself still game for battle and critical of how little had been achieved: " 'Social security is not social security when it reaches only the destitute'" (cited in Fitzpatrick, 1991:216). In that statement, she articulated the vision of the welfare state that the Chicago Women's School of Sociology had been moving toward in their social theory. We turn now to that theory.

GENERAL SOCIAL THEORY

Assumptions

The members of the Chicago Women's School shared many assumptions with their major theorist, Jane Addams: Progressivism, the women's movement, philosophic pragmatism, the settlement house philosophy of democratic participation, and an essentially midwestern Protestant sense of duty (see Chapter 3). And they assumed some of the main points in the sociology Addams herself was formulating: the duty of the sociologist to work for social amelioration; the need to take account of the individual actor's understandings; the understanding of the individual as embodied, agentic, self-interested, sociable, and ethical; and the analysis of society as patterned by ethics and material production. Additionally, three other sets of ideas affected their thinking—Marxian socialism, empiricism, and jurisprudence.

While only Kelley had a strong grounding in formal Marxism, the other women (including Addams) all identified economic class position as the main variable explaining the human misery they saw around them, unfettered capitalist greed as the primary cause of that misery, and labor organization and legislation as critical to worker emancipation. Marxist theory was debated at Hull-House clubs, Addams was reading Marx, and the members of the Chicago Woman's Club studied *Capital* as part of their general preparation for beginning to "manage large endeavors" (Scott, 1993:120). Kelley, the other major theorist of the School, had become a socialist in Zurich in the mid-1880s, and published the first English translation of Engels's *The Conditions of the Working Class in England in 1844*. The impact of socialism on Kelley's thinking is shown in a remarkable work of her own, also published in 1887, "The Need for Theoretical Preparation for Philanthropic Work," which applies Marxist theory to philanthropy, arguing that

> [o]ur bourgeois philanthropy, whatever form it may take, is really only the effort to give back to the workers a little bit of that which our whole social system, systematically, robs them of, and so to prop up that system yet a little longer. . . . It is the workers who produce all values; but the lion's share of what they produce falls to the lion—the capitalist class. . . . [F]or the capitalist class as a whole, all philanthropic effort is a work of restitution for self-preservation. (Kelley (1887/1986:94)

The debate resulting from this publication focused on the problem that underlay the work and the thought of the Chicago Women: intensifying class divisions in the United States.[5]

The Chicago Women assumed that one contribution social scientists could make to the problem of class division was to provide accurate descriptions of the conditions of the working classes and of all groups living in dire poverty: immigrants, sweatshop workers, African Americans, and the old, sick, and mentally ill. In arriving at a standard for accuracy, they were influenced by two developing traditions of empiricism. One was the tradition represented by Carroll Wright, in his work first at the American Social Science

Association, and later as first chief of the US Bureau of Labor Statistics. Wright helped Emily and Marion Talbot analyze the data for the ACA 1882 survey (see Theme 2, following). He hired Kelley to run the Chicago portion of his seventh Bureau of Labor Statistics report, *The Slums of Baltimore, Chicago, New York, and Philadelphia* (1894), which gave her access to some of the data for *Hull-House Maps and Papers* (see Theme 2, following). Wright's particular interest seems to have been in developing the range of variables—especially of social conditions—that could be collected and tabulated by statisticians. These statistics were used by social reformers as "hard" evidence to advance the Progressive agenda. The second influence was that of British pioneers in empirical research, most particularly Charles Booth and Beatrice and Sidney Webb, who were interested in the general problem of how to use facts to generate policy-relevant theory. Booth's masterwork *The Life and Labour of the People of London* (1892–1902) was well-known in US social science circles. Beatrice Webb helped in that work and later, with her husband Sydney, founded the London School of Economics; Edith Abbott studied there, taking their course "Methods of Social Investigation" and attending lectures by both Webbs during the time of Beatrice's heated involvement with the Poor Law Commission (see Chapter 8). One finds references to Booth and Beatrice Webb in the writings of Addams, *Hull-House Maps and Papers,* and the publications of Edith Abbott, Breckinridge, and Kelley. Like Booth and the Webbs, the Chicago Women sought those indicators that would best measure urban poverty and serve as a guide to reform legislation. Underlying that quest was a faith that it was possible to establish norms of social science research on whose validity researchers, policymakers, and the public could agree (see Chapter 8). The Chicago Women's School was at first more influenced by these empiricist trends in social science than were their male contemporaries in the University of Chicago Department of Sociology, who, within the division of academic labor, regarded empirical studies as "women's work." Thus, for instance, Edith Abbott for many years taught the course in social statistics as a marginal lecturer in the Chicago Sociology Department (Deegan, 1991).

The Chicago Women had an ongoing interest in jurisprudence, which for them was the philosophy that law is a medium for social reform—a generally accepted Progressive faith. Lathrop, Kelley, Breckinridge, and the Abbotts had fathers who were lawyers and legislators. Kelley for her Cornell senior thesis wrote "On Some Changes in the Legal Status of the Child since Blackstone." Kelley, Breckinridge, and Kellor all got law degrees themselves, and Lathrop and Grace Abbott both read law for a time. The Chicago Women had a keen interest both in the drafting of reform legislation and in its implementation and administration. They viewed legislation as the means to implement a caring and democratic social state. Kelley's major statement, *Some Ethical Gains Through Legislation,* is a paradigmic working through of this shared view—that vulnerable social groups experienced structurally produced pain, that an ethical public informed by social research would be impelled to mitigate that pain, and that law, properly written and administered, was the instrument of this ethical concern.

Major Themes

The Chicago Women's School of Sociology defines a problem as "social" if its origins lie in the organization of society rather than in human nature or individual character, and the purpose of sociology as the discovery of those societal arrangements that lead to social inequity and human suffering. The duty of the researcher is both to discover such arrangements and to advocate measures for their reform. To study a problem out of only abstract scientific interest with no attempt at remedy is, for the Chicago Women, practically illogical and morally indefensible. We explore their sociology in terms of three themes: a focus on the social-structural causes of human pain, the invention of a research methodology that accurately portrays such structural arrangements, and the role of the sociologist as an advocate for change.

1. For the Chicago Women's School, the subject of sociology is the systemic social arrangements producing human pain. The Chicago Women vary in their working through of this principle, but overall their studies are marked by four qualities: (1) the concretization of a social problem through vivid individual examples of human pain; (2) the demonstration that that pain occurs not randomly but in patterns; (3) the investigation of the structural causes of inequity and suffering; and (4) the determination to produce remedies (discussed in Theme 3).

The Fact of Individual and Collective Pain   The duty to bear witness to individual pain is the emotional if not the presentational beginning of research and activism for the Chicago Women. In her study "The Cook County Charities," in *Hull-House Maps and Papers,* Lathrop wonders if "[t]here is . . . a certain satisfaction to the philanthropist and sociologist alike, in having touched bottom, reached ultimate facts" (Lathrop, 1895:144).* Reaching one such ultimate fact, Lathrop graphically illustrates the principle that total institutions are organized for staff rather than inmates in her analysis of the administrative rule separating husbands and wives into the male and female quarters of the county poorhouse. She describes the terror this produced in "an old Irish couple" pleading not to be sent to the county poorhouse: "the old woman; who is ninety odd, said, 'Oh, he'll have to go in with the men; I'll have to go in with the women, and all our own clothes will be taken away from us. I can somehow sort o' do for myself; but he . . . he can't. I'll feel sorrier for him than for me'" (1895:149–150).* In the same volume, Kelley gives a vivid example of old age produced not by living to "ninety odd" but by years of overwork begun in childhood in the case "of a cloakmaker who began work . . . at the age of fourteen years, and was found, after twenty years of temperate and faithful work, . . . too feeble to be of value to any sweater" and was declared by "two competent physicians" to be "suffering from old age . . . at thirty-four" (1895:37). Grace Abbott in a study of employment agencies which systematically defraud immigrant workers, notes not only the physical price but the blows to self-esteem that the workers experience: "This is one of the most pathetic things in connection with the work [of the researcher]. The men are ashamed to tell their story. 'Everyone cheats a greenhorn,' they say, and want to hide, from those who are anxious to help them, what they consider a reflection on their intelligence" (1908:298–299).*

---

*An asterisk following a citation in the text means that the passage quoted is given in fuller context in the "Readings" at the end of the chapter.

Correlates of Human Pain   The Chicago Women understand and demonstrate that the scenes of individual deprivation they portray result from the intersection of dimensions of oppression—class, gender, ethnicity, race, age—in individual but typical biographies: the working-class child, the elderly working-class woman, the immigrant man trying to provide for a family without knowledge of language, law, or customs. Lathrop analyzes the ethnic background and social class of persons who end up at the Cook County Charities, finding they are persons who have worked for "an average wage-rate so low as to render thrift . . . an ineffective insurance against emergencies" (1895:143). MacLean looks at the intersection of gender and class in the lives of department store salesgirls (1899) and at configurations of ethnicity, class, gender, and age in sweat shop labor (1903). Grace Abbott (1908) and Kellor (1905a,b,c, 1915) explore the intersection of class and race/ethnicity in the practices of employment agencies used by immigrants, African Americans, and women seeking domestic service positions. Breckinridge describes how race overrides class in the housing discrimination faced by black Americans: "every man who is black," whether "rich or poor," is forced to pay "extortionate rents" and to live in areas dangerous because of their proximity to the "disreputable white element . . . forced upon him" (Breckinridge, 1913:575).

The most stunning example of this effort to show the correlates of poverty may be the extraordinarily detailed color maps in *Hull-House Maps and Papers* (1895) which present, house by house, the race/ethnicity and family incomes of the Hull-House neighborhood (see Theme 2). Breckinridge and Edith Abbott's studies of housing conditions continue this tradition, portraying with maps, statistics, photographs, and words the quality of life in various ethnic slums. They describe the district known as "back of the yards," located between the Chicago stockyards and the city dump: "In the Stockyards . . . are the mingled cries of the animals awaiting slaughter, the presence of uncared-for-waste, the sight of blood, the carcasses naked of flesh and skin, suggestion of death and disintegration—all of which must react in a demoralizing way, not only upon the character of the people, but the conditions under which they live" (1911:434–435).* Their study shows the correlation between "pain"—indicated by death, disease, and destitution—and class, skill level, immigrant status, language, and cultural barriers. They see as the intervening variable in this correlation terrible housing in a nightmarish setting.

Structural Causes of Pain   The Chicago Women seek the systemic social arrangements which produce these correlations. Their governing analytic principle is that all social conditions are interrelated: one cannot talk separately of industry, family, gender, education, domestic service, household, factory, government, consumer, or immigrant. Their typical mode of analysis is to begin from a condition of human pain, analytically as well as sympathetically described, moving to show both its causes in social structure and its consequences for the larger community and society. They then look for the changes that can be made to ameliorate that pain. They identify three general structural arrangements that cause pain: (1) the workings of the industrial order under capitalism; (2) the patterning of access by discriminatory practices; and (3) a maladjustment between the processes of production and the ethical responsiveness of the community.

Grace Abbott, in her study of employment agencies dealing with immigrants, recognizes that in the larger employment pattern "seasonal work must be done in the United States. . . . The work cannot easily be made attractive or desirable, but some system of handling these men honestly must be devised. This study of employment has given only a superficial insight into a much larger problem of American industrial life" (1908:300). This line of argument is also developed by MacLean in her studies of coal miners, and hop-pickers, as well as in the Breckinridge and Edith Abbott study of work in the stockyards. Later in her career, in a 1939 lecture to social workers, Grace Abbott broadens her analysis to the general problem of unemployment within capitalism: "Unemployment may, therefore, be regarded in greater or lesser degree as the inevitable result of our industrial system. Our economic life is based upon it. A democracy which supports this system should, therefore, make adequate and democratic provision for its victims, recognizing the costs of their care as the price it pays for the continuance of the capitalist system" (G. Abbott, 1941/1966:4–5).

The Chicago Women show the patterning of employment and destitution by class, ethnicity/race, gender, and age. MacLean considers how class and gender keep women shop workers at such low wages that they are forced to prostitution (1899). Kellor explores the exploitation of rural southern black women trying to find work in the North (1905a,b,c). Breckinridge and Abbott (1911) attempt to account for why the immigrants come to live "back of the yards." New immigrants, lacking money and knowledge of both the English language and American customs, need to live near their work and with people who speak their language, thus intensifying the housing problem. Kelley connects housing patterns with the issue of worker hours: "In those occupations in which long hours of work prevail, the employees are obliged to live near their place of work, and . . . congestion is thus intensified" (Kelley, 1905:109).

The Chicago Women locate much of the cause of systemically produced pain in the disjuncture, identified by Addams (Chapter 3), between the material organization of industry and the ethical organization of social relations. Industrial production is socially organized, but social relations remains anchored in individualistic ethics and family claims, making greed acceptable. Studying the criminal justice system in the South, Kellor shows how individual greed, enshrined in law, can corrupt the state: "There can be no doubt that Southern penal laws are unequally administered. . . . The office of justice is shunned by the better class of men and few honest persons accept it. The salary is small, and the rule is: no conviction, no fee for either justice or jurors. This is a direct bribe for conviction" (Kellor, 1901b:421). Kelley locates the primary agents of greed at the pinnacle of the economic system, with the capitalist manufacturer. She describes how the sweating system which allows clothing to be made in tenements is part of a much larger system of labor. The manufacturer of clothing, seeking to cut costs, finds it "cheaper" to hire out various jobs and thus reduce his own overhead in keeping a plant.

> A millionaire philanthropist, at the head of one of the largest clothing-houses in the world, was once asked why he did not employ directly the people who made his goods, and furnish them with steam-power, thus saving a heavy drain upon their health, and reducing the number of sweaters' victims found every winter in his pet hospital. "So far," he replied, "we have found leg-power and the sweater cheaper." (Kelley, 1895:40)

2. For the Chicago Women, the method of sociology is the use of multiple research strategies to achieve empirically accurate accounts of socially produced human pain. A major challenge for the Chicago Women was to create methods that would give them the empirically grounded, generalizable information they needed to formulate policy initiatives. In meeting this challenge, they were remarkably inventive; one of their lasting achievements is the variety of data-gathering techniques they pioneered. With only a few earlier studies to guide them (see "Assumptions," preceding, and Chapter 8), the Chicago Women often invented their research procedures as they went along, driven by their curiosity but restrained by a self-imposed standard for empirical rigor. A representative sample of their data-gathering strategies is presented in Figure 7-3, which lists techniques of direct observation and textual analysis of documents for both quantitative and qualitative data. Four qualities of the research of the Chicago Women are especially noteworthy: (1) a willingness to start from immediate lived experience; (2) the use of multiple research strategies to explore a given issue; (3) a critical attitude toward both the data collected and the ethical implications of research design; and (4) a vivid and accessible presentation of data in which the researchers keep themselves present to their readers.

The Chicago Women bring into the research area their own experience as citizens living ordinary lives—going home late on the trolley (Kelley, 1905); helping with voter registration (E. Abbott, 1915); remembering childhood (MacLean, 1903); judging institutional food and needs (Lathrop, 1895). They also draw on their experience in official positions. For instance, Kelley uses her experiences as Illinois Inspector of Factories as a major source of data about labor relations; Lathrop draws on her own experience as a visitor for the Illinois State Board of Charities to write a guide for other such volunteers; Grace Abbott's studies of immigrants begin with her experiences as Assistant Director of the Immigrants' Protective League; and Talbot draws on untold faculty meetings to carve out this timeless description of faculty politics over the curriculum:

> Whence comes this tyranny of the curriculum? Largely from traditional conceptions of the inherent value of certain subjects of study . . . [and] the pressure for their continued recognition [from] . . . scholars and heads of departments. . . . In debate and discussion, in regulation and act, . . . [m]embers of college faculties often seem on the one hand atrophied in their judgment of human needs, and on the other ignorant of the constant change in the content and method of subjects taught. (Talbot, 1910:183–184)

In any single study, the researcher typically combines qualitative accounts of people's lives, quantitative statements about distribution of traits, and analyses of key texts. In her 1899 *AJS* study of life as a department store saleswoman, MacLean uses participant observation; composes tables giving the working women's occupation, income, ethnicity, and length of time in present job; and offers overviews of state legislative attempts to regulate women's work. In their 1911 article "Back of the Yards," Breckinridge and Edith Abbott and their students combine photographs, maps, verbal descriptions, interviews, physical measurements of room size and number of windows, statistical profiles of ethnicity and occupation, and analysis of housing codes to present a multi-dimensional account of life in a desperately poor area.

The Chicago Women take a critical attitude both toward data collected by others and toward the ethics of their own data collection strategies. Edith Abbott and Breckinridge

FIGURE 7-3   Methods of the Chicago Women

Data type	Technique	Sample study and source	Description
Observations, quantitative	Survey	Association of Collegiate Alumnae 1882 (see Rosenberg, 1982); MacLean, 1910	Marion Talbot, working with mother, Emily, mailed survey to 1,290 women college graduates about health; got 705; MacLean surveyed over 13,000 women employed in 400 work sites in some 20 cities, using five survey schedules and supervising some 29 interviewers
	Interviews	Breckinridge and E. Abbott, 1911	In studying housing conditions in Chicago, Breckinridge and Abbott had students go door to door to find out occupations, ethnicity, numbers of persons in residences, etc.
	Physical measurement	Breckinridge and E. Abbott, 1911; Kellor, 1901a	Breckinridge and Abbott students measured room size and doors and windows; Kellor did measurements of prisoners' heads to test (and disprove) Lombroso's theory that criminal behavior is a result of biological characteristics revealed in physiognomy
	Personal budget keeping	MacLean, 1899	MacLean kept track of the budget she worked off of using her wages earned as a salesgirl in a department store
Observations, qualitative	Participant observation	MacLean, 1899, 1903; Kellor, 1904	MacLean did research working as a salesgirl in a department store and as a sweatshop seamstress; Kellor investigated employment agencies by acting as an employer in some agencies and an employee in others
	Field observation and interviews	Lathrop, 1895, 1905; G. Abbott, 1908; Kelley, 1905	Lathrop did field observation and interviews in her charity service and wrote a pamphlet on how to be an effective "visitor"; G. Abbott visited employment agencies specializing in immigrants; Kelley did both field observation and interviews with employees in her work as Illinois State Inspector of Factories
	Self-reporting	Talbot, 1910	In *the Education of Women*, Talbot draws on firsthand experience at faculty meetings to explain curriculum requirements
Documents, quantitative	U.S. census data	E. Abbott and Breckinridge, 1906	Abbott and Breckinridge study women's employment patterns in industry over time
	Court records	Breckinridge, 1910	Breckinridge uses court records and traces problems back to delinquent child's home situation, mother's work demands, and husband's support
	Voting records	E. Abbott, 1908, 1910	E. Abbott does an early study of gender gap in voting in municipal elections
	Surveys by others	Kelley, 1899	Kelley uses New York Consumers' League survey of 1,400 businesses
Documents, qualitative	Memoirs and diaries	E. Abbott, 1908; Talbot, 1910	E. Abbott traces information about employment from private memoirs; Talbot looks at women's education beginning with a young girl's diary for 1771
	Catalogues and syllabi	Talbot, 1910	Talbot incorporates requirements from various schools and courses to give an overview of educational objectives for women
	Laws	Kelley, 1905; Kellor, 1901b; Breckinridge, 1934	Kelley studies laws governing employment and working conditions; Kellor studies laws governing working of legal system itself; Breckinridge does huge casebook on laws governing family and state

(1906) point out that the various parts of the census data for 1900—*Population; Occupations, Employees, and Wages;* and *Manufacturers*—were prepared under two different directors and that the breakout and definitions of categories do not match, so that comparisons across data sets are problematic. As head of the Children's Bureau, Lathrop (1912) is concerned that many official studies have been neither read by nor made accessible to the general public and sets the editing of such studies as a first goal for the Bureau (see Theme 3, following). The Chicago Women's general sensitivity to the ethics of social data gathering is suggested in the introduction to *Hull-House Maps and Papers:* "The painful nature of minute investigation, and the personal impertinence of many of the questions asked, would be unendurable and unpardonable were it not for the conviction that the public conscience when roused must demand better surroundings for the most inert and long-suffering citizens of the commonwealth" (Holbrooke, 1895:13–14). Kellor discusses the issue of honesty in participant-observation research into businesses: "No private business can be investigated, with even a remote approach to accuracy, by any one who goes openly and avowedly as an investigator; and this is especially true of enterprises that are in the least degree questionable." She regrets the need for dissembling but asks, "Does not the end justify the means? Is it not right to employ this, the only accurate method of investigation, rather than to continue the present conditions?" (1904:2, 3).

In their presentation of their findings, the Chicago Women strive to be accessible and to keep themselves present to their readers in their accounts. Their desire for accessibility is most marked by their use of visual aids, both quantitative and qualitative, of which the maps in *Hull-House Maps and Papers* remain a landmark achievement. These maps pattern data, from a Department of Labor survey, to show in color codes the ethnicity/race and average family weekly wage of each household in the Hull-House neighborhood. On separate maps, they use six colors to represent wage ranges and eighteen colors for nationalities. (A building may contain several households; businesses are not noted except for brothels.) By comparing the different maps, the reader may locate, for any given building, the diversity of income and ethnicity, and within the neighborhood, ethnic enclaves and intermingling as well as gradations of poverty.

As researchers, the Chicago Women are typically present as embodied persons in their narratives, and they use this presence both to bear witness to the pain of the situation described and to suggest possible limitations to their data. Kelley testifies about her own eyesight in describing the work now expected of women in some power-operated manufacture:

> In the capacity of inspector for the National Consumers' League it has been the fortune of the writer to visit and inspect a large number of factories. . . . In the course of that time there has occurred a development of machinery . . . significant in its consequences[:] . . . the speed of the sewing-machines has been increased so that they set, in 1905, twice as many stitches in a minute as in 1899. Machines which formerly carried one needle now carry from two to ten. . . . Thus a girl using one of these machines is now responsible for twice as many stitches at the least. . . . The strain upon the eyes is . . . far more than twice what it was. . . . Now, when the needle set twenty-two hundred stitches a minutes, as was the case in 1899, the writer, whose eyes are unusually keen, could see the needle when the machine was in motion. At the present speed, the writer, whose eyes have remained unimpaired, is wholly unable to see the needle, discerning merely the gleam of light where it is in motion. (Kelley, 1905:121–122)

In a different tack, MacLean uses her reflections on her experience to admit to possible shortcomings in her report on her experience in a sweatshop. She admits to absolute exhaustion from the work but allows that "it would be necessary to charge much of my discomfort to inexperience." Yet there remains the fact that sweating is "a system vocal with the sobbing of children and the groans of weary women" (MacLean, 1903:307–308). MacLean goes on to charge her readers as morally obligated as consumers to learn the origins of what they are buying: "And we who buy need not soothe our consciences with the belief that we are helpless in the matter, while the people who give out the work are the only sinners. This may be comfortable, but it is criminal. The contractor gives us what we are willing to take" (MacLean, 1903:300).

3. For the Chicago Women, the duty of the sociologist is to use research to mobilize the people and the state for reform of inequitable social arrangements. The Chicago Women's School understood that to change the social conditions producing human pain, they had to mobilize two potential actors, the people and the state. Mobilization presented at least four theoretical problems: the nature of the people; the ideology of "public versus private"; the invention of forms of association necessary to the expression of a reform agenda; and the organization of the state. Their appeal to the people is guided by their understanding of the individual human being, conceptualized much as Addams does (see Chapter 3): as an embodied agent motivated by practical interests, a desire for sociability, and an ethical need to judge action as "right" or "wrong." They relate to the people through an appeal to both conscience and self-interest, critiquing the ideology of public versus private, analyzing the need for new associational forms, and explicating the workings of the state.

The Critique of Public versus Private Within the ideology of "private versus public," which still permeates American policy debates, "private" is understood as lying within the province of the individual and outside the right of the state, while "public" is understood as affecting the whole community to such a degree as to override private interest and be subject to state intervention. The Chicago Women use empirical studies to support their theoretical claim of the interrelatedness of private and public. Breckinridge (1910) calls this argument "the theory of public interest"; Kelley (1905), the theory of "the ethical standards of the community." Breckinridge reasons that "public interest justifie[s] the enforcement of . . . obligations on the part of the husband" to the wife and family, for the public is affected by the educational limitations and possible delinquency of children raised by "the unsupported mother," who, bearing "the double burden of earning the support and of performing the domestic duties," is often forced into conditions of "poverty, the crowded home, the congested neighborhood" (Breckinridge, 1910:54–55). Kelley discussing the necessity of legislation to prohibit child labor, regardless of parental preference, reasons that "[t]he care and nurture of childhood is thus a vital concern of the nation. . . . An unfailing test of the ethical standards of a community is the question 'What citizens are being trained here'" (Kelley, 1905:3–4). Talbot (1910) argues for higher education for women because a changing world is propelling women into relationships far beyond their homes, giving them a new power resource as consumers. But she and Breckinridge point out that for women to use any power they have, "The housekeeper must be present in her own person or in the person of her agent where the concerns of her family are at issue" (Talbot and Breckinridge, 1912:85).

Inventing Associations   The Chicago Women theoretically and practically realize that people have to invent new forms of association to bring pressure to bear on the perpetrators of injustice. The theoretical significance of association in the cause of reform is presented in Kelley's 1899 *AJS* article "Aims and Principles of the Consumers' League." Kelley seeks to call consumers into being as a conscious social force to redress the imbalance between capital and labor.

> Those of us who enjoy the privilege of voting may help, once or twice in a year, to decide how the tariff, or the currency, or the local tax rate shall be adjusted to our industries. But all of us, all the time, are deciding by our expenditures what industries shall survive at all, and under what conditions. Broadly stated, it is the aim of the National Consumers' League to moralize this decision, to gather and make available information which may enable us all to decide in the light of knowledge, and to appeal to the consciences, so that the decision when made shall be a righteous one. (Kelley, 1899:289–290)*

The essential principles of the sociology of the Chicago Women are all in this article: that social science must act for change; that all citizens, including women still denied suffrage, are nevertheless morally responsible for the welfare of the country; that every action ties a person to other people; that effective personal virtue today must be realized through associations because it is only in associations that people can gain both the knowledge and the power to make their individual action truly "righteous"—that is, both democratic and effective.

Kelley's appeal to the consumer is made both on moral grounds and on the basis of self-interest. Customers, she says, are mistaken in believing that by buying the most expensive item they are protecting themselves from both the danger of disease and any charge of responsibility for the exploitation of the worker. Kelley narrates a story from her days as Illinois Inspector of Factories, telling how an expensive coat ordered in Helena, Montana, ended up in the workroom of a tailor in a smallpox-infected tenement in Chicago. She stresses that the tailor who made this coat was forced to conceal the fact of smallpox out of fear of losing even a day's wages, and that many items of production have now moved to such a "ready-made" status that all consumers are potentially threatened by "injurious chemicals . . . in milk, bread, meat, home remedies" (Kelley, 1899:293–294).

She then turns to direct actions the Consumers' League should undertake: working for uniform legislation—important because the US Constitution forbids any state to deny the import of goods from any other; translating government statistical reports into guides for consumers by naming manufacturers in violation of labor regulations; and marking products with its own "League" label, certifying that the product contains what it is supposed to contain and that no workers were exploited in its production. "The consumer," she claims, "ultimately determines all production" (Kelley, 1899:290). But for their power to be felt, consumers must form a unity of demand large enough to affect the manufacturers—power for consumers can come only through association.

Reform through Government   The Chicago Women's analysis of the role of the state in social amelioration reflects a hardheaded empiricism earned in their long years as researchers and activists. They argue that the state can and will act responsibly only *if*—government agencies are energized, mobilized, and monitored by concerned citizen associations; social science research is used in the formation of strategies for reform; and there is open, accessible communication among agencies, citizen publics, and social scientists. The citizen must mobilize not only for the passage of a law but for its enforcement. Noting how many inspectors are supplied to enforce New York City's Tenement House Commission and how few staff the Chicago sanitation department have to enforce similar regulations, Breckinridge and Edith Abbott conclude "Back of the Yards" with the stern admonition: "When the community conscience has been sufficiently aroused to demand changes in the content of the law, it seems little short of dishonest not to make possible its enforcement. To substitute the shadow for the substance in dealing with the problem of city housing leads quickly to criminal neglect" (Breckinridge and G. Abbott, 1911:468). The thesis that social science research should inform government decisions scored one of its most famous victories in a case supported in part by the Consumers' League headed by Kelley. In *Muller v. Oregon,* 1908, a case on the legality of an Oregon law limiting the maximum hours that women could work, Louis Brandeis formulated what became known as "the Brandeis brief"—an argument that used statistics and sociological and economic data as evidence in addition to traditional legal arguments.

In setting her agenda for the Children's Bureau, Lathrop, in a July 1912 speech to the General Federation of Women's Clubs (GFWC), stresses that for government reform to proceed, the constituencies that supported the creation of the Bureau (which included the members of the GFWC) must stay consulted, motivated, and mobilized. She outlines her role for them in the first major project before the Bureau—the accurate registration of births. Seeing that an attempt at massive registration by the federal government will be resisted on states' rights grounds, she calls on progressive women's associations to assist in the data collection effort at the local level and to lobby for state legislation. She then describes the relation among social science researchers, government agencies, voluntary associations, and individual citizens needed to solve social problems. The Bureau must synthesize the hundreds of already existent social science studies and publish them in a form useful to the lay reader: "Those responsible for the work of the Bureau . . . are ready to accept the function of popularizing the wisdom of others . . . [as the] task [that] should precede original work on the part of the Bureau itself" (Lathrop, 1912:320–322). In carrying out this task, Lathrop followed the woman-centered approach that characterized her administration of the Bureau. While getting advice from male medical experts, she turned for the actual writing of the pamphlet to a widow with five children—Mary Mills West's "publications [on child care] became the best-selling pamphlets of the Government Printing Office in the 1910s" (Muncy, 1991:55).[6]

THE RELEVANCE OF THE CHICAGO WOMEN'S SCHOOL OF SOCIOLOGY FOR THE HISTORY AND PRESENT PRACTICE OF SOCIOLOGY

The Chicago Women and the Canon of Sociology

In locating the Chicago Women's School of Sociology in the history of the discipline of sociology, the first point to be noted is that we have here a genuine "school" of sociologists, understood as a group of thinkers and researchers located essentially in the same space, working in close relationships, guided by the ideas of a major theorist, Addams, and modifying those ideas in various ways that remain true to the basic theory while still reflecting the biographies, personalities, intellectual interests, and research findings of the group over time. If only for this fact, the Chicago Women's School of Sociology deserves its place in our understanding of our past. Such schools are rare in the history of the profession. In the history of Western sociology the best-known schools are the ones that sprang up around Emile Durkheim in Paris before World War I; the male "Chicago School" that developed around Robert E. Park between the two World Wars; the Frankfurt Institute in Germany in the 1920s; and the group of students, eminent sociologists in their own right, who studied with Talcott Parsons at Harvard during the 1940s and early 1950s. Studied as a school, the Chicago Women exemplify the way in which "normal science" (Kuhn, 1962), that is, scientific work based in a shared theoretical perspective, is done. The Chicago Women's School of Sociology created many of the methodological and data-gathering strategies that would by the 1930s become criteria—adopted without acknowledgement—of male professionalized sociology. If only to redress this situation, to give them "patent" to what they invented and male sociologists appropriated, it is necessary to reinstate them to the canon (see Bulmer, Bales, and Sklar, 1991 for a historical perspective on a part of this methodology).

The next point to be noted is that the Chicago Women were researchers first, theorists only secondarily. Adding them to the canon of sociology's history of itself makes us see, as does the addition of Beatrice Webb (see Chapter 8), that there is another way for this history to be told—as the story of sociology's great empirical works rather than that of its major theories. As a school developing a theory through major empirical works, the Chicago Women believed that research is for social change, that it should not be value-neutral, that certain problems come to the researcher's attention because the conditions in question are causing pain, and that the researcher begins with a general allegiance to a principle of fairness or equity in society and allows the specific configuration of equity to emerge out of the research. This School played an important role in shaping US social policy as its members helped to produce, through the National Conference of Charities and Corrections, the landmark position paper "Social Standards for Industry." That paper outlined much of what we today associate with the welfare state: government regulation of industry to achieve for all citizens a living wage, a wage paid biweekly, an eight-hour day, a six-day week, a ban on homework (that is, the sweating system), unemployment insurance, old-age pensions, workmen's compensations, protection for women and children in certain conditions of work. The paper became part of the 1912 Progressive Party platform, and its ideas underlay much New Deal legislation.

The third point to be noted is the Chicago Women's eclectic relation to ideas in the major male theoretical traditions. They share with functionalism a fascination with society as a system of interrelation and pursue the possibility of achieving some degree of equilibrium in society; they focus, like Durkheim, on the law and its texts, and they believe, like later functionalists, that the legal process should serve an integrative function by adjudicating social conflict. Yet in their critique of social inequity, their focus on problems produced by social inequity, and their moral commitment to a value-infused sociology of advocacy, they are fundamentally different from the functionalists. The

Chicago Women trace much social conflict to the exploitative practices of modern industrial capitalism, in which they hold the state complicitous. They stand as advocates on behalf of those exploited by capitalism and define that exploitation primarily in terms of class. All this links them to Marxian conflict theory. But, with the exception of Kelley, the Chicago Women were not Marxian. They see ethnicity and gender, as well as age, as major factors in the patterning of exploitation, and they believe that class differences can be bridged and society reformed by an appeal to the public conscience to transform the state. Like the interpretive paradigm, the Chicago Women focus on groups—in distinctive work sites, neighborhoods, ethnic communities. They view these groups as people in interaction, in symbolic communication, and engaged in courses of meaningful action. What separates the Chicago Women from the interpretive tradition, however, is their understanding that meanings are not produced by an equal exchange between parties, that power is ever present, manifesting itself in measurable, objective physical realities—money, organizational resources, space, time, health—and determining the outcome of negotiations over meaning.

The Chicago Women and the Tradition of Feminist Sociology

A Feminist Research Methodology   The Chicago Women begin their researches in the situation at hand, quite literally in their own backyards—Hull-House, voter registration, a Consumers' League discussion of the plight of saleswomen in department stores, a major garment workers' strike. They develop their theory in the manner forcefully articulated by Maria Mies (following Mao Tse-tung): "If you want to know a thing, you must change it'" (1983:125). Repeatedly in their empirical studies they make clear that they have reached an understanding of a social condition by having tried to change it. In deciding on strategies for data collection, the Chicago Women are early examples of that eclecticism and inventiveness that contemporary feminist scholars view as characteristic of feminist research methods (Fonow and Cook, 1995; Reinharz, 1992). They move easily between primary and secondary data and between quantitative and qualitative expressions of those data. Their quantitative skills are sophisticated, their qualitative techniques reflective and ingenious, and—unlike some modern feminists—they express no ideological tension in choosing between these modes. This may be because they interweave so many data sources, qualitative and quantitative, in their reports. They often worked in teams and wrote collaboratively.

Importance of Women   Gender is not always the first or key variable in the Chicago Women's work; but it is always a variable. They are always conscious of the possibility of differences between men's and women's experience in the same category—immigrant, unemployed, worker, family member, institutional inmate. It is from women's experience that they comment on the vast changes in social organization brought by industrialization: changes in the home and family in all classes of society, in the role of women in industry, in looking for work and being out of work, in the needs of mothers for financial support, in the increasing interdependence of people in urban life, in the problems created by a failure to act upon impulses of kindness across barriers of nationality and race, in the need for suffrage, and in the problems of difference and inequality increasingly exacerbated by the growing discrepancies in wealth. And they call on women to be agents of social change through organizations like the Consumers' League, the General Federation of Women's Clubs, the Women's Trade Union League, and the National American Woman Suffrage Association.

An exemplar of the convergence of many of these predispositions and concerns is Breckinridge's analysis of pay equity in "The Home Responsibilities of Women Workers and the 'Equal Wage'" (1923). Breckinridge notes the complexity of relations covered in such phrases as "family responsibility" and "equal wage" in her opening statement, "The demand on the part of women workers for 'equal pay' to men and women for 'equal work' is likely not only to raise the question what is 'equal work' and what is 'equal pay,' but also to lead swiftly to the question of the relative burdens in the way of family obligation carried by men and by women wage-earners" (Breckinridge, 1923:521). She then proceeds to argue that it is widely acknowledged that women rarely receive equal pay and rarely have the opportunity to do work that is the same as men's. She points out as a corollary of these twin conditions that "the difference between the pay of the one and of the other group is greater than the difference between the value to their employer of their respective product" (1923:521). She says the social consequence of this is that women become "the perpetual scab in industry" (1923:523). Analyzing the conditions that lead to less pay for women, she notes first that women are more likely to follow a pattern of working and then marrying and stopping work; second, that they are less likely to be well organized into wage-negotiating units; and third, and most critically, that the man's wage is defined in terms of what will let him support himself and his family, while the woman's wage is defined on the assumption that she has only herself to support. Yet many young women workers who live with their parents typically contribute to the "composite family wage." Married women workers present a problem for the total society.

> The point is that the employment of mothers of young children often passes from a problem in industrial organization to a problem in poverty or dependency. In such cases, the doctrine of dependents with which men bolster their claims would certainly apply to them. . . . [I]n the labor market, their presence can be prevented from becoming a catastrophe only by the payment of a family wage. (Breckinridge, 1923:533–534)

The great bulk of the studies to emerge from the Chicago Women focus on women and children, but they nearly always extend the discussion to the plight of men as well, and especially to that of immigrants. Their research reveals an implicit awareness of the need to cross variables of race, class, gender, geopolitical location, and age in understanding a person's situation. Repeatedly they trace these intersections: in the problems of the elderly poor, in the discrimination against blacks in housing, in the housing conditions of immigrant workers, and in the childhoods of working-class children.

Conclusion   The Chicago Women are important to us today both for the content of their sociology and as role models who successfully combined disciplined research with a commitment to ameliorative social change. Yet it is helpful to remember that they did not all start with a commitment to Progressive ideals or social change. Some—especially, the Abbotts, Breckinridge, Kellor, and MacLean—came to a commitment to use social research for social amelioration only after they had had university study—and, as Muncy (1991) argues, only after university study had failed to yield university employment. Edith Abbott is perhaps the prime example of a change in orientation. Trained at the University of Chicago and then the London School of Economics, she was in 1908, when she began to live at Hull-House, committed to the growing ideal of value neutral research. But the Hull-House environment—an environment she seems to have found only because of a lack of academic career possibilities for women—changed her. In a 1932 tribute to Lathrop, Abbott "rejected the academic theory that social research could only be 'scientific' if it had no regard for the finding of socially useful results and no interest in the human beings whose lives were being studied" (cited in Muncy, 1991:73).

ENDNOTES

1. The women's movement to Chicago is indicative of many of the changes taking place in America in this period—the women's movement in general, urbanization, the growth of the status of Chicago itself, and improvements in transportation.

2. Some sense of the interlocking ties of the women's network in the United States is given by the fact that Kelley was directed to Hull-House through a contact with the Women's Christian Temperance Union. The union had, under the leadership of Frances Willard, expanded its program to include social goals such as the regulation of child labor, and Kelley had worked on a pamphlet, *Our Toiling Children,* published by the union.

3. She selected Alzina P. Stevens, a Hull-House resident, as her chief deputy. Stevens had long experience in the labor movement; family financial disaster had forced her to work at thirteen, and she had lost a finger in a factory accident, a constant reminder to her of the need for safety legislation.

4. Muncy extends this critique to suggest that sometimes, unaware, these women may have exploited the needs of other women and of those weaker than themselves in order to have careers. A careful review of their careers does leave one with the conundrum with which Muncy concludes: "that even the female professionalism of women in the dominion was fraught with the arrogance of power. . . . [Is it] possible to reconcile professionalism and feminism, to bend the privilege of professionalism toward the empowerment of all" (1991:165).

5. Kelley's essay was first read to a meeting of the New York chapter of the Association of Collegiate Alumnae. One wonders what her listeners made of this extraordinary vision of philanthropic work; Kelley biographers Blumberg (1966) and Sklar (1995) report no extant minutes of the ACA meeting. But when the essay was published in the June 1887 *Christian Union,* Kelley wrote to Engels that "[t]he editors received over eighty letters of inquiry and remonstrance and I was showered with books, pamphlets and letters from all parts of the country, while the Christian Union printed three editorial protests and two several-columns long protests from readers" (cited in Blumberg, 1966:79).

6. Lathrop, like the other Chicago Women, had a long history of criticizing the patronage system of hiring that controlled nearly all Chicago social service agencies; she concluded her *Hull-House Maps and Papers* study with the cry, "It is as tiresome as that Carthage must be destroyed, but it is as true, that the charities of Cook county will never properly reform their duties until politics are divorced from them" (1895:161). But as Chief of the Children's Bureau, she took a very broad view of civil service law and used the powers she had to hire an overwhelmingly female staff and often to tailor examinations for women she thought particularly well suited. Muncy (1991) gives an excellent account of Lathrop's exercise of her power of appointment and its interface with civil service law.

READING 7-1

Excerpt from "The Cook County Charities" by Julia Lathrop

This selection is excerpted from pages 143–153 and 158–161. Lathrop opens with a contextualized comment about what the maps in the volume show about the population of the Hull-House neighborhood. She then explores what happens to people when their all-too-meager incomes confront emergencies and they must turn to charities for help. She looks at several charities; our excerpt focuses on the infirmary and the outdoor relief agency. She emphasizes the role of class, the need for an aroused public, and problems of state patronage.

As the study of these maps reveals an overwhelming proportion of foreigners, and an average wage-rate so low as to render thrift, even if it existed, an ineffective insurance against emergencies, we are led at once to inquire what happens when the power of self-help is lost. . . . When we inquire, then, what provision is made to meet sickness, accident, non-employment, old age, and that inevitable accident, death, we are asking what some outside agency performs. . . .

. . . There is, doubtless, a certain satisfaction to the philanthropist and the sociologist alike, in having touched bottom, reached ultimate facts; and this in a sense we have done when we have reached the county institutions. These are the infirmary, the insane asylum, the hospital, the detention hospital, and the county agency. . . . To show the relation of the infirmary population to the population of this district [Hull-House], it is enough to state that of its 5,651 admissions during the year 1893, there were 3,563 persons of foreign birth. . . .

The infirmary is a great brick building, with many well-lighted wards, steam-heated, and clean. . . .

Source: Julia Lathrop, "The Cook County Charities," in *Hull-House Maps and Papers,* (Boston: Crowell, 1895), pp. 143–161.

A very little work is required of each inmate to keep the place in order. There is a hired attendant in every ward, . . . The infirmary and the insane asylum are both under the control of one superintendent. . . .

The women's wards are never crowded as are the men's. By some curious law of pauperism and male irresponsibility, whose careful study offers an interminable task to any loving collector of data, men are in a great majority in the poorhouses. . . .

A curious indication of the effect of hard times is shown in the sudden increase of 299 in the male population, and of only 16 among the women,— nearly 25 per cent in the first case, and a little over 4 per cent in the second, from January, 1893, to January, 1894. . . .

In a winter so unprecedented as that of 1893–1894, the men's wards are always full, many of them fearfully over-crowded, and certain of the hallways are sometimes nightly filled with straw ticks for sleepers who cannot be accommodated in the wards. . . .

. . . There are [in the surgical wards] usually from fifty to seventy-five children, of whom a large proportion are young children with their mothers. . . . The remainder, perhaps, a third, are the residuum of all the orphan asylums and hospitals, children whom no one cares to adopt because they are unattractive or scarred or sickly. . . .

And now what impression does the visitor receive who sees the infirmary, not as to the great problems of pauperism and crime, for the study of which this place offers infinite opportunity; not upon the value or efficiency of our system of caring for the dependent, but simply as to whether the work undertaken is adequately and reasonably performed? Do we have difficulty in understanding the universal dread of the "County"? . . .

. . . The absolute lack of privacy, the monotony and dulness, the discipline. . . . [A]ny provision for homely comfort, for amusements or distractions from themselves and their compulsory neighbors, is wanting alike for the most decent and the most worthless.

If husbands and wives are obliged to come to the infirmary, they are always separated, no matter how aged and infirm, nor how blameless. How painful this separation may be, is indicated by the attitude of an old Irish couple of my acquaintance. . . . When [the county poorhouse] was suggested to them they were panic-stricken; and the old woman; who is ninety odd, said, "Oh, he'll have to go in with the men; I'll have to go in with the women, and all our own clothes will be taken away from us. I can somehow sort o' do for myself; but he is somehow sort o' shiftless like, and he can't. . . . Let us stay here [at home]." . . .

. . . [I]n the infirmary, as in the other three county institutions, the pivot upon which turns the question of . . . the care and nursing of these feeble beings, is the change in the *personnel* of the county board . . . the appointment of all the persons who have charge of this community is made and changed solely according to political preference. . . .

. . . [I]f the constant succession of new attendants is prejudicial to the proper work of the infirmary, what must it be . . . where insane people are to be cared for? A man or a woman overcome with an infirmity, which the laws of Illinois at last recognize as a disease, is placed in constant care night and day of—nurses trained for such are? Not at all. But of some one who has a "pull." . . .

The most spectacular proof of the poverty entailed upon Chicago by the general business depression of 1893, and locally the inevitable human *débris* left by the World's Fair, could be daily seen during all the severer months of the winter of 1893 and 1894. It was a solid, pressing crowd of hundreds of shabby men and shawled or hooded women, coming from all parts of a great city . . . standing hour after hour with market-baskets high above their heads held in check by policemen, polyglot, but having the common language of their persistency, their weariness, their chill and hunger. . . . When once the applicant penetrates the office, he is in the great dingy waiting-room of the Cook County Agency, from whence is dispensed out-door relief. He furnishes

his name and address, and is called upon later by a paid visitor, upon whose report the fuel and ration are allowed or refused. Or, if the application has been granted, . . . the allowance of food and one bar of hard soap is carried hence, the coal being sent later from the contractor. . . .

There is a constant criticism of the county relief office from the recipient's point of view. He says the coal is delivered slowly and in scant measure, that favoritism is shown by visitors, that burials are tardy and cruel; and the facts justify him. But any one acquainted with the daily work of this office must feel that the wonder is that the $100,000 allotted for its work is really as fairly divided as we find it. The methods of this office, with its records kept as each changing administration chooses, its doles subject to every sort of small political influence, and its failure to co-operate with private charities, are not such as science can approve.

These institutions cost the county for running expenses alone, nearly $700,000 annually, providing salaried positions for five hundred persons or more, and of course do in some degree meet the necessities of a great dependent population which is at present an unavoidable factor in our social problem. Yet such a state of irresponsibility as investigation now and again discloses must discourage us. We are impressed with the lack of system and classification among the beneficiaries of the infirmary and the country agency for out-door relief. We are shocked by the crudeness of the management which huddles men, women, and children, the victims of misfortune and the relics of dissipation, the idle, the ineffective criminal, the penniless convalescent, under one roof and one discipline. . . .

. . . How many persons in the city of Chicago whose incomes make them safe from the possibility of a personal interest in these places ever visit them, or perhaps know where they are? More, how many of them realize that their visits, their intelligent interest, are all that is necessary to make these institutions give really good service? There is no mal-administration so strong that it can persist in the face of public knowledge and attention. The public now has and will have exactly such institutions as it demands, managed exactly as its discrimination requires. It is as tiresome as that Carthage must be destroyed, but it is as true, that the charities of Cook County will never properly perform their duties until politics are divorced from them.

Excerpt from "Two Weeks in Department Stores" by Annie Marion MacLean

This selection is excerpted from pages 721–739. This is one of the first pieces of participant observation research. MacLean connects research and advocacy in her ties to the Consumers' League. She sees the relation between gender and class in determining the quality of life of the department store saleswoman.

It is so common for those who purchase goods to think nothing at all about the clerk in attendance, or the conditions under which the goods were produced, that it seems timely just now, when the Consumers' League†, has started upon a crusade of educating the public, to give a true picture of some conditions existing in Chicago. . . .

. . . With a view to ascertaining some things which could be learned only from the inside, the investigation which is to form the subject-matter of this paper was undertaken. It seemed evident that valuable information could be obtained if

---

†The Consumers' League of Illinois was organized by the collegiate alumnae of this city in February, 1897, when a standard was adopted and a provisional constitution drawn up. A permanent organization with Mrs. Charles Henrotin as president, was effected at a meeting held in Hull-House, November 30, 1898. The league at the present time has about eight hundred members.

Source: Annie Marion MacLean, "Two Weeks in Department Stores," *American Journal of Sociology* 4 (1899), pp. 721–741.

---

someone were willing to endure the hardships of the saleswoman's life, and from personal experience be able to pass judgment upon observed conditions. The urgency of the need, coupled with an enthusiastic interest in the work for which the Consumers' League stands, led me to join the ranks of the retail clerks for two weeks during the rush of the holiday trade. . . . The consumer should know how far his Christmas shopping works hardship for the clerks. . . .

. . . From 1830 to 1874 agitation for the protection of women and children in the factories was kept up, till finally, at the latter date, the Massachusetts Act became a reality. The other states followed the example set, until, at the present time, almost all the states having large manufacturing interests have very good factory laws. Illinois is a notable exception. . . . We are just on the eve of an agitation for amelioration of the conditions under which a vast army of saleswomen and cash children work. . . . And to help, in a small way, the educative movement here, my labor was undertaken. . . .

. . . [I]t was not until several visits had been made that I was promised a position at three dollars a week. . . . Employment being promised, it seemed desirous to engage board in some home for working women; for the environment which such a place would provide gave promise of the best results. I was fortunate in finding a most satisfactory place not far from the heart of the city, and there I went as a working-woman. . . . A large proportion of the sixty-five residents were saleswomen, and they, in the course of conversation, gave me much useful information. . . .

This, then, was the place from which I started out to work on the appointed Monday morning. . . . I reached my destination promptly at eight, the time of opening. . . . But the manager had changed his mind about wages, and said he would give me two dollars a week plus 5 per cent. commission on sales, instead of the regular salary he had mentioned in our former interview. . . . I was sent to the toy department, where I found sixty-seven others who were to be my companions in toil. . . .

We all served in the double capacity of floor walkers and clerks, and our business was to see that no one escaped without making a purchase. . . . The cause of such watchful activity on the part of so many employés was the 5 per cent commission which was to eke out the two or three dollars a week salary. . . .

One of the difficult things at first was keeping track of the prices, for they were frequently changed during the day. . . .

Every morning there were special sales. . . . But we soon learned what things were to be "leaders" from day to day, and the manager's brief instructions each morning were sufficient to keep us posted on the bargains. . . .

Oh, the weariness of that first morning! The hours seemed days. "Can I possibly stand up all day?" was the thought uppermost in my mind, . . . there was not a seat of any kind in the room and the only way one could get a moment's rest was to sit on the children's furniture that was for sale on one part of the floor. . . . [Those found so resting were firmly warned.] By night the men as well as the women were limping wearily across the floor, and many sales were made under positive physical agony.

. . . [O]ur house was open every evening till about ten o'clock, and the only compensation given for extra work was a supper. . . . We were fed in droves and hurried away before the last mouthful was swallowed. The menu consisted of a meat dinner and an oyster stew. . . . [T]he said stew consisted of a bowl of hot milk, in the bottom of which lurked *three* oysters, except on that memorable day when I found *four*.

The days in the store were much the same, with their endless fatigue. At time the rush would be great; then again we would have nothing to do but stand around and talk. Thus we became surprisingly well acquainted in a short time. We talked about our wages and compared index sheets on every possible occasion. . . . The mental anguish of some of the girls when they saw at night how small their sales had been is impossible to describe.

One may elect to become a worker, and endure the hardships of the toil, and live the life of the laborer, and receive the same starvation wages, but he can never experience the abject wretchedness of not knowing where to turn when the last dollar is gone. Three dollars a week to a girl alone in the city means starvation or shame. . . .

The cloak-, toilet-, and lunch-rooms were the gloomiest and filthiest it was ever my misfortune to enter. . . . And that was where the girls who brought lunches had to eat them. . . . [At night] there were always men on the street corners ready to speak to a girl alone, and one hesitating step meant danger. Almost every morning the girls had some story to tell of encounters with men of that class; and that they were not exaggerating was proved satisfactorily to me by an experience of my own. I stepped from the [tram]car late one night after midnight, and soon found that I was being followed. The chase continued for two blocks, when I staggered breathless into my doorway, with my pursuer not five feet away. My terror had given me power to outrun him. . . .

Sunday in the home was a quiet day. Everybody was tired and discouraged. . . . Most of the girls . . . guarded their small earnings carefully. I guided my expenditures by theirs and kept an accurate account of my expenses for the week. The items are here presented:

Board for one week. $2.50
Car fare, 6 days @ 10c 60
Lunch 5 days, @ 15c 75
"   one day, @ 10c. 10

[MacLean gives a detailed account producing total expenses of $4.79.]

What I earned for the week was as follows:

Wages. $2.00
Commission $3.25
                                                                  $5.25
Less fines 30
                                                                  $4.95

Thus I had a balance of sixteen cents after my bills were paid, and that was as much as many had. At that rate it would take a long time to earn enough to buy a pair of boots. . . .

The hours were very long. We worked from eight in the morning till eleven at night, with the exception of Christmas eve, when we worked until twelve. . . .

. . . It seemed to me that my thoughts were always centered on my feet! Our arms got tired, too; we had to reach a good deal for the stock. A man made me open and take the dolls from nineteen boxes to see if I could not find one with black eyes and yellow hair. I told him they were all gone, at the price he desired, but he wanted me to verify my statement. As if it would matter to a two-year-old baby. . . .

. . . [T]he wages were woefully insufficient. From four dollars to five dollars a week was the average. . . . It was an openly acknowledged fact among the girls that the paths of dishonor were traversed to supplement their small incomes. . . . They viewed the matter solely from a commercial standpoint, and justified their conduct by the urgency of the need. The girls themselves said . . . "If I don't get more wages I'll have to go bad. But I'd hate to disgrace my family.". . . "*We have to earn our living.*"

. . . All the hardships of the shop girl's life fade into insignificance before this grave danger she has to face. Adequate support is the first necessity. Improved sanitary conditions and opportunity for rest may well take a second place. They can be secured by legislation; the other must come from united action on the part of the buyers and the organization of the saleswomen themselves. The trades-union spirit should be fostered, and the working-women taught the power of united effort. . . .

In the two weeks I was employed I worked one hundred and seventy-five hours and received eleven dollars and eighty-eight cents, or a little less than six cents an hour. . . . I am going to present just here in tabulated form some information I gathered from my fellow-workers regarding themselves. . . . [MacLean's table describes her respondents in terms of employment, hours of work, overtime, weekly wages, additional compensation, cost of living per week, marital status, and health.]

READING 7-3

Excerpt from "Aims and Principles of the Consumers' League" by Florence Kelley

This selection is excepted from pages 289–299. Kelley appeals to both ethics and self-interest and urges the need to organize.

Throughout our lives we are choosing, or choice is made for us, as to the disposal of money. . . . As we do so, we help to decide, however unconsciously, how our fellow-men shall spend their time in making what we buy. Few of us can give much in charity; . . . But whatever our gifts may be, they are less decisive for the weal or woe of our fellows than are our habitual expenditures. For a man is largely what his work makes him—an artist, an artisan, a handicraftsman, a drudge, a sweater's victim, or scarcely less to be pitied, a sweater. All these and many more classes of workers exist to supply the demand that is incarnate in us and our friends and fellow-citizens.

Those of us who enjoy the privilege of voting may help, once or twice a year, to decide how the tariff, or the currency, or the local tax rate shall be adjusted to our industries. But all of us, all the time, are deciding by our expenditures what industries shall survive at all, and under what conditions.

Source: Florence Kelley, "Aims and Principles of the Consumers' League," *American Journal of Sociology* 5 (1899), pp. 289–304.

Broadly stated, it is *the* aim of the National Consumers' League to moralize this decision, to gather and make available information which may enable all to decide in the light of knowledge, and to appeal to the conscience, so that the decision when made shall be a righteous one.

The Consumers' League, then, acts, upon the proposition that the consumer ultimately determines all production, since any given article must cease to be produced if all consumers ceased to purchase it. . . .

While, however, the whole body of consumers determine, in this large way and in the long run, what shall be produced, the individual consumer has at the present time, for want of organization and technical knowledge, no adequate means of making his wishes felt, of making his demand an effective demand. . . .

It is sometimes questioned whether, . . . it is not true that in a general way the laws protect the purchaser, and the producer bends all his energies to meet the consumers' wishes. . . . These are really two questions, and must be answered separately.

First, as to the producer, and his effort to meet the wishes of the consumer. It is true that every manufacturer studies the market; he is constrained, if he would succeed in his business. . . . The failure of an enormous percentage of manufacturers shows how difficult is this task of inference. . . . The difficulties of the manufacturer are greatly intensified by the extraordinary incompetence of the "average" purchaser to judge the desired articles on their merits. What housewife can detect, alone and unaided, the injurious chemicals in her supplies of milk, bread, meat, home remedies? . . .

 . . . [T]he great mass of producers have long had recourse to the more simple device of advertising. This can lay no claim to any educational quality. It is distinctly not meant to educate or instruct but to stimulate, persuade, incite, entice, and induce the indifferent to purchase. Much of the current advertisement . . . is directly aimed at the ignorance of the purchaser. . . .

To the producer the league offers that which he needs more than any other one condition of success—a somewhat stable body of customers. In Great Britain, where the cooperative movement has grown slowly to gigantic proportions, the purchasers by pooling their interests have been enabled to employ expert buyers who can stipulate in advance as to conditions of manufacture as well as prices and qualities; and obtain in return for the stable demand which they represent goods produced by manufacturers aware, in advance, of the wishes of this part of their purchasing public. In this country, in the absence of such an organization, supply and demand are left to regulate themselves automatically, ruining in the process large numbers of merchants and manufacturers who guess unsuccessfully as to the wishes of the public. . . .

The Consumers' League recognizes the fact that this blind guessing, inferring, deducing the wishes of the consumer from his action in the past, while now almost universal in this country, is not an inevitable consequence of any natural or social law. All factory legislation is enacted in recognition of the fact that the human relations of supply and demand are susceptible of beneficent modifications; the cooperative movement is a further witness to the same fact; the Consumers' League, latest comer in this field, aims at still another demonstration of this truth.

As to the second part of the query, whether the consumer is not substantially protected by the laws . . . [o]ne of the most important considerations is the fact that legislation is by no means uniform throughout the states. . . . [And] under the constitution of the United States no one state can forbid the importation of goods made in another state, however far the standard of conditions of manufacture in that state may fall below its own. For the promotion of uniform legislation for the protection of the consumer, if for no other purpose, there seems to be room for the work of the National Consumers' League.

Nor is this all. . . . The Department of Labor at Washington, the state bureau of labor statistics, the state inspectors of factories, the municipal boards of health all publish . . . information designed for the enlightenment and instruction of the public. . . . [But] not one of these officials publishes the list of the kitchen tailors to whom the merchant tailor gives his goods to be made up; just as not one of them can possibly give information whereby adulterations of foods can be successfully detected in the private kitchen. There is urgent need for a private society to investigate certain specified branches of industry . . . , guaranteeing the product made under clean and wholesome conditions. . . .

Incidentally, it is true that the community is likely to enjoy the benefit of a more rigid enforcement of its ordinances and statutes just in proportion as it cooperates through volunteer agencies with the officials who write these reports; . . .

The National Consumers' League acts upon the proposition that, to constitute an effective demand for goods made under right conditions, there must be numbers of consumers sufficiently large to assure purchases steady and considerable enough to compensate for the expense incurred by humane employers. . . . The standard adopted for the present embraces four requirements, viz.: that all goods must be manufactured by the manufacturer on his own premises; that all the requirements of the state factory law must be complied with; that no children under sixteen years of age shall be employed; and that no overtime shall be worked. It is hoped that within a reasonable time it may be possible to include a requirement as to minimal wages. . . .

Since the exodus of manufacture from the home, the one great industrial function of women has been that of the purchaser. . . . It is, therefore, very natural that the first effort to educate the great body of miscellaneous purchasers concerning the power of the purchaser should have been undertaken by women, among women, on behalf of women and children. Having proved successful, within moderate limits, in that field, it is now extending among people irrespective of age and sex.

READING 7-4

Excerpt from "Psychological and Environmental Study of Women Criminals" by Frances Kellor

This selection is excerpted from pages 671–682. This is the second of two articles by Kellor; in the first she reported the results of her doing physical measurements of criminals as suggested in the theory and research of Italian sociologist Cesare Lombroso, who argued that criminality was innate in some people and that the social scientist could discover the potential criminal by detecting physiological and mental traits. Kellor works here to establish the social and environmental factors that cause people to commit criminal acts, questioning the theory of a genetic predisposition to crime. Her research was partly funded by the Chicago Woman's Club.

Though . . . often closely interrelated with psychical conditions, what are some of the facts [about women criminals] ascertained by the sociological investigation? The sources and methods included these . . . the habitats of the criminals, . . . such facts as institution records show, possession of such observations as lay within the matrons' grasp, and an interrogation of the criminal and her associates. . . . The interrogation of the criminals and their associates is most frequently conducted . . . during seemingly chance conversations with the women in the prisons. . . .

The results obtainable from these sources and by these methods may be grouped under the following topics: nature of crime, age, nationality, religion, conjugal condition, number of children, occupation, education, habits, recidivism, degradation, moral sense, economic influence, parents and

---

Source: Frances Kellor, "Psychological and Environmental Study of Women Criminals," *American Journal of Sociology* 5 (1900), pp. 671–682.

their occupation, industriousness, associates, disease, biological influences.

The question often arises: What crimes do women most frequently commit? . . . The crimes of the workhouse inmates are . . . against public morals, public peace, and public policy. . . . [I]n the penitentiaries, . . . the crimes are largely against property and public safety. . . . Where the public safety is threatened, as in homicides, emotional conditions in woman, as contrasted with motives of gain in man, are often at work.

With reference to the age of the women criminals almost nothing can be said. This depends entirely upon their statements, which are untrustworthy. . . .

Records of institutions place stress upon nationality and religion. These seem of negative value as compared with some other facts . . . unless the nativity of the parents, and the time spent by parents and criminals in America are known. The social forces and their effect upon them are otherwise unascertainable.

The first objection to deductions from statistics upon religion is that it is closely related to nationality. . . .

. . . Numerically whether more married women or unmarried women are criminals is not so much the important question as is the fact that so large a number of married women are found in prisons. Often these women are mothers. . . . [F]igures vary with locality, but they show that . . . [t]he marriage of many of these women does not withdraw them fully from the competitive world, for they must frequently contribute to the support of the family. . . . [C]onversations with some of the women reveal a high degree of domestic infelicity . . . a harshness of environment and a brutality of associates. . . .

Occupation, for many reasons, I consider important. Of the 1,451 at Blackwell's Island, 1,208 were domestics, 125 housekeepers (usually a doubtful occupation and closely related to courtesanship). . . . An analysis of the domestic class, as found in cities, may suggest [that]

[f]or the following reasons, there is no occupation among women which includes so many criminals: (1) the large number of women in the occupation; (2) many of the lowest classes go into this occupation when other means fail; (3) inadequate salaries for the gratification of tastes in dress and amusements, . . . ; (4) the easy route which this occupation furnishes to prostitution, through its temptations, almost all cases of prostitution resulting from seduction being from this class; (5) the employment bureaus for servants which are often but procuring places for prostitution; (6) the limited education and erroneous perception of the relation of things, especially true of the foreign class. . . .

. . . [D]ata regarding education . . . I found . . . most confusing. . . . [E]ducation must be tested, and not [left to] the criminal's verbal assurance. . . . [For instance,] in my tests, I learned the grade and reader in use when the subject left school. . . .

. . . It is a prevailing opinion that when women are criminal they are more degraded and more abandoned than men. From the observation of the two sexes, this seems due rather to the difference in standards which we set for the two sexes. We say woman is worse, but we judge her so by comparison with this ideal of a woman, not with a common ideal. . . . Licentiousness in conversation and manner, uncleanliness in habits and person, do exist to a high degree; but the men and women come from the same classes, have the same standards, and know the same life. Thus from this point of view the woman is not more degraded than the man. . . .

From the number of children in the criminal's family, combined with such knowledge of financial condition as was obtainable, I attempted to gather some light upon the opportunities as a child. . . .

The number of children, together with the occupation of the parents, which was usually one of the trades or unskilled labor, and the early age at which many of them sought work, show that the opportunities for self-advancement must have been less than where good educations obtain.

The industriousness of the women furnishes another interesting condition. Out of 115 recorded, 60 admitted they were idle when the crime was committed. . . .

That the economic conditions of woman render her liable to immorality has been so fully discussed elsewhere that I give only one illustration, the result of an investigation in New York. Clipping from the newspaper some thirty advertisements for clerks, stenographers, bookkeepers, etc., I had an assistant answer them. Although she visited only a little more than half the places, almost every one of them was a snare for immoral purposes, and the proposals were so bluntly made that she declined answering more. To a girl dependent upon herself in a large city an opportunity for immorality is thus offered in an attractive way. . . .

While presenting such factors as the preceding, . . . no attempt is made to negative the biological side of crime. . . .

. . . [But] there remains much work here and in investigating the classes which are not criminal, but from which criminals come. . . .

. . . Two things are needed in a study of criminal sociology: such a presentation of facts as shall make possible a more rational, helpful attitude upon the part of the non-criminal class; legislation which shall be compelled to recognize these facts, and not revert to the precedents of the Middle Ages for its initiative. The needs are such as to press into the service of social investigation any science which renders it more trustworthy and liberal, and which relieves it from the charge of mere theorizing.

READING 7-5

Excerpt from *Some Ethical Gains through Legislation* by Florence Kelley

This selection is excerpted from Chapter 3, "The Right to Leisure," pages 105–126. In this book, Kelley presents the arguments for certain basic rights for all people, such as the right to childhood, or in this case, the right to leisure. She offers an analysis in separate chapters of particular legislation that has attempted to enforce acts guaranteeing such rights, and of the fate of such legislation in the courts. Here she makes the case both for voluntary associations and for the state to enforce a right to leisure.

The effort to establish the right to leisure was a distinctive movement of the nineteenth century, accompanying the development of machinery . . . Sunday rest, the Saturday half-holiday, Decoration Day, Labor Day, Lincoln's birthday, . . . [t]he early closing of stores. . . . The prohibition of the work of women and minors at night . . . , the effort on behalf of child labor legislation . . . towards securing fourteen free years for school and wholesome growth . . . , the ten hours movement, and later . . . the eight hours movement.

The struggle for the shorter working day is commonly described as the effort of the laborer to give as little exertion as possible in return for the pay which he receives and many workingmen passively accept this statement of the animus of their movement. It is, however, susceptible of interpretation as the effort of wage-earning people to obtain, in the form of leisure, a part of their share of the universal gain arising from the increased productivity of every occupation, and due to the incessant improvement of machinery.

Source: Florence Kelley, *Some Ethical Gains through Legislation* (New York: Macmillan, 1905).

Obviously the characteristic feature of the industrial life of the nineteenth century was the unprecedented increase in the output of all branches of production. . . . The fundamental ethical question of the century was, in essence, the equitable distribution of these newly acquired possessions of the human race.

More precious, perhaps, than any of those enumerated is the immaterial, imponderable human by-product—leisure. . . . Yet, by reason of its inequitable distribution, it remained, in the crude and unsocial form of unemployed time, the bane and sorrow of large sections of the working-class, who were constrained to devote generations of organized effort to regulating, equalizing, and redistributing their working-time and their free time, . . .

Assured daily leisure is an essential element of healthy living. Without it childhood is blighted, perverted, deformed; manhood becomes ignoble and unworthy of citizenship in the Republic. Self-help and self-education among the wage-earners are as dependent upon daily leisure as upon daily work. Excessive fatigue precludes the possibility of well-conducted meetings of classes, lodges, co-operative societies and all other forms of organized effort for self-improvement. . . .

As machinery becomes increasingly automatic and the work of the machine-tender reduces itself . . . to . . . the wholly monotonous performance . . . leisure becomes indispensable for him in order to counteract the deadening effect upon his mind exercised by his daily work. . . . Without regular, organized leisure, there can be no sustained intelligence in the voting constituency.

In those occupations in which long hours of work prevail, the employees are obliged to live near their place of work, and that congestion is thus intensified which is one of the more unfortunate features of life in large manufacturing cities. Shortening the hours of labor gives to working people a wider range of selection in location of their homes, thus benefitting wives and children as well as the operatives themselves.

Daily assured leisure serves a purpose of the highest social value by enabling the wage-earner to husband that resource of nervous energy which is required to continue active working-life after the passing of youth. In the garment-trades, men are old at forty and women are superannuated at thirty, largely by reason of the alternations of overwork and enforced idleness, and the absence of that regularly recurring sufficient period of rest between the close of one day's work and the beginning of the next, which alone permits body and mind to bear years of continuous work without wearing out. . . .

It may be fairly claimed, then, that the establishment of a regular daily leisure contributes to the health, intelligence, morality, lengthened trade life, freer choice of home surroundings, thrift, self-help and family life of working people. Granted that not all workers make equally valuable use of free time, just as members of the leisure class vary in the uses to which they apply their leisure, it remains true that, without free time, these benefits are impossible. To be deprived of leisure is to be deprived of those things which make life worth living.

Leisure seems to have come to different groups of people in different ways;—to some automatically without exertion on their part; to others as the result of long, painful struggle; to many not at all. The portion of society to which leisure has not come consists, on the one hand, of the great body of children and young girls in the textile and other industries in states in which no laws yet define the limit of their working day and working week; and on the other hand, of the mass of unskilled workingwomen as unorganized and defenseless as the children themselves. . . .

By the education of public opinion something has been accomplished towards establishing leisure in certain occupations. . . . The hours of labor of the clerks and cash children in the stores of many cities have been improved in consequence of the efforts of the Consumers' Leagues in some places, and of the Retail Clerks' Protective Associations in others, to induce the shopping public to exercise consideration of the employees in arranging the hours of shopping.

The cigar-trade has long enjoyed the benefits of the short working day by reason of . . . the principle which all trade unionists acknowledge, and upon which thousands of them conscientiously act. Millions of dollars have been spent in advertising their label; cigars bearing it are made only in shops in which the working day is limited to eight hours; and working men of all trades . . . buy the cigars thus recommended. . . . It is an interesting and significant fact that the organizations mentioned as using this method are among the most persistent advocates of legislation restricting the hours of labor, acting on the principle that not one but all methods of protecting the workers in their right to leisure must be followed, and taught by experience how far more effective is their effort when directed towards the enforcement of statutes than when confined to persuasion alone.

READING 7-6

Excerpt from "The Chicago Employment Agency and the Immigrant Worker" by Grace Abbott

This selection is excerpted from pages 289–298 and 305. Abbott explores an agency of much concern to the Chicago Women, that of employment agencies, which their researches repeatedly showed to be questionable operations, often defrauding immigrants and serving to procure women for prostitution rings. Abbott makes

clear that her knowledge comes from her efforts to change this system and emphasizes the connections between poverty and discrimination.

Ignorant of our language, the country, and the American standard of wages, and compelled by his poverty to accept the first possible work, the immigrant is especially defenseless when he offers himself in the labor market. . . . [H]e is dependent in most cases upon the private employment agent and he becomes, because of his ignorance and necessities, a great temptation to an honest agent and a great opportunity to an unscrupulous one. For this reason an investigation of Chicago agencies was made in order to determine what kinds of work this means, in what ways they are exploited, and what changes in the laws are necessary to reduce such an exploitation to a minimum. [Investigation was narrowed to] 110 agencies . . . [as] the only ones in the city which handle immigrants in any large numbers. Of these fifty-six furnished work for men, thirty-three for women, and twenty-one for both men and women. As the conditions and difficulties of the immigrant man and woman are quite different their relation to the employment agent must be separately considered.
. . . The problem . . . so far as the immigrant girl is concerned, is to secure for her work where she will be morally protected. . . . So long as

Source: Grace Abbott, "The Chicago Employment Agency and the Immigrant Worker," *American Journal of Sociology* 14 (1908), pp. 289–305.

TABLE SHOWING KIND OF WORK SUPPLIED IMMIGRANT WOMEN BY CHICAGO EMPLOYMENT AGENCIES

	Agencies supplying women only
Number of agencies offering housework	28
Number of agencies offering hotel or restaurant work	18
Number of agencies offering factory work	4
	50
Agencies counted twice	17
Total number of agencies	33

there is . . . an overdemand and undersupply of houseworkers . . . she always has this work to fall back on.

With the immigrant man the situation is much more difficult . . . because of his ignorance of English . . . he cannot work without an interpreter. Interpreters can be profitably employed only when large groups of immigrants work together. Such groups are employed by the foundries, at the stock yards, in mines, on railroads, car-line and building construction, in the harvest fields, in ice and lumber camps. . . . Much of this work is seasonal and is located at a great distance from the city. . . . The pay is not good. . . . Board is expensive and poor in quality. . . . [T]he men must get back to Chicago to get their next work, so return railroad fare must be counted on. . . . [Yet] it is work the immigrant can do, and, because in most cases he must have work immediately, he takes it gladly. This means that whatever his training or experience may be he must serve an apprenticeship in the ranks of the unskilled seasonal laborers. . . .

Forced to obtain work through the private employment agent the immigrant usually suffers in one of three ways: (1) he is over-charged for the services rendered; (2) the work obtained is not as represented by the agent either in character, permanency or remuneration; (3) he fails to get work or the work lasts only a few days leaving him at an enormous distance from the city labor markets. . . .

. . . Several concrete cases . . . have come to the attention of the [Immigrant's Protective] League. . . . One [such case] . . . was made up of Hungarians. There were fifty-three men and two women—one of these had a baby—who expected to be cooks for the gang. They were shipped April 14, by a Chicago agent, through a St. Louis agent. They paid the Chicago agent fourteen dollars apiece and were promised steady work at $1.40 a day. When they reached Leslie [Arkansas] . . . , [t]hey were told that the work was twenty-five miles from there. They walked to this place but the foreman only laughed at them and said he had no work for any such number. He finally put to work fifteen men and the woman who was unencumbered with the baby. The rest . . . started to walk back to Chicago. . . . At the end of the third day the woman gave out and the men pooled their money and sent her home on the railroad. Then they scattered so as to find work on the way. Two of them were shot by the police in St. Louis and when last heard from were in a hospital there. The rest of them eventually reached Chicago. . . .

Ten Polish laborers from one house on the west side went to Wyoming last winter expecting to work in a lumber camp. They paid an agent ten dollars apiece. When they were put off the train in Wyoming they found no work of the character described but were given work for a short time on the railroad. Then they started to walk back. One of the men, a bright young fellow of twenty-two, froze his foot. With no money to pay for a doctor for treatment and compelled to walk on, when he finally reached Chicago blood poisoning had set in and it was necessary to amputate the foot. Although crippled for life, he feels not so much resentment against the agent who sent him as shame that he should have been so ignorant of the climate of Wyoming and humiliation that he should have proved such an easy victim. This is one of the most pathetic things in connection with the work. The men are ashamed to tell their story. "Everyone cheats a greenhorn," they say, and want to hide, from those who are anxious to help them, what they consider a reflection on their intelligence. . . .

. . . [A]ll this reacts upon the city, for it makes Chicago the headquarters of what is truly an army of casual laborers who keep down the wages of the regular unskilled workers in the city. Worse than this, after experiences such as many of these men suffer when sent out of the city, it becomes increasingly difficult to reduce city poverty and congestion by distribution throughout the country and these disappointed seasonal workers become the material out of which a degraded working class is made.

The . . . remedy suggested for this situation is . . . some modification of the present employment agency law. Those suggested are that the fees charged should be public and uniform, that there should be no division of fees with contractors, that statements containing detailed information about the work and the employer should be furnished the applicant in a language he can understand, that damages should be allowed when work is not secured or not as represented, and that fees should be promptly refunded when no work is secured or when it lasts only a short time. These reforms are asked not only as a protection to the immigrant, but to the community in which he lives.

READING 7-7

Excerpts from *The Education of Women* by Marion Talbot

These selections are excerpted from pages 10–49. Talbot offers in this work a complete overview of the education of women in the United States up to 1910. Her focus in the first part of the book, excerpted here, is on how material changes in production make education for women an increasing social necessity. Her arguments bring together many of the analyses by other women in this volume.

EXCERPT FROM CHAPTER 2, "THE INDUSTRIAL AND COMMERCIAL CHANGE"

The change in the interests of women which is most striking is that due to the industrial revolution or the introduction of the factory system. The removal of household industries from the home has gone on rapidly . . . until only the remnants of these occupations remain, so that if the house is now a workshop, it is frequently one hardly worthy of the name, so much of the work that is retained being unskilled or "belated."

With . . . unimportant exceptions the home has ceased to be a center of production, and women workers have followed their work out of the home into the factory . . . and other wage-earning occupations. . . .

The list of occupations scheduled by the Twelfth Census (1900) contains 303 separate employments, in 295 of which women are found. . . .

There were, however, only eighteen occupations each of which employed 1 or more than 1 per cent. of the total number of women gainfully employed, and these eighteen together employed 86.8 per cent. of the total. . . .

When these figures are compared with those of 1890, it is found that in four occupations there is a decrease of women employed as compared with the population, and these occupations are the ones which are popularly supposed to belong to women, viz., dressmakers, seamstresses, tailoress, servants, and waitresses.

> Of the other fourteen occupations in this group, one, "stenographers and typewriters," had more than tripled its numbers; . . . "saleswomen," "bookkeepers and accountants," and "nurses and midwives"— had more than doubled; four—"musicians and teachers of music," "boarding- and lodging-house keepers," "housekeepers and stewardesses," and "laundresses" had increased by more than one-half.‡

Because of this change, women have now the great function of directing how the products of other people's labor shall be consumed . . . [for] the center of consumption is the home. This is a

---

Source: Marion Talbot, *The Education of Women* (Chicago: University of Chicago Press, 1910).

‡Edith Abbott and Sophonisba P. Breckinridge, "Employment of Women in Industries," *Journal of Political Economy,* January, 1906.

new and serious responsibility, requiring . . . a knowledge of fabrics and other materials, of methods of production, of laws governing different industrial processes, of standards of fitness in the article and of efficiency in the workman. It should also include such an appreciation of human needs as will help determine the conditions under which goods are produced, and will demand workshops free from disease, prohibition of child labor, reasonable hours and decent wages for the workman. . . . At the present time girls are receiving no training to meet these new duties commensurate with their importance. . . .

Fortunately, there are some who see ways of serving as an intelligent directive power in this field. The Consumer's League and the Woman's Trade Union League are instances of experiments in this direction.

EXCERPT FROM CHAPTER 3, "THE EDUCATIONAL CHANGE"

New educational standards for women form another influence which has been at work affecting their position and interests. In the first half of the eighteenth century fewer than 40 per cent. of the women of New England who signed legal papers wrote their name; the others made their mark. . . .

. . . Free elementary and secondary schools were established quite generally in the few decades preceding the Civil War. The employment of women teachers in comparatively large numbers can be traced to the effects of the Civil War. . . . The opening of higher institutions of learning to women began in 1833 with the founding of "Oberlin Collegiate Institute," which from the beginning admitted women as well as men. Antioch College followed in 1853, and the state universities beginning with Utah in 1850 have all opened their doors to women, with the exception of Florida, Georgia, and Virginia. In many colleges and universities women hold teaching positions, although as yet mostly of inferior rank, al-

ways with slower promotions, and frequently with salaries lower than those given to men of the same rank. . . .

. . . [T]he movement proceeded with a force which marked it as one of the great characteristics of the last century. . . .

. . . Whatever modifications may be made as to limiting the number [of women] in an institution, as in Leland Stanford Jr. University, or giving instruction separate from men, as in the University of Chicago, or even refusing longer to grant [women] admission, as in Wesleyan University, the principle has been established that will never be sacrificed, that women shall have, if they wish it, the best intellectual training the world knows. . . .

. . . [F]igures taken from the *Report of the United States Commissioner of Education for 1907–08* measure in part the force of this educational movement. . . . [Talbot gives several pages of charts showing the presence of women.]

Of the teaching staff in the school enrollment of the United States, 78 per cent. are women.

Of the teaching staff in the high schools, 56 per cent. are women, . . .

Of the supervising officers 52 per cent. and of the teachers 91 per cent. in cities of 8,000 and over are women. . . .

Of the collegiate students in universities, colleges, and technological schools open to both sexes 34 per cent. are women. . . .

Out of 543 professional schools 268 are attended by women.

EXCERPT FROM CHAPTER 4, "THE CIVIC CHANGE"

The new industrial era and the increased facilities in transportation are agencies which have led to a remarkable development of urban life. The total population of the United States in 1790 was 3,929,214 of whom 131,472 people, or 3.35 per cent., lived in towns of 8,000 inhabitants and over, and the number of such towns was only 6. In 1900 the population was 76,303,387 of whom 24,992,199 or 33.1 per cent., lived in towns, and the number of the towns had increased to 545. . . .

This development of urban life has very largely modified the activities and responsibilities of women. . . .

Groups of families . . . living together in cities have found it necessary to provide a common supply of water and of light, to co-operate in disposal of wastes, and in control of food supplies, buildings, plumbing, contagious diseases, and care of the sick, the infirm, the insane and the criminal. . . . [T]here arises here a new duty for women, that of intelligently and effectively co-operating with the other members of the community for the welfare of the individual households. The right education gives women not only specific knowledge, but vigor and breadth of view, discipline of character, and a freedom of mind which comes from the scientific attitude. . . . It has been said that the home does not stop at the street door—it is as wide as the world into which the individual steps forth.

The determination of the character of that world . . . constitute[s] a real duty resting upon woman. This means the control over the streets, the schools, the street-cars, the shop, the park, the public library, the art gallery, the theater, the very air itself. . . .

As a result of these changes the social instinct of women has found expression in part through a movement for some years characteristic of the United States, but now rapidly extending through all . . . countries. The club movement[¶] . . . bring[s] women together in social relations though a common organization. . . . More important than the broadened intellectual life which has come to women through their interest in clubs is the larger and deeper social spirit which is fos-

tered through the club movement. . . . The enumeration of some of the great women's national organizations is sufficient to prove that this power of social organization is tremendously effective. The General Federation of Women's Clubs, the Association of Collegiate Alumnae, the Congress of Mothers, the National Council of Jewish Women, the National Woman's Trade Union League, . . .

Their power of co-operation may be judged from the participation of women with men in such organizations as the National Education Association, the Conference of Charities, the National Child Labor Committee, the Religious Education Association, the American Federation of Labor. . . . as well as organizations devoted to . . . science or art, such as the American Chemical Society, . . . the American Philosophical Society. . . .

This larger social spirit also manifests itself in the movement looking toward co-operation in government control through suffrage, a movement which has assumed proportions indicated by the facts that there are four states which grant to women the same political rights as to men, viz., Colorado, Idaho, Utah, and Wyoming, and that the right to vote on some or all school questions is granted to women in Arizona, Colorado, Connecticut, Delaware, Iowa, Illinois, Idaho, Kentucky, Kansas, Michigan, Massachusetts, Minnesota, Mississippi, Montana, Nebraska, New Hampshire, New Jersey, New York, North Dakota, Oklahoma, Ohio, Oregon, South Dakota, Utah, Vermont, Wyoming, and Wisconsin.

Kansas, in addition to the states which grant full suffrage, grants municipal and bond suffrage to women, New York gives tax-paying women in all towns and villages the right to vote on questions of local taxation, and Montana and Louisiana give tax-paying women the right to vote upon all questions submitted to the taxpayer. In Minnesota, women have the right to vote for library trustees.

[¶]The General Federation of Women's Clubs in 1908–9 had a membership of 967 individual clubs with 77,544 active members and 8,592 associate members. There were 5,312 clubs in the state federations with 358,497 members.

Excerpt from "Housing Conditions in Chicago, III: Back of the Yards" by Sophonisba Breckinridge and Edith Abbott

This selection is excerpted from pages 435–467. This article was part of a series of studies of housing conditions being done by Breckinridge and Edith Abbott and their students at the Chicago School of Civics and Philanthropy. It is representative of the principle of using multiple research strategies which the Chicago Women used in their study of the causes of "social problems." The full article contains maps, photographs, and charts.

In the Stockyards . . . are the mingled cries of the animals awaiting slaughter, the presence of uncared-for-waste, the sight of blood, the carcasses naked of flesh and skin, the suggestion of death and disintegration—all of which must react in a demoralizing way, not only upon the character of the people, but the conditions under which they live. . . .

The territory back of the "Yards" is, then, so unfortunate in its blighted surroundings that great interest was felt as to what actual living conditions might be in a dismal region with the city dumps, the brickyards, and "Bubbly Creek" on one side, and the greatest slaughter-houses in the world on the other. Its very peculiarities, as compared with other neighborhoods, seemed to justify a study of its housing conditions. . . . The records of the United Charities show that a large proportion of the applicants for relief come from this territory. . . . [A] map published by the commissioner of health shows that large numbers of babies die here every year, and tuberculosis, high infant mortality, poverty, and bad housing and sanitary conditions will generally be found together. . . .

The homes of this district have always been workmen's homes. Small frame cottages have gradually been displaced or outnumbered by tenements built for two or more families; but it has continued to be almost solidly occupied by those who depend upon the yards for work and by those upon whose work the industry, in turn remains dependent. . . .

. . . In the earlier days, the workers in the yards and the dwellers in the neighborhood were almost exclusively Irish; but as they gradually found their ways into higher-grade work, they were succeeded first by the Germans and later by the Slavs, . . .

Two groups of blocks were selected for a house-to-house canvas, one Polish and one Lithuanian, and an attempt was made to select those which contained, not the poorest, but the typical homes of the neighborhood. . . . The accompanying map shows the whole neighborhood in its relation to the blocks investigated.

The following table . . . indicates how largely Slavic the population back of the yards has become [and] is given by blocks because it shows how the Poles and Lithuanians tend to segregate.

The fact of chief interest . . . is that 1,167 out of 1,562 heads of households are Polish or Lithuanian. When the large number of lodgers are added to these family groups, it is clear that this is now a district almost exclusively made up of Slavic immigrants, many of them newly arrived and unable to speak any English. The problem of the adjustment of the newly arrived immigrant is very closely connected with the housing problem. It almost uniformly happens that the families which are most foreign are most exploited in the matter of their housing situation. They pay the highest rents for the poorest apartments, and they seem quite unable to understand that they have a right to insist on needed repairs or a decent standard of cleanliness. . . . The student investigators who made the house-to-house canvass reported that their authority was rarely questioned among the less Americanized

Source: Sophonisba Breckinridge and Edith Abbott, "Housing Conditions in Chicago, III: Back of the Yards," *American Journal of Sociology* 16 (1911), pp. 433–468.

NATIONALITY OF HEADS OF HOUSEHOLDS

	Polish	Lithuanians	Bohemians	German	Slovak	Irish	Other	Total
Block 1	49	12		1	5	6	10	83
Block 2	60	74		4	3	4		145
Block 3	52	124			2		1	179
Block 4	26	12	4	7	3	9	18	79
Block 5	17	37	1	10	1	9	15	90
Block 6	32	63	14	3	2		2	116
Block 7	67		12	2	15	4	6	130
Block 8	119		8	8	7	1	1	144
Block 9	131		13	6	17		2	169
Block 10	72		38	10	10		4	230
Whiskey Row West Side	171	11	2	9	10	12	15	230
East Side	38		1	8	6	7	3	63
Total	**834**	**333**	**93**	**92**	**81**	**52**	**77**	**1,562**

groups; the people were uniformly submissive, and apparently it never occurred to them that they had a right to ask why strangers could come in and measure their doors and windows.

It is a well-known fact that the unskilled work in the yards is largely done by the members of these foreign groups. Additional evidence, however, is found in the following table which shows that of the 876 heads of families (men) whose occupations were learned, only 152 did work requiring any considerable degree of skill. . . .

[P]rimitive sanitary arrangements . . . still exist in this neighborhood. . . . The needs of the families in . . . 1,119 apartments which were without water-closets were met in part by the primitive yard closets and privies but in the majority of cases by closets in the basements or cellar which were used either by several or by all of the families in the building. In 127 buildings the tenants used water-closets in the basement or the cellar and in 155 buildings the water-closets were in the halls. In one building there was one water-closet for five families, in another one for six families and in another one for seven families.

. . . It is clear that the insanitary accommodations which are only too often dark, out-of-order, offensive, used by large groups of men lodgers, and often by other families not clean in their habits, are mostly a degrading and contaminating influence which could easily be prevented. . . .

Conditions within the apartment are supposedly governed by certain regulations bearing upon the question of light and air, and cubic air space per person. The most important of these, though undoubtedly the most difficult of enforcement, is the provision which attempts to prevent overcrowding by requiring for each occupant a definite minimum of space. . . .

[The] table [a cross-tabulation giving room occupancy and cubic footage] shows that in 1,981 cases the law against over-crowding was violated, and that in many instances the number of cubic feet in the room was shockingly below the number of cubic feet required by law. . . .

One of the worst features of this overcrowding is the demoralizing lack of privacy. . . .

It appears from [the] table [giving cross-tabulation of blocks with rooms used for sleeping] that in 106 families even the kitchen was used as a bedroom at night. In 508 cases all the rooms except one were used as bedrooms at night.

Out of the 1,616 apartments which were visited . . . [a] large number were found to be inadequate in light as well as in area. The ordinance prescribes for rooms in new tenement houses a minimum height of eight and a half feet, but 935 rooms were found which failed to conform to this requirement. . . .

. . . The large number of immigrants, both men and women, who find it easy to get employment in the yards wish, when they first come to this country, to live near their work, and among people of the same nationality. The families who live in the neighborhood are therefore constantly tempted to add to their income by taking in one more lodger. Only 768 out of the 1,616 families visited said that they had no lodgers. That is, more than one-half of the families added to their income by filling up their rooms to the utmost capacity with the men and women who were too new to this country to realize that they could demand anything more than a place to sleep. . . .

The fact that there are several lodgers in a family means serious overcrowding in these small apartments . . . , it means a great deal of additional work for the overburdened wife and mother, . . . It also means a sacrifice of privacy; for in many cases the lodgers sleep in the same room with some member of the family. . . . Sometimes men and women lodgers slept in the same room. . . . In other cases men lodgers slept in the same rooms with the young daughters of the household, and no one seemed aware of danger or improprieties. . . .

The practice of taking lodgers is, of course, to be explained by the fact that the families are large, the earnings are small, and the rents high. The lodger, however, is as much the cause as the effect of high rents; the landlord finds it easy to excuse a high rental by pointing out that the families will surely take lodgers and earn enough to pay it. . . .

. . . Reference has already been made to the fact that conditions in the yards must be a demoralizing influence on the people who live near; but along with the influence of the Stockyards should be reckoned that of the great city "dump.". . .

Obviously the material deposited in these dumps is of several kinds: ashes and other substances . . . ; cans, bottles, old junk, wooden boxes . . . ; old mattresses, worn garments, and articles of personal use . . . which may easily convey infection; . . . and finally waste food. . . . It should be added that the articles of real value are not infrequently mixed in with the refuse by mistake. . . .

. . . This reference to the city dumps has been made because in presenting an account of housing conditions in this neighborhood it seemed important to call attention to this great stretch of territory. . . . In spite of foul odor, heavy clouds of dust, and dreary ugliness, women who hope to add to their meager supply of furniture and fuel, are tempted to search here, and children who grow accustomed to these conditions find here their adventure and play.

READING 7-9

Excerpt from "Are Women a Force for Good Government?" by Edith Abbott

This selection is excerpted from pages 437–439. Edith Abbott did a number of analyses of what we today

Source: Edith Abbott, "Are Women a Force for Good Government?" National Municipal Review 4 (1915), pp. 437–443.

would term the "gender gap" in voting, using her statistical skills to answer charges that women voters made no difference. Here she focuses on the Chicago mayoral election, making the important point that the only moment at which voters had a real choice was in the Republican primary—in this period the Republican party was the more liberal, or "progressive," party— and that is where one had to look for women's impact.

What effect did the women's vote actually have on the recent municipal elections in Chicago? Were any candidates nominated or elected who would not have been nominated and elected without the women's vote? If the women did not actually change the result of the election, did they vote more largely than the men for the best candidates?

In attempting to answer these questions, which have been so frequently asked in so many parts of the country since the election, it is not necessary to indulge in speculation. The women of Illinois have only limited suffrage, and special "women's ballots" are provided for their use and these ballots are counted separately from the men's. How the women vote is, therefore, all a matter of official record, and it is only necessary to study the returns in order to determine the facts.

A study of the influence of the women's vote upon the mayoralty election must necessarily begin with the choice of candidates at the primary election. . . . The two leading candidates for the Republican nomination were William Hale Thompson, since elected and inaugurated mayor, and Chief Justice Harry Olson, of the Chicago municipal court,—the fusion candidate agreed upon by the Progressives, led by Professor Charles E. Merriam, who has been for many years the leader of the good-government forces in Chicago. . . . As to which was the better candidate there could be no possible question. The significance, therefore, of the figures given in the following tables [sic] cannot be overestimated.

This table shows that the women gave a decisive plurality of more than 7,700 votes to the better candidate while the men gave a still larger plurality to the less desirable candidate. Fifty-five per

NUMBER AND PER CENT OF VOTES CAST BY MEN AND WOMEN FOR CANDIDATES IN REPUBLICAN PRIMARY

	Number		Per Cent	
	Men	**Women**	**Men**	**Women**
Thompson	61,506	25,827	53.0	42.7
Olson	51,255	33,570	44.2	55.6
Hey	3,264	1,019	2.8	1.7
Total	116,025	60,614	100.0	100.0

cent. of the women voted for Judge Olson, but the men's plurality for Mr. Thompson was large enough to out-weigh the women's vote. If the men had stayed away from the polls on the day of the primary and left to the women their business of choosing a candidate, the fate of Chicago would have been different.

In the contest between Mayor Harrison and Mr. Sweitzer for the Democratic nomination, there was no such distinct line of cleavage between the good and bad elements. Both were "machine" candidates, although the mayor's machine was considered less undesirable than Mr. Sweitzer's. . . .

The contrast between the situation on the day of the primary and the day of election was very striking. When the primary was held, there was chance to nominate a reform candidate for mayor, and the women made the choice in favor of Judge Olson and good government. The men chose differently, and on election day there the choice was between an undesirable Democrat and an equally undesirable—or slightly less undesirable—Republican. Men and women alike had to do the best they could with the hopeless situation created by the men voters. If the men had stayed home on the day of the primaries, it will be remembered, the men and women would have had a choice between Judge Olson and Mr. Sweitzer. Since there was no "good" candidate to vote for, the best that could be done by the men or the women was to vote for the *least undesirable* candidate.

Beatrice Potter Webb (1858–1943)— Sociology as Critical Positivism

BIOGRAPHICAL BACKGROUND

Beatrice Potter Webb was born on January 2, 1858, near Gloucester, England; she died at Passfield Corner, Surrey, on April 30, 1943. On December 12, 1947, her ashes and those of her husband, Sidney Webb, were ceremoniously interred in Westminster Abbey, with British Prime Minister Clement Atlee declaring, "Millions are living fuller and freer lives today because of the work of Sidney and Beatrice Webb" (Muggeridge and Adam, 1968: 258). The emphatic word here is "work"; for Beatrice Potter Webb was what she set out to be, a "brain worker," a social investigator, whose tireless labor with her husband Sidney left a policy-oriented body of empirical research that is not only unsurpassed in social science but that served as a blueprint for the great humanitarian enterprise of the British welfare state. The best single source for Webb's life are her two autobiographical volumes, the highly acclaimed *My Apprenticeship* (1926) and the posthumous *Our Partnership* (1948). There are numerous biographies of Webb and the Webbs. The best feminist accounts are Deborah Epstein Nord's clear and insightful *The Apprenticeship of Beatrice Webb* (1985) and a fine summary article by Barbara Caine, "Beatrice Webb and the 'Woman Question'" (1982). The best account setting Webb in the political context of her time is Margaret Cole's sympathetic and eminently readable *Beatrice Webb* (1946). There is also the lively and intimate *Beatrice Webb: A Life, 1858–1943* (1968) by her niece Kitty Muggeridge and Ruth Adam.

Webb is an anomaly in this text. Unlike the other women studied here, she has not been forgotten in traditional male-centered accounts of the history of sociology; as a recognized partner with Sidney, she has been included in discussions of sociology's empirical tradition. The bulk of her writing was done in a complex partnership with Sidney, so that it is difficult to isolate Webb's contribution. Further, that contribution was shaped by

277

her alignment with an intensely male-dominated discourse, the British reworking of socialist ideas known as Fabian socialism; she not only failed to achieve, she seems to have rejected both a gendered standpoint in her own writing and feminism as an independent movement. Yet to omit her would be an injustice. Alone and in partnership with Sidney, she created some of the enduring works in the tradition of empirical sociology, which taken in combination with the Webbs' political activities, are an exemplar of a critical sociology as a force in social policy. This chapter attempts to deal with this anomaly by tracing, in writings done before or independent of Sidney, the development of Webb's radical empiricism with its growing critique of capitalist society. Occasional references to their joint works are to those where we can show the connection between the content of those writings and Beatrice Webb's own theory. Wherever ease of communication permits, to keep attention focused on her, we refer to her as Webb and her husband as Sidney (she did not retain Potter in her name after her marriage).

Our purpose in this biographical sketch is to consider how Webb came to be a sociologist and the kind of sociologist she was. To this end, we focus the biography most particularly on the years up to 1892, when she marries Sidney—a period of intellectual growth and development which she recalls autobiographically in *My Apprenticeship,* a sociological account of the making of a sociologist. In its opening pages she states the questions that led her to sociology: "Can there be a science of social organisation . . . , enabling us to forecast what will happen, and perhaps to alter the event by taking action . . . ? And . . . is man's capacity for scientific discovery the only faculty required for the reorganisation of society . . . ? Or do we need religion as well as science . . . ?" (1926:xiv). To explain how these questions came to be critical to Webb, we focus on three interrelated factors: accident of birth; a temperamental predilection for intellectual order; and the conundrum of gender and career, finally resolved in her partnership with Sidney.

Accident of Birth

Webb, the eighth of nine daughters, was four years old when a son and male heir was born to her parents Richard and Laurencina (Heyworth) Potter and she was seven years old when he died. A few months after his death, Webb's last sister was born and became a solace for her mother's grief. Webb summarizes her childhood as lived "in the shadow of my baby brother's birth and death" (1926:58). It is possible to see in Webb's early life a reworking of the male child's oedipal experience: where he must reject the mother because he is not a girl, Webb was distanced from her mother by the fact that she was not a boy—first by the brother's birth, then by his death, then by the birth of the sister. Had Webb been a boy, the birth of the sister would not have removed her from the center of her mother's attention and the circumstances of the family during her early life would not have let Webb slip from view—as she reports herself as having done (noting that her mother regarded her as the only ungifted child in the family). She seems to have experienced some basic discomfiture in gender identity, which while not the determining factor in her life, certainly left her with mixed feelings about being female. The particularity of her response is perhaps demonstrated by the fact that all of her sisters made conventionally good marriages and went on to live lives of conventional female service.

It is equally important to realize that the household she grew up in was one of immense material privilege, secured by a father she remembers as at once indulgent and a skilled capitalist speculator. Richard Potter's particular genius was for entrepreneurial activity—he could see how to make deals, though he had little interest in overseeing the details once the deal was struck. Thus, the death of the son took place in the context of a family in which a male heir might have laid claim to the family business, and in which the support of servants meant that the grieving mother could turn her attention away from her children. Further, the fact of material privilege meant an opportunity to converse at the dinner table with such luminaries as longtime family friend Herbert Spencer, a part of Webb's growing up, a living stage in her intellectual journey. Most important, the class position of the family meant that Webb early distinguished between

Beatrice Potter Webb, age 33

classes of people who were "order givers" and classes of people who were "order takers."

While Webb would devote an extraordinary amount of labor to improving the lives of those persons who were habitually order takers, she perhaps never successfully ceased to identify herself as an order giver. This class sense of being an order giver was at odds with the gender position of being an order taker in relations with men of her own class. The accidents of birth that shape Webb's life are, thus, an intersection between particular experiences of gender identity and her own deeply felt though ambiguously regarded class identity.

Temperament: A Desire for Order and Purpose

All the Potter daughters were educated at home by a series of governesses. Webb was often ill and could rarely do a full term in the schoolroom and so increasingly came to educate herself, using her father's library and forming an intellectual friendship with Spencer.[1] Webb recalls the intellectual atmosphere of her home as one of questioning and challenging. Her self-education reached a key moment at fifteen in 1873, when she was reading Goethe and making her own translation of *Faust,* beginning to keep the comprehensive diary that became part of her ordering of her life for the next seventy years, and traveling with her father on business to America. She confides to her diary that it was all right to question conventional religion but one then had a duty to create a belief system of one's own. For most of her life, Webb worked conscientiously to make a faith—sometimes finding it in the craft of the social investigator, sometimes in Sidney's persistent optimism that their work mattered and that time and progress were on their side; at other times, longing for some religious creed. She writes in her diary of her belief that "'the two big forces for good in the world were the scientific method applied to the process of life, and the use of prayer in directing the purpose of life'" (cited in Nord, 1985:221). Webb temperamentally wished for a personal intellectual ordering of the world; she perhaps found that ordering in the creation of written texts—the private diary, the autobiography, the public sociological analysis.

The Conundrum of Gender and Career

Writing in 1926, Webb asserted that "I had never suffered the disabilities assumed to arise from my sex" (1926:355). But no matter how much she may have denied that being a woman inhibited her life choices, Webb had to be aware that only a certain number of career options were open to a woman of her class. In age, she just missed the opening of the British universities to women. At her mother's death in 1882, she had four obvious life choices: to remain with her father, managing the family home;[2] to marry; to be a spinster dedicating herself to good works; or, perhaps, to try to be a "lady novelist."

But Webb could begin to imagine another option, one not well worked out for men, much less women: the possibility of being a social scientist. She had grown up knowing and studying Spencer and been led by this study to Auguste Comte. She knew the intellectual debates in political and social science circles, debates focused in the 1880s on the overriding question of how there could be "poverty amidst riches" (Webb, 1926:216). She could see where the coming action would be—in social science and social reform. And she began by a zigzag path to work her way there.

In the period between 1883 and 1887, Webb made her way into the world of social investigation. She first experimented with charity work, which struck in her both a chord of compassion and an intense desire to know more and to know more accurately about the people who made up the manual working class, of whom she felt the charity cases might be only a fraction. Her first step toward gathering this information was to return to the original home of the Potters and Heyworths—Bacup, Lancashire—where she still had distant relatives. Disguising herself and her purposes in order to observe the spontaneous life of the community, she discovered that her Bacup relatives were a self-sufficient and seemingly happy group of working-class people, their lives centered in the Nonconformist Chapel and the Consumers' Co-operative, the local, community-owned, democratically managed store. This research experience was the turning point in her decision to become a social investigator.

Two separate pieces of her life came together to give her the opportunity she sought. She returned to London and became a supervisor and "rent collector" in the Katherine Buildings, part of an experiment in low-cost housing for the poor near the East London docks. She found the work frustrating: the buildings were so bare (lacking even a sink in the apartments) that they further demoralized the people forced by poverty to live there;

and there seemed to be no records, no information, no sense of who ended up there and why. She questioned how she could morally justify urging people in such hopeless conditions to do better.

In the meantime, through a family connection, she began to work with Charles Booth, who was drafting the plan for his social science achievement, *The Life and Labour of the People of London.* She joined Booth's research project not out of philanthropic impulse but out of a wish to work as a scientific investigator. The Booth study, which combined quantitative and qualitative research methods and data, came to be for Webb a standard of excellence in the practice of social research. In the course of it, she had opportunities to try out several methods of social research—personal observation, interviewing, statistical compilation, the use of documents and literature, and participant observation. (See "Assumptions" and Theme 1 later in this chapter.)

In 1889, at the end of her work on part of Booth's study, Webb was determined to be "a brain worker," a phrase she frequently uses, to establish identity with other workers. Convinced by the Booth study that the capitalist system was slowly destroying the British working class, she wanted to study manual workers who were managing their lives successfully and in whose success there might be hopes of an alternative socio-economic strategy. She returned to her Bacup experience and to the subject of working-class consumer co-operatives. She had already acquired a modest reputation from three journal publications on working-class conditions. One, "Pages from a Working Girl's Diary" (1888), although the slightest piece sociologically, was perceived as gender appropriate and people categorized Webb as a specialist in issues of women's work. Thus, when she approached two male mentors, Booth and Alfred Marshall, a distinguished Cambridge economist, about a study of the co-operative movement, they both urged her to study women's work. Marshall's response in March 1889 especially rankled: *"'A book by you on the Co-operative Movement I may get my wife to read to me in the evening to while away the time, but I shan't pay any attention to it,'"* (Webb, 1926:352).[3] Two months later, Webb signed an anti-suffrage petition, the publication of which effectively discredited her to most people as an investigator into women's issues. She was perhaps propelled by a need to distance herself from women's issues in order to be seen as a woman brain worker, that is, a social investigator who happened to be a woman. She did not try publicly to reverse this anti-suffrage stance until 1906 (see "Webb and the Tradition of Feminist Sociology," following).

Webb did do her study of co-operatives and produced her most influential single-authored book, *The Co-operative Movement in Great Britain* (1891)—which was translated into twelve languages (see Chapters 3 and 7 and "Webb and the Tradition of Feminist Sociology," following). During her work on the co-operative movement, she converted to socialism—a change in belief she recorded in her diary on February 1, 1890. She became a socialist out of her experience as a social investigator, and the conversion was seen by herself and her peers as a radical one. Yet the socialism to which she converted was not revolutionary but reformist. Her most basic principle at the moment of conversion seems to have been that there had to be collective or state action to stop the destructive impetus of free competition and guarantee to each individual member of society a minimum standard of quality of life.

Partnership with Sidney

Webb met Sidney, a prominent Fabian socialist, in the spring of 1890; he was a career civil servant from a distinctly less privileged background than the Potters. But he had an encyclopedic memory, a willingness to work hard, and a quality Webb names with admiration as "disinterestedness," that is of a genuine desire to promote right rather than himself (cited in Cole, 1946:42). In Webb's account (1926), Sidney was neither the source of her conversion to socialism nor a major love interest. What attracted her to him—and him to her, though he also apparently found her physically appealing—was the chance to make a partnership with another brain worker. Sidney's political views made him seem wildly radical to much of Webb's family and she waited until after her father's death in 1892 to marry.

From 1892 to the end of her life in 1943, Beatrice and Sidney Webb worked in a remarkable partnership—but a partnership that called for change, adaptation, and sacrifice by Beatrice Webb, a partnership in which Sidney seems to have assumed directorship. They published a set of massively detailed empirical studies, many of which are still required readings, most especially in labor history. Their first two works built on an interest Beatrice Webb had been pursuing, collective organizations outside the state—*The History of Trade Unionism* (1894) and the companion volume, *Industrial Democracy* (1897). They then turned their attention to what was to become a monumental work, a history of English local government, as a way of exploring the history of co-operative collective activity within the state. This work they began in the spring of 1899; it would eventually run to eight major books and ten volumes, encompassing some 4,212 pages (Cole, 1946:96–97): *The History of Liquor Licensing in England* (1903), *The Parish and the County* (1906), *The Manor and the Borough* (1908), *The Story of the King's Highway* (1913), *Statutory Authorities for Special Purposes* (1922), *English Prisons under Local Government* (1922), *English Poor Law History: The Old Poor Law* (1927), and *English Poor Law History: The Last Hundred Years* (1929). Additionally, in those years, they would write *The Prevention of Destitution* (1920), *A Constitution for the Socialist Commonwealth of Great Britain* (1920), *The Decay of Capitalist Civilization* (1923), *Methods of Social Study* (1932), their last major work of social science, and a parting shot, *Soviet Communism: A New Civilization* (1937).

Besides these mammoth works of scholarship, the Webbs were also active in British politics. They helped, with other Fabians, to organize the London School of Economics (where Edith Abbott studied; see Chapter 7), and they were prime movers in beginning the *New Statesman,* one of the most important of British left-wing intellectual journals. Beatrice Webb was a key actor in one of the major controversies in British politics in the years before World War I: the drafting of the influential Minority Report of the Poor Law Commission. Despite a rocky history and its failure in Parliament, that Minority Report became the basis for the Beveridge Report of 1942, which ushered in a welfare state for Great Britain. Sidney became a member of Parliament and then a Cabinet minister in the 1920s in the first two Labour Party governments in British history. As part of the maneuverings for the Cabinet minister post, Sidney was given a peerage; he took the title Baron Passfield, but Beatrice resisted unsuccessfully the title Baroness Passfield (Muggeridge and Adam, 1968:228–229).

About the partnership with Sidney, which brought the vicissitudes of political battle and the extraordinary achievements in empirical research, Webb had deeply mixed feelings. In a series of diary entries, cited by Nord (1985:225), Webb reveals her sense of loss of control in the partnership: "'I never write, except in my diary in my own style'" (8 December 1913); "'I have constrained my intellect, forced it to concentrate on one subject after another; on some of the dullest and least illuminating details of social organisation. . . . I vividly remember the nausea with which, day after day, I went on with this task'" (22 December 1918). As Nord (1985:236) says, "It is perplexing and profoundly revealing that while the first Labour government in Britain's history was being established, Beatrice Webb was longing to be left alone to devote herself to her autobiography." And it is perhaps for this autobiography, *My Apprenticeship,* that she should be especially appreciated by today's generation of women sociologists; for despite her unconfronted discomfiture with gender discrimination, it is a remarkably reflective sociological account of a woman's intellectual journey to a vision of society.

The Labour governments fell far short of the Webbs' hopes, and they increasingly looked to the Soviet Union for a model. Beatrice Webb died in the midst of World War II, having expressed the hope that the family home, Passfield Corner, should become "a haven where tired sociologists could rest and discuss" (Muggeridge and Adam, 1968:254).

GENERAL SOCIAL THEORY

Assumptions

Four concerns in British intellectual life shaped Webb's work: (1) the intertwined Victorian ideas of science and progress; (2) the tension between the doctrine of individualism and the fact of poverty amidst prosperity; (3) the emerging tradition of empirical sociology; and (4) the growing doctrines of socialism, especially Fabian socialism.

"The Mid-Victorian Time-Spirit"   Webb remembers her family life as infused with the ideas she calls the "mid-Victorian time-spirit," in which science and progress were intertwined themes. An individual had only to look around to see that "progress" was occurring and that that progress was the result of science, or—more accurately, perhaps—the application of science to technological achievement. Technological changes made possible the growth of capitalism which became in the popular mind associated with material progress. For instance, the expansion of the railroads, from which Webb's father, Richard Potter, made his considerable fortune, was seen as the miracle of the age, a prime indicator of progress through the practical application of science. The railroads transformed Britain—most visibly by making possible the growth of the commercial and industrial centers that made the country the economic and political power of the nineteenth-century world: where in 1800 there had been one city with a population of over 100,000 (London, 865,000), by 1850 there were nine, and by 1891, twenty-three such centers. "Greater" London grew to over four million by 1900 (Altick, 1973:75–76). Further, in the Victorian mind, science came to be associated not only with progress but with salvation. Darwin reverently concluded *The Origin of the Species* (1859): "There is a grandeur in this view of life, with its several powers, having been originally breathed by the Creator into a few forms or into one . . . and that from so simple a beginning endless forms most beautiful and most wonderful have been, and are being evolved."

The Debate over Poverty   Victorian England in Webb's intellectually formative years was racked by a debate about the causes of poverty, in which age-old views were reinforced by Herbert Spencer's application of evolutionary theory to social life. The traditional view held that a person's prosperity or destitution resulted from his or her own individual actions; that "the iron law of wages" set the amount of money available for wages at any given moment in any country's economic development, so that if part of that money went to support the unemployed, there was less for the worker; and that Malthusian theory demonstrated that acts of charity could produce over-population by allowing the unfit to multiply beyond the capacity of the land to support them. Spencer reinforced these views by arguing that the best social world is that in which the individual, the basic unit of society, is allowed to function unhampered. Capitalism as one expression of evolution rests on each individual cell or unit of society acting in its own best interest. Collectivist interference with individual competition would produce chaos and disorder, and lead to retrogression, a return to a more primitive state of society in which all would suffer. Thus, state intervention on behalf of the poor would subvert the principle of survival of the fittest by increasing the numbers of persons who could not survive on their own to such a point that those more adapted for survival would be overwhelmed. While individual acts of charity might be good for the character of the individual giver—and even this was called into question—the charitable action of the state would only induce ultimate ruin as it interfered with evolutionary progress. If one wished wealth for the nation, one must accept that there must be poverty for some individuals. These debates were absolutely real, and they informed the transactions of the various charitable societies with which Webb began her social scientific career, as well as the thinking of such pioneers as Canon Barnett, the founder of Toynbee Hall, which had influenced Jane Addams.[4]

The Tradition of Empirical Sociology   One response to this debate was to look to science for solutions to poverty or for guides to ways to do charity. As Webb was tutored by Spencer in an individualistic theory of society, she was trained by Charles Booth in an empirical methodology—and in the end the findings of the latter would derail, for her, the policy directives of the former. The tenets of Booth's thinking about the problems of empirical research are contained in his letters to Webb, the only one of Booth's disciples who really shared his concern with the methodology of social science inquiry (Simey and Simey, 1960). Booth's first concern was to develop a system of data collection that would yield theory rather than be shaped by theory. The second was to properly weight the significance of any piece of data in the context of the entire system of empirical information. The third was to find ways to verify that data did indeed show the "facts"—a challenge he met by the strategy of collecting and comparing data from as many sources as possible. The fourth was the issue of separating fact from opinion in these data, not necessarily dismissing the opinion but noting it as opinion. Finally, as he began to do trial runs to see if this methodology would work, Booth struggled with the problem of establishing reliable categories of classification. What is critical in Booth's approach, and what inspired

Webb, was the focus on finding ways to get at the "real facts" of the conditions of a set of people, most particularly the complex aggregate of poor people in urban settings.

Fabian Socialism   In the course of her empirical research, Webb became genuinely convinced that the problem of poverty was structural, not individual, and she converted to socialism. With her involvement with Sidney, Webb became part of an organized group of British thinkers, the Fabian socialists, who by the late 1880s had moved to sufficient consensus to present their ideas in a surprisingly popular book, *Fabian Essays in Socialism* (Shaw, 1889b). The theoretical position in this book was "eclectic" (Cole, 1961), willing to borrow and piece together from a variety of sources and to adopt middle-of-the-road positions. Socialism was presented as essentially pragmatic and "British," rather than radical and Marxist. The Fabians argued that what Marx calls "surplus value" is really "rent"—the profit made by landowners and capitalists—and should either be returned to labor or be turned over to the community at large. The private claiming of this "rent" leads to waste (Shaw, 1889a). The Fabians' position was that "rents" or "surplus value" should be used to run large centralized enterprises like the post office and the railroads, and even more significantly, that this money should be turned over to local governments, understood as " 'the democratically elected representatives of the community'—whatever the community was" (Cole, 1961:30). They saw the ultimate management of civic affairs being carried out by skilled experts hired by the democratically elected representatives of the community. In his essay in this collection, Sidney Webb presents the goal of socialism in terms of the time-honored British Benthamite principle of "the greatest good for the greatest number"; he acknowledges that Marx is right, that the material or economic workings of society determine its political form; but he says that socialism will come about not through class warfare or revolution but through the gradual evolution of public opinion working through the democratic process (S. Webb, 1889:35). Fabians believed that the way to produce change was through the strategy Sidney names "permeation." At all levels of government and cooperative organization, Fabian members took whatever policy initiative was being advanced and attempted to shape it in a socialist or collectivist direction. Essential to permeation was the production of competent, accurate analyses of social conditions, so that Fabianism would become associated in the public mind with a fair and thoughtful presentation of issues. Sharing the general faith in progress of the Victorians, Fabians believed that social evolution would go the direction they were charting—though they would have to work to make it happen. While there were active women members in the Fabians, it was a male-dominated discourse. Only one woman, Annie Besant, contributes to the *Essays*. And when a few years later the society produced a book entitled *What Every Intelligent Woman Needs to Know about Socialism,* it was authored by George Bernard Shaw.

Major Themes

Webb wanted above all to explore the possibility of creating a science of society that could describe, explain, and predict social relations. The focal issue for such a science was the anomaly that surrounded her and puzzled the intellectual members of her class: the problem of growing human destitution despite an increasingly prosperous economy.

We describe her sociology in terms of three themes: that empirical research should ground theory; that society is a system of structures; and that the project of sociology is to help create a society characterized by economic equity and democratic decision-making.

1. For Webb, sociology begins with the proposition that any social science claim must be arrived at inductively and grounded in the practice of rigorous empirical investigation. To understand this proposition as a beginning point, it is necessary to appreciate the mixture of responses with which Victorians confronted the problem they described as "poverty amidst riches": disbelief, denial, puzzlement, blame, guilt, patchwork remedies, calls for massive change. In one of her earliest published analyses, "The Dock Life of East London," Webb describes some of the positions in this debate:

> The economist in his study frowns sternly as he deplores the attractions of low-class labour into London. The philanthropist, fresh from the dock gate, pleads with more sensational intonation the guilt of the dock and the waterside employer in refusing to this helpless labour more inducement to remain, more possibility to live decently and multiply freely. The indifferentist alone stands by the side of the existing institution, and talks glibly of the inevitable tendency of inevitable competition in producing an inevitable irregularity of employment; failing to realise that these so-called 'inevitables' mean the gradual deterioration of the brain and sinew of fellow-countrymen. (1887:483)*

Webb's response was both epistemological and methodological: some way needed to be found to determine if there were significant inequities in the society or if the issue was a case of what Webb would later describe as the "fallacy of the individual instance" (1907:347), such as newspaper stories of incredible individual hardship, designed to touch the public conscience about *social* conditions but really only reflecting an instance of *individual* bad luck. The first duty of the sociologist is to arrive at a true picture of the situation-at-hand, starting with the commonly accepted understanding of that situation and moving by investigation to uncover either the complexity behind the commonplace or the underlying commonalities between conditions popularly thought to be diverse.

The "picture" of the situation-at-hand has two elements, its immediate facts and the historical and statistical framing of those facts. Webb draws on three sources for the immediate facts: direct personal observation by the investigator, interviews, and the use of documents and literature. Personal observation is most accurately done, Webb says, when the people observed are unaware of the observation and thus behave spontaneously. Thus, working as a rent collector at the Katherine Buildings was a better field method than standing as a social science observer at the gate to the East London docks. Webb holds up as a model of the interview Booth's work in *The Life and Labour of the People of London* (1892–1902), which used as a key resource the School Board Visitors who called on every home in a neighborhood to collect data as to family size, occupation, and income. Booth and his staff interviewed the School Board Visitors in depth, going over their collected data with them, a method Webb characterizes as "wholesale interviewing"

---

*An asterisk following a citation in the text means that the passage quoted is given in fuller context in the readings at the end of the chapter.

(1926:277). She sees this technique as a way to reduce bias: the idiosyncracies in the School Board Visitors' reports are evened out in the process of interviewing them all; the Visitors' purpose in collecting is offset by the different purpose of Booth's interviewers; and none of the interviewers themselves grasp or control the full direction of the project. Thus, respondents' and interviewers' tendencies to shape their statements according to their own predispositions are progressively sifted out of the data. Webb hopes that the interview data will lead the researcher to documents and literature; "a document is a written testimony which is unconsciously secreted by a social organisation for the purpose, not of influencing thought, but of influencing action," while literature is designed to influence thought and is "the personal impression of the individual who writes" (1907:348–349).

Any picture of a situation-at-hand must be set in context, both statistically and historically. The statistical context helps the researcher know whether a condition is social, preventing distortion of any particular observation, interview, or document—for the essence of statistics for Webb is that all the units are regarded as equal. But one can only determine the nature and equality of the units in one's aggregate if one has made repeated personal observations of individual cases. The historical context establishes the past actions by human beings that seem to have called this situation into being. The researcher does not presume that these actions were undertaken to produce these conditions but only that these actions seem germane or salient to the fact of the existence of the conditions. In looking at the London docks, Webb establishes the role of historically created structures in shaping the destinies of the present dockworkers. For instance:

> The substitution of steam for sailing vessels, while it distributes employment more evenly throughout the year, increases the day to day and hour to hour uncertainty. In bygone days at certain seasons of the year a fleet of sailing vessels would line the dock quay. The work was spread over weeks and months, and each succeeding day saw the same number of men employed for the same number of hours. . . . Now the scene is changed. Steamers come and go despite wind and tide. (1887:485)*

The researcher must also begin inductively to create possible typifications or classifications of these data by grouping them in relation to one another. Webb repeatedly emphasizes the importance of note-taking and of reshuffling and realigning one's notes so that descriptive and causal patterns appear. Her careful presentation of the mechanics of note-taking is a way in which Webb concretizes the mental process that must be gone through in moving from fact to classification to cause-and-effect.

The effectiveness of this method of inductive movement from data to claim is illustrated in Webb's study "How to Do Away with the Sweating System" (1892/1898). Webb opens with her essential proposition that the first duty is accurate presentation of the situation: "First, we must decide what we mean by sweating and the sweating system; and secondly, we must determine the cause of these evils" (1892/1898:139). She reports that when she began her work, sweating was misunderstood to be an arrangement that turned on the presence of the subcontractor. Investigating shop after shop, recording her findings, and reviewing her data, Webb found that the subcontractor was *not* a constant factor. Her empirical work convinced her—and her testimony along with that of others managed to convince the House of Lords Committee on Sweating—that "sweating was no particular method of remuneration, no peculiar form of industrial organisation, but certain conditions of employment—viz., *unusually low rates of wages, excessive hours of labour, and insanitary work-places*" (1892/1898:140). Thus, legislation aimed at the sub-contractor to correct sweating as an employment practice was in point of fact looking to the wrong solutions. Webb then goes on to present what her data show about the right places to look for solutions.

2. Webb's basic sociological claim is that empirical investigation shows society to be a system of emergent social structures rather than the by-product of individual action. In arriving at this claim, Webb made an intellectual journey from an individualistic interpretation of social organization to a collectivist interpretation, that is, from a view of the individual as the primary social unit and the cause of his or her own fate, to a view in which the individual is shaped by social organization. This claim resolves part of the problem that originally inspired Webb to social research: the causes of destitution amidst prosperity. Webb's empirical researches show her that the causes of poverty are not in individual character but in social structure. But Webb stresses that she herself did not begin from this premise but from the premise that individual character among the poor needed somehow to be strengthened.

The explanation she labels "individualism" sees poverty as an inevitable outcome of individuals pursuing their interests in free competition, a process upon which social evolution depends (as does its "most progressive" manifestation, capitalism). Against this individualistic argument is the theoretical position Webb labels "collectivism," which says that the cause of poverty is precisely in the failure of people to act collectively to control competition and capitalism and to produce an equitable distribution of goods and services. By logical extension, of course, collectivism argues that not only is the cause of poverty in social structure or collective arrangements but so is the source of capitalism and wealth. Webb came completely to break with Spencer's libertarian sociology over what she saw as intellectual fallacies in his theorizing. The most blatant of these she identifies as his arbitrary labeling of corporate or individual capitalism as "natural" while attempts by trades unions or co-operative movements are 'artificial' meddling with the macro process of social evolution. Webb argues that "there is no such thing as a social structure apart from human beings, or independent of their activity. Thus, strictly speaking, every development of social structure and function, from the family . . . to the most complicated Act of Parliament, is alike 'artificial,' that is to say, the product of human intervention" (1926:342). It is essential in understanding Webb's sociology to see that she considers the preceding argument to be the product not of "theory" but of "discovery"—she arrives at it through scientific empiricism, that is, an inquiry into the facts guided by the scientific method. Indeed, a further quarrel with Spencer is that he has used data not to arrive at theory but to illustrate pre-conceived theories, that he does not practice the scientific method he proclaims.

Webb is intensely aware of herself, and others, as products of particular class backgrounds which give them certain interests in the situation they investigate. This is for her perhaps the distinguishing feature of sociology: that the sociologist cannot really be outside the frame of what he or she investigates, in the way Webb imagines the chemist or the biologist to be. What seems critical to Webb is that her own class position does not change, rather her position is changed by the solid fact of empirical experience; the work of social investigation leads her whether she likes it or not to increasingly collectivist interpretations of cause. Thus Webb's basic argument is that sociology can convince if its methods are rigorously and intelligently empirical.

But Webb does admit that science alone cannot account for her interest or the interest of her contemporaries in the problem of the co-existence of poverty and wealth. Sociology might present a picture of innocent people suffering because of collective failures and the society might still feel that there was nothing it wished to do. But this is a position Webb allows for only in theory, arguing that in practice one must act " 'as if' the individual soul . . . were in communion with a superhuman force which makes for righteousness" (1926:344).

Webb's theory that social structures are primary causal factors is central to all her sociology, but it is not focal. Once she established through empirical investigation her own confidence in the collectivist interpretation, she focused on using empirical social research to guide social policy.

3. For Webb, the project of sociology is to discover how economic equity can be arrived at through democratic decision-making.

Webb's empiricism led her from a critique of existing conditions of exploitation to an exploration of alternative ways of social organization, which she finds in various "social experiments." Webb argues that social experiments are taking place all the time as collectivities, businesses, and governments try different actions to see if they will produce desired effects on various groups of people. These efforts are not typically named as "experiments," but that is nevertheless what they are.

> As a matter of fact we are always applying our knowledge of society to predict events, and we base our knowledge on the prediction. Imagine what would happen if you had a statesman who was haunted by philosophic doubt, in charge of the post office just before Christmas, who would refuse to authorise the employment of additional postmen on the ground that there was no reason to suppose that the same increase of work would occur as in former years? I suggest that we can ascertain with sufficient certainty to base action upon it, what the conduct of the average man will be under ordinary circumstances. It is upon this kind of knowledge that the whole of successful government is based. (1907:350–351)

Webb seeks through social science research to analyze those social experiments that bring political democracy to economic life.

The first such experiment she turns to, as an alternative to the libertarian model of unfettered individual interests and competition, is the already successful consumer co-operative movement she knew firsthand from her early work in Bacup (Webb, 1891). She is interested in this movement because it seems to have begun with the people themselves, understood here as manual workers; because it recognizes basic principles of self-governance; and because it offers an economic system different from capitalism for the production and distribution of goods.

Webb sees the co-operative store movement as having developed by a system of trial and error, or social experiment, combining the best ideas of two revered British visionaries—economic utopian Robert Owen (1771–1858) and democratic Parliamentary reformer William Cobbett (1763–1835). In Webb's telling, Owen saw the need to eliminate "the profit on price," that is, the selling of items at more than they cost to manufacture, the practice that is the base of capitalism; he wanted to establish factories to support workers in a comfortable lifestyle rather than to realize monetary profit for an owner who then used it to create more money. But Owen saw no place for democratic decision-making by the workers. Cobbett, on the other hand, did not care about economic issues but tried to focus the attention of the masses on Parliamentary reform and suffrage, believing that democracy would cure the evils of the economy.

Webb presents the co-operative store as a successful experiment in using a democratic decision-making process to govern the provision of goods. In broad outline, co-operative stores were associations of working-class consumers who elected their own managers, charging them to negotiate, with the advice of the membership, the purchase of goods the membership wanted. Bulk buying for a large collectivity enabled the managers to strike a good bargain with producers. At the end of the year, if the stores turned a profit, that profit was returned to the co-operative members as a dividend based on the amount of items they had purchased from the co-operative during the year.

Webb uses the co-operative store as a launching point for a vision of a society organized along lines other than those of capitalist competition, a society organized democratically around the twin economic roles of producer and consumer and the process she names "the collective bargain." Webb sees the collective bargain as a stage in industrial evolution, replacing both the ancient system of exchange directly between individuals, made obsolete by the industrial revolution, and the exploitative exchange of capitalism now in place.

> Barter between individuals must be superseded by negotiations, through authorized representatives, between groups of workers and consumers. . . .
>
> To gain a clear conception of the collective bargain—of the social relation which will supersede the individual relation—let us imagine, therefore, that this industrial democracy were fully developed and that industry were organized by associations of consumers (whether voluntary or compulsory, the Store, the Wholesale Societies, the municipality and the State), while all workers were united in Trades Unions. Then the official of the weavers' Union would debate questions of wages and technical training with the official of the Store or the municipality. . . . The official of the Trade Union and the official of the community would, it is true, represent the rival interests of different sections of the community. But as members of one State the interests of their constituents are ultimately identical. (1891/1904:216–218)*

Working with Sidney after 1893, Webb developed a theory of the history of municipal government not as a history of the enforcement of laws but as a history that began with a group of citizens wishing to procure a collective rather than an individual good—such as roads and parks. The municipal government can then be seen not in terms of issues of votes and law enforcement but in terms of people attempting to find ways to meet collective material needs. This view of the state led Webb to claim that in the crisis of destitution amidst wealth, government both local and national had the right to act through various forms of graduated regulation to reduce the exploitation and degradation that capitalism produced among the working classes.

But the first step in intelligent state regulation, for Webb, remains a knowledge of actual working conditions. The great duty of the sociologist in public policy is empirical: to gather facts and arrange facts without bias until they form descriptive and causal patterns that can be used by policymakers to direct the course of society. But the direction of that course, Webb concludes, depends finally on the values the society elects.

WEBB'S RELEVANCE FOR THE HISTORY AND PRESENT PRACTICE OF SOCIOLOGY

Webb and the Canon of Sociology

Introducing Webb into the canon leads us to two reformulations: (1) that of the relation of theory and research in the history of sociology and (2) that of the Webbs' place as contributors to the theoretical tradition of analytic conflict theory.

The Empirical Tradition   Unlike the other women presented in this book, Beatrice Webb has been, in partnership with her husband Sidney, a part of the canon of sociology. But the part to which the Webbs have been assigned—empirical sociology and more particularly the British tradition in empirical sociology—has itself been marginalized. In *A History of British Empirical Sociology* (1981), Raymond Kent takes as an exemplar of the movement from empirical data to theory, the Webbs' crowning study *Industrial Democracy* (1897/1902), an exploration of trade unionism in Great Britain. In the very plan of the book, the Webbs tried to use empirical data to generate theory and to avoid allowing theory to shape investigation. Only late in the work, on the basis of their empirical findings, do they turn to theory. In the introduction to the 1902 edition of *Industrial Democracy,* they offer a rigorous statement of this principle of letting one's data guide one to theory:

> To begin with the student must resolutely set himself to find out, not the ultimate answer to the practical problem that may have tempted him to the work, but what is the actual structure and function of the organisation about which he is interested. Thus, his primary task is to observe and dissect facts, comparing as many specimens as possible, and precisely recording all their resemblances and differences whether or not they seem significant. This does not mean the scientific observer ought to start with a mind free from preconceived ideas as to classification and sequences. If such a person existed, he would be able to make no observations at all. (1897/1902:ix–x)

They suggest three main sources for data, sources Webb (1907) has repeatedly returned to—the document, the personal observation, and the interview. They then offer, as Webb has done from her earliest days, advice about the use and taking of notes. In their 1932 methods book, *Methods of Social Study*—which had as one base Webb's earlier writings, including memoranda she wrote to herself in the 1880s—they describe how they achieved their theory of trade unionism by a constant shuffling and reshuffling of their notes. About this methodology, Kent offers the intriguing hypothesis: "It may not be so far-fetched to suggest that here in this . . . were the beginnings of what contemporary sociologists would call multivariate analysis, that is the rearrangement of data in many different ways so as to reveal patterns and relationships between phenomena which, at first sight, were not at all apparent" (1981:116). This is a fitting tribute to Webb's careful instructions on note-taking, which make concrete the mental experience of patterning relationships in the data. Focusing on the Webbs shows again that the definition of sociology in terms of its theories is a choice—not arbitrary but also not inevitable. In making that choice, students of the history of sociology have moved to the edge of their vision work like that of the Webbs, work important to the discipline and to the wider society.

The Tradition of Analytic Conflict Theory   In *Industrial Democracy,* the Webbs present a theory we today might recognize as a form of "analytic conflict theory"—a theoretical perspective that in substance though not in name Beatrice used earlier in *The Cooperative Movement in Great Britain* (1891). In their analysis in *Industrial Democracy,* the Webbs see three kinds of decisions having to be made about production: what to produce, how to produce it in terms of materials and skills needed, and under what working conditions. And they place those three decisions essentially in the hands of three different interest groups: consumers' associations, directors of industry, and trades unions. The Webbs award the first consideration, the issue of what shall be produced, to the consumers. They argue that the trades unions have "no more to do with this determination of what is produced than any other citizens or consumers" (Webb and Webb, 1897/1902:818). Further, the Webbs are especially concerned to bar the trades unions from the second consideration—that of processes, material, and human labor—because they see the trades unions as being deeply biased in favor not of the whole community but of the particular interests of their membership. This second decision the Webbs would award to "the directors of industry," whether capitalists or public salaried employees. But the interest of these directors may be in achieving a cheapness of production that could harm "the Standard of Life" of the manual workers. Thus, the Webbs see the trades unions as the primary actors in the third determination, the establishment of the conditions under which this production—once decided upon in terms of product, materials, and processes—shall occur. What they see is the complexity of interrelation among these three decisions, the decisions of product, process, and conditions.

In this model, the Webbs may offer a significant though unexplored early statement of analytic conflict theory—a statement consistent with many generalizations by modern theorists like Randall Collins (1975) and Ralf Dahrendorf (1968). The Webbs' model locates groups in society that seem to have inimical interests: producers and consumers, workers and capitalists, citizens and producers, citizens and capitalists. They show, however, that there are significant overlaps in those categories, which are not necessarily mutually exclusive, save that people are encouraged to identify their interests with one particular category, often because the other categories lack organization and collective voice. The Webbs insist that these conflicting interests, while real, must by any logic ultimately be reconciled by the fact that every single person is a member of the "community," however defined. They feel that there is no way a person could escape geographic residency, and that the fact of being physically present means that one has ultimately to care about roads, water, air, and the possibility of epidemic disease—issues which press as urgently on societies today. In such an arrangement of inimical and shared interests, a system could succeed by an open acknowledgement of what the Webbs usually called "bias" and we would call "interest" on the part of the constituent groups. Their project is to form an "industrial democracy" by realizing anew the constituent groups that make up a society; realizing those groups in terms of the processes of production, distribution, and consumption of goods and services, and integrating those economic processes with a politically democratic decision-making system so that material life is democratically governed.

Webb and the Tradition of Feminist Sociology

As we have already suggested, Webb did not actively identify as a feminist; indeed, upon occasion she seemed to actively identify as anti-feminist. We might expect or hope that her empiricism would have led her to see that particular conditions in the organization of society affected women in particular ways. But her personal needs and the Fabian socialism she adopted seem to have stopped the open empirical investigation that marked her most daring intellectual journeys. Once committed, through a process of empirical investigation, to the theoretical principle of collectivism, she found it difficult, as Barbara Caine has concluded, "to recognise that women's needs were not identical with those of the community as a whole" (1982:41).

She did occasionally make efforts on behalf of women. In 1906, in a letter intended for publication at a key moment of suffrage mobilization, she moved to retract her 1889 anti-suffrage stance and align herself with the cause by arguing that her case for women's suffrage rested not in a natural rights doctrine but in the thesis that life is "'a series of obligations'" and that for women to "'fulfill their . . . particular obligations'" they needed to exercise the franchise (Caine, 1982:35). In 1908, she helped to found the Fabian Women's Group, which over the years, despite male Fabian commitment to traditional family roles, made some significant efforts; Webb supported but rarely participated in the group (Caine, 1982). In 1918 she wrote a minority report on the question of equal wages in which she recommended, characteristically, that wages be set by occupation regardless of who held a particular position. This was a positive move, but it sidestepped the difficult question of the fact that men and women rarely held the same position—a point she herself had argued earlier (Webb, 1895/1896/1898).

Webb's work, though essentially *non*feminist (but perhaps not *a*feminist), influenced many of the more feminist thinkers in this volume. She visited Hull-House in 1898. In Chapter 7, we noted some of her influences on the Chicago Women in methodology and in the idea of the consumer as a social actor. But as early as 1891, Addams was reading *The Co-operative Movement in Great Britain* (Addams 1910b). It is interesting to compare Addams's rhetoric and thought in "The Subjective Necessity for Social Settlements"(1893) and *Democracy and Social Ethics* (1902/1907) with Webb's analysis of Robert Owen, William Cobbett, and the founding of the co-operative movement. In *The Co-operative Movement in Great Britain,* Webb writes of Owen: "For in contradiction to the competitive formula, 'each man for himself and the devil take the hindmost,' he declared 'that the happiness of self clearly understood can only be attained by a direct and conscious service of the community'" (1891/1904:25). Webb argues that Owen's downfall was that "[h]e had not grasped the significance of Democracy as a form of association whereby the whole body of the people acquires a collective life—the internal Will to transform institutions preceding the external act of reform" (1891/1904:31). Much of Addams's articulation of her theory of the social ethic is in the line of argument developed here by Webb, and

Owen could have been one model for Addams's critiques of philanthropists who presume they know better what is good for people than do the people themselves (see Chapter 3). Additionally, Webb met Charlotte Perkins Gilman who later contributed to Webb's most radical venture into feminism in an issue of the *New Statesman*. And Marianne Weber cites Webb in a 1904 essay on women's place in the creation of knowledge.

The piece of analysis by Webb that contemporary feminists may find most provocative or sympathetic is a 1913 article for the *New Statesman* which introduced a special supplement on the "woman question," "The Awakening of Women." In that "Introduction" Webb writes powerfully because she sees, however momentarily, a connection among women's movements, labor movements, and the nationalism of subject-peoples. She begins,

> We shall never understand the Awakening of Women until we realise that it is not mere *feminism*. It is one of three simultaneous world-movements towards a more equal partnership among human beings in human affairs. . . . [T]he movement for woman's emancipation is paralleled, on the one hand, by the International Movement of Labour—the banding together of the manual working classes to obtain their "place in the sun"—and, on the other, by the unrest among subject-peoples struggling for freedom to develop their own peculiar civilisations. (1913: iii)*

She then identifies the dominant who oppresses all three groups as one and the same person, showing that domination is at the heart of the world system of stratification.

This piece, reproduced in the readings, is an extraordinary feminist analysis. It is also pretty much a one-time shot. Webb's essential discomfiture, we would argue, was not with the idea of herself as a woman but rather with the idea of herself as an order taker rather than an order giver—no matter how much she sought to better the lot of the classes who habitually take orders. To identify with women as a class was to admit the possibility of belonging not to the category of order giver but to the category of order taker, not to be the dominant fighting for the rights of the oppressed but to be the much riskier thing—the subordinate resisting oppression. That was perhaps the leap she could not make.

ENDNOTES

1. That friendship was strong enough that Spencer named her his literary executor—until her conversion to socialism in 1892. Even then they remained friends and she agreed to work with the man he finally named as executor. Webb's autobiography and diaries show a personal loyalty to Spencer the human being even as she is with increasing incisiveness debating and breaking with his sociological theory.
2. She reports in her autobiography that her father suggested that she might want to join him in business if she did not marry. But this is a single sentence, and it is unclear how serious the offer was. It is clear that Webb found Richard Potter's business, which involved risky speculations, to be highly stressful during the period in which she did manage it after his stroke in 1885.
3. Despite denials of having experienced sexual discrimination, Webb was troubled enough by Marshall's response that she not only reports the conversation at length in her diary but thirty-five years later in her autobiography she reproduces those diary pages and adds a footnote. The footnote reports on an obituary of Marshall written by a male professor who recalls that when he

was a graduate student Professor Marshall had taken a special interest in him and advised him to pursue the co-operative topic but not to be affected by Beatrice Potter's *The Co-operative Movement in Great Britain.*

4. Responding to this moral problem, Webb engaged at various points in "charitable work" through the Charity Organisation Society, most particularly as a manager of the Katherine Buildings. She found charitable work itself enmeshed in the vast debate overtaking Victorian society about why this was all happening. The philanthropist, whom she came to know through her charity work, was trying any variety of solutions to the problem. A first approach was to help the deserving poor; but it was discovered that the deserving were often unhelpable—being, for instance, chronically ill and broken down and demanding more resources than the charitable society could give. A second approach was to help the helpable, although it seemed often that those who might most easily get back on their feet in some way were perhaps among the least inclined to do so. A third approach was to give out aid in a scientific manner, judging each case in terms of what aid would most help this person and this class to stand on their own—though this, of course, did not solve the basic problems that the deserving need too much and the helpable often seem willing to be helped indefinitely. Further, there was the always present caution to be careful not to dispense charity indiscriminately, as that would encourage people to become dependent. Finally, there was the uneasy sense that no matter how much charity was dispersed, the actual poverty seemed to stay the same. Amidst these conflicting opinions, Webb was especially frustrated by the absence of any hard data, any real facts about what was going on. She came to admire most the women who simply did what they felt was right—such as one Emma Cons who abandoned Charity Organisation Society prescriptions and organized music hall entertainments for the poor; but Cons had little or no interest in data collection.

READING 8·1

Excerpt from "The Dock Life of East London"

This selection is excerpted from pages 483–494. Webb's earliest sociological publication shows many of the enduring traits of her sociology—the focus on manual workers and issues of poverty, a fairly traditional definition of women's roles, and an intense interest in empirical research as a means of informing the public about the complex reality behind a stereotypical and simplistic understanding of a "social problem." Webb uses historical, statistical, observational, and interview data to identify the categories of working-class groups involved in dock work.

[T]he popular imagination represents the dock labourer either as an irrecoverable ne-er-do-well, or as a down-fallen angel. It does not recognise that there are 'all sorts and conditions' here as elsewhere in the East End. . . . The economist in his study frowns sternly as he deplores the attractions of low-class labour into London. The philanthropist, fresh from the dock gate, pleads with more sensational intonation the guilt of the dock and the waterside employer in refusing to this helpless labour more inducement to remain, more possibility to live decently and multiply freely. The indifferentist alone stands by the side of the existing institution, and talks glibly of the inevitable tendency of inevitable competition in producing an inevitable irregularity of employment; failing to realise that these so-called 'inevitables' mean the gradual deterioration of the brain and sinew of fellow-countrymen. But happily the democracy has a taste for facts, and we may hope a growing sense of proportion. I venture therefore to describe the life of the East London Docks and to distinguish between and characterise the different classes of

Source: Beatrice Potter Webb, "The Dock Life of East London," *Nineteenth Century* 22 (1887), pp. 483–499.

labour. And I am enabled, through the courtesy of dock officials, to give the actual numbers of those employed, and to preface this sketch by a short notice of the circumstances which have led to the present state and methods of employment.

The three docks of East London are the London and St. Katherine, the West and East India, and the Millwall. The two former were opened at the end of last and the beginning of this century respectively, and during the first fifty years of their existence possessed the virtual monopoly of the London trade. . . . In 1868 the Millwall Dock covered the space left over by the West and East India in the Isle of Dogs. The competition of the wharves had at that time become severe, and the Millwall was started with all the newest appliances and methods of saving labour and reducing the cost of operations. . . . But even during the good times the two big companies were beginning to scrutinise their paymaster's sheets. . . .

And the fierce competition for a declining business was not the only agency at work in producing spasmodic and strained demands for labour. The substitution of steam for sailing vessels, while it distributes employment more evenly throughout the year, increases the day to day and hour to hour uncertainty. In bygone days at certain seasons of the year a fleet of sailing vessels would line the dock quay. The work was spread over weeks and months, and each succeeding day saw the same number of men employed for the same number of hours. . . . Now the scene is changed. Steamers come and go despite wind and tide. The multitudinous London shipowners show no sign of wishing to organise their business so as to give as regular employment as is practicable. . . .

Such, in briefest outline are the trade events which have helped to bring about the present state of dock employment in East London, and which are still at work effecting further transformation. The futility of the attempt to separate the labour question from the trade question is becoming every day more apparent; and unless we understand the courses of trade we shall fail to draw the correct line between the preventable and the inevitable in the deepening shadows of East End existence. For all things are in the process of becoming, and the yesterday vies with the to-day as a foreteller of the to-morrow. And I think it will add reality to a picture of life in and about the docks if the reader will follow me in a short account of . . . the classes of men employed and on the methods of employment. . . .

I herewith give the numbers of those employed by the three East London docks, classed according to regularity or irregularity of employment.

WEST AND EAST INDIA DOCKS

Outdoor staff:
    Foremen, &c. 457
    Police . . . . 114 Total 818
                                       regularly
                                       employed
    Permanent labourers 247
      Irregularly employed:
          Maximum 2,355
          Minimum . . . . 600 Average
                                 <u>1,311</u>
                                 irregularly
                                 employed
      Preferred for employment   2,129
      or 'Royals'. 700

LONDON AND ST. KATHERINE DOCKS

Outdoor staff:
    Foremen, &c. 400
    Police . . . . 100 Total 1,070
                                         regularly
                                       employed
    Artisans 150
    Permanent labourers 420
      Irregularly employed:
          Maximum 3,700
          Minimum. . . . . 1,100 Average
                                 <u>2,200</u>
                                 irregularly
                                 employed
      Preferred for employment   3,270
      or 'Royals' 450
[She also gives Millwall.]

It will be seen from the foregoing that the two big dock companies employ three classes of workers—

permanent, preference, and casual. . . . I shall attempt to describe the larger features distinguishing these social strata; and I shall try to give the more important economic, social, and moral conditions under which they are formed and exist. . . .

. . . The foreman is distinctly the official. Directly the day's work is over he hurries from a disreputable neighborhood back into the odour of respectability which permeates a middle-class suburb. There, in one of those irreproachable houses furnished with the inevitable bow window, and perchance with a garden, or at least with a back-yard, wherein to keep and ride the hobby, he leads the most estimable life. Doubtless he is surrounded by a wife and family, perhaps keeps a maid-of-all-work, and has a few selected friends. He meddles little with public business . . . , lives unto himself . . . [and obeys] the eternal formula of the individualist creed: Am I my brother's keeper? . . .

. . . The 'permanent' man of the docks . . . [w]ith a wage usually from twenty to twenty-five shillings a week and an average family, exists above the line of poverty, though in times of trouble he frequently sinks below it. . . . As a rule the permanent men do not live in the immediate neighbourhood of the docks. They are scattered far and wide in . . . outlying districts; the regularity of their wage enabling them to live in a small house rented at the same figure as one room in Central London. . . . In common with all working men with a moderate but regular income, the permanent dock labourer is made by his wife. If she be a tidy woman and a good manager, decently versed in the rare arts of cooking and sewing, the family life is independent, even comfortable, and the children may follow in the father's footsteps or rise to better things. If she be a gossip and a bungler—worse still a drunkard—the family sink to the low level of the East London street. . . .

But the foremen and permanent men are, after all, the upper ten of dock life, and our interest is naturally centered in the large mass of labour struggling for a livelihood, namely, in the irregular hands employed by the docks, warehouses, and wharves of

East London. I have not been able to collect complete statistics. . . . But from the evidence I gathered . . . [t]he average of irregular hands employed by the three dock companies stands at 3,000 . . . a large wage one week and none the next, . . . are not favourable conditions to thrift, temperance, and good management. . . . Many of the [irregular but permanent] dock labourers live in common lodging-houses of the more reputable kind. If married, they must submit to the dreariness of a one-roomed home which, even in its insufficiency, costs them from 3s. to 4s.6d., out of their scanty earning. More likely than not the wife spends her day by straining, by miserably paid work, to meet the bare necessities of existence. . . .

. . . [The husband] may stave off starvation but he cannot rise to permanent employment. . . . And apart from work, and away from the comfortless and crowded home, neither husband nor wife, nor children have any alternative or relief except the low level of monotonous excitement of the East End street.

READING 8·2

Excerpt from *The Co-operative Movement in Great Britain*

This selection is excerpted from Chapter 7, "The Ideal and the Fact," pages 205–221. This book made Webb famous in progressive circles worldwide and influenced the theories of Jane Addams (Chapter 3) and the Chicago Women (Chapter 7). It represents also, for Webb, a remarkable theoretical journey and transformation of values—from the capitalist values of her own affluent family and the tutelage in "libertarian"

Source: Beatrice Potter Webb, *The Co-operative Movement in Great Britain* (London: Swan, Sonnenschein and Company, 1891/1904).

politics by Herbert Spencer, to advocacy of collectivist and socialist solutions for improving working-class lives. Webb's description of late-nineteenth-century society driven by unfettered capitalism—characterized by job insecurity, underpaid manual workers, a deteriorating standard of living for the average citizen, growing poverty in one sector of society, disproportionate income for the few at the top of the economic ladder, shoddy consumer goods, and arbitrary pricing of goods and services—is still timely. Her socialist solution is non-Marxian and nonviolent, calling for organizations of workers and consumers; the elimination of private or corporate profit; and the public regulation of production and of the distribution of money, goods, and services. Webb uses several interesting political strategies in making her case—she bases it on research, especially research into an "experiment" already being attempted by workers, the co-operative consumer movement, and she shows that the arguments for socialism are time-honored and British, originating with Robert Owen, not Marx. Because the co-operative takes no "profit on price," it can price competitively. Her reference to the "Poor Laws" is to the system of public relief for the destitute, which was begun in the seventeenth century and was still in place in Britain in her own time, and which she would work to radically reform in the early twentieth century.

We are now in a position to estimate how far the modern Co-operative movement has realized Robert Owen's Co-operative system of industry.

The reader will remember that the keystone of Owen's New System of Society was the elimination of profit on price and the substitution of a salaried official for the profit-maker. Profit on price he regarded as the forbidden fruit of industry—as the potent poison exciting the economic man to fraudulent devices and selfish monopoly—in short, as the origin of industrial warfare. And he imagined that profit-making as a method of adjusting supply to demand might be superseded by a scientific ascertainment of the needs of the workers.

Now with regard to the first point—the elimination of profit on price—the democratic form of Co-operation has been entirely successful. The absorption of profit by the community has had a twofold effect. The actual seller of an article within the Co-operative system has no personal interest in defrauding the customer. The devices of the credit and tally system, the dodges and deceptions of leading articles and second prices of adulterated or fraudulent goods together with the more modern and statesmanlike policy of great trusts and capitalist combinations, boldly dictating prices—all these monstrous or pigmy forms of industrial tyranny have been effectually checkmated within the area of its influence by the democratic form of Co-operation.

This is the immediate and direct result of eliminating profit on price. But the ultimate effect on the organization of industry of selling at cost price is of greater importance. It is the unique, and I say advisedly, the glorious achievement of the democratic form of Co-operation, that through extinguishing profit as well as eliminating the profitmaker, it destroys the occasion—it roots up and extirpates the very foundations—of the art of wealth-gaining apart from rendering services to the community. For if all industry were organized according to the democratic form of Co-operation, gambling in shares—all such operations as "Bearing," "Bulling," and cornering the market would be relegated to the work of an economic antiquarian. The Stock Exchange would come to be superseded by a mutual Banking Department. . . .

In the open democracy of the Store and the dependent federal institutions all surplus over and above cost of production, together with the "unearned increment" of superior sites or trade fluctuations, is shared with all those who choose to enter, even at the eleventh hour, or else is accumulated in the form of extra depreciations of land and buildings, and heavy reserve funds for the use of future generations of citizens. . . .

. . . In short, the whole body of consumers refuse a tribute to a minority of capitalists in excess of the market rate.

It is, however, a more difficult and delicate question whether the democratic form of Co-operation has effectually and finally demonstrated that individual profit-making is an unnecessary method of adjusting supply to demand. . . . Thus, at the quarterly meetings of the Wholesale Society, and at conferences of buyers held in different parts of the country, the directors and officials of the federal institution undergo the wholesome ordeal of listening to the criticism of expert customers—to the opinions of men whose profession in life is to ascertain the wants, and to supply the needs of individual consumers; while the buyers and directors of the central institutions have ample opportunity of instructing the consumer's representatives as to the real value of articles apart from their competitive price, together with the conditions of employment needful in the production of cheap commodities. At monthly and quarterly meetings of the members of the individual Stores, their officers and delegates are forced to submit in their turn to detailed complaints as to the fit of a Leicester boot, the flavour of a packet of tea, and the colour of a slice of bacon. The members require a satisfactory explanation or insist on a prompt remedy. Without doubt this close and constant tie between the *entrepreneur* and the customer accounts for the unmistakable rise in the standard of taste, for the knowledge of real value, and consequently for the stability of demand that is a characteristic of consumption in Co-operative districts. Here we perceive a near approach to a scientific ascertainment of the wants of the community.

But I freely admit that so long as the Co-operative movement forms a "State within a State," and the Co-operative system is surrounded by an individualist and competitive society, it is impossible to assert dogmatically that democratic control would be an effective alternative to individual profit-making in lowering the price and improving the quality of commodities. At the present time the officials of Stores are stimulated by the efforts of the shopkeepers to underbid them. The Wholesale Societies live in wholesome fear of the private trader and manufacturer. Moreover, the members of the Store, the delegate to the Wholesale Society, can clinch his complaints of inefficient management by tangible proof in the form of an article of better quality or lower price bought in the open market. Whether efficiency of administration would survive a monopoly of custom by associations of consumers, is a matter upon which none of us can dogmatize. I venture, however, to offer a few suggestions towards the solution of this all-important question.

First, let me remind the reader that competition between individuals and communities is not necessarily connected with profit-making. Public officers, from ambassadors to village schoolmasters, are chosen among many competitors. . . .

. . . [And] we can imagine many instances of effective competition without profit-making. The municipalities of Leicester and Northampton might both undertake to provide gas, water, education, and amusement to their inhabitants. If the affairs of Leicester were better administered, it would be quickly apparent to the citizens of both towns, and would lead to dissatisfaction among the citizens of Northampton, and consequent immigration to the more favoured town. . . . Emulation among localities would, in these instances, supersede competition among individual traders. In fact, if each municipality provided its citizens with all the necessaries of life at cost price, the law of "the survival of the fittest" would tell with extended force on human intelligence and character. For the efficient service of the community would not, in that case, depend on the chance appearance of a Harrod or a Whitely in one municipality rather than another, but on the general capacity of all citizens for democratic self-government. . . .

. . . In associations of consumers all those who are interested possess, if they choose to use it, complete material for a sound judgment as to the relative excellence of services rendered by individual producers and professionals. The members can estimate the expenditure of faculty as well as the satisfaction of desire; they can compare social cost with social value. Hence emulation among officials to secure the confidence and goodwill of their constituents replaces profit-seeking. . . . Granted, therefore, that the whole commerce and industry of the country were to be undertaken by the community in the form of stores, municipalities, counties, or states, whatever other difficulties we might encounter, competition between individuals would still be an effectual method in the selection of officers, and a potent stimulus to ability and industry in the service of the community by various classes of producers.

We may therefore say that the cardinal principle of Robert Owen's New System of Society, *the elimination of profit on price,* has been realized in the modern Co-Operative movement. But the reader will remember that . . . Robert Owen . . . objected equally to competition between individuals for employment as a method of determining *the price* at which they should work. To quote the words of the first chapter: "He held that labour (which included all forms of human effort) should be rewarded according to its needs; that is, according to the expenditure required to keep it in a full state of efficiency, providing, at the same time by education, in its widest sense, for the progressive improvement of the physique, intellect and character of the individual and the race; and including an allowance for the risk of illness or incapacity, and for the decrepitude of old age."

Now in the great competitive and commercial system of to-day we note two facts utterly at variance with Robert Owen's view of a proper method of remunerating human effort. In the first place, brain-workers extract from the community incomes altogether out of proportion to their needs; secondly, whole classes of manual workers are reduced to bare subsistence—to a standard of life degrading to their faculties as wealth-producers, citizens and parents.

The democratic form of Co-operation has obviated the first evil. For a multitude of competing self-seekers, each intent on amassing a great fortune, or adding to a little heap, we see a complete civil service of industry—an army of officials with fixed salaries ranging from the £2 a week of the village storekeeper to the £400 a year of heads of departments handling goods to the tune of a few millions. These salaries, we are told by merchant princes and great financiers, are quite inadequate to attract that calibre of brain which secures sound financial operations. . . . The rising tide of Co-operative enterprise, the steady progress of the Store system with its federal institutions, adding year by year to the multiplicity of their operations in industry and commerce, are a sufficient answer to this biassed or theoretical view of human motive. The goodwill of a great community, the political power and social influence equitably earned by the able and energetic official of a powerful and growing organization have proved as efficient a form of remuneration as the unknown gains and lawless expenditure of the capitalist *entrepreneur,* or the exorbitant salaries given by middle-class shareholders to middle-class officials, consequent on an extravagant estimate of the conventional outlay due to social position. . . .

But while it has been easy for Co-operators to extinguish the profit of the middleman, it has been impossible for the Co-operative employer struggling in the midst of a competitive system to raise the wages of the manual workers to the level of effective citizenship. It is in this endeavour that Co-operators need the constant, and, I fear sometimes unwelcomed assistance of Trade Unions.

For no organization, except a Trade Union, or as the French more aptly term it—*an association of professionals,* possesses at once the technical knowledge and experience to determine and the power to secure a standard of technical education and scale of living for all its members. A Trade Union offers to the community a rough and ready estimate of the expenditure needful to a certain class of faculty; it ensures through a standard wage that the endurance and capacity of one individual will not lower the remuneration of all to a level at which efficiency in that particular industry is impossible to the average man. . . .

Once again, therefore, by a conjunction of Co-operative and trade union organization, we must bring the producer and consumer face to face. I do not mean that the bootmaker can sell his boots to the weaver, while the weaver disposes of his cloth to the farmer's wife; this personal relationship is not longer possible in a commercial system transformed by the industrial revolution. Barter between

individuals must be superseded by negotiations, through authorized representatives, between groups of workers and consumers. Individualist exchange must follow individualist production, and give place to collective bargaining.

To gain a clear conception of the collective bargain—of the social relation which will supersede the individual relation—let us imagine, therefore, that this industrial democracy were fully developed and that industry were organized by associations of consumers (whether voluntary or compulsory, the Store, the Wholesale Societies, the municipality and the State), while all workers were united in Trade Unions. Then the official of the weavers' Union would debate questions of wages and technical training with the official of the Store of the municipality; the college of surgeons or physicians would, as at present, determine the standard and subjects of examination for the medical student and fix fees for medical attendance, subject perhaps to the democratic control of a Minister of Health.[1] The official of a Trade Union and the official of the community would, it is true, represent the rival interests of different sections of the community. But as members of one State the interests of their constituents are ultimately identical. For under a democratic organisation of industry it will be recognised that the well-being of each individual will be indissolubly bound up in a high standard of capacity among the whole body of citizens.

Nor is it difficult to discover the practical basis for a compromise between the immediately conflicting interests of the consumer and producer of special commodities or services, supposing that these different groups of citizens should persistently refuse to

---

[1] It is noteworthy that this determination by a Trade Union or Association of Professionals of the price at which they will work, or the educational qualifications upon which they will insist, is not demurred to by the capitalist class in professions such as the Law and Medicine, of which they have practically the monopoly. But the limited and broken authority of working-class Unions, the attempt on their part to secure a full subsistence wage for their members, is bitterly resented as an interference with individual liberty.

recognize the "larger expediency" of efficient citizenship among all classes of the community. . . .

Thus if the National Union of Boot and Shoemakers were to raise wages above the point of efficient citizenship the Wholesale Society or municipality would import boots and shoes and manufacture other articles instead; or if the gas stokers proved unreasonable, we might prefer petroleum or electric light rather than submit to their dictation. Barristers and medical men might even be brought to modest terms by free justice and municipal dispensaries. For if the issues between the producer and consumer of commodities or services were uncomplicated by the unknown profits and losses of individual capitalists and brain-workers, public opinion would be a final and irresistible court of appeal. For while the community would possess all the materials for a judgment, they would also have an absolute power to enforce it. . . . In a democratic organization of industry—such as we are, for the purposes of our argument, assuming to exist—all men alike would be in one capacity or another, servants of the community. . . . And if one special group of workers were singled out for oppression, it hardly needs even the intelligence of the *a priori* economist to perceive that the recruits to that profession or industry would not be very numerous. If the services of this class were of use to the community, the terms would have to be raised. . . .

Again, it is objected that this form of industrial organization, with its standard rates of wages and prices, is applicable only to the well-disciplined and efficient workers of the industrial army. In other words that the organization of industry for the benefit of the community will leave no place for those who, for one reason or another, can render no efficient service to the community. . . . Is it necessary to remark that the unfit, the men and women who have fallen from the ranks, are dealt with in the end, under the present system, by a Poor Law; and that under any conceivable industrial system these unfortunates could only be *effectually* dealt with (unless we permitted them to die on the streets) under a reformed Poor Law? . . .

But the social value of this form of society would not consist solely or even principally in a more equitable diffusion of the necessaries and comforts of life. If this were all, it would be a poor result for generations of human effort; a goal unworthy of the disciples of Robert Owen. For Co-operators have always been inspired by the ancient doctrine of human fellowship, by the new spirit of social service, by a firm faith that the day would come when each man and woman would work, not for personal subsistence or personal gain, but for the whole community. This service of the community by the citizens—this free ministering of all by all—constitutes the moral ideal of the British Co-operative movement, and one of which most assuredly Co-operators have no reason to stand ashamed. An organization of society in which the community—not any profit-making individual—would always be the employer—an organization of labour whereby the immediate and ultimate welfare of the workers would be guarded by a representative personally uninterested in the question of wages and intent on a general high standard of effort and enjoyment in the class he represents—this fully-developed industrial democracy alone provides, in a complete form, the economic basis for the future religion of humanity.

READING 8-3

Excerpt from "Introduction to 'The Awakening of Women'"

Webb's introduction to this issue on "the woman question"—which contained papers by many feminists, including Charlotte Perkins Gilman, referred to in Webb's statement—is a theoretically rich analysis of the

Source: Beatrice Potter Webb, "Introduction to 'The Awakening of Women,'" *A Special Supplement to the New Statesman* 1 November (1913), pp. iii–iv.

multiple oppressive practices of North Atlantic, propertied-class, white men towards women, the working class, people of color, and subjugated societies; and of the growing, multi-dimensional resistance to that oppression. The explicit and feminist line of argument used in this statement makes it, as we have discussed in this chapter, atypical, as Webb usually prefers a class analysis of society and is ambivalent about gender issues.

We shall never understand the Awakening of Women until we realise that it is not mere *feminism*. It is one of three simultaneous world-movements towards a more equal partnership among human beings in human affairs. To future historical philosophers we may leave the analysis of how far these three simultaneous movements all over the world are parts of one another. For the moment it is enough to note that the movement for woman's emancipation is paralleled, on the one hand, by the International Movement of Labour—the banding together of the manual working class to obtain their "place in the sun"—and, on the other by the unrest among subject-peoples struggling for freedom to develop their own peculiar civilisations. And all three movements are progressing towards achievement. Within the great streams there are, in each case, cross-currents of method and immediate aim, oft-times appearing in mutual opposition, but swinging eventually in the same general direction. Carefully conceived and persistently pressed schemes of reform are crossed by heroic outbursts of impatient revolt. Both serve, as the subsequent historian narrates, the same general end—the transformation of the ideas, customs and laws accepted by the bulk of apathetic and preoccupied humans. Naturally, there are, in all three streams, all sorts of obstacle-raisers—reactionaries of sex, class, or race—who assert, with every degree of candour and conviction, that the oppressed are unqualified for freedom, that those who have been denied participation in the good things of this life are not really injured by their deprivation, and that it is fundamentally out of kindness and humanity that the strong have been taking care of the weak!

It is interesting to trace this parallelism of the three movements in the lively pamphlet just published by the frankest, and I am inclined to think the most honest, of these reactionaries. The testimony is all the more convincing in that it is seemingly unself-conscious. Probably Sir Almroth Wright has even now not realised that in almost every page of his *Unexpurgated Case Against Women Suffrage* his naive insolence towards women is interspersed with an insolence as naive and uninformed toward the whole manual-working, wage-earning class, and towards every race in the wide world that differs in colour from himself. There is a certain simple charm in the way that this male white property-owner sums up all three prejudices. He denounces, as "unworthy of a virile and Imperial race," the very notion of holding the scales of justice even—the very ideal that "in the distribution of wealth or political power, or *any other privileges which it is in the power of the State to bestow,* every man should share equally with every other man and every woman with every other woman, and that in countries where Europeans and natives live side by side these latter share all privileges with the white" (p. 11). Sir Almroth Wright cannot, indeed, always be explicitly classing together in one and the same sentence the subject-class, the subject-race, and the subject-sex. But we may trace the idea right through his argument. In the following passage I have inserted only the words necessary to show how easy it is to use all the arguments in favour of the dominance of the male sex as reasons for a similar dominance of a class of property owners or a white race:

"The failure to recognise that man [the capitalist, the white man] is the master and why he is the master lies at the root of the suffrage [labour, nationalist] movement. By disregarding man's [the capitalist's, the white man's] superior physical force, the power of compulsion upon which all government is based is disregarded. By leaving out of account those powers of the mind in which man [the capitalist, the white man] is the superior, woman [the labourer, the coloured man] falls into the error of thinking that she [he] can really compete with him [them] and that she [he] belongs to the self-same intellectual caste. Finally, by putting out of sight man's [the capitalist's, the white man's] superior money-earning capacity the power of the purse is ignored" (p. 71).

This acceptance of an amalgam of physical force and the power of the purse as the right foundation for social organisation is characteristic of the baser types of Imperialism and Commercialism, as it is also of the "disorderly house." In short, we have here merely an outburst of the insolence of conscious power, and the curious identification, which is sometimes the outcome of a cultivation limited to physical science, of that which is with that which ought to be.

Those reactionaries who, like Sir Almroth Wright, thus argue in a circle—deducing from the very effects of subjection on the subject sex, class, or race a justification for continued subjection—may perhaps not realise how effectively they are making out their opponents' case. To those who find themselves handicapped in the struggle, whether by disadvantages of sex, class, or race, . . . Mrs. Gilman's article . . . will help to convince them that what they are suffering from is really an artificially intensified arrest of development, which the reactionary male (or the reactionary white man or the reactionary capitalist, as the case may be) tries, consciously or unconsciously, to perpetuate. For this hypothesis of an artificial arrest of development there is only too much evidence. . . . There are doubtless Indian physicians who argue that the smaller stature, enfeebled frame, and undeveloped intelligence of the secluded Indian woman unfit her to emerge from the zenana; that it would be dangerous for the girl to remain unmarried until she is an adult; that it would be unbecoming and contrary to "immemorial" ethics for her to appear unveiled before even the majority of men in her own family. The Indian physician . . . might even believe that the emerging of the woman from the zenana would trouble men's feeling to such an extent as to make social

life impracticable. Much the same arguments have been used about the emerging of the manual working class from their subjection. Scarcely a century ago a reactionary House of Commons applauded the contemporary Wyndham when he pleaded against the education of the wage-earners, in favour of retaining the immemorially sanctioned orgies of bull-baiting and cock-fighting, on the ground that the less sensual and ignorant labourers became the more there would be of "sedition." One notices the same ring of nervous self-assertiveness among the more reactionary members of the Indian Civil Service, who will tell you in the same breath that the Bengalees are incapable of running their own local administration, and that if we make the mistake of training them in administration, the English officials will be got rid of. None of these obstacle-raisers produces any argument against the hypothesis that it would be of advantage to the world if we ceased to arrest the development, or that, with that cessation, the human beings concerned would fail to grow.

. . . We do not adequately realise how much of the work of the world is now performed by women. For good or for evil, the capitalist system has forced millions of women out of a position of economic dependence on husband or father into the position of independent wage-earners, often responsible for the livelihood not of themselves alone, but also of family dependents. The tragedy of the situation is that, whilst we have forced these millions of women to walk along the wage-earning road, we have not unbound their feet! By continuing to brand the woman as the social inferior of the man, unworthy of any share in the direction of the country, upon the economic development of which we have made her directly dependent; by providing for her much less technical training and higher education than for the boy; by telling her that she has slighter faculties and smaller needs, and that nothing but toil of routine character is expected from her; by barring her out, . . . from the more remunerative occupations—perhaps in order to make her acquiesce in what Sir Almroth Wright calls "women's intrinsically inferior money-making capacity"—man has made woman not merely into a wage-earner, but, taken as a whole, in the world of labour, unfortunately, also into a "blackleg," insidiously undermining the wages of man himself.

On the other hand, where positions involving brain-work and responsibility have been thrown open to women—where they have been welcomed as honourable colleagues on equal terms—they have shown how much they can respond to the stimulus, even whilst still handicapped by the fetters of custom and by a professional training in many ways imperfect. In medicine and in public administration, . . . in the great profession of teaching, in literature and in scientific research, the comparatively few women who have had equal opportunities with men have more than justified their admission to that competition in public service which freedom secures. It is interesting to notice that in all these professions the women, taken as a whole, have distinguished themselves for those qualities of sterling public worth which their new detractors would deny them—for unwearied persistent industry, for sane and measured judgment, for accuracy and insight, and (to the mere man perhaps most incredible of all) for a sense of honour and *esprit de corps* equalling, if not excelling, that of their male colleagues.

Some critics may object that the sobriety and quiet industry for which women in the brain-working professions have been distinguished have been more than offset of recent years by the activities of the "militant" demands of Woman Suffrage. Taken as a whole, it is interesting to note that the Woman's Movement all over the world, in comparison with the other two strivings after freedom, the Labour Movement and the Nationalist Movement, has been singularly free from "militancy."

For the last three-quarters of a century women have been steadily making their way, in all parts of the world, to economic, social and political emancipation, and with remarkable success. In one country after another they have gained access, often in face of the strongest opposition, to higher education, to the medical profession, to local government, to various branches of the public service, even to the franchise; whilst in the North, in the South, and in the West—in Scandinavia, Australia, Western America—they have attained full and free citizenship. This progress has been achieved without "insurrectionism" or appeal to physical force. In the United Kingdom alone within the last few years do we find an attempt to force open the door otherwise than by persuasion. And even among those who nowadays are proud to call themselves "militants" there has been throughout a singular tenderness towards human life or the giving of pain—always excepting the voluntarily sacrificed life and comfort of the "militants" themselves. . . . We object to insurrectionism and violence because we think the appeal to physical force is just as lowering and inconclusive when made by women as it is when made by men. We know that outbreaks of disorder degrade public manners, for which we all still share the responsibility, just as we all find our lives conditioned by them, women as well as men. . . . We realise, indeed, that it is one of the sorrowful reactions of the world that the denial of justice always evokes, somewhere and at some point, a wild exasperation in the oppressed. We are not called upon to condemn an exasperation which, equally with the injustice, we deplore. We condemn rather those in positions of power who themselves appeal to a physical force domination as the only possible basis of efficient governmental and social life.

Epilogue—Tests of Significance

We need to learn how to treat what . . . women say as a source and basis for our own work and thinking . . . as the authoritative speakers of our experience and concerns.
—Dorothy E. Smith

"**S**o what?" remains the most demanding question in scholarship, whether one asks it of oneself or is asked it by others. The question came to us early, after we had presented on Jane Addams; a thoughtful male discussant described various themes in contemporary sociology which he saw her work "anticipating," and then posed his key questions: "What you must address, both for yourselves and others, is what difference Jane Addams's sociology might make to us today? How might it change what we do?"[1] This epilogue is a response to those questions, generalized to all the women discussed in this book: *what significance does the recovery of the women founders have for contemporary sociology?* We give two answers: one about the significance of a change in the discipline's understanding of its history; the other about the significance of the women's theories—for despite much variation, they share important common themes. Our discussion begins with the issue of a reconfigured understanding of sociology's past, and moves, in stages, to the issue of the significance of the women's theories for us today.

The initial significance of our research for us was that it satisfied our intellectual curiosity—a curiosity that was neither disembodied, disinterested, nor uniquely ours. As feminists we began with feminism's basic and radical question—*and what about the women?* As sociologists with an interest in the history of the discipline, we knew from the pioneering work of Mary Jo Deegan and many other feminist researchers that there had been early women sociologists. As feminist sociologists with a particular interest in social theory, we wanted to know not only that these women had lived *but what they had thought.* But our curiosity was permeated by what Dorothy E. Smith (1979, 1987) calls "bifurcated consciousness," an occupational hazard for women trained as we have been: on the one hand, we wished to know what the women thought, we thought what women thought mattered; on the other hand, our own thinking was circumscribed by our training in American sociology. An archeological metaphor may describe our changing consciousness as the research proceeded. We began by expecting to find a few interesting, unique, female temples in "the Valley of the Kings"—for we had been well socialized in the American sense of sociology's canon which was and is a masculinist interpretation. We found instead a vast lost world of female scholarship in social theory, sociology, and social science, a discovery that forced us to reconfigure, in stages, what we thought we had known: our understandings of the importance of the history of sociology for the contemporary practice of sociology: the form and voice in which one can do theory; the ways the lens of gender shapes social theory; the possibilities of feminist scholarship and practice; and the future of sociology in the present period which Charles Lemert (1995) names "after the crisis."

Further, our initial reading of the women founders was shaped by an anachronistic expectation that we might encounter a female Durkheim or a nineteenth-century Dorothy Smith; that we would find "anticipations" of the theories we know today. We had to learn to read the women as themselves, to understand that they were participants in the *creation* of sociology and, thus, free from the conventions of thinking that bind us today to particular ways of doing sociology and writing social theory. They were designing their own ways, producing a sociology and a social theory done "in a different voice." Our initial judgment of the women founders as "anticipating" later developments in sociology is not wrong, but it is shallow, and in its shallowness it distorts the significance of their achievement. For its effect is to suggest that somehow the original statements of the women founders are more schematic, less encompassing of social reality than what follows, important only because of what comes later. We now think the women founders are better understood not as "anticipations" but as the beginnings of a tradition which if not timeless, is certainly not ephemeral. The social theory of the women founders reaffirms the claim for a tradition of a critical and feminist sociology.

Discovering this tradition is especially significant for women sociologists seeking to do feminist work. For discovering the women founders of sociology is part of the larger project of women's history: "to restore women to history and to restore our history to women" (Kelly-Gadol, 1976/1983:11). This is not a small ambition, for history may be a source of vicarious courage; when we find ourselves—that is, people like us—in history, we may also find courage to try to do the things they did, the things we already aspire to do. Feminist writer Tillie Olsen has described the particular courage it takes to be a writer, to craft a more or less permanent statement of one's thoughts and share those thoughts with a public: "How much it takes to become a writer. Bent (far more common than we assume), circumstances, time, development of craft—but beyond that: how much conviction as to the importance of what one has to say, one's right to say it. . . . Difficult for any male not born into a class that breeds such confidence. Almost impossible for a girl, a woman" (1972:8). Recovering the early women creators of sociological theory may give a source of conviction and confidence to women sociologists and women students today seeking to speak theoretically and authoritatively on any issue of social import. For the women founders did not limit their sociology to the exploration of "gender as a variable." Rather they began from the fact of themselves as women and then proceeded to do analysis from that standpoint, with the conviction that that standpoint mattered. As Anna Julia Cooper said of the Black Woman: "[G]reat social and economic questions await her interference, . . . problems of national import, . . . the management of school systems, . . . the tone of public institutions, . . . the far reaching influence of prisons and reformatories . . . the treatment of lunatics and imbeciles,—. . . mooted questions in political economy, . . . the relations of labor and capital" (1892: 134–135, 138). The women founders asserted that women had views about everything, that those views could not be subsumed under men's, that their gender—a term they did not have—was a lens through which they inescapably viewed the social world and created social theory.

Their understanding that they did social analysis from a woman's standpoint led the women to some shared and distinctive theoretical practices—an unwillingness to make universal claims about human behavior, a preference for societally specific analysis, and a sensitivity to the effects of gender, class, race, ethnicity, and age in any situation being discussed. This is true of Martineau's analysis of morals and manners in historically specific cultures; of Addams's focus on the varying effects of age, ethnicity, gender, and class for individuals' adjustments to the complexities of industrial capitalism in America; of Cooper's contrast of white and black feminisms; of Wells-Barnett's use of a matrix of gender, race, and region in analyzing sexuality; of Gilman's critique of the differences in women's and men's experience of productive human work; of Weber's analysis of class variations in women's experience of work; of the Chicago Women's School's advocacy on behalf of specific disempowered constituencies in U.S. society; and of Webb's nuanced understanding of economic variations in working-class lives.

The women founders' use of gender leads us to see that the male founders, though unconscious of the fact, also see through the lens of gender—a phenomenon in social theory explored by other feminist sociologists (e.g. Bologh, 1990; Kandal, 1988; Lehmann, 1995; Sydie, 1987). Thus, Mead's analysis of the self is really an analysis of the development of the self from the masculine point of view—as is Weber's analysis of authority. An interesting gender contrast is Max Weber's use of the word *"herrschaft,"* translated by Parsons and others as "authority," a word that carries with it in German the sense of "an expectation that one's words will be obeyed"; Marianne instead chooses the word *"autöritat"* which has as its meaning that "one must comply." In this contrasting vocabulary we see encapsulated the truth that all sociological theory is created through a lens of gender (and of class, race, and culture).

Collectively, the women founders produced a social theory and a sociology characterized by a distinctive or different voice from that typical of the texts in sociology's canon. While the phrase "different voice" is associated with Carol Gilligan's work on gender differences in ethical decision-making (1983); we use it here, for our own purposes, to describe the relation the social theorist establishes among self, audience, and subject matter. The chief characteristics of the women's voice, as contrasted with that of the male founders, are that it is embodied rather than generalized, engaged rather than abstracted, specific rather than universal, accessible rather than arcane. The woman founder typically presents herself as a woman and usually as a woman of a particular class and ethnicity. She is aware that these facts about herself influence her perception of events. She explains the position from which she addresses her readers, establishing the basis in lived experience of her knowledge. She further presents herself as concerned with ethical standards of "right conduct," "fairness," and "equity." She is interested in these in the society she studies and as part of her own understanding of the role of sociologist. The morality she invokes has as a basis the idea that humans have some right to happiness and that social structures should be examined in terms of whether they promote that right. The women founders write with a desire to communicate with an audience larger than that of professional sociology, and they experiment with presenting sociological ideas in many forms—in travel books, magazine columns, novels, poetry, and editorials, as well as the formal treatise. In pursuit of accessibility, they mix abstract ideas with a rich imagery of everyday life and an underlying sense of humor. Examples of this mix abound in the readings sections of the preceding chapters.

Rediscovering the women founders can sensitize contemporary sociologists to the range of "voices" and genres in which social theory may be expressed. This awareness takes us back to the past with new questions and quests, but it is equally significant to our orientation to contemporary theory. The women founders strengthen sociology's claim to a tradition, hitherto associated almost exclusively with Marx, engaged with the project of constructing a critical sociology. They also give a distinctive patterning to the project of critique—one is not only morally opposed to social inequality and to socially produced human pain; one is also morally committed to the realization of human joy. Martineau, for instance, treats as key indicators of a society's well-being its patterned arrangements of recreation, domesticity, and leisure; Addams argues that society in her own day has mistakenly focused only on organizing production while neglecting the issue of promoting pleasure; Gilman sees human joy as experienced through meaningful work in community, a potential subverted by faulty social arrangements of gender and class stratification; Cooper's critique of gender and race oppressions is fuelled by the recognition that "[a] bird cannot warble out his . . . most joyous notes while the wires of his cage are pricking and cramping him at every heart beat" (1892:223); Kelley in her study of ethical gains made through legislation focuses on leisure as an imperative human right.

The inclusion of the women founders within the canon of sociology's history expands the possibilities for sociology's future, giving us exemplars of what Lemert (1995) has called "extramural sociologists," that is, social theorists outside the academic professional code. Accepting this practice and possibility in our history makes it possible and practicable for our present sociological and theoretical community "to relinquish its rigid adherence to the traditional disciplinary standards" and reach out to contemporary extramural theorists—people such as Trinh T. Minh-ha, Henry Louis Gates, Toni Morrison, Mary Daly, Spike Lee, Gloria Anzaldùa—who are "writing the sociologies of our time" (Lemert, 1995:208–209). What the "extramural" social theorists, both past and present, most have in common is an ability to convey that they are actively engaged with problems that matter to people in their immediate everyday lives. What the women founders empower us to ask is whether we as sociologists, if judged, for instance, by any current issue of a major professional journal, are doing this. In a study entitled "The Main Drift of Sociology between 1936 and 1984," Patricia Wilner (1985) argues that sociology moved steadily away from an engagement with what she identified as "the momentous events" of that time period—the Great Depression, McCarthyism, social movements between the late 1950s and early 1970s, and "the decline of the U.S. national economy and global hegemony." Looking for articles in the *American Sociological Review* that were "directly relevant" to these events, Wilner found for the total period 130 articles out of 2,559, or 5.1 percent, that focused on these major events. And the trend that Wilner documents has continued in professional publications. It is the trend that Lemert despaired of in 1995, the trend that leads him to turn to the "extramural sociologists." Including the women founders in our canon of classic texts may help us all to take stock of the disassociation between "professional" sociological activity and issues of pressing public concern.

Finally, the rediscovery of the women founders presents sociological theorists with a specific test of their claims to inclusivity. To make good on these claims, sociologists, as writers and teachers, would have to move to incorporate the ideas of the women founders into their presentations of the classic texts. This is at one level a practical challenge. We have been asked many times in this project, "How can we add anything more to our syllabi, our readings, our expectations about the number of texts a student can afford to buy? Which currently 'canonized' texts will we have to delete if our canon is, practicably, to be inclusive of the women founders?" Our response to these questions is that they pose a false dilemma, perhaps because they operate out of the flawed logic that to add something means giving something else up, rather than expanding and enriching people's range of choices. For while courses are restricted by the time limits of the academic calendar, curricula choices and requirements are very malleable—as anyone knows who has taught sociology through the last decades of expanding computer technology, statistical sophistication, paradigmic multiplication, and the emergence of new subspecialties like the sociologies of gender, of sexuality, and of various ethnicities. Courses can be added, requirements altered, program choices offered. If the topic is considered significant these changes can be made—they have been. So one comes to a more fundamental issue—is the *will* to be inclusive really there? Can the sociological community grant authority to women's voices, to feminist theories, and by extension, to the voices and understandings of all those "Others" who work as sociologists and social theorists on the margins of a discourse dominated by white, male, heterosexual, privileged-class, North Atlantic understandings? This is an issue currently being debated in the profession with utmost seriousness (see, for example, Alway, 1995; Bhavnani, 1996; Collins, 1996; Ingraham, 1996; Lemert, 1995; McCarthy, 1996; Smith, 1996; Stacey and Thorne, 1996). The women founders of sociology present an immediate and pressing instance of the need for strategies of inclusion on terms of equal authority.

Six criteria for assessing the degree to which such full and empowered inclusion has occurred are offered by Arthur Stinchcombe in a 1982 article entitled "Should Sociologists Forget Their Mothers and Fathers?"—which regrettably discusses only sociology's "fathers." Stinchcombe describes six uses of classic theory texts: "(1) as a "touchstone" offering "a beautiful and possible way of doing one's scientific work"; (2) in "developmental tasks" teaching students to make hitherto unrecognized theoretical connections; (3) as "small coinage" to indicate through citation the intellectual tradition in which one is working; (4) as a discussion of "fundamental ideas" addressing a basic principle "the great minds of the past have addressed"; (5) in "routine science" as a source of testable hypotheses; and (6) in the "ritual function" of providing a common history.

Using these criteria, we can measure the degree to which any of the women founders begin to serve as classics in the sociological canon. They will have "touchstone" status when, either individually or collectively, they are used as paradigms that frame our thinking: when, for example, we find "beautiful and possible" Martineau's balance between a stoic pursuit of empirical indicators and a passionate and critical concern with social injustice; or Addams's broad vision of an ethical *and* productive industrial society; or the women founders' combined and nuanced tradition of woman-centered theorizing. They will serve the developmental task of training in complex thinking when, for instance, sociologists begin to confront Gilman's analysis that women's oppression is a cause of alienation under capitalism, not a consequence of it; or when sociologists trace the interaction of hate and love, race and gender, that is Wells-Barnett's understanding of American race relations. The women founders will be paid intellectual small coinage when—again illustratively—Cooper becomes as routine a citation as Collins in referring to the tradition of black feminist theory, or when Edith Abbott, Breckinridge, and Talbot are remembered by citation in empirical studies of women's economic, political, and educational status. They will be treated as a source of fundamental ideas when Marianne Weber's views of power and authority are included along with Max's, as a distinct and foundational theoretical position, or when Addams's claim about the human being's quest to give and receive kindness is incorporated into sociological discussions of the individual in society. They will provide us with routine hypotheses for research whenever we pause to take any of them seriously, for a commitment to empirical investigation is as essential to their social theory as is their understanding of the significance of the lens of gender. Examples of such hypotheses include Martineau's thesis that a society's treatment of its disabled, pauperized, or deviant members is a sure measure of its overall practices of, and ethical commitments to, social liberty; Gilman's claim that the "false concepts" of capitalist theories of economic motivation misdirect people's collective potential for productive work; Cooper's argument that manners have a functional role in the management of social conflict; or Webb's empirical demonstration that ordinary people in the modern world order have repeatedly invented effective collectivist and cooperative associations. Finally, they will become part of our rituals of community when the facts and legends of their lives become part of the stories we all tell ourselves and our students about sociology—when we imagine Gilman (as well as Max Weber) sitting in nervous exhaustion staring at the wallpaper; when Addams's choice of a social science career is recalled, as she recalls it, as a moment of moral clarity when she stared down from the top of a London omnibus on the outstretched hands of the London poor; when the Chicago Women's practice of sociology as advocacy is linked to the drama of Kelley and Lathrop shaming the Chicago health authorities and risking their lives during a smallpox epidemic, as they entered infected tenements to bring relief to the inmates and to remove infected sweatshop garments; and when Wells-Barnett's sociological exposé of lynching is associated with her pistol-carrying field trips to the scenes of white terrorism and her oft-stated resolve, "I felt that one had better die fighting against an injustice than to die like a dog or a rat in a trap. I had already determined to sell my life as dearly as possible if attacked. I felt if I could take one lyncher with me, this would even up the score a little bit" (Wells-Barnett, 1970:62).

But the most basic test of significance—the ultimate response to the "so-what test"—is that we are not made complacent by adding these women as a new bevy of icons in sociology's story of itself. Instead, their recovery requires that we go on to answer the question, "Who else is there waiting to be discovered?" What other women and men, of what race, class, age, or nationality, had something important to say about sociology and social theory—and still await our discovery to speak once more, adding to sociology's multiple meanings?

REFERENCES

1. We are indebted to Professor James Ennis for his thoughtful and probing response to our paper at the 1996 Eastern Sociological Association Meetings in Boston. His questions stayed with us throughout our work.

References

Abbott, Edith
  1908 "A Study of the Early History of Child Labor in America." *American Journal of Sociology* 14, pp. 15–37.
  1910 *Women in Industry: A Study of American Economic History.* New York: Appleton.
  1915 "Are Women a Force in Good Government? An Analysis of the Returns in the Recent Municipal Election in Chicago." *National Municipal Review* 4, pp. 437–443.

Abbott, Edith, and Sophonisba Breckinridge
  1906 "Employment of Women in Industries: Twelfth Census Statistics." *Journal of Political Economy* 14, pp. 14–40.
  1910 "Chicago's Housing Problems: Families in Furnished Rooms." *American Journal of Sociology* 16, pp. 289–308.

Abbott, Grace
  1908 "The Chicago Employment Agency and the Immigrant Worker." *American Journal of Sociology* 14, pp. 289–305.
  1941/1966 *From Relief to Social Security.* New York: Russell Sage.

Addams, Jane
  1881 "Cassandra." In *Essays of Class of 1881, Rockford Seminary,* pp. 36–39. DeKalb, IL: "News" Steam Press.
  1893 "The Subjective Necessity for Social Settlements." In *Philanthropy and Social Progress,* ed. Henry C. Adams, pp. 1–26. New York: Thomas Y. Crowell & Company Publishers.
  1895 "The Settlement as a Factor in the Labor Movement." *Hull-House Maps and Papers: A Presentation of Nationalities and Wages in a Congested District of Chicago, Together with Comments and Essays on Problems of the Social Conditions,* by Residents of Hull-House, pp. 183–204. Boston: Thomas Y. Crowell.
  1896 "A Belated Industry." *American Journal of Sociology* 1, pp. 536–50.
  1907 *Democracy and Social Ethics.* New York: Macmillan.
  1905 "Problems of Municipal Administration." *American Journal of Sociology* 10, pp. 425–44.
  1906 *The Modern City and the Municipal Franchise for Women.* New York: National American Woman Suffrage Association.
  1907 *Newer Ideals of Peace.* New York: Macmillan.
  1909 *The Spirit of Youth and the City Streets.* New York: Macmillan.
  1910a "Charity and Social Justice." *North American Review* 192, pp. 68–81.
  1910b *Twenty Years at Hull-House.* New York: Macmillan.

1910c "Why Women Should Have the Vote." *Ladies Home Journal*, January, pp. 21–22.

1912 *A New Conscience and an Ancient Evil.* New York: Macmillan.

1915 *Women at The Hague.* New York: Macmillan.

1916 *The Long Road of Woman's Memory.* New York: Macmillan.

1922 *Peace and Bread in Time of War.* New York: Macmillan.

1930 *The Second Twenty Years at Hull-House.* New York: Macmillan.

1932 *My Friend Julia Lathrop.* New York: Macmillan.

Altick, Richard

1973 *Victorian People and Ideas.* New York: Norton and Company.

Alway, Joan

1995 "The Trouble with Gender: Tales of the Still-Missing Feminist Revolution in Sociological Theory." *Sociological Theory* 13:3, pp. 209–226.

Anzaldua, Gloria, ed.

1990 *Making Face, Making Soul/Hacienda Caras: Creative and Critical Perspectives by Women of Color.* San Francisco: Aunt Lute Foundation Books.

Baker-Fletcher, Karen

1994 *A Singing Something: Womanist Reflections on Anna Julia Cooper.* New York: Crossroad.

Bannister, Robert

1987 *Sociology and Scientism.* Chapel Hill: University of North Carolina Press.

Becker, Ernest

1971 *The Lost Science of Man.* New York: Braziller.

Beecher, Catharine

1844/1977 "From *Miss Beecher's Domestic Receipt Book.*" In *The Female Experience: An American Documentary,* ed. Gerda Lerner, pp. 122–24, Indianapolis: Bobbs-Merrill Press.

Bellamy, Edward

1888/1917 *Looking Backward.* New York: Modern Library.

Benjamin, Jessica

1988 *The Bonds of Love: Psychoanalysis, Feminism, and the Problem of Domination.* New York: Pantheon.

Bennett, Joan

1957 *Four Metaphysical Poets.* Cambridge: Cambridge University Press.

Bernard, Jessie

1964 *Academic Women.* University Park: Pennsylvania State University Press.

Bernard, L. L. and Jessie

1943 *Origins of American Sociology: The Social Science Movement in the United States.* New York: Thomas Y. Crowell, Co.

Bhavnani, Kum-Kum

1996 "Impact Is Not the Same as Revolution." *Perspectives: The ASA Theory Section Newsletter* 18, pp. 7–8.

Blair, Karen J.

1981 *The Clubwoman as Feminist: True Womanhood Redefined,* 1868–1914. New York: Holmes & Meier.

Blumberg, Dorothy

1966 *Florence Kelley: The Making of a Social Pioneer.* New York: Augustus M. Kelley Publishers.

Bologh, Roslyn W.

1990 *Love or Greatness: Max Weber and Masculine Thinking—A Feminist Inquiry.* New York: Unwin Hyman.

Booth, Charles

1892–1902 *The Life and Labour of the People of London.* 17 vol. London: Macmillan.

Breckinridge, Sophonisba

1910 "Neglected Widowhood in the Juvenile Court." *American Journal of Sociology* 16, pp. 53–87.

1913 "The Color Line in the Housing Problem." *Survey* 29, pp. 575–76.

1921 *New Homes for Old.* New York: Harper and Brothers.

1923 "The Home Responsibilities of Women Workers and the 'Equal Wage.'" *Journal of Political Economy* 31, pp. 521–43.

1934 *The Family and the State.* Chicago: University of Chicago Press.

Breckinridge, Sophonisba, and Edith Abbott

1911 "Housing Conditions in Chicago III: Back of the Yards." *American Journal of Sociology* 16, pp. 433–68.

Britton, Anne Camden

1979 "The Life and Thought of Marianne Weber." Master's thesis, San Francisco State University.

Broschart, Kay

1991a "Beatrice Webb." In *Women in Sociology: A Bio-Bibliographical Sourcebook,* ed. Mary Jo

Deegan, pp. 425–31. Westport, CT: Greenwood Press.

1991b "Ida B. Wells-Barnett." In *Women in Sociology: A Bio-Bibliographical Sourcebook,* ed. Mary Jo Deegan, pp. 432–39. Westport, CT: Greenwood Press.

Bryan, Mary Lynn McCree and Nancy Slote and Maree de Angury

1996 *The Jane Addams Papers: A Comprehensive Guide.* Bloomington, IN: Indiana University Press.

Bulmer, Martin, Kevin Bales, and Kathryn Kish Sklar, eds.

1991 *The Social Survey in Historical Perspective, 1880–1940.* Cambridge: Cambridge University Press.

Buxton, William, and Stephen P. Turner

1992 "From Education to Expertise: Sociology as a 'Profession.'" In *Sociology and Its Publics,* ed. Terence C. Halliday and Morris Janowitz, pp. 373–407. Chicago: University of Chicago Press.

Caine, Barbara

1982 "Beatrice Webb and the 'Woman Question.'" *History Workshop Journal* 14, pp. 23–43.

Campbell, Thomas F.

1988 "Edward W. Bemis." In *Historical Dictionary of the Progressive Era, 1890–1920,* ed. John D. Buenker and Edward R. Kantowicz, pp. 49–50. Westport, CT: Greenwood Press.

Caraway, Nancie

1991 *Segregated Sisterhood: Racism and the Politics of American Feminism.* Knoxville: University of Tennessee Press.

Carter, Susan

1981 " 'Academic Women' Revisited: An Empirical Study of Changing Patterns in Women's Employment as College and University Faculty, 1890–1963." *Journal of Social History* 14, pp. 675–99.

Ceplair, Larry, ed.

1991 *Charlotte Perkins Gilman: A Non-Fiction Reader.* New York: Columbia University Press.

Chodorow, Nancy

1978 *The Reproduction of Mothering: Psychoanalysis and the Sociology of Gender.* Berkeley: University of California Press.

Cole, Margaret

1946 *Beatrice Webb.* New York: Harcourt, Brace.

1961 *The Story of Fabian Socialism.* Stanford, CA: Stanford University Press.

Collins, Patricia Hill

1990 *Black Feminist Thought: Knowledge, Consciousness, and the Politics of Empowerment.* Boston: Unwin Hyman.

1996 "Sociological Visions and Revisions: Review of Charles Lemert, *Sociology After the Crisis* and Donald Levine, *Visions of the Sociological Tradition.*" *Contemporary Sociology* 25, pp. 328–331.

Collins, Randall

1975 *Conflict Sociology.* New York: Academic Press.

Cook, Blanche Wiesen

1977 "Female Support Networks and Political Activism: Lillian Wald, Crystal Eastman, Emma Goldman." *Chrysalis* 3, pp. 35–53.

Cooper, Anna Julia

1892 *A Voice from the South by a Black Woman from the South.* Xenia, OH: Aldine Press.

1925/1988 *Slavery and the French Revolutionists, 1788–1805.* Trans. Frances Richardson Keller. Queenston, Canada: Edwin-Mellen Press.

1951 *Personal Reflections of the Grimké Family and the Life and Writings of Charlotte Forten Grimké.* Washington, DC: Privately printed.

Coser, Lewis

1977 "Georg Simmel's Neglected Contributions to the Sociology of Women." *Signs* 2, pp. 869–76.

Costin, Lela

1983 *Two Sisters for Social Justice: A Biography of Edith and Grace Abbott.* Urbana: University of Illinois Press.

Dahrendorf, Ralf

1968 *Essays in the Theory of Society.* Stanford, CA: Stanford University Press.

Darwin, Charles

1859/1962 *The Origin of the Species.* London: Collier Books.

Davis, Allen F.

1967 *Spearheads of Reform: The Social Settlement and the Progressive Movement 1890–1914.* New York: Oxford University Press.

1973 *American Heroine.* New York: Oxford University Press.

DeBeauvoir, Simone

1947/1963 *The Second Sex.* New York: Vintage Books.

Deegan, Mary Jo

1988 *Jane Addams and the Men of the Chicago School, 1892–1918.* New Brunswick, N.J. Transaction Books.

1996 " 'Dear Love, Dear Love': Female Pragmatism and the Chicago Female World of Love and Ritual." *Gender & Society* 10, pp. 590–607.

Deegan, Mary Jo, ed.

1991 *Women in Sociology: A Bio-Bibliographical Sourcebook.* Westport, CT: Greenwood Press.

Degler, Carl

1966 Introduction to 1966 edition of *Women and Economics,* by Charlotte Perkins Gilman. New York: Harper and Row.

Dewey, John

1922 *Human Nature and Conduct.* New York: Henry Holt.

Diner, Steven J.

1980 *A City and Its University.* Chapel Hill: University of North Carolina Press.

DuBois, W. E. B.

1903/1989 *The Souls of Black Folks.* New York: Bantam.

Durkheim, Emile

1895/1938 *The Rules of Sociological Method.* Ed. George E. G. Catlin, trans. Sarah A. Solovay and John H. Mueller. New York: Free Press.

Ellison, Ralph

1952/1972 *Invisible Man.* New York: Vintage Books.

Engels, Friedrich

1846/1887 *The Condition of the Working Class in England in 1844.* Trans. Florence Kelley. New York: L. Weiss.

Evans, Richard J.

1976 *The Feminist Movement in Germany, 1894–1933.* Vol. 6, *Sage Studies in 20th Century History.* Beverly Hills, CA: Sage Publications.

Faderman, Lillian

1991 *Odd Girls and Twilight Lovers: A History of Lesbian Life in Twentieth-Century America.* New York: Columbia University Press.

Festinger, Leon

1957 *A Theory of Cognitive Dissonance.* Evanston, IL: Row, Peterson.

Fish, Virginia Kemp

1981 "Annie Marion MacLean: A Neglected Part of the Chicago School." *Journal of the History of Sociology* 3, pp. 43–62.

1985 "Hull House: Pioneer in Urban Research During Its Creative Years." *History of Sociology* 6, no. 1, pp. 33–54.

Fitzpatrick, Ellen

1990 *Endless Crusade: Women Social Scientists and Progressive Reform.* New York: Oxford University Press.

Fonow, Mary Margaret, and Judith A. Cook, eds.

1995 *Beyond Methodology: Feminist Scholarship as Lived Research.* Bloomington: Indiana University Press.

Forster, E. M.

1927/1955 *Aspects of the Novel.* New York: Harcourt, Brace, & World.

Fout, John C.

1984 "Current Research on German Women's History in the Nineteenth Century." In *German Women in the Nineteenth Century: A Social History,* ed. John C. Fout, pp. 3–54. New York: Holmes & Meier.

Furner, Mary

1975 *Advocacy and Objectivity: A Crisis in the Professionalization of American Social Science, 1865–1905.* Lexington: University of Kentucky Press.

Gabel, Leona C.

1982 *From Slavery to the Sorbonne and Beyond: The Life and Writings of Anna Julia Cooper.* Northampton, MA: Smith College, Department of History.

Gates, Henry Louis

1988 "Introduction to *The Schomburg Library of Nineteenth-Century Black Women Writers.*" In *A Voice from the South,* by Anna Julia Cooper, ed. Mary Helen Washington. New York: Oxford University Press.

Giddings, Paula

1984 *Where and When I Enter: The Impact of Black Women on Race and Sex in America.* New York: William Morrow.

Gilligan, Carol

1983 *In a Different Voice.* Cambridge: Harvard University Press.

Gilman, Charlotte Perkins

1887 "The Right to Earn Money." *Woman's Journal,* 18 (January 8), p. 12.

1892/1973 *The Yellow Wallpaper.* New York: Feminist Press.

1898 *Women and Economics.* Boston: Small and Maynard.

1900 *Concerning Children.* Boston: Small and Maynard.

1903 *The Home: Its Work and Influence.* New York: Macmillan.

1904 *Human Work.* New York: McClure and Phillips.

1911 *The Man-Made World, or Our Androcentric Culture.* New York. Charlton Company.

1923 *His Religion and Hers: A Study of the Faith of Our Fathers and the Work of Our Mothers.* New York: Century.

1935 *The Living of Charlotte Perkins Gilman.* New York: D. Appleton-Century Company.

1994 *The Diaries of Charlotte Perkins Gilman.* 2 vols. ed. Denise Knight. Charlottesville: University Press of Virginia.

1995 *A Journey from Within: The Love Letters of Charlotte Perkins Gilman, 1897–1900.* ed. Mary A. Hill. Lewisburg, PA: Bucknell University Press.

Gordon, Linda
1994 *Pitied But Not Entitled: Single Mothers and the History of Welfare.* New York: Free Press.

Green, Martin
1974 *The Von Richtofen Sisters: The Triumphant and the Tragic Modes of Love: Else and Frieda von Richtofen, Otto Gross, Max Weber, and D. H. Lawrence.* New York: Basic Books.

Halbwachs, Maurice
1992 *On Collective Memory.* Trans. and ed. Lewis Coser. Chicago: University of Chicago Press.

Halliday, Terence, and Morris Janowitz, eds.
1992 *Sociology and Its Publics.* Chicago: University of Chicago Press.

Hamilton, Alice
1943 *Exploring the Dangerous Trades.* Boston: Little, Brown and Company.

Haraway, Donna
1988 "Situated Knowledge: The Science Question in Feminism and the Privilege of the Partial Perspective." *Feminist Studies* 14, pp. 575–600.

Harper, Frances Ellen Watkins
1891/1976 "Duty to Dependent Races." *Transactions.* Philadelphia. National Council of Women of the United States. In *Black Women in Nineteenth-Century American Life: Their Words, Their Thoughts, Their Feelings,* ed. Bert James Loewenberg and Ruth Bogin, pp. 247–50, University Park: Pennsylvania State University Press.

Harris, Trudier
1991 "Introduction" to *Selected Works of Ida B. Wells-Barnett,* ed. Trudier Harris. In *The Schomburg Library of Nineteenth-Century Black Women Writers.* New York: Oxford University Press.

Heilbrun, Carolyn
1988 *Writing a Woman's Life.* New York: Norton.

Hill, Mary A.
1980 *Charlotte Perkins Gilman: The Making of a Radical Feminist, 1860–1896.* Philadelphia: Temple University Press.

Hill, Michael R.
1989 "Empiricism and Reason in Harriet Martineau's Sociology." Introduction to *How to Observe Morals and Manners,* by Harriet Martineau, ed. Michael R. Hill. New Brunswick, NJ: Transaction Books.

Hoecker-Drysdale, Susan
1992 *Harriet Martineau: First Woman Sociologist.* Oxford, England: Berg Publishers, Inc.

Hofstadter, Richard
1955 *Social Darwinism in American Thought.* Boston: Beacon Press.

Holbrooke, Agnes Sinclair
1895 "Map Notes and Comments." In *Hull-House Maps and Papers: A Presentation of Nationalities and Wages in a Congested District of Chicago, Together with Comments and Essays on Problems Growing Out of Social Conditions,* by Residents of Hull-House, pp. 3–23. Boston: Thomas Y. Crowell.

Holt, Thomas
1982 "The Lonely Warrior: Ida B. Wells-Barnett and the Struggle for Black Leadership." In *Black Leaders of the Twentieth Century,* ed. John Hope Franklin and August Meier, pp. 39–61. Urbana: University of Illinois Press.

Howells, William Dean
1892 *An Imperative Duty.* New York: Harper.

Hughes, Helen McGill
1975 "Women in Academic Sociology, 1927–1975." *Sociological Focus* 8, no. 3, pp. 215–22.

Hutchinson, Louise Daniel
1981 *Anna J. Cooper: A Voice from the South.* Washington, DC: Smithsonian Institution Press.

Ingraham, Chrys
1996 "You've Come a Long Way Baby . . . or . . . the Revolution Will Not Be Televised." *Perspectives: The ASA Theory Section Newsletter* 18, pp. 8–9.

James, Henry
    1888/1985 "The Art of Fiction." In *The Norton Anthology of American Literature,* 2 ed., (ed.) Nina Baym et a l., pp. 430–46. New York: W.W. Norton & Company.

James, William
    1907 *Pragmatism.* New York: Longmans, Green, and Company.

Johnson, Miriam
    1988 *Strong Women, Weak Wives: The Search for Gender Equality.* Berkeley: University of California Press.
    1989 "Feminism and the Theories of Talcott Parsons." In *Feminism and Sociological Theory,* ed. Ruth A. Wallace, pp. 101–18. Newbury Park, CA: Sage.
    1993 "Functionalism and Feminism: Is Estrangement Necessary?" In *Theory on Gender/Feminism on Theory,* ed. Paula England, pp. 118–30. New York: Aldine de Gruyer.

Kandal, Terry R.
    1988 *The Woman Question in Classical Sociological Theory.* Miami: Florida International University Press.

Käsler, Dirk
    1981 "Methodological Problems of a Sociological History of Early German Sociology." Paper presented at the Department of Education, University of Chicago, November 5.

Keith, Bruce
    1991 "Charlotte Perkins Gilman." In *Women in Sociology: A Bio-Bibliographical Sourcebook,* ed. Mary Jo Deegan, pp. 148–56. Westport, CT: Greenwood Press.

Keller, Evelyn Fox
    1985 *Reflections on Gender and Science.* New Haven: Yale University Press.

Kelley, Florence
    1887/1986 "The Need for Theoretical Preparation for Philanthropic Work." In *Notes of Sixty Years: The Autobiography of Florence Kelley,* ed. Kathryn Kish Sklar, pp. 91–104. Chicago: Charles H. Kerr.
    1895 "The Sweating System." In *Hull-House Maps and Papers: A Presentation of Nationalities and Wages in a Congested District of Chicago, Together with Comments and Essays on Problems Growing Out of Social Conditions,* by Residents of Hull-House, pp. 3–23. Boston: Thomas Y. Crowell.

    1899 "Aims and Principles of the Consumers' League." *American Journal of Sociology* 5, pp. 289–304.
    1905 *Some Ethical Gains Through Legislation.* New York: Macmillan.

Kelley, Florence, trans.
    1887 *The Condition of the Working Class in England in 1844,* by Fredrich Engels (1846). New York: L. Weiss.

Kellor, Frances
    1900 "Psychological and Environmental Study of Women Criminals." *American Journal of Sociology* 5, pp. 671–82.
    1901a "The Criminal Negro." *Arena* 25, pp. 59–68, 190–97, 308–16, 419–28.
    1901b *Experimental Sociology.* New York: Macmillan.
    1904 *Out of Work.* New York: G. P. Putnam.
    1905a "Assisted Emigration from the South: The Women." *Charities* 15, pp. 13–14.
    1905b "Associations for the Protection of Colored Women." *Colored American Magazine,* 9 (December), pp. 695–99.
    1905c "Southern Colored Girls in the North." *Charities* 13, pp. 584–85.
    1915 *Out of Work.* Rev. ed. New York: G. P. Putnam.
    1920 *Immigration and the Future.* New York: Macmillan.

Kelly-Gadol, Joan
    1976/1983 "The Social Relation of the Sexes: Methodological Implications of Women's History." In *The Signs Reader: Women, Gender, and Scholarship,* ed. Elizabeth Abel and Emily K. Abel, pp. 11–25. Chicago: University of Chicago Press.

Kent, Raymond A.
    1981 *A History of British Empirical Sociology.* Aldershot, England: Gower Press.

Kirchen, Elizabeth
    1997 Conversation. Ann Arbor, MI, March 17, 1997.

Knight, Louise Wilby
    1991 "Jane Addams and Hull-House: Historical Lessons in Nonprofit Leadership." *Nonprofit Management and Leadership* 2, pp. 125–41.

Kuhn, Thomas
    1962 *The Structure of Scientific Revolutions.* Chicago: University of Chicago Press.

Kuklick, Henrika
  1973 "A 'Scientific Revolution': Sociological Theory in the United States, 1930–1945." *Sociological Inquiry* 43, pp. 3–22.
Lane, Ann J.
  1990 *To Herland and Beyond: The Life and Work of Charlotte Perkins Gilman.* New York: Pantheon.
Lathrop, Julia
  1895 "The Cook County Charities." In *Hull-House Maps and Papers: A Presentation of Nationalities and Wages in a Congested District of Chicago, Together with Comments and Essays on Problems Growing Out of Social Conditions,* by Residents of Hull-House, pp. 3–23. Boston: Thomas Y. Crowell.
  1905 *Suggestions for Visitors to County Poorhouses and to Other Public Charitable Institutions.* Chicago: Public Charities Committee of the Illinois Federation of Women's Clubs.
  1912 "The Children's Bureau." *American Journal of Sociology* 18, pp. 318–29.
Lehmann, Jennifer
  1993 *Durkheim and Women: The Problematic Relationship.* Lincoln: University of Nebraska Press.
  1995 "The Question of Caste in Modern Society: Durkheim's Contradictory Theories of Race, Class, and Sex." *American Sociological Review* 60, no. 4, pp. 566–95.
Lemert, Charles
  1995 *Sociology after the Crisis.* Boulder, CO: Westview Press.
Lemert, Charles, and Esme Bahn, eds.
  1998 *The Voice of Anna Julia Cooper.* Boulder, CO: Rowman and Littlefield.
Lengermann, Patricia Madoo
  1979 "The Founding of the *American Sociological Review:* The Anatomy of a Rebellion." *American Sociological Review* 44, pp. 185–98.
Lengermann, Patricia Madoo, and Jill Niebrugge-Brantley
  1995 "Intersubjectivity and Domination: A Feminist Analysis of the Sociology of Alfred Schutz." *Sociological Theory* 13, pp. 25–36.
  1996 "Early Women Sociologists." In *Classical Sociology,* by George Ritzer, pp. 294–328. New York: McGraw-Hill.
Lerner, Gerda, ed.
  1972 *Black Women in White America: A Documentary History.* New York: Vintage.

Leuchtenberg, William E.
  1958 *The Perils of Prosperity, 1914–1932.* Chicago: University of Chicago Press.
Levine, Daniel
  1971 *Jane Addams and the Liberal Tradition.* Madison: State Historical Society of Wisconsin.
Levine, Donald
  1995 *Visions of the Sociological Tradition.* Chicago: University of Chicago Press.
Linn, James Weber
  1935 *Jane Addams.* New York: Appleton-Century-Crofts.
Lorde, Audre
  1984 *Sister Outsider.* Trumansburg, NY: Crossings Press.
MacLean, Annie Marion
  1899 "Two Weeks in Department Stores." *American Journal of Sociology* 4, pp. 721–41.
  1903 "The Sweat-Shop in Summer." *American Journal of Sociology* 9, pp. 289–309.
  1905 "The Significance of the Canadian Migration." *American Journal of Sociology* 10, pp. 814–23.
  1910 *Wage-Earning Women.* New York: Macmillan.
  1916 *Women Workers and Society.* Chicago: McClurg.
  1920 *Some Problems of Reconstruction.* Chicago: McClurg.
  1922 *Our Neighbors.* New York: Macmillan.
  1923 "Twenty Years of Sociology by Correspondence." *American Journal of Sociology* 32, pp. 461–72.
  1925 *Modern Immigration.* Philadelphia: J. B. Lippincott.
  1932 "I Become an American." *Sociology and Social Research* 16, pp. 427–33.
Madge, John
  1963 *The Origins of Scientific Sociology.* London: Tavistock.
Majors, Monroe
  1893 *Noted Negro Women: Their Triumphs and Activities.* Chicago: Donohue and Henneberry.
Marilley, Suzanne M.
  1995 *Woman Suffrage and the Origins of Liberal Feminism in the United States, 1820–1920.* Cambridge: Harvard University Press.
Martineau, Harriet
  1822 "Female Writers on Practical Divinity." *Monthly Repository* 17, pp. 593–96.

1832–34 *Illustrations of Political Economy.* 9 vols. London: Charles Fox.

1836/1837 *Society in America.* 2 vols. New York: Saunders and Otley.

1838a "Domestic Service." *London and Westminster Review* 29, pp. 405–32.

1838b *How to Observe Morals and Manners.* London: Charles Knight and Company.

1838c "The Martyr Age of the United States." *London and Westminster Review* 32, pp. 1–59.

1838d *Retrospect of Western Travel.* 3 vols. London: Saunders and Otley.

1839/1892 *Deerbrook: A Novel.* London: Smith, Elder, and Company.

1841a *The Hour and the Man: An Historical Romance.* 3 vols. London: Cassell.

1841b *The Playfellow.* 4 vols. London: Charles Knight and Company.

1844 *Life in the Sick-Room: Essays by an Invalid.* London: Edward Moxon.

1845 *Letters on Mesmerism.* London: Edward Moxon.

1848 *Eastern Life: Past and Present.* 3 vols. London: Edward Moxon.

1849 *Household Education.* London: Edward Moxon.

1852 *Letters from Ireland.* London: John Chapman.

1853 *The Positive Philosophy of Auguste Comte, Freely Translated and Condensed by Harriet Martineau.* London: John Chapman.

1859 "Female Industry." *Edinburgh Review* 109, pp. 293–336.

1862 "Modern Domestic Service." *Edinburgh Review* 115, pp. 409–39.

1877 *Harriet Martineau's Autobiography, with Memorials by Maria Westin Chapman.* 3 vols. London: Elder.

Martineau, Harriet, and Henry George Atkinson
1851 *Letters on the Laws of Man's Nature and Development.* London: John Chapman.

McCarthy, Doyle
1996 *Knowledge as Culture: The New Sociology of Knowledge.* London and New York: Routledge.

McDonald, Lynne
1994 *The Women Founders of the Social Sciences.* Ottawa, Canada: Carleton University Press.

Mies, Maria
1983 "Towards a Methodology for Feminist Research." In *Theories of Women's Studies,* ed. Gloria Bowles and Renate Duelli Klein, pp. 117–39. London: Routledge and Kegan Paul.

Mills, C. Wright
1959/1977 *The Sociological Imagination.* New York: Oxford University Press.

Minnich, Elizabeth K.
1990 *Transforming Knowledge.* Philadelphia: Temple University Press.

Misra, Joya, Ivy Kennelly, and Marina Karides
1997 "'Of Course *You* Got a Job': Race, Gender, and the Academic Job Market Strategy." Paper presented at American Sociological Association annual meeting, Toronto.

Mitzman, Arthur
1970 *The Iron Cage.* New York: Alfred A. Knopf.

Morgan, J. Graham
1983 "Courses and Texts in Sociology." *Journal of the History of Sociology* 5, no. 1, pp. 42–65.

Muggeridge, Kitty, and Ruth Adam
1968 *Beatrice Webb: A Life, 1858–1943.* New York: Alfred A. Knopf.

Muncy, Robyn
1991 *Creating a Female Dominion in American Reform, 1890–1935.* New York: Oxford University Press.

Murphy-Geiss, Gail
1995 "Jane Addams: Social Gospel Token?" Paper presented at National Women's Studies Association annual meeting, Norman, OK.

Nord, Deborah Epstein
1985 *The Apprenticeship of Beatrice Webb.* Amherst: University of Massachusetts Press.

Oakes, Guy, ed.
1984 *Georg Simmel on Women, Sexuality, and Love.* New Haven: Yale University Press.

Oberschall, Anthony
1972 "The Institutionalization of American Sociology." In *The Establishment of Empirical Sociology: Studies in Continuity, Discontinuity, and Institutionalization,* ed. Anthony Oberschall, pp. 187–251. New York: Harper and Row.

Olsen, Tillie
1972 "Women Who Are Writers in Our Century: One Out of Twelve." *College English* 34, no. 1, pp. 6–17.

O'Neill, William
1971 *Everyone Was Brave: A History of Feminism in America.* Chicago: Quadrangle Books.

Park, Robert E., and Ernest Burgess
  1921 *Introduction to the Science of Sociology.* Chicago: University of Chicago Press.

Parsons, Talcott
  1937 *The Structure of Social Action.* 2 vols. New York: Free Press.

Pichanick, Valerie Kossew
  1980 *Harriet Martineau: The Woman and Her Work, 1802–1876.* Ann Arbor: University of Michigan Press.

Platt, Jennifer
  1996 *A History of Sociology Research Methods in America, 1920–1960.* Cambridge: Cambridge University Press.

Quataert, Jean H.
  1979 *Reluctant Feminists in German Social Democracy.* Princeton University Press.

Rauschenbusch, Walter
  1907/1963 "Excerpt from *Christianity and The Social Crisis.*" In *The Progressive Movement 1900–1915,* (ed.) Richard Hofstadter, pp. 368–71. New York: Simon & Schuster, Inc.

Reinharz, Shulamit,
  1983 "Experiential Analysis: A Contribution to Feminist Research." In *Theories of Women's Studies,* ed. Gloria Bowles and Renate Duelli Klein, pp. 162–90. London: Routledge and Kegan Paul.
  1989 "Teaching the History of Women in Sociology: Or, Dorothy Swaine Thomas, Wasn't She the Woman Married to William I?" The *American Sociologist* 20, no. 1, pp. 87–94.
  1992 *Feminist Methods in Social Research.* New York: Oxford University Press.

Reinharz, Shulamit, ed.
  1993 *A Contextualized Chronology of Women's Sociological Work.* Waltham, MA: Brandeis University Press.

[Residents of Hull House]
  1895 *Hull-House Maps and Papers: A Presentation of Nationalities and Wages in a Congested District of Chicago, Together with Comments and Essays on Problems Growing Out of Social Conditions.* Boston: Thomas Y. Crowell.

Richards, Dell
  1993 *Superstars: Twelve Lesbians Who Changed the World.* New York: Carroll and Graft Publishers.

Richards, I. A.
  1929/1962 *Practical Criticism.* New York: Harcourt, Brace and World, Harvest Books.

Riis, Jacob
  1890/1924 *How the Other Half Lives.* New York: C. Scribner's Sons.

Roby, Pamela
  1992 "Women and the ASA: Degendering Organizational Structures and Processes, 1964–1974." *American Sociologist* 27, pp. 18–48.

Rollins, Judith
  1985 *Between Women: Domestics and Their Employers.* Philadelphia: Temple University Press.

Rosenberg, Rosalind
  1982 *Beyond Separate Spheres: Intellectual Roots of Modern Feminism.* New Haven: Yale University Press.

Rosenberg-Smith, Carroll
  1975 "The Female World of Love and Ritual." *Signs* 1, pp. 1–29.

Ross, Dorothy
  1991 *The Origins of American Social Science.* Cambridge: Cambridge University Press.

Roth, Gunther
  1990 "Marianne Weber and Her Circle." *Society* 127, pp. 63–70.

Scharnhorst, Gary
  1985 *Charlotte Perkins Gilman: A Bibliography.* Metuchen, NJ: Scarecrow Press.

Schutz, Alfred
  1967 *The Phenomenology of the Social World.* Evanston, IL: Northwestern University Press.
  1973 *Collected Papers I: The Problem of Social Reality.* The Hague: Martinus Nijhoff.

Schutz, Alfred, and Thomas Luckmann
  1973 *The Structure of the Life World.* Trans. Richard M. Zaner and H. Tristram Engelhardt Jr. Evanston, IL: Northwestern University Press.

Scott, Joan Firor
  1964 "Introduction to *Democracy and Social Ethics,* by Jane Addams." Cambridge: Harvard University Press.
  1992 *Natural Allies: Women's Associations in American History.* Urbana and Chicago: University of Illinois Press.

Shaw, George Bernard
  1889a "The Economic Basis of Socialism." In *Fabian Essay in Sociology,* ed. George Bernard Shaw, pp. 128–60. New York: Humboldt Publishing Company.
  1889b *Fabian Essays in Socialism.* New York: Humboldt Publishing Company.

Silva, Edward T., and Sheila A. Slaughter
1989 *Serving Power: The Making of the Academic Social Science Expert.* Westport, CT: Greenwood Press.

Simey, T. S., and M. B. Simey
1960 *Charles Booth, Social Scientist.* Oxford: Oxford University Press.

Sklar, Kathryn Kish
1973 *Catharine Beecher: A Study in American Domesticity.* New Haven: Yale University Press.
1995 *Florence Kelley and the Nation's Work, 1830–1900.* New Haven: Yale University Press.

Skocpol, Theda
1992 *Protecting Soldiers and Mothers: The Political Origins of Social Policy in the United States.* Cambridge: Harvard University Press, Belknap Press.

Small, Albion
1895 "The Era of Sociology." *American Journal of Sociology* 1, pp. 1–15.
1916 "Fifty Years of Sociology in the United States." *American Journal of Sociology* 21, pp. 721–864.

Smith, Dorothy E.
1979 "A Sociology for Women." In *The Prism of Sex: Essays in the Sociology of Knowledge,* ed. J. A. Sherman and E. T. Beck, pp. 135–87. Madison: University of Wisconsin Press.
1987 *The Everyday World as Problematic: A Feminist Sociology.* Boston: Northeastern University Press.
1990 *The Conceptual Practices of Power: A Feminist Sociology of Knowledge.* Boston: Northeastern University Press.
1996 "Response to Judith Stacey and Barrie Thorne." *Perspectives: The ASA Theory Section Newsletter* 18, pp. 3–4.

Smith, Mark C.
1994 *Social Science in the Crucible.* Durham, NC: Duke University Press.

Sprague, Joey
1997 "Holy Men and Big Guns: The Can[n]on in Social Theory." *Gender & Society* 11, no. 1, pp. 88–107.

Stacey, Judith, and Barrie Thorne
1996 "Is Sociology Still Missing Its Feminist Revolution?" *Perspectives: The ASA Theory Section Newsletter* 18, pp. 1–3.

Stead, William
1894/1995 *If Christ Came to Chicago.* Evanston, IL: Chicago Historical Bookworks.

Steffens, Lincoln
1904/1957 *The Shame of the Cities.* New York: Hill and Wang.

Stetson, Charles Walter
1985 *Endure: The Diaries of Charles Walter Stetson.* ed. Mary A. Hill. Philadelphia: Temple University Press.

Stinchcombe, Arthur L.
1982 "Should Sociologists Forget Their Mothers and Fathers?" *American Sociologist* 17, pp. 2–11.

Sydie, Rosalind
1987 *Natural Women, Cultured Men: A Feminist Perspective on Sociological Theory.* New York: New York University Press.

Talbot, Marion
1910 *The Education of Women.* Chicago: University of Chicago Press.
1936 *More than Lore: Reminiscences of Marion Talbot, Dean of Women, the University of Chicago, 1892–1925.* Chicago: University of Chicago Press.

Talbot, Marion, and Sophonisba Breckinridge
1912 *The Modern Household.* Boston: Whitcomb-Barrows.

Tarbell, Ida
1904 *History of Standard Oil.* New York: Macmillan.

Terry, James L.
1983 "Bringing Women . . . In: A Modest Proposal." *Teaching Sociology* 10, no. 2, pp. 251–61.

Tijssen, Lietake van Vucht
1991 "Women and Objective Culture: Georg Simmel and Marianne Weber." *Theory, Culture and Society* 8, pp. 203–18.

Tocqueville, Alexis de
1835/1840 *Democracy in America.* London: Longmans, Green.

Townes, Emilie
1993 *Womanist Justice, Womanist Hope.* Atlanta: Scholars Press.

Turner, Stephen and Jonathan Turner
1990 *The Impossible Science.* Newbury Park, CA: Sage.

Wade, Louise C.
1977 "Julia Lathrop." In vol. 2, *Notable American Women,* ed. Edward T. James, Janet Wilson

James, and Paul S. Boyer, pp. 370–72. Cambridge: Harvard University Press, Belknap Press.

Washington, Mary Helen
1988 "Introduction" to *A Voice from the South,* by Anna Julia Cooper, ed. Mary Helen Washington. In *The Schomburg Library of Nineteenth-Century Black Women Writers.* New York: Oxford University Press.

Webb, Beatrice Potter
1887 "The Dock Life of East London." *Nineteenth Century* 22, pp. 483–99.
1888 "Pages from a Working Girl's Diary. *Nineteenth Century* 23, pp. 301–14.
1891/1904 *The Co-operative Movement in Great Britain.* London: Swan, Sonnenschein and Company.
1892/1898 "How to Do Away with the Sweating System." In *Problems in Modern Industry,* by Sidney and Beatrice Webb, pp. 139–55, London: Longmans, Green.
1895/1896/1898 "Women and the Factory Acts." In *Problems in Modern Industry,* by Sidney and Beatrice Webb, pp. 82–101, London: Longmans, Green.
1907 "Methods of Investigation." *Sociological Papers* (Sociological Society, London) 3, pp. 343–54.
1913 "Introduction to 'The Awakening of Women.'" *A Special Supplement to the New Statesman,* 1 November, pp. iii–iv.
1926 *My Apprenticeship.* London: Longmans, Green.
1948 *Our Partnership.* ed. Barbara Drake and Margaret Cole. London: Longmans, Green.

Webb, Robert K.
1960 *Harriet Martineau: A Radical Victorian.* New York: Columbia University Press.

Webb, Sidney
1889 "The Historic Basis of Socialism." In *Fabian Essays in Sociology,* ed. George Bernard Shaw, pp. 1–43. New York: Humboldt Publishing Company.

Webb, Sidney, and Beatrice Potter Webb
1894 *The History of Trade Unionism.* London: Longmans, Green.
1897/1902 *Industrial Democracy.* London: Longmans, Green.
1932 *Methods of Social Study.* London: Longmans, Green.

Weber, Marianne
1900 *Fichte's Sozialismus und sein Verhältnis zur Marx'schen Doktrin.* Tübingen: J. C. B. Mohor.
1905/1919 "Jobs and Marriage." In *Frauenfragen und Frauengedanken,* pp. 20–37. Tübingen: J. C. B. Mohr.
1907 *Ehefrau und Mutter in der Rechtsentwicklung.* Tübingen: J. C. B. Mohr.
1912/1919/1997a "Authority and Autonomy in Marriage." In "Selections from Marianne Weber's Reflections on Women and Women's Issues," trans. Elizabeth Kirchen, pp. 27–41. Unpublished manuscript. Originally published in *Frauenfragen und Frauengendanken,* pp. 67–79, Tübingen: J. C. B. Mohr.
1912/1919/1997b "On the Valuation of Housework." In "Selections from Marianne Weber's Reflections on Women and Women's Issues," trans. Elizabeth Kirchen, pp. 42–58. Unpublished manuscript. Originally published in *Frauenfragen und Frauengedanken,* pp. 80–94, Tübingen: J. C. B. Mohr.
1913/1919 "Women and Objective Culture." In *Frauenfragen und Frauengedanken,* pp. 95–134. Tübingen: J. C. B. Mohr.
1917/1919/1997 "Types of Academic Women." In "Selections from Marianne Weber's *Reflections on Women and Women's Issues,*" trans. Elizabeth Kirchen, pp. 67–73. Unpublished manuscript. Originally published in *Frauenfragen und Frauengedanken,* pp. 179–201. Tübingen: J. C. B. Mohr.
1918/1919/1997a "The Forces Shaping Sexual Life." In "Selections from Marianne Weber's Reflections on Women and Women's Issues," trans. Elizabeth Kirchen, pp. 59–66. Unpublished manuscript. Originally published in *Frauenfragen und Frauengedanken,* pp. 202–37, Tübingen: J. C. B. Mohr.
1918/1919/1997b "Women's Special Cultural Tasks." In "Selections from Marianne Weber's Reflections on Women and Women's Issues," trans. Elizabeth Kirchen, pp. 1–26. Unpublished manuscript. Originally published in *Frauenfragen und Frauengedanken,* pp. 238–61, Tübingen: J. C. B. Mohr.
1919 *Frauenfragen und Frauengedanken,* Tübingen: J. C. B. Mohr.

1926/1975 *Max Weber: A Biography.* Trans. and ed. Harry Zohn. New York: Wiley.

1929 *Die Idee der Ehe und die Ehescheidung.* Frankfurt: Frankfurter Societats-Druckerie, Abteilung Buchverlag.

1930 *Die Ideale der Geschlechtergemeinschaft.* Berlin: F. A. Herbig.

1935 *Frauen und Liebe.* Koonigestein in Taunus: K. B. Langewissche.

1948 *Lebenserinnerungen.* Bremen: J. Storm.

Wells-Barnett, Ida B.

1892/1969 *Southern Horrors.* Reprinted in *On Lynchings,* New York. Arno.

1893/1991 *The Reason Why the Colored American Is Not in the World's Columbian Exposition.* Reprinted in *Selected Works of Ida B. Wells-Barnett,* ed. Trudier Harris. In *The Schomburg Library of Nineteenth-Century Black Women Writers.* New York: Oxford University Press.

1895 *A Red Record.* Chicago: Donohue and Henneberry.

1900/1969 *Mob Rule in New Orleans.* Reprinted in *On Lynchings,* New York: Arno.

1970 *Crusade for Justice: The Autobiography of Ida B. Wells.* Ed. Alfreda M. Duster. Chicago: University of Chicago Press.

Welter, Barbara

1966/1973 "The Cult of True Womanhood: 1820–1860." In *Our American Sisters: Women in American Life and Thought,* ed. Jean E. Friedman and William G. Shade, pp. 96–123.

Williams, Fannie Barrier

1893/1976 *The Present Status and Intellectual Progress of Colored Women.* Pamphlet, privately printed. In *Black Women in Nineteenth-Century American Life: Their Words, Their Thoughts, Their Feelings,* ed. Bert James Loewenberg and Ruth Bogin, pp. 271–79. University Park: Pennsylvania State University Press.

Wilner, Patricia

1985 "The Main Drift of Sociology between 1936 and 1984." *Journal of the History of Sociology* 5, no. 2, pp. 1–20.

Wirth, Louis

1947 "American Sociology, 1915–47." *American Journal of Sociology, Index to Volumes I–XLII,* pp. 273–81.

Yates, Gayle Graham, ed.

1985 *Harriet Martineau on Women.* New Brunswick, NJ: Rutgers University Press.

Index